Leviathan Undone?

Leviathan Undone?
Towards a Political Economy of Scale

...... Edited by Roger Keil and Rianne Mahon

UBCPress · Vancouver · Toronto

© UBC Press 2009

All rights reserved. No part of this publication may be reproduced, stored in a retrieval system, or transmitted, in any form or by any means, without prior written permission of the publisher, or, in Canada, in the case of photocopying or other reprographic copying, a licence from Access Copyright (Canadian Copyright Licensing Agency), www.accesscopyright.ca.

16 15 14 13 12 11 10 09   5 4 3 2 1

Printed in Canada on ancient-forest-free paper (100% post-consumer recycled) that is processed chlorine- and acid-free, with vegetable-based inks.

Library and Archives Canada Cataloguing in Publication

    Leviathan undone : towards a political economy of scale / edited by Roger Keil and Rianne Mahon.

Includes bibliographical references and index.
ISBN 978-0-7748-1630-4

    1. Canada – Politics and government. 2. Constitutional law – Canada. 3. Canada. Canadian Charter of Rights and Freedoms. I. Keil, Roger, 1957- II. Mahon, Rianne, 1948-

JL15.L49 2009　　　　　　　320.971　　　　　　　C2009-900930-7

Canadä

UBC Press gratefully acknowledges the financial support for our publishing program of the Government of Canada through the Book Publishing Industry Development Program (BPIDP), and of the Canada Council for the Arts, and the British Columbia Arts Council.

This book has been published with the help of a grant from the Canadian Federation for the Humanities and Social Sciences, through the Aid to Scholarly Publications Programme, using funds provided by the Social Sciences and Humanities Research Council of Canada.

UBC Press
The University of British Columbia
2029 West Mall
Vancouver, BC V6T 1Z2
604-822-5959 / Fax: 604-822-6083
www.ubcpress.ca

Contents

Preface / vii

Introduction / 3
RIANNE MAHON AND ROGER KEIL

Part 1: The Scalar Turn

1 A Thousand Leaves: Notes on the Geographies of Uneven Spatial Development / 27
NEIL BRENNER

2 Is Scale a Chaotic Concept? Notes on Processes of Scale Production / 51
BYRON MILLER

3 Why the Urban Question Still Matters: Reflections on Rescaling and the Promise of the Urban / 67
STEFAN KIPFER

Part 2: Political Scales

4 Avoiding Traps, Rescaling States, Governing Europe / 87
BOB JESSOP

5 Scaling Government to Politics / 105
WARREN MAGNUSSON

6 Producing Nature, Scaling Environment: Water, Networks, and Territories in Fascist Spain / 121
ERIK SWYNGEDOUW

7 Getting the Scale Right? A Relational Scale Politics of Native Title in Australia / 141
RICHARD HOWITT

Part 3: Re/Productive Scales

8 The Cult of Urban Creativity / 159
JAMIE PECK

9 State Spaces of "After Neoliberalism": Co-Constituting the New Zealand Designer Fashion Industry / 177
WENDY LARNER, NICK LEWIS, AND RICHARD LE HERON

10 Public Health and the Political Economy of Scale: Implications for Understanding the Response to the 2003 Severe Acute Respiratory Syndrome (SARS) Outbreak in Toronto / 195
S. HARRIS ALI AND ROGER KEIL

11 Of Scalar Hierarchies and Welfare Redesign: Child Care in Four Canadian Cities / 209
RIANNE MAHON

Part 4: The Scale of Movements

12 The Spatiality of Contentious Politics: More than a Politics of Scale / 231
HELGA LEITNER AND ERIC SHEPPARD

13 Regional Resistances in an Exurban Region: Intersections of the Politics of Place and the Politics of Scale / 247
GERDA R. WEKERLE, L. ANDERS SANDBERG, AND LIETTE GILBERT

14 Revolutionary Cooks in the Hungry Ghetto: The Black Panther Party's Biopolitics of Scale from Below / 265
NIK HEYNEN

15 The Empire, the Movement, and the Politics of Scale: Considering the World Social Forum / 281
JANET CONWAY

Conclusion / 301
RIANNE MAHON AND ROGER KEIL

References / 309

Contributors / 347

Index / 353

Preface

This book originated in separate but connected discussions at Carleton University, the University of Ottawa, and York University on matters of political economy and scale. Political economists from the varied and rich traditions of Canadian political economy had begun to engage with extant debates on geographic aspects of power, the state, capitalism, etc. Earlier publications (Jenson, Mahon, and Bienefeld 1993) had already noted these connections in the context of the Canadian discourse, but the newer discussions on scale and topologies, which mushroomed over the past decade, necessitated a fresh look. Out of the local conversations in Ottawa and Toronto grew the idea of holding the annual Studies in Political Economy conference on the subject of scale in 2005. Headed by the editors of this volume in conjunction with Caroline Andrew of the University of Ottawa, an organizing committee prepared a large and vibrant conference at York University in February of that year. This conference laid the groundwork for the book before us. European and American experts on scale joined a large contingent of Canadian scholars for an exciting and groundbreaking debate on the notion of scale in the practice of political economy.

In an innovative format, the conference combined two forms of paper contributions. In order to demonstrate our commitment to the support of junior academics and graduate students, we held a workshop of graduate student papers, which were discussed by senior scholars. The main section of the conference was structured around keynote presentations by leading thinkers on scale and topical sessions on various theoretical and empirical *problematiques* related thereto. We subsequently invited some of the contributors to the conference to submit papers for an edited collection, the results of which you are holding in your hands.

A project like this cannot succeed without help from a number of people and institutions. Our project was generously supported by a conference grant from the Social Sciences and Humanities Research Council of Canada (SSHRCC) and by individual contributions from various departments and faculties at Carleton University, the University of Ottawa, and York University. We are grateful to our colleagues on the editorial board of *Studies in Political Economy* for their encouragement and assistance. We thank Joseph Roman for his work on the abstracts and the program and Clara Morgan for creating the website at Carleton University. The conference was meticulously organized by Stefanie Primeau at York University. She deserves our special recognition. Patrick Laceby and Carol Altilia were instrumental for logistics at York University before and during the event.

Ahmed Allahwala carefully edited and formatted the manuscript to fit the style of the publisher. We could not have carried the project through to completion without the expert and patient assistance of Emre Uckardesler and Lindsey McKay. Melissa Pitts at UBC Press provided her unrelenting support to the project. We are extremely grateful to them for their patience, professionalism, and flexibility.

Leviathan Undone?

Introduction

Rianne Mahon and Roger Keil

This book is an intervention into several ongoing debates in political economy and the critical social sciences. It contributes to the development of a new language and sensibility to questions of space, scale, and topology in critical political economy. Caught in "the territorial trap" (Agnew 1994) of the nation-state, and frozen in the bloc logic of the Fordist post-World War II period, critical political economy has often failed to problematize space. Rather than taking the spatial as given, this book brings into focus the highly contested reconfiguration of relations among and across scales of action and the invention of new ones, so characteristic of the contemporary period. We are treating scale in this context as *one* form of spatialization of political economies that has its own contradictions and dynamics but is also articulated with other related spatialities such as topologies, places, territories, and levels (of government).

The fundamental shifts in the economic space of post-Fordism, globalization, and the post-Cold War rejigging of the Westphalian nation-state system have brought supra- and subnational spatial entities to the fore of sociospatial regulation, setting in motion strong real historical-geographical transformations. These changes have, however, often been understood as simply *institutional* realignments, while their *spatial* or *territorial* implications are ignored. Thus, the end of the Cold War was primarily recognized as a systemic event: the liberal democratic capitalist system won over the state socialist system of the Soviet Bloc. Such thinking was (and still is) replete with spatializing metaphors – the wall, the iron curtain – but rarely were the spatial implications of the "system competition" problematized. They were simply taken for granted. Similarly, while the post-1990 developments were acknowledged for their tremendous impacts on the lives of people and the conditions for the expansion of globalized capital were freed from previous boundaries, political economy rarely understood these developments in spatial, scalar, or topological terms. When the spatial implications were considered, they were viewed in either/or terms: either the national state remained central to the construction of the current phase of imperialism (Hirst and Thompson 1995; Panitch and Gindin 2003), or it disappeared, to be replaced by a "global space of flows" (Castells 2000) or a Foucaultian vision of empire (Hardt and Negri 2000).

Nevertheless, a strong and pervasive spatial – and now one can add scalar and topological – turn has entered the realm of political economy, both metaphorically and analytically. Our book draws on and develops this important work. The volume includes contributions from some of the leading theorists of scale as well as from newer scholars who are pushing the research agenda forward. A crucial shared insight is that contemporary developments should not be understood as a zero sum process that, in a parody of Marx's prophecy, entails the withering away of the nation-state. Rather, we need to recognize the existence of multiple and overlapping scales and of changes in the relations among them. Rescaling involves a complex, highly contested reconfiguration of interscalar arrangements, including the invention of new scales of action and emancipation. Here we offer an introduction to the concepts of space, place, and scale and outline some of the key debates that run through this rich literature.

Space, Place ...

It is no accident that geography, which has often been looked at as a useful but intrinsically unimportant "auxiliary science" *(Hilfswissenschaft)* by political economists, has recently become a leading source of ideas for political scientists, sociologists, and environmental studies and cultural studies scholars. This is not the place to reiterate the full extent of the spatial revolution in the social sciences, but let us draw in broad strokes a few of the determining real developments and intellectual tendencies in political economy regarding the notion of space in the twentieth century.

In the painting *The Red Cavalry* by Casimir Malevich, painted between 1928 and 1932, red riders gallop purposefully across the Russian tundra.[1] Beneath them, abstractly striped geological layers of history lie solid and unmoved. Above them, there is only open blue sky. This depiction of revolutionary action, which has dynamic history as its ontological centre, was typical of the twentieth century. In this case, the riders provide the agency to propel revolutionary Soviet Russia on its mission to abolish all class rule.

Geography remains the immobile and passive quarry from which historical action takes its ammunition and energy. Space appears as an empty canvas to be filled by historical events. The twentieth century believed in progress: space is overcome by time, made irrelevant by it. Political economists have, for the most part, subscribed to this worldview.

That the spatial was underdeveloped can be credited to two diametrically opposed yet linked movements, revolution and counterrevolution at a world scale. For the most part, the metaphorics and geography of revolution, which determined long periods of the nineteenth and twentieth centuries (Hobsbawm 1962, 1994), were able to do without reference to, or problematization of, space, scale, or topology.

Carried over from Marx's critique of Hegel's spatial fetishism in the nineteenth century, space remained suspicious to the critics and revolutionaries of the twentieth century. Space was about the state. Time was about revolution. Moreover, the science of space – geography – can hardly deny its origins in the military logic of territorial rule and expansion (Lacoste 1990). History transports its contents over more or less defined geographies, whose landscapes and people are literally wiped away by waves of modernization (Berman 1982). In the concretization of the Russian Revolution, the central question about the chances for "socialism in one country" to succeed is not one of space but one of the *historical* readiness of the "weakest link" in the chain of imperialism.

On the other side of the history of the twentieth century, capitalism spread itself as a world system imperialistically across entire continents. Here, too, this expansion occurred under the pretexts of modernization, civilization, and colonization: that is, *historical* processes. Only German National Socialism was a deliberately spatialized intervention into the history of colonization. The search for "life space" *(Lebensraum)* itself became the motivation for historical movement. History, in fact, was suspended with the declaration of the Thousand Year Empire of the Nazis – for twelve years, it changed the geography of the world. The stillborn Nazi Empire rested on the expansion of Germany towards the East, which became the main aspect of military action in World War II. It went with the extermination of people, countries, and landscapes at an unprecedented scale. In geographer Walter Christaller's geopolitical theory of central places, the colonization of the East obtains a scientifically rationalized principle of order (Rössler 1989). Small wonder, then, that much of critical theory of the postwar period kept its distance from space.

In Canada, the prewar work of the first generation of critical political economists, led by Harold Innis, had laid the foundation for a political economy that brought together time and space to produce a critical analysis of capitalist development. As Janine Brodie (1989, 144) reminds us, "Innis asked us to think about geographic space abstractly and relationally. It was as if Canadian history could be represented as a series of transparencies, each representing a different matrix of economic growth and political organization, laid on geographic space ... as the international political economy changed. Each staple led to different geographic configurations that were unstable across time. Boundaries – whether national or regional – were not 'in the land' but rather tied to the pattern of staples exploitation." In the early postwar years, political economists carried this tradition forward, albeit with a greater emphasis on the role of the state (Fowke 1957) and politics (Macpherson 1953). Yet, critical political economy in Canada, as elsewhere in the West, was marginalized by the growth of a positivist, discipline-bound social science that flourished in the Cold War era. While prepared to challenge this, for the most part, critical social scientists contributed to the "silenced spatiality of historicism" in which "an already made geography sets the stage, while the wilful making of history dictates the action and defines the story line" (Soja 1989, 14).

After World War II, of course, spatial metaphors were built directly into the new world order. This historical systems competition between East and West created relatively inert, immobile territorial entities, symbolically and materially cordoned off from each other through walls and armed frontiers. The relative immobility of the double hegemony of the USSR and the United States stood in contrast to the virulent anticolonial wave of revolutions of the global South. They aimed for new kinds of spatialization in independent nation-states but potentially entailed a permanent revolutionizing of the colonial and imperialist state system. When the youth of the Western world in the 1960s picked up the slogan "create one, two, many Vietnams," they signified the moment – Paris, 1968 – when the revolution of geohistorical relationships was put back on the agenda of the metropolitan countries of the West. "Space" as a sociotheoretical problematic of critical theory in the second half of the twentieth century was rarely recognized. If it was, it remained a metaphor of world historical calcification.

In the context of the rapidly changing structure of Fordist societies, space moved to the centre of theoretical interest in the social sciences in the 1970s, the crisis of neoimperialism, which became manifest in various liberation struggles; the crisis of Fordism, a self-consciously spatialized regime of accumulation ("the suburban solution"); the crisis of the cities; the ecological *problematique;* the identity debates of postmodernism; and the rescaling of spatial arrangements, economies, and society-nature in the process of globalization. Intellectual developments such as the success of human ecology in large parts of urban and regional sciences, sociology, and geography, as well as realism in international relations scholarship, created the specific conditions for the rediscovery of critical theories of space and society first as critique of spatial determinism (e.g., Manuel Castells) and later as critical spatial theory (David Harvey, Henri Lefebvre, Neil Smith, Edward Soja). In Canada, too, the "rediscovery" of political economy by the New Left spawned a revival of interest in theories of uneven spatial development. Classes were understood to be constituted at multiple scales – regional, national, and continental. Brodie's work (1989, 1990) in particular sought to bring together insights from the older Canadian tradition and newer work being done by critical geographers such as Doreen Massey.

Since the tectonic shifts in Western capitalist societies since the 1960s (Boltanski and Chiapello 2006), it has become increasingly impossible to explain social developments in non-spatial terms and to devise appropriate strategies for social change if space itself is treated as an unproblematic category. The rapid acceleration of the restructuring of the post-World War II global order into a new industrial division of labour gradually chipped away at the traditional hesitancy in the critical social sciences to space (and its derivatives, scale and topology) as an important category of explanation. Although a healthy distancing from spatial determinism remains, critical political economy has opened up to the relevance of the spatial to the construction and sustainability of modern capitalist societies. "The production of space" (Lefebvre 1991) itself became a dominant metaphor of societal change in the post-Cold War period.

The rediscovery of space has called for the development of a more refined vocabulary. One such concept is that of "place" – "a more or less bounded site of face-to-face relationships among individuals and/or other forms of direct interaction among social forces ... Place is generally closely tied to everyday life, has temporal depth, and is linked to collective memory and social identity" (Jessop, this volume). Political economists and others have often associated place-based politics and identifications with a xenophobic politics of nostalgia, in contrast to the universalism of working-class revolutionaries – or the cosmopolitanism of the intelligentsia (Harvey 1996). For Massey, however, a progressive sense of place is dynamic and connected; it is a "meeting place" of a whole series of complex networks and social relations. Its boundedness is understood not as forming a simple enclosure but as being permeated by the multiple relations that stretch across the globe. The specificity of place is not linked to a unique, place-based identity, for places are traversed by unequal relations of power and struggles to contest these relations. Rather, specificity "derives from the fact that each place is the focus of a distinct *mixture* of wider and more local social relations" (Massey 1994, 155). We will return to the concept of place later, when we reflect on contemporary debates on the core concept in this book – scale.

... and Scale

An important variant or offshoot of the spatial turn has been the recognition of the centrality of scale to the perpetuation of capitalist societies. Scale is thus understood not cartographically, as the relation between distance on a map and distance on the ground, but as socially constructed. For John Agnew (1997, 100), scale refers to "the focal setting at which spatial boundaries are defined for a specific social claim, activity or behaviour." This definition is useful in highlighting the way in which space is differentiated, carved out as spaces for particular actions and relations. Yet, it fails to bring out the critical relational – or multiscalar – dimension (Brenner 2001a). In other words, each scale needs to be understood in terms of its relation to other scales. Scale thus defined provides a better way of grasping the ever-changing and contested world of globalization. Rather than assuming set dimensions of social reality and the structuring of the human condition, scales are socially produced and reproduced through myriad, sometimes purposeful, sometimes erratic, social, economic, political, and cultural actions (Brenner 2004; Herod and Wright 2002; McMaster and Sheppard 2004; Swyngedouw 2004a).

The scalar turn in geography specifically, and in the social sciences generally, has been initiated by political economists. Neil Smith, Erik Swyngedouw, Bob Jessop, and Neil Brenner have been leading voices in the scale debate, with strong roots in the historical-geographical materialism spearheaded by David Harvey in the 1970s. As McMaster and Sheppard (2004, 16) note, "the strongest tradition, emerging out of Marxist-inspired political economic theories of the space economy, stresses the *production* of scale; i.e. how economic and political processes shape the emergence of scale. Processes include the geographic strategies of capitalist firms, of political institutions such as the nation-state, and of labor organizing to improve livelihood conditions in the face of challenges posed by capital mobility and/or state strategies."

Along with Peter Taylor, Neil Smith is credited with initiating the political economy of scale in the 1980s. Concerned to understand unequal geographical development, Smith (1984) located the production of scales in relation to the dialectics of equalization within a scale and differentiation across scales. Particular "scalar fixes" – for example, the national state – were identified as sites for the temporary resolution of the competing requirements of cooperation and competition among capitals (Smith and Dennis 1987). In subsequent work, Smith (1992b) engaged with the postmodernist critique of marxism to reflect on the construction of identities and the ways in which not only capital but also other social forces, including the homeless, could "jump scale" to further their power positions.

While the early scale theorists focused on capital accumulation, scale, and the national state as the Fordist scalar fix, feminists have rightly insisted that the "messy world" of social reproduction and consumption should also be included (Marston 2000; McDowell 2001). Thus, it is important not only to analyze the way in which scale intersects with, and helps to channel, the flow of goods, capital, and people but also to examine the scalar arrangements governing the development of social infrastructure and the way that this intersects with the "small world" of the neighbourhood and the household. While Linda McDowell illuminates the ways in which scale, class, and gender intersect in the contemporary service economy, Sallie Marston (2004, 182) has analyzed the ways in which white, middle-class American women learned to use lessons drawn at the scale of the household to redesign the nineteenth-century US state system, "enlarging its functions and responsibilities and creating a new scale of state territoriality in the process." The feminist critique also brought into view other scales, such as the body, which earlier scale theorizing, with its macro political economy roots, tended to ignore.

Social reproduction is articulated not only with class and gender relations but also with race-ethnicity. Fiona Williams' (1995, 143) classic essay on welfare state formation establishes how the construction of social citizenship at the national scale occurred "within a context in which the policies and discursive practices attached to the provision of social rights were exclusionary and/or differentiated along lines of class, race, gender, ability and sexuality." Similarly, today, the construction of "social Europe" is drawing lines between insider-bearers of rights and those who, at best, are second-class citizens. The politics of inclusion/exclusion play into the dynamic of welfare state restructuring. As care responsibilities are reassigned to markets and families, the latter turn to immigrants whose vulnerable position makes them cheap sources of labour (Lister et al. 2007).

Feminists are not alone in pointing out the need to extend scale theorizing beyond the boundaries of classic Marxist political economy. Political economy needs to get beyond the conception of nature as a passive object for "man" to master, as Harvey (1996) and others have argued. For Swyngedouw (2004b, 129), "the transformation of nature is embedded in a series of social, political, cultural, and economic constellations and procedures (i.e. social relations) that operate within a nested articulation of significant, but intrinsically unstable, geographical scales." The newer literature on political ecology has, in fact, been at the forefront of rethinking scale as a critical concept (Gibbs, Jonas, and While 2002; Keil 2005; Swyngedouw and Heynen 2003). The rescaling of societal relationships with nature has become a central topic in the restructuring of economic and social spaces, such as metropolitan regions, as the metabolism of cities is reorganized deliberately to fit into a world defined by the tensions of global economic interterritorial competition and bioregional ecological limits (Debbané and Keil 2004; Heynen, Kaika, and Swyngedouw 2005; Keil and Boudreau 2005; Keil and Debbané 2005).

Beyond the National to a Multi-Scalar Perspective

Westphalian blinders hindered a creative opening towards the kinds of questions beyond the territorial cage. This is not surprising, as the rise to prominence of the national state coincided with the foundation of modern social sciences. The modern centrality of the nation state has powerfully influenced their horizons, including those of political economy. As Peter Taylor (2000, 8) notes, "the 'society' which sociologists study, the 'economy' which economists study, and the 'polity' which political scientists study all share a common boundary, that of the [national] state ... From a geographic perspective, the trinity provides 'one scale' social knowledge." This national centrism – or "methodological nationalism" (Brenner 2004, 38) – has bedevilled not only mainstream social science but also critical political economy, from Poulantzasian state theory and other left critiques of the world systems theory of Immanuel Wallerstein and Gunder Frank to contemporary regime theorists. Nor did world systems theory offer a viable alternative, for it simply shifted the focus from one scale – the national – to another – the world system. Instead, what is needed is a multiscalar approach.

A recent contribution to the empirical literature – Darel E. Paul's *Rescaling International Political Economy* – attempts to do just that. This book discusses the scales of international political economy that are usually left out of the picture by focusing on world city formation processes in Quebec, Georgia, and Minnesota. Paul is rightly critical of the scalar fixation of international political economy (IPE) on the global scale, from which is derived all relevant change. Noting that "social scientists interested in the political-economic implications of globalization have for the most part ignored" the "actions and authority of subnational states," Paul (2005, 3) sets out to emphasize the multiscalar politics that constitute both the global and the local, in which the local is not simply acted upon by global forces. Rather, "by thinking of rescaling rather than simply globalization, one makes visible the invisible, finally seeking the subnational and its contributions both to the recapitulation of the global in conventional ways as well as to efforts to alter it through practices which contradict established patterns. One also sees subnational institutions, including subnational states, in a new light, as sites in and through which actors defined at any scale interact with global structures to produce and reproduce the global political economy" (8).

Paul's book represents an important attempt to integrate subnational scales into a multiscalar analysis. Yet, it fails comprehensively to challenge the containerized view of territorial space in IPE. This failure may have much to do with his preoccupation with the local as the prism of multiscalar analysis. Atlanta, Montreal, and Minneapolis become far more than case studies of glocalization processes; they become critical pivots of the global order. As sites of glocalization, they absorb the entire multiscalar process topologically. While Paul subjects the traditional nation-state centrism of the political economy literature to useful and biting critique, he is too quick to downscale the national to subnational, losing sight of the continued Westphalian skeleton on which the skin of rescaled metropolitan regions is draped. He thus underrates some of the critical work that has been done on the capitalist state and the politics of scale.

Jessop's (2002a) work has been important in this respect, locating the shift in scalar fix from the Keynesian welfare national state to the Schumpeterian-workfare post-national regime as a response to the crisis of Atlantic Fordism. In other words, the postwar period can be seen as the heyday of the national state – a political form that had slowly, and often violently, become the dominant form in Western Europe in the nineteenth century, then spread to the rest of the globe through colonization and decolonization. Yet, even at its peak, the national state never actually operated as the single policy-relevant scale. Advanced capitalist countries could be called upon to heed the "advice" of the International Monetary Fund. For developing countries, the World Bank and major donor countries often played a substantial role in shaping national policy "choices." In both unitary and federal systems, moreover, subnational scales retained a certain, if variable, importance. Nevertheless, the national scale occupied a pivotal position in the Keynesian welfare states of the advanced capitalist countries, the "developmental" states of Asia, Latin America, and Africa, and the Soviet and Chinese Communist regimes.

The crisis of the Keynesian welfare national state involves more than a shift from Keynesian demand management to the Schumpeterian competition state and from "passive" welfare to the "activation" strategies of the workfare state.[2] It also entails the "relativisation of scale": "The national scale has lost the taken-for-granted primacy it held in the economic and political organization of Atlantic Fordism; but this does not mean that some other scale of economic and political organization (whether the global or the local, the urban or the triadic) has acquired a similar primacy" (Jessop 2002b, 112). In other words, while the national state is no longer the pivotal scale, no other scale has succeeded in taking its place. The notion of a "postnational regime" thus refers not to the withering of the national state but to a redefinition of its place within a tangled set of hierarchies. This insight was already embedded, if rarely explicitly developed, in the early literature on the crisis of the Fordist-Keynesian regime of accumulation, which saw the end of the nation-state's primacy linked to its internal rescaling into a multilevel regionalized competition state and to the recalibration of its external relations to supranational modes of regulation (see, e.g., Hirsch 1997; Hirsch and Roth 1986; Lipietz 1987, 1992).

The destabilization of the national state's place within the hierarchy of scales is often seen as a result of neoliberal "glocalization." For Swyngedouw (1997b, 160), glocalization refers to an uneven (and contested) process involving the "upscaling" of the circuits of capital and the simultaneous downscaling of the regulation of work and social reproduction. Peck and Tickell (2002, 315), however, would draw attention to the role of neoliberal "extralocal rule regimes" and the way that they "undermine the potential of non-neoliberal programs at the local scale, while engendering a lemming-like rush towards urban entrepreneurialism." Liberalization of financial flows certainly helps to shape these new regimes, but market mechanisms are reinforced by the global flow of policy ideas or "fast policy transfer" wherein "policy advocates, consultants and evaluation foster and circulate essentialized readings of effective local programs in which a small number of supposedly decisive (and potentially replicable) design features are ... promoted" (Peck 2002b, 349).

Brenner has done much to illuminate the place of the urban scale in the rapidly shifting multiscalar world of today, without losing sight of the continued importance of national states. In his book-length treatment of the rescaling of after-Fordist European spaces, Brenner (2004, 180) insists on the special role played by metropolitanization as it has created "(a) high value added socioeconomic capacities, advanced infrastructures, industrial growth, inward investment, and labor flows [that] are increasingly concentrated within major metropolitan regions, and (b) territorial disparities between core urban regions and peripheral towns and regions [that] are significantly intensifying across Europe." In particular, his conception of "state spaces" is designed to come to grips with a post-Weberian "relativized" statehood in which urban spaces are given a new prominence. This is not because urban sites have "slipped anchor" and now float free of national states in a space of global capital flows. Rather, the new prominence of the urban reflects a strategic turn in state policy from a strategy aimed at spatial equity through standardization/homogenization to spatial differentiation and the interurban networks of competition and cooperation thrown up in response.

The absence of a privileged scale does not mean that anarchy prevails, however. Countertendencies are at work, including the elaboration of new mechanisms of multiscalar metagovernance, involving the rearticulation of primary, nodal, and marginal scales. One of them is the formation of new supranational structures at the regional/continental scale. The most advanced example is the European Union. Jessop (2004b) has looked at the implications of the attempts to consolidate the European Union for contemporary statehood, criticizing state-centric views of liberal intergovernmentalism and supranationalism as well as governance-centric views of multilevel governance and network states.

It is no longer appropriate to try to understand the world with single-scale theoretical lenses. Comparative and international political economy need to adopt a multiscalar approach. Adoption of such a perspective does not mean that the national state has literally been hollowed out. As we have suggested, rescaling, or the "relativization of scale," is not a zero sum process in which new policy roles at the supranational scale and the rediscovery of the urban mean the eclipse of the national state. Rather, what is at stake is a reconfiguration of a complex set of hierarchical arrangements. This is, moreover, a contested process but one that is not without a certain order as new, multiscalar arrangements are superimposed upon and displace those forged during the nineteenth and twentieth centuries. In the process, the national scale, far from withering away, often retains an important role as "scale manager" in the emergent structures for metagovernance.

Scale, Hierarchy, Network

Metaphorically, political economists rarely moved beyond the Russian doll conception wherein each doll/scale is understood as largely capable of being considered on its own, even while located in its (fixed) position within a preordained hierarchy (Herod and Wright 2002; Keil 1998). Such a conception was inadequate even in the heyday of the nation-state-centred hierarchy, and it is even more so today as interscalar arrangements are being reconfigured in complex ways. Scale theory seems to offer a more nuanced approach, one focused on the construction, destruction, and reconstitution of scales and interscalar arrangements. Some argue, however, that scale theorists have also remained trapped in the nesting metaphor and thus fail to grasp the complex horizontal connections, or networks, that traverse scalar arrangements (Amin 2002; Marston, Jones, and Woodward 2005).

Certainly, scale is not the only way to think about space. As we have suggested, the concept of place captures different dimensions of the spatial. To this we might add recent thinking about topologies. Critics such as Ash Amin have noted that the understanding of socially constructed scales is still too fixed a notion of human relationships to explain the globalized world in which we live: "Overlapping near-far relations and organizational connections that are not reducible to scalar spaces" have to be taken into account (2002, 386). For some, a "topological" ontology offers a better way to grasp these connections (Amin and Thrift 2002; Latham 2002; Marston, Jones, and Woodward 2005). The obvious advantage of this way of thinking is that it offers an alternative to a narrowly territorial understanding of globalized spatial relationships. Many contemporary social realities seem to be subject to such a topological or relational logic. Thinking in spatialized but non-territorial terms can thus provide insight into the realities of many social collectives in a globalized world.

One of the most explicit statements in this context is Richard Smith's recent work on global cities. Smith (2006, 401) engages with Deleuze, Guattari, Latour, and other poststructuralist thinkers to invoke a language of "folds" rather than scales: "What interests Deleuze are (un)folds, the infinite labyrinth of fold to fold, that produces the world's topology as one of processes that overwhelms the fictions of boundaries, limits, fixity, permanence, embedment. What is important to realize ... is that all folds are equally important, there are no masters and no servants." In eschewing scale as too static a concept, Smith sees space as "rather messy, complex, juxtaposed, or perhaps that there are many kinds of space" (401).

The global is not just "out there"; networks of varying reach are very much co-present in, and play a role in structuring, the everyday practices that constitute the urban (Flusty 2004). The literature on such networks has developed parallel to the work on scale. Leitner, Pavlik, and Sheppard (2002), in a thorough review of the relevant literature, identify three discourses of importance: (1) *networks in economic geography and regional development*, where the notion of network has been used to describe the relationships of firms in industrial sectors, learning regions, etc., in post-Fordist economies, where firms are described as "constellations of network relations" and "circulatory networks" (Amin and Thrift 2002, 64-65); (2) *policy networks*, which have gained prominence as alternatives to hierarchical or market modes of organization and governance (Leitner, Pavlik, and Sheppard 2002); and (3) building on the work of Bruno Latour and John Law, Leitner, Pavlik, and Sheppard (2002, 284) present *actor-network theory*, which considers individuals as constituted by and constitutive of "complex, ever-changing, heterogeneous" networks of "actants" of various origin and "with potentially equal power to influence collective outcomes." "Individual action should be evaluated as connected to, and contingent upon, relative position, rather than as endogenously determined by characteristics of individuals or by macro-level conditions applying to all agents" (Leitner, Pavlik, and Sheppard 2002, 285).

In his most recent work, Latour could not be clearer on this point. Building on Boltanski and Thévenot, Latour (2005, 184-85) notes that "if there is one thing you cannot do in the actor's stead it is to decide where they stand on a scale going from small to big, because at every turn of their many attempts at justifying their behavior they may suddenly mobilize the whole of humanity, France, capitalism, and reason while, a minute later, they might settle for a local compromise." He adds this terse assessment: "Scale is the actor's own achievement. Although this is the oldest, and in my view, the most decisive proposition made by A[ctor] N[etwork] T[heory], I have never encountered anyone who could accept to even glance at the landscape thus revealed – no more, if I dare the parallel, than Galileo could tempt his 'dear and respected colleagues' to have a look through his makeshift telescope. The reason is that we tend to think of scale – macro, meso, micro – as a well-ordered *zoom*" (185). Of course, Latour's notion of scale as employed here is of the metric kind, less complex than the notions that many authors extol in this book. But the point is made – scales and agency through networks of actors are entwined and not ontologically separable.

The literatures on network and scale have hitherto rarely been explicitly connected, but there is much to be gained from weaving together insights drawn from both. Leitner, Pavlik, and Sheppard (2002, 287) identify several distinctive social and geographical attributes of networks: they "span space but do not cover it"; they "transcend the boundaries dividing the spaces of hierarchical modes of governance"; the "flexibility of network membership means that the geographical boundary of any network, separating the places which are part of the network from those which are not, may frequently change"; and "network spaces can overlap and interpenetrate one another," unlike the non-overlapping conventional political spaces. Networks, however, exist in a dialectical relation to hierarchies and markets, which they come from but which they also influence. And networks are scaled: "The scale of a network is not fixed but is a consequence both of how that network evolves and of other processes shaping its territorial and social extent" (Leitner, Pavlik, and Sheppard 2002, 286).

Marston, Jones, and Woodward (2005, 422) reject these attempts at synthesis. For them, scale theory is fundamentally flawed: "In spite of efforts ... to build complex relational understandings that crisscross these levels ..., research projects often assume the hierarchy in advance, and are set up a priori to obey its conventions." Scale, they argue, should be abandoned in favour of a "flat ontology" of social sites. Yet, they (420) and other critics admit that vertical hierarchies do exist. For example, Amin (2002, 396) recognizes that

> those concerned with the politics of regulation and governance associated with globalization are right to note the very real and felt contest of jurisdiction and control between local, national and global state and non-state organizations. They are right to stress that globalization ... has unleashed a rigorous restructuring of the rationale and spaces of formal politics ..., including the rise of new forms of economic and political regionalism, experiments to regulate a new global regime of capital accumulation, [and] the reorganization of the state towards the imperatives of global competition ... All of these aspects do represent a politics

mobilized around redrawn institutional boundaries and fixities, including scalar ones.

For Amin, the concept of governmentality – networks of spatial connectivity governing "action at a distance," drawn from Foucault and Latour – offers a better alternative to scale. Yet, such networks are structured by scalar hierarchies. They are not free-floating alternatives to scalar arrangements but are embedded in them.

Contra the misrepresentation of scalar hierarchies in Marston, Jones, and Woodward (2005),[3] moreover, scale theorists also clearly recognize that there is more than one single hierarchy, moving from the global down to the local, and that the relations among them are complex. As Brenner (2001a, 605) argues, "the meaning, function, history and dynamic of any one geographical scale can only be grasped relationally, in terms of its upwards, downwards, and sidewards links to other geographical scales situated within tangled scalar hierarchies and dispersed interscalar networks." More broadly, Sheppard and McMaster (2004b) have clearly shown the ways in which the notion of hierarchy employed by political economists differs from that of the physical geographers and cartographers. They show how, in the political economy of scale, hierarchy is understood in quite a different way than it is in biophysical geography.

1 In the political economy of scale, *the units are not fixed but mutable*. Scales and the units of which they are comprised are not determined once and for all but are shaped and reshaped by socioeconomic processes and political struggles. This is, in fact, a core premise of the political economy of scale.
2 *Causality does not begin at the smallest scale but runs in all directions.* "Social collectivities and individuals are mutually constituted so causality can run in all kinds of directions within and across scales" (Sheppard and McMaster 2004, 261).
3 *There is not a single hierarchy; rather, there is a multiplicity of hierarchies.* As Brenner (2001a, 606) suggests, "processes of scalar structuration do not produce a single nested scalar hierarchy, an absolute pyramid of neatly interlocking scales, but are better understood as a mosaic of unevenly superimposed and densely interlayered scalar geometries." In other words, a multiplicity of differently structured, tangled scalar hierarchies operates in and across diverse spheres of life.

4   While there may be a plurality of hierarchies, pluralism does not prevail. There are what Peck (2002b, 341) has called *interscalar rule regimes* that "envelop, constrain or animate" action at any particular scale. While both the supra- and the subnational scales have assumed a greater prominence today, the national state retains an important role as "scale manager," especially as organizer of the complex of hierarchies governing different aspects of everyday life. As a consequence, there are important cross-national differences in these regimes. Nationally centred interscalar regimes contribute to the path dependencies noted by Brenner (2001a) and Jessop (1993).
5   In the political economy of scale, *it is possible and desirable to ask how scaled processes can be shaped in ways that promote equality and democratic control.* In other words, dealing with the world "as it is" does not rule out thinking about the way the world ought to (and can) be. In fact, as Gramsci (1971) recognized, critical theorists need to develop a dynamic perspective on "effective reality" in order to transform it.

Marston, Jones, and Woodward (2005) fail to take these crucial qualifications into account. They reject any conception of hierarchy even while they acknowledge (in passing) the argument that "nesting seems to be imposed by legal, juridical and organizational structures without our having to accept the legitimacy of the hierarchy that did the ordering" (420). Rejecting scalar hierarchies in favour of a "flat ontology" of "localized and non-localized event-relations productive of event-spaces," they claim to liberate agency from the shadows of scalar structures (424). Hierarchies exist, and, *pace* Marx (or famously Harvey extending Marx's historical view to geography and space), they do structure the world in which individual and collective agents make their choices. The concept of scale and the mutable, contested, but nonetheless real hierarchies that it brings into focus are critical to understanding the political world in which social movements have to operate. Smith (2005, 897) has put it more pungently: "If hierarchies vanish today in our academic theories, then so too vanish most of the targets of our political critique. One can't fight what one can't see or identify."

Contestations and Resistances

A key point in the literature on scale is that struggles for emancipation necessarily involve contesting, and sometimes using, scalar arrangements. Scale theorists are thus interested in how interscalar arrangements not only operate to reinforce but also to contest class, gender, and racial-ethnic inequality as well as environmental degradation. Precisely because such interscalar arrangements have an impact on social relations of power, they can become the target of struggles designed to profoundly alter those relations. In reflecting on the politics of scale, theorists have debated the relative weight given to structure versus agency. Brenner (2001a), Collinge (1999), and Jessop (2002a) have tended to focus on the structural forces driving rescaling, whereas others, such as Herod (1997), Kurtz (2003), and Miller (1997), have concentrated on social movements, as they incorporate interscalar arrangements into their strategic calculations.

Smith's (1992b) concept of "jumping scale" has been important here, pointing to the ways in which those who sought to challenge existing power relations often incorporate scale into their strategic repertoires, shifting scales (upward and downward) to gain advantage. Kurtz (2003) and Miller (2000) have shown how scale figures in the strategies of social movements.

Engels (1958 [1884]) earlier highlighted the way in which the labour movement's power was dependent on its capacity to operate across scales. More recent work by scale theorists highlights the way that it has sought to strike a balance between centralization to reap the benefits of organization at the national scale and maintenance of a vital presence in the local workplace (Herod 1997; Swyngedouw 2004a). While some would suggest that, in the current round of globalization, workers must shift their horizons to transnational scales, Noel Castree (2000a) argues that the national and local scales remain vital to the success of workers' struggles even today. This is not to suggest a unidirectional "leap" from the local to the national (and supranational). For example, while the Swedish unions were successful in developing their power resources at the national scale in the postwar period, today they find it essential, on the one hand, to regenerate local power resources to counter the move by big capital in the engineering branch to decentralize wage formation and, on the other, to develop the capacity to act at the European or even global scale (Mahon 1999).

Richard Howitt's work on Aboriginal land claims in Australia shows how they have created new scales and altered scalar arrangements in that country. In Canada, Jean Rousseau (2000) has documented the ways in which the Quebec Cree as well as environmental movements in that province successfully utilized scale in their struggles over construction of the James Bay hydroelectric projects. Rousseau's analysis brings out the important transnational dimension to scalar strategies. Janet Conway's research (2004) on antiglobalization movements shows how a local social justice movement such as the Metro (Toronto) Network for Social Justice was able to develop an innovative social praxis that contributed to the constitution of the antiglobalization movements of the 1990s. As Debbané and Keil (2004) and Keil and Debbané (2005) have pointed out, notions of (environmental) justice are similarly scaled, complex, and both path and place specific in real politics and political discourse alike.

Outline of the Book

The contributions to this volume provide a wide-ranging yet profound argument for the value of spatial perspectives in political economy. Political economy is understood here as a colourful collection of complementary and competing intellectual projects, unified in their joint interest in critically commenting on, and ultimately changing, contemporary capitalism. The book is also self-consciously Canadian in that it evokes the Innisian and Marxist political economies of this country. Half of the contributors to this collection use Canadian examples to illustrate the ways in which scale illuminates contemporary challenges/struggles. Such a single country focus has its limits, however, as the world of "permeable Fordism" (Jenson 1989) has turned into the "porous post-Fordism" of the Canadian experience today. From the multinational, multicultural, pervasively globalized reality of contemporary Canada, new views have opened up not least because of the rescaled and retopologized dimensions of all aspects of life in this highly urbanized country. From the perspective of an almost exemplary world society of diversity and difference, deprivation and opportunity, rabid neoliberalism and civic reform, new views have opened up. With authors and topics from many regions around the world, this book combines rich empirical analyses with cutting-edge theoretical *tour du mondes*, taking us through the rescaled new topologies of global capitalism. Defiantly local at times, and provocatively global in other sections, the authors have created a kaleidoscope of the political economy of neoliberal capitalism and its discontents.

Exploring the scalar turn in theoretical terms opens the volume with a broadside of theoretical accounts and innovations, which succinctly summarize the state of the art in debates on the political economy of scale. In different ways, the chapters in this section address the "limits to scale" as a singular concept for grasping the spatial while at the same time mounting strong arguments for scale as part of a broader conceptual toolkit. Miller takes on the thesis that scale is a "chaotic concept" – one that has been stretched to encompass often unrelated objects and processes, concluding that it is better understood as an "umbrella term for a set of commonly intertwined relations." In his opening contribution to this volume, Brenner uses the image of a thousand leaves to remind us of the complex and multilayered spatial realities with which we are dealing. He subsequently reflects on a generation of spatial theory and the consecutive and equally layered concepts that political economists have invited into their theoretical home. Kipfer explores the way in which scale is complemented by level in the pathbreaking work of Henri Lefebvre.

The section on political scales gives the state its due. Jessop, too, takes up the "limits of scale," identifying four fallacies marring current scalar debates. He goes on to offer a working hypothesis for future research, that the relative weight of different moments of spatiality in state strategies has shifted from the postwar primacy of place-territory to the current primacy of scale-network. In this way, he seeks to put scale "in its place" within a broader spatiotemporal framework and to move beyond the political economy of scale to a more complex-concrete analysis of restructuring. For Magnusson, the nation-state still exercises a serious hold on contemporary political imaginaries because of its promise of a universal justice tailored to the particularities of place. Yet, there are other political projects that have the potential for scaling government to a more fulfilling politics. Of particular interest in this regard are cities – the classic scale of democratic politics in ancient Athens, whose time may have come again. And cities are reemerging from under the shadow of the national state, as several other contributions to this volume suggest.

Using the example of the scalar politics of water in Franco's Spain, Swyngedouw develops his thesis that scalar reconfigurations produce new sociophysical ecological scales that determine who gets access to what kind of nature and shape the trajectories of environmental change. He demonstrates how the scalar politics of this fascist "modernization" project was predicated upon a profound reworking of the socionatural organization of Spain and a redefinition of its internal and external scalar arrangements. In his chapter, Howitt examines recent developments in relations between Aboriginals and non-indigenous Australians, relations in which he was involved. He shows how the concept of scale can be put to use by those aiming to construct new spaces of sociality, governance, and accountability.

The third section takes a closer look at contemporary processes of competition and social reproduction. Peck offers an incisive critique of Richard Florida's flat world of "creative cities" and the growing intraurban inequalities into which it plays. He shows how the interlocal competition generated by the contemporary extralocal rule regime creates favourable conditions for its rapid diffusion. Larner, Lewis, and Le Heron pick up on the theme of "creativity" in an era of "after-neoliberalism," focusing on the way in which the designer fashion industry has become the focus of diverse political projects, each with its own spatial imaginary. Their approach shows that the glocalizing dimensions of the designer fashion industry have been co-constituted through sites in diverse places. After-neoliberalism thus needs to be understood not as a coherent strategy but as *ex post facto* connections between discrete, even contradictory, projects.

Swyngedouw and others have suggested that social reproduction is of decreasing salience in state practices today. Yet, neoliberalism is not the only force restructuring and rescaling welfare regimes. Changing gender relations are putting new needs, such as non-parental child care, on the agenda (Mahon 2002). These needs are often experienced earlier and more intensely in major urban areas, where they have given rise to new attempts to remodel welfare regimes from below. Mahon's analysis of child care in four of Canada's largest cities shows that the expansion of local alternatives remains constrained by the interscalar arrangements that constitute the very scaffolding of existing welfare regimes. Health care is another important component of the social reproduction puzzle. The chapter by Ali and Keil uses the SARS "epidemic" to locate bodies within the scaled hierarchy of global health governance, from the World Health Organization (WHO) to local hospitals. They argue that this scalar structure intersects with the topological nature of global city formation to produce the accelerated and erratic movement of ideas, practices, policies, things, people, and non-human natures across the planet. A post-Westphalian political pathology of emerging disease now forces us to rethink the global political economy of health in fundamental ways.

The final section on social movements confronts our political economies of today with "a spatiality of contentious politics," in the words of Leitner and Sheppard. This group of chapters paints a rich picture of a world of social movements, simultaneously restrained and enabled by the current refractions of a political economy of scale, going beyond the biophysical, historical, and geographical limits of the definitions associated with a politics of place. Leitner and Sheppard argue that successful contentious politics frequently involves both a "politics of place" and the construction of networks of spatial connectivity that stretch across and challenge the nested territorial nature of political scale. Their analysis of the Immigrant Workers Freedom Ride in the

United States provides a nice illustration of how place, scale, and network were simultaneously deployed. Heynen's analysis of the Black Panther Party's "biopolitics from below" reveals how the leadership clearly saw the strategic connections between hungry bodies, ghetto communities, and resistance to empire.

Wekerle, Sandberg, and Gilbert focus on the intersection of capitalist development and nature, highlighting environmental opposition to urban sprawl waged on the ex-urban fringe of the Greater Toronto Area. In the Oak Ridges Moraine, the politics of scale and the politics of place intersected to create a bioregional identity and an alternative vision for the region. Environmental movements strategically utilized discourses of ecosystem management to mobilize resistance to development and to pressure the provincial government to enact legislation to control sprawl by preserving nature and the countryside. Conway's chapter assesses the World Social Forum as a site of transnational emancipatory practice. Conway argues that the forum needs to be seen not as a unitary entity but as a "worldwide movement-based multiscale cultural process involving a wide variety of civil society entities, themselves operating at a variety of geographical scales."

NOTES

1 To view this painting, go to http://www.auburn.edu/academic/liberal_arts/foreign/russian/art/malevich-cavalry.html. Some of the ideas in the next paragraphs have been previously expressed in Keil and Brenner (2003).
2 On the workfare state, see also Peck (2001b, 2003).
3 Although their article begins well, they slide into caricature when they construct the supposed "binaries" of scalar reasoning. See their Tables I and II on pages 420 and 421.

PART 1
The Scalar Turn

1
A Thousand Leaves: Notes on the Geographies of Uneven Spatial Development

Neil Brenner

The experience of geographical difference – that is, the recognition that spaces across the world differ from one another – lies at the heart of capitalist modernity. While geographical difference is hardly unique to the modern age, it can be argued that the ability of populations to travel long distances, and thus to encounter otherness, has intensified qualitatively during the capitalist epoch. It continues to be enhanced in the early twenty-first century, as worldwide flows of capital, trade, and migration acquire ever greater densities and speeds.

Some commentators have claimed that, in our current moment of "globalization," geographical differences are being annihilated as new information technologies, transnational corporate strategies, free-market politics, and cultural imperialism homogenize the landscapes of everyday life around the world. Most critical geographers reject such claims, arguing that late modern capitalism has been premised upon an intensification of differences among places and territories, even as the mobility of capital, commodities, and populations is enhanced (Cox 1997; Lee and Wills 1997; Smith 1997). Struggles for a sense of place, for territorial rootedness, and for a unique geographical niche remain as intense as ever in a world of sometimes disturbing volatility (Massey 1994). Precisely as interconnections among dispersed spaces around the globe are thickened, geographical differences are becoming more rather than less profound, at once in everyday life and in the operation of social, political, and economic power. In short, spatial unevenness remains endemic to the contemporary global capitalist (dis)order (Smith 1997).

During the past three decades, critical geographical scholarship has confronted the problem of geographical difference in a systematic, theoretically reflexive way. The concept of *uneven spatial development* lies at the heart of such analyses. This concept is derived from Marx's (1976) foundational account of capital circulation in *Capital*, where the notion of uneven development was used to describe the existence of differential growth rates among various sectors (or "departments") of the capitalist economy. The concept was reinvented in the early twentieth century by socialist intellectuals such as Lenin, Luxemburg, Bukharin, Trotsky, and (decades later) Mandel, who were concerned to understand the global expansion of the capitalist mode of production through imperialism and colonialism (Smith 1984). The concept of uneven *spatial* development was introduced by radical geographers in the late 1970s and early 1980s, thanks to the pathbreaking contributions of writers such as Harvey (1982), Lefebvre (1991 [1974]), Massey (1985), Smith (1984), and Soja (1985). Through their work on uneven spatial development (USD), these scholars and others in their intellectual milieux developed new ways of conceptualizing the production of geographical difference under modern capitalism. The theoretical foundations forged during this period have also proven useful for scholars concerned to analyze various aspects of geographical differentiation that cannot be fully derived from the logic of capital accumulation (Brenner 2004; Harvey 2003, 2006b; Taylor 1993).

Building upon this expansive, increasingly sophisticated literature, this chapter considers a specific question: how are the *geographies* of USD to be conceptualized? In his classic book on the topic, Neil Smith (1984) suggested that USD is deeply imbricated in the production of geographical scale. Indeed, it was his attempt to decipher the "see-saw movement" of USD that appears to have led him, in a brilliant intellectual manoeuvre, to theorize about geographical scale on its own terms rather than subsuming it under other geographical concepts such as territory and place. The very differentiation of global, national, regional, and urban scales, Smith argued, must be understood at once as a medium and a product of the process of USD under capitalism.

Smith's justifiably influential conceptualization inspired a generation of critical geographical scholarship not only on USD but also, more generally, on the production of scale and its associated politics. Against the background of recent debates on the new political economy of scale (see Mahon and Keil, this volume), this chapter revisits the intellectual terrain of Smith's initial theorization of USD. While I build closely upon the foundations constructed by Smith, I also argue for a broader, polymorphic conceptualization. Drawing upon a metaphor introduced by Lefebvre (1991, 87), I suggest that the geographies of USD resemble "a thousand leaves": that is, a multilayered fusion of several distinct *dimensions* of sociospatiality (for a closely related conceptualization, see also Jessop, this volume). While Smith's insight that

USD is scale-differentiated remains foundational, any adequate, historically nuanced conceptualization of this phenomenon must also consider its place-based, territorial, and networked dimensions. Paradoxically, it is precisely the progress of debates on the new political economy of scale during the past two decades, which have provided a differentiated conceptual vocabulary for the analysis of scalar structuration, that now enables us to reconsider processes of USD in their full geographical complexity.

Following a general overview of the theory of USD, I develop this theorization through a stylized analysis of its four most essential geographical dimensions during the geohistory of modern capitalism – namely, place, territory, scale, and networks. My argument underscores what I have elsewhere termed "the limits to scale" (Brenner 2001a). While I would agree with the contention of other contributors to this volume that processes of rescaling are central to the political economy of late modern capitalism (Brenner 2004), this chapter is intended to caution against the tendency to overextend scalar concepts.

Foundations

Reflexive theorizing on USD began in the 1970s and has subsequently flourished in the writings of critical geographical political economists. While this literature is now quite multifaceted, it contains at least four core theoretical propositions regarding the nature of USD under modern capitalist conditions, which can be briefly summarized as follows.

First, under capitalism, the existence of geographical difference is not simply an expression of the discrete qualities of particular places, of inherited differences among territories, or of the fact that sociospatiality is intrinsically heterogeneous. As the capitalist division of labour is deepened and extended, spaces throughout the world are simultaneously connected and distinguished in a see-saw movement of equalization and differentiation (Smith 1984). Rather than extinguishing the distinctiveness of places and territories, this dialectic of simultaneous interconnection/differentiation reworks inherited geographical differences, which can now only be understood in relational terms. From this point onward, geographical difference no longer represents the spatialization of particularity. It instead demarcates the distinctive positionality of any given space within an evolving, worldwide grid of interdependencies. In the most general terms, then, USD represents the aggregate, macrogeographical expression of such positionalities within each configuration of global capitalist development (Sheppard 2002).

Second, each historical framework of USD entails the differentiation of cores and peripheries, spaces of centrality and marginality, zones of inclusion and exclusion (Lefebvre 1991; Smith 1984; Soja 1985). Accordingly, in this conceptualization, spatial positionality refers not only to absolute geographical location but also to the relational situatedness of particular spaces within broader, asymmetrically organized frameworks of power (Sheppard 2002). The notion of USD is therefore intended to capture the deeply polarized distribution of socioeconomic assets, forms of geopolitical influence, ideological hegemony, and conditions of everyday life not only among different populations but also among spaces positioned differentially within the global capitalist system.

Third, patterns of USD are mediated through large-scale institutional forms (e.g., the modern state) and diverse social forces (e.g., capitalist firms, business organizations, trade unions, property owners, and place- or territory-based social movements). This means that the analysis of geographical difference necessarily entails an inquiry into the "politics of space" (Lefebvre 1976) through which historically specific structures of sociospatial polarization are produced. Capitalist accumulation strategies play a central role in the structuration of USD, but so do political institutions, territorially based alliances, social movements, and households (Cox 2002).

Fourth, during the historical evolution of capitalism, certain deep structures of USD have been entrenched. They include the core/periphery division on which the international division of labour has long been grounded (Amin 1979; Wallerstein 1974) and the city/countryside opposition (Williams 1973). Despite this, however, USD is always articulated in historically and contextually specific forms. Global inequality and the urban/rural divide remain persistent, durable features of capitalism, but their precise geographical contours have been reshaped during the past three centuries. Moreover, even as certain dimensions of USD under capitalism have proven relatively durable, others have been qualitatively modified during the process of historical development. Examples of the latter include the configuration of urban and regional settlement patterns, the geographies of industrial development, networks of infrastructural investment, and the concentration of political-economic hegemony (Harvey 1985; Soja 1985). Patterns of USD can thus be said to crystallize at the interface between inherited sociospatial configurations and emergent spatial strategies intended to transform the latter (Brenner 2004; Massey 1985).

A Thousand Leaves

Up to this point, my discussion has deployed the term "space" as a generic category for describing all aspects of geographical difference. I have thus referred to "spaces," "spatial differentiation," and, most generally, "uneven spatial development" without delineating the specific forms in which they are articulated. At this stage, it is essential to examine more closely the fabric of social space and, specifically, the contours of USD. To this end, Lefebvre's (1991) emphasis on the *polymorphic* character of social space within capitalist modernity provides a useful methodological starting point. From this point of view, the geographies of any social process – such as urbanization, state power, capital accumulation, or uneven development – cannot be understood with reference to a singular principle or all-encompassing pattern. Instead, several intertwined yet analytically distinct dimensions of sociospatiality may be distinguished (Brenner et al. 2006a, 2006b; Sheppard 2002).

For example, the principle of *place*, which entails geographical proximity, the embedding of social relations within particular locations and patterns of areal (horizontal) differentiation (Massey 1994; Paasi 2004), represents an important dimension of each of the aforementioned social processes, but it cannot capture all aspects of their geographies or serve as a generic metaphor for sociospatiality as such. To proceed otherwise entails the methodological error of *place-centrism:* that is, the treatment of social space as if it were composed completely and uniformly of places.

Similarly, the principle of *territoriality*, which entails the enclosure, bordering, and parcelization of social relations (Sack 1986; Taylor 1993), is powerfully implicated in diverse aspects of macrogeographical development. However, it would be a serious mistake to reduce all aspects of social space to this form. Indeed, even the geographies of the modern state, which has been routinely defined as a territorial power-container (see, e.g., Giddens 1984; Mann 1988), cannot be understood in exclusively territorial terms (Agnew 1994; Brenner et al. 2003). This fallacy, which has been quite pervasive within mainstream political studies, may be characterized as *methodological territorialism* (Agnew 1994; Brenner 2004).

The principle of *scaling*, which entails the vertical differentiation of social relations among, for instance, global, supranational, national, regional, urban, and/or local levels (Smith 1995; Swyngedouw 1997b), likewise represents an essential, but not comprehensive, element of modern sociospatial organization. To reduce sociospatiality as a whole to its scalar dimension leads to the methodological dead-end of *scale-centrism*.

Finally, the principle of *networking*, which entails the establishment of transversal interconnections across geographically dispersed locations or organizational units, is an increasingly significant dimension of contemporary sociospatiality (Castells 1996; Sum 1997; Whatmore and Thorne 1997). However, the fallacy of *network-centrism* must likewise be avoided insofar as the proliferation of long-distance, transversal linkages (e.g., through the deployment of new information technologies) does not necessarily erode the importance of place, territoriality, and scale as co-constitutive dimensions of social space (Bulkeley 2005; Leitner 2004).

Thus, in contrast to reductionist, isomorphic, and monodimensional approaches, it is methodologically imperative to view every sociospatial process as a complex crystallization of multiple, intertwined geographical dimensions and consequently to subject each of the latter to sustained analysis. In *The Production of Space*, Lefebvre (1991) develops this point through his thesis of the "superimposition and interpenetration of social spaces" (88). In one particularly vivid formulation, he likens the superimposed dimensions of social space to the intricate, asymmetrical layerings within a *mille-feuille* pastry – a powdery French dessert that means, literally, "a thousand leaves" (88). While Lefebvre's somewhat fanciful culinary metaphor may distract us momentarily from the intricacies of sociospatial theory, it has direct implications for the discussion at hand. Like the *mille-feuille*, formations of USD are composed of complex articulations among multiple patterns, contours, lines,

FIGURE 1.1
Mille-feuille cake
SOURCE: http://en.wikipedia.org/wiki/Image:Mille-feuille_01.jpg.

> ### Henri Lefebvre on the polymorphic character of sociospatiality
> (excerpts from Lefebvre 1991, 85-88)
>
> "How many maps ... might be needed to deal exhaustively with a given space, to code and decode all its meanings and contents? It is doubtful whether a finite number can ever be given in answer to this sort of question."
>
> "We are confronted not by one social space but by many – indeed, by an unlimited multiplicity or uncountable set of social spaces which we refer to generically as "social space." No space disappears in the course of growth and development: the *worldwide does not abolish the local* ... Thus social space, and especially urban space, emerged in all its diversity – and with a structure far more reminiscent of a flaky *mille-feuille* pastry than of the homogeneous and isotropic space of classical (Euclidian/Cartesian) mathematics."
>
> "The places of social space are very different from those of natural space in that they are not simply juxtaposed: they may be intercalated, combined, superimposed ... Consequently the local ... does not disappear, for it is never absorbed by the regional, national, or even worldwide level. The national and regional levels take in innumerable "places"; national space embraces the regions; and world space does not merely subsume national spaces, but even (for the time being at least) precipitates the formation of new national spaces through a remarkable process of fission."
>
> "The principle of the interpenetration and superimposition of social spaces has one very helpful result, for it means that each fragment of space subjected to analysis masks not just one social relationship but a host of them that analysis can potentially disclose."

folds, points, clusters, and edges. Drawing upon the distinction between place, territory, scale, and networks introduced above, the remainder of this chapter elaborates this contention through a series of macrogeographical generalizations regarding the evolutionary patterning of USD during the *longue durée* history of capitalism. A schematic summary of this discussion is provided in Figure 1.2, which links major accounts of the *sources* of USD under capitalism

Figure 1.2

Geographies of uneven spatial development under capitalism

Underlying tendencies and tensions within the geographies of capitalism
- Tension between space-annihilating tendencies of capital (promoting spatial dispersal) and its endemic space-dependency (promoting spatial concentration)
- Tension between capital's drive towards equalization (promoting spatial redistribution) and its drive towards differentiation (promoting spatial inequality)
- Endemic tendency towards the "creative destruction" of sociospatial configurations
- Recurrent quest for a "spatial fix" or "structured coherence" to secure the provisional stabilization of sociospatial configurations
- Chronically unstable, temporary character of spatial fixes: geographies of capitalism remain fundamentally inconstant, discontinuous, and uneven

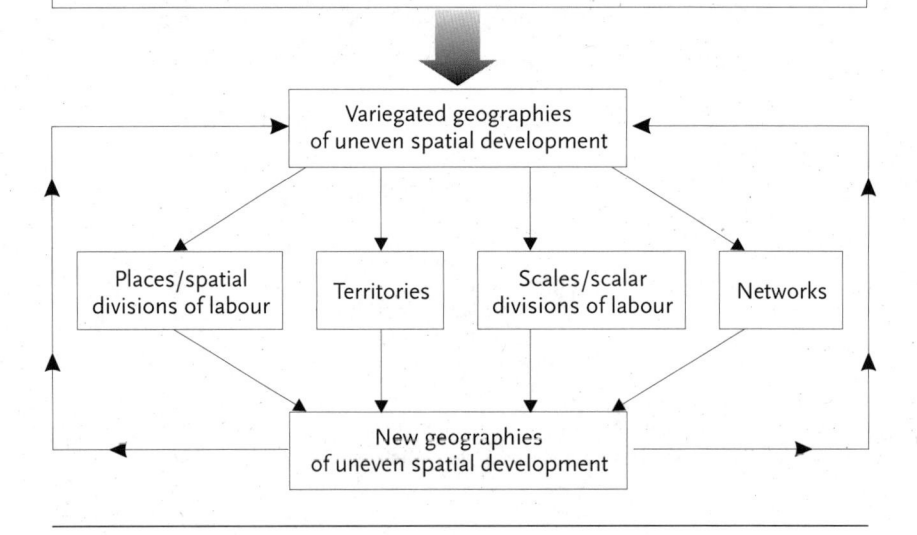

⬇

Variegated geographies of uneven spatial development

| Places/spatial divisions of labour | Territories | Scales/scalar divisions of labour | Networks |

New geographies of uneven spatial development

(Harvey 1982; Smith 1984) to the analysis of its polymorphic *geographies* that is elaborated below.

Places and Uneven Spatial Development

Capitalism emerged within a differentiated geographical landscape inherited from previous modes of production. Nonetheless, even in its incipient stages, capitalist expansion entailed profound transformations of places, above all through the establishment of new spatial divisions of labour in which dispersed geographical locations were assigned specific functional roles within the expanding capitalist world market. Initially, under merchant capitalism (1600-1750), these spatial divisions of labour were articulated with circuits of precapitalist trade and the geographies of inherited resource endowments – for example, the locations of waterways, raw materials, mineral supplies, and so forth. However, with the progressive industrialization of capital since the mid-eighteenth century, and the increasing integration of the production process into circuits of accumulation, specifically capitalist spatial divisions of labour emerged that have been based predominantly upon socially constructed economic assets ("agglomeration economies"). Under these circumstances, beginning in the core zones of Western Europe and eventually extending throughout the world economy, urbanization processes dramatically accelerated as capital and labour were concentrated within large-scale, specialized production complexes and long-distance trade networks were at once expanded and thickened. On a macrogeographical level, these trends also entailed the consolidation of a worldwide grid of places differentiated according to their particular functions, specializations, and positions within the spaces of global accumulation (Läpple 1978; Storper and Walker 1989). This differentiated landscape of place-making processes has articulated patterns of USD in at least five key ways.

First, new spatial divisions emerged within the expanding centres of capitalist production through residential segregation, the functional division of urban space, and the consolidation of new urban infrastructures for production and social reproduction. As capitalist urbanization has intensified and accelerated during the past two centuries, these intraplace divisions have continued to evolve, albeit always in contextually specific forms (Gordon 1978).

Second, the urban/rural divide was exacerbated as rapid industrialization fuelled large-scale urbanization and an increasing peripheralization or "underdevelopment" of rural spaces (Williams 1973). The division between two distinct *types* of places – capital-rich, industrializing urban centres and capital-poor, predominantly agrarian peripheries – thus became an essential axis of capitalist USD (Myrdal 1957). Even as settlement patterns have been differentiated among an ever broader range of types, this basic division has persisted, albeit in a continually evolving form, throughout the past two centuries (McMichael 2006).

Third, as capitalist industrialization accelerated in the global core zones, places across the global periphery were transformed into sites for the primary extraction, processing, and export of raw materials, generally through a process of "accumulation by dispossession" in which surpluses were violently or coercively appropriated (Harvey 2003). In this manner, spatial divisions of labour articulated a worldwide pattern of USD in which core, capital-rich zones of large-scale industrialization (the "global North") were differentiated from peripheral, capital-poor areas of relative underdevelopment (the "global South") (Amin 1979; Wallerstein 1974).

Fourth, as industrial restructuring and technological change have accelerated since the nineteenth century, new forms of interplace differentiation have rippled across the global system. The spatial divisions of labour produced through the first wave of capitalist industrialization have been subjected to rounds of "creative destruction" in conjunction with each period of crisis-induced restructuring – hence the increasingly chronic instability of places and interplace relations under capitalism since the nineteenth century. Such restructuring processes have, in fact, seriously unsettled the concrete patterns associated with each of the three previously mentioned forms of place-based USD (intraurban, urban/rural, and global core/periphery). The creative destruction of spatial divisions of labour has not, however, eroded the basic significance of place as an axis for the articulation of geographical difference.

Fifth, and finally, places may become basing points and arenas for social mobilizations that destabilize or otherwise modify broader patterns of USD (Harvey 1989c). This is because, even as capital strives to transform places, place-based attachments persist in the form of everyday routines, regimes of social reproduction, institutionalized political compromises, and socio-cultural identities. Such place-based commitments are often articulated quite sharply when broader processes of capitalist restructuring destabilize patterns of interplace relations. Consequently, capital's impulsion to rework spatial divisions of labour in search of new opportunities for profit making may encounter intense resistance from those whose everyday lives, livelihoods, and identities are tightly enmeshed within particular places. The resultant forms of place-based "revulsion and revolt" may assume reactionary or progressive forms (Harvey 1989c), but whatever their political valence, the cumulative impact of such mobilizations is to insert an element of friction into capital's process of creative destruction. Places, in other words, cannot be creatively destroyed according to the whim of capital; rather, their evolution is an object and stake of intensive sociopolitical contestation and negotiation

(Hudson 2001). The concrete shape of place-based USD is therefore powerfully mediated through social struggles regarding the form, pace, rhythm, and trajectory of capital's process of creative destruction.

Territories and Uneven Spatial Development

The capitalist space-economy emerged in medieval Europe within a fragmented, decentralized mosaic of political-economic spaces. This mosaic encompassed small city-state enclaves, interurban networks, bishoprics, duchies, principalities, and a patchwork of absolutist state structures lacking fixed territorial boundaries (Spruyt 1994). However, following the Peace of Westphalia of 1648, the principle of territoriality became an increasingly foundational basis for organizing political life. Despite continued institutional and geographical diversity among them, states were now understood to occupy mutually exclusive, non-overlapping, contiguous, and sovereign territorial spaces and were reflexively monitored as such (Giddens 1984; Ruggie 1993). Borders were now seen clearly to separate the "inside" from the "outside" of states, and the domestic/foreign divide came to serve as a basic reference point for political-economic activity (Agnew and Corbridge 1994; Walker 1993). With the consolidation of mercantile capitalism, this grid of state territories was entrenched as both statesmen and capitalists attempted to expand international trade, to consolidate national markets, and thereby to increase national wealth (Braudel 1984). The territorialization of worldwide social space continued during the first wave of capitalist industrialization through (a) the intensified regulation of interstate boundaries; (b) the increasing internal parcelization of state space among intergovernmental administrative hierarchies; (c) the development of enhanced infrastructural capacities through which states could attempt to extend their authority over all "points" within their jurisdictional borders; and (d) the imperialist conquest and territorial division of peripheralized zones of the world economy under the yoke of colonial rule (Lefebvre 1978; Maier 2000).

These territorializations were maintained during subsequent rounds of capitalist industrialization in the nineteenth and twentieth centuries, even through phases of profound geoeconomic and geopolitical instability. This is not to suggest that territoriality has remained static within the Westphalian system; its specific roles have evolved significantly. The power and wealth containers of early modern territorial states were superseded by new forms of state developmentalism, nationalism, and welfarism that were likewise grounded upon distinctively territorial structures and strategies (Taylor 1994).

Concomitantly, the concrete geographies of interstate borders and intrastate jurisdictional divisions have periodically been modified, whether through warfare, internal rebellions, legal decisions, or social protest. And, as interstate relations have evolved in relation to the broader dynamic of worldwide capitalist development, new, large-scale territorial institutions (e.g., the European Union, NAFTA, ASEAN, and Mercosur) have been introduced that encompass multiple (national) state structures. Nonetheless, even in the midst of these macrohistorical realignments, the underlying principle of territoriality has been reproduced (Sack 1986). Most crucially, for my purposes, the differentiated landscapes of state territorial organization have articulated, mediated, and modified forms of USD in at least five central ways.

First, as the Westphalian interstate system has been globalized, territory has come to serve as a taken-for-granted category for the understanding of sociospatial organization more generally (Agnew 1994; Häkli 2001). As a result, patterns of USD have been widely conceptualized in territorial terms, whether in institutionalized forms of data collection (e.g., in national censuses, OECD statistical tables, or World Bank development reports), in political discourse (e.g., in debates on spatial inequalities within territorially demarcated areas such as Europe, Britain, the South East of England, or London), or in everyday life (e.g., in popular representations of "Africa" or "the ghetto"). In each case, a unit of analysis is defined with reference to the jurisdictional boundaries of states, territorially demarcated substate areas, or groups of territorial states. It is then treated as a relatively coherent, integrated whole and contrasted to other, formally equivalent units with reference to a particular socioeconomic indicator (e.g., population, unemployment, GDP, or crime rates) or a perceived characteristic (e.g., wealth or poverty, order or disorder). Thus, even though territory represents only one among several constitutive dimensions of USD, it has generally been treated as the most fundamental sociospatial form in terms of which geographical inequalities are to be understood and acted upon.

Second, within the modern interstate system, state territorial structures demonstrate considerable rigidity and, therefore, frequently act as a drag upon the capitalist impulsion to relocate investment activity (Harvey 1985, 2003). In other words, the territorial borders delineated and controlled by states have been much less malleable than the spatial imprints of capital circulation that interpenetrate them. Consequently, such borders impose determinate locational constraints upon the capitalist drive to creatively destroy established sociospatial configurations. Even when the concrete geographies of capital have been rearranged, the modern interstate system has provided a relatively fixed, stable, and immobile grid of institutionalized sociospatial divisions – a world of parcelized, bordered spaces – for the process of capital circulation. To be sure, state territorial borders and internal jurisdictional arrangements have been modified during the course of capitalist development, in some cases quite significantly (e.g., after major military conflicts, civil wars, or revolutions). Once institutionalized, however, the concrete spatial parcels demarcated by state boundaries are relatively difficult to modify, even as their political-economic functions continue to evolve (Cox 1990; Taylor 1994). As discussed previously, patterns of USD are intimately intertwined with the endemic tension between capital's dependence upon fixed sociospatial arrangements and its equally chronic tendency to creatively destroy those very arrangements in pursuit of fresh possibilities for accumulation. The consolidation of state territoriality as a deep structure of sociospatial organization within modern capitalism directly impacts this contradictory dynamic: it imposes a certain element of fixity, embodied in the worldwide grid of state territories, upon an otherwise restlessly changing geographical landscape (Harvey 1985).

Third, actually existing state territorial borders and internal jurisdictional boundaries have direct, durable implications for the concrete forms in which place-based inequalities and spatial divisions of labour are articulated. This is because different types of state territorial structures and regulatory arrangements organize widely divergent conditions for capital circulation. For instance, the relative costs and availability of labour power, equipment, land, and raw materials, the nature of transportation and communication infrastructures, and the level of taxation and tariffs may diverge significantly among state territories as well as among intrastate (regional or local) political jurisdictions. Such inter- and intraterritorial differences are likely to have profound ramifications for the locational geographies of capital and, by implication, larger-scale spatial divisions of labour. Capitalists in search of cost-competitive locations are most likely to invest in territories (whether neighbourhoods, cities, regions, countries, or superregions) that provide the lowest costs of production and exchange. By contrast, capitalists whose accumulation strategies hinge upon more specialized forms of labour power, interfirm relations, infrastructural conditions, institutional relays, and technological resources are more likely to sink their investments into territories that provide such non-substitutable, territorially embedded socioeconomic assets (Storper and Walker 1989). In this sense, the geographies of (state) territories do not only interpenetrate place-based patterns of USD but also directly shape them. Consequently, as Cox (2002, 253) notes, there is frequently "some congruence between patterns of geographically uneven development ... and the territorial structure of the state."

Fourth, in significant measure due to their territorially centralized institutional structures, state institutions have the capacity to mobilize political strategies to influence patterns of USD both within and beyond their borders (Brenner 2004). States may pursue this goal through diverse policy instruments, including industrial policies, economic development initiatives, infrastructure investments, spatial planning programs, labour market policies, regional policies, urban policies, housing policies, international trade agreements, and imperialist interventions, all of which have direct or indirect ramifications for intra- and suprastate geographies of production, reproduction, and circulation. During the twentieth century, national-developmentalist state institutions came to promote the entire state territory as an integrated framework for economic growth. Relatively non-industrialized rural and peripheral regions were targeted in redistributive policies that aimed to spread urban industrial growth more evenly throughout the national territory. Most recently, across much of the world economy, major urban and regional economies have become strategically important targets for a range of spatially selective policies intended to enhance national competitive advantages in the context of accelerated geoeconomic integration. Throughout these periods, diverse forms of state-led imperialism, colonialism, and neocolonialism profoundly influenced patterns of USD beyond the state's jurisdictional borders, whether through the expropriation of raw materials, the construction of markets, or, most recently, the imposition of regulatory conditions favourable to foreign direct investment (Harvey 2003). While the concrete effects of such interventions have varied considerably, and have often been considerably at odds with their declared purpose, these examples illustrate the multifarious ways in which state institutions have attempted to influence patterns of USD both within and beyond their territorial jurisdictions.

Fifth, the territorial structures of the state provide various overlapping institutional arenas in and through which social movements may attempt to modify inherited forms of USD. Insofar as places represent the most immediate geographical terrain on which the disruptive consequences of capitalist creative destruction are experienced, social movements frequently assume a place-based form. Crucially, however, the "nested hierarchical structures" of the state (Harvey 1982, 430) may likewise become important platforms for social forces concerned to confront the dislocations of creative destruction. Insofar as place-based mobilizations attempt to harness the institutional capacities of the state in pursuit of their agendas, they necessarily assume at least a partially territorial form. Under these circumstances, state institutions (whether national, regional, or local) may be mobilized against capital's strategies of place transformation or at least as a means to reshape the latter to accommodate popular or sectional demands. But meanwhile, capitalists may adopt territorial strategies of their own, harnessing state institutions in order to preserve, modify, or transform the spatial divisions of labour upon which their current or projected accumulation strategies depend. In this manner, the territorial structures of the state become a terrain of political contestation in which diverse social forces struggle to influence the geographies of capital accumulation (Cox 1990). The processes of territorial alliance formation that ricochet throughout all levels of the state apparatus may thus have profound implications for the contextually specific forms in which USD is articulated.

Scales and Uneven Spatial Development

The preceding discussion of places, territories, and geographies of USD has presupposed a third, equally foundational dimension of sociospatial differentiation – geographical scale. In addition to the "horizontal" or areal differentiation of social practices across places and territories (or geographical scope), there is also an equally fundamental "vertical" differentiation in which social relations are hierarchically articulated among, for instance, global, supranational, national, regional, metropolitan, and/or local scales (Collinge 1999; Swyngedouw 1997b). Insofar as any social, political, or economic process or institutional form is internally differentiated into a vertical hierarchy of relatively discrete spatial units, the problem of its scalar organization arises. Thus understood, like other macrogeographical processes under capitalism, USD is profoundly scale-differentiated. Indeed, all of the aspects of USD discussed above under the rubric of place and territory are articulated in profoundly scale-differentiated forms.

The establishment of distinctively capitalist spatial divisions of labour and the territorialization of political power during the course of capitalist industrialization entailed not only the transformation of places, the consolidation of new intra- and interplace divisions, the territorial extension of capitalism beyond its European heartlands, and the territorial segmentation of sociospatial inequality throughout the capitalist space-economy. These developments were also closely intertwined with qualitatively new forms of scalar differentiation, including, most centrally, three aspects.

First, the *urban* and *regional* scales were institutionalized as key spatial niches for agglomerations of capital and labour, as embodied in major metropolitan centres (Harvey 1982). This urban and regional scaling of USD was constitutively intertwined with the production of the intra- and interplace inequalities described above but cannot be reduced to the latter. It involved not only the polarization of urban spatial organization and the differentiation of cities and city-regions from other types of settlement spaces but also their strategic positioning within a broader hierarchy of sociospatial forms stretching from the local scale to the global scale.

Second, the *global* scale was consolidated as the ultimate geographical horizon for capitalist expansion, as embodied in the world market (Wallerstein 1974). This globalization of capital circulation necessarily entailed a territorial extension of the capitalist system into hitherto unincorporated zones and the crystallization of new forms of core/periphery polarization. It also helped to consolidate the global scale as an encompassing geographical niche within the emergent capitalist interscalar hierarchy.

Third, the *national* scale was consolidated as an institutionalized terrain of mediation within the process of intercapitalist competition, as embodied in the political-institutional hierarchies of the territorial state (Smith 1995). This nationalized scaling of political–economic space has already been examined above, through the analytical lens of (national) territoriality. It contributed to, and was in turn reinforced by, the various forms of interplace differentiation and territorial inequality that were surveyed previously.

In close conjunction with the latter trends, processes of USD have been articulated onto several additional geographical scales as well, including (a) the *neighbourhood* scale, embodied in intraurban zones of association and political jurisdiction, and (b) the *supranational* scale, embodied in institutionally demarcated spaces of capital circulation and political regulation that encompass multiple national states (e.g., the European Union, NAFTA, ASEAN). Each of the latter scalings of USD has been intertwined with place-based and territorial inequalities, yet their scalar dimension cannot be reduced to either of the latter. Insofar as each of the aforementioned scales provided an additional niche within the broader interscalar hierarchies of modern capitalism, it contributed to the further differentiation of processes of USD.

Because scales are defined relationally, the institutional and spatial coherence of those listed above can be grasped only with reference to their distinctive roles and positions within interscalar hierarchies. Concomitantly, because the functions, institutional expressions, and interconnections among these scales have evolved historically, their differentiation should not be treated as an absolute functional requirement for the reproduction of capital. Nonetheless, because the differentiation among the neighbourhood, urban, regional, national, supranational, and global scales has been reproduced even as historically specific spatial divisions of labour and territorial arrangements have been creatively destroyed, they must be viewed as deep structures within capitalism's restlessly changing geographical landscape. In this sense, the process of USD under capitalism at once presupposes and reinforces a historically specific formation of scale differentiation (Smith 1984), which has been intimately intertwined with place-based and territorial articulations of sociospatial difference.

However, just as place-based and territorial patterns of USD have been reworked during the geohistory of capitalism, so too have its scalar geographies. Beyond the initial wave of scale differentiation discussed above, in which specifically capitalist instantiations of the urban-regional, national, and global scales were produced, the scalar configuration of USD has assumed historically specific forms *within* the capitalist system and, concomitantly, has been periodically junked and rewoven. These successive waves of "rescaling" (Brenner 1998a; Swyngedouw 1997b) represent an essential medium and expression of USD under capitalism.

Mercantile and early industrial capitalism involved a generalized condition of "scale relativization" (Collinge 1999) in which no single scale prevailed as the dominant level of political-economic organization. Patterns of USD were articulated at multiple spatial scales, from the urban and the national to the imperial and the global. Within the newly consolidating geographies of early modern capitalism, spatial scales provided a relatively malleable scaffolding in and through which USD could be differentiated among diverse types of places, territories, and zones of exchange.

This situation of scale relativization was rearticulated during the period of territorial state consolidation that began in the eighteenth century and continued through successive waves of capitalist industrialization well into the twentieth century. From this broad period until the termination of national-developmentalist capitalism (early 1970s), the national scale gradually became predominant at once as a crystallization point for USD and as an institutional locus for political strategies to manage the latter. As Taylor (1994) notes, the effort to impose a spatial congruence between economic processes and political life within each state's territory also entailed a growing nationalization of key aspects of socio-institutional existence (see also Cerny 1995). To be sure, patterns of USD were articulated at other spatial scales, from the global to the local, but the increasing territorialization of political-economic life during this epoch was inextricably linked to a generalized nationalization of sociospatial inequality (Maier 2000). Consequently, inequality among cities and regions, or in the international arena, was increasingly understood and acted upon as if it could be neatly aggregated upward or collapsed downward into the national scale of political-economic organization. Despite significant geoeconomic crises, military conflagrations, and waves of industrial restructuring that periodically unsettled sociospatial arrangements, this nationalized scalar configuration lasted until the crisis of national-developmentalist capitalism in the late twentieth century.

The most recent round of worldwide capitalist restructuring of the post-1970s period has decentred the nationalized "scalar fix" (Smith 1995) and engendered a renewed situation of scale relativization. The expansion of the role of transnational corporations and global finance capital since the early 1970s, coupled with the consolidation of a new international division of labour, the emergence of post-Fordist forms of industrial agglomeration, the intensification of international diasporic flows, and the growing importance of new information technologies in mediating worldwide economic transactions, are among the most blatant indicators of this systemic sociospatial realignment (Agnew and Corbridge 1994). Some scholars have characterized these trends with reference to the purported ascendancy of a single spatial scale – as, for instance, in accounts of the "new globalism," "triadization," "Europeanization," the "new regionalism," the "new localism," or the "local-global nexus" (for an overview, see Lee and Wills 1997). By contrast, the argument proposed here is that the scalar architecture of capitalism as a whole – and, specifically, of USD – is being contested and reworked in unpredictable, often uncontrollable, ways (Brenner 2004; Jessop 2000; Swyngedouw 1997b). This line of interpretation builds upon the observation that previously nodal, subordinate, or marginal spatial scales are acquiring a renewed significance in contemporary political-economic processes. The key claim, however, is not that the national scale is being superseded or that any other scale has now acquired a dominance akin to that of the national during previous phases of capitalist geohistorical development. Rather, the significance of the national is now ever more tightly linked to other supra- and subnational scales of political-economic organization than was previously the case. Concomitantly, patterns of USD are no longer configured around a single, predominant scale of political-economic organization.

In sum, this discussion suggests five key ways in which scaling processes may influence, and in turn be shaped by, processes of USD. First, the *differentiation of scales* under capitalism generates a hierarchical, but often tangled, scaffolding of sociospatial forms in and through which processes of USD may be organized and reproduced.

Second, scalar configurations are themselves internally differentiated insofar as they contain specific divisions of labour among their constitutive tiers (*scalar divisions of labour*). Whether they appear within political or economic organizational forms, such scalar divisions of labour are one of the key scalar expressions of sociospatial inequality (Collinge 1999).

Third, *scalar fixes* may emerge insofar as interscalar relations are provisionally stabilized around a relatively established scalar division of labour. They thus represent a mechanism through which scale-articulated and scale-dependent forms of USD may be further entrenched (Smith 1995).

Fourth, insofar as scalar fixes are destabilized and interscalar relations are unsettled, *rescaling processes* ensue in which new scales of political-economic organization and new interscalar hierarchies are produced (Swyngedouw 1997b). Rescaling processes may thus undermine established patterns of USD while also producing qualitatively new forms of sociospatial inequality and sociospatial differentiation.

Fifth, insofar as interscalar arrangements are contested, a *politics of scale* emerges in which diverse social forces actively struggle to reorganize the functions, organizational embodiments, and/or interconnections among spatial scales (Smith 1995). Indeed, like place and territory, scale can likewise serve as a basing point for social movements concerned with challenging established patterns of USD. Thus, the specific configuration of scale-based patterns of USD must be viewed as both object and stake of sociopolitical contestation.

Networks and Uneven Spatial Development

These considerations bring us to one final dimension of USD that has attracted considerable attention in recent years – namely, the role of networks and networking as the basis for an alternative, topological mode of sociospatial organization based upon "points of connection and lines of flow, as opposed to ... fixed surfaces and boundaries" (Whatmore and Thorne 1997, 289). According to Leitner (2004, 248), networks "span space" by establishing horizontal, capillary-like interlinkages among geographically dispersed nodal points. Consequently, "the spatial surface spanned by networks is ... fluid and unstable" insofar as (a) the degree of connectivity among network nodes may fluctuate; (b) patterns of network membership may fluctuate; and (c) multiple networks may overlap, interpenetrate, and crosscut one another (Leitner 2004, 248-49).

Network geographies have long figured centrally in the geohistory of capitalism, and they have been tightly enmeshed with the uneven geographies of places, territories, and scales in nearly all of their concrete forms. Indeed, interfirm networks, diasporic networks, intercity networks, infrastructural networks, interstate networks, and network-based social movements have thoroughly interpenetrated the place-based, territorial, and scalar geographies of mercantile, industrial, and globalizing capitalism that were surveyed above. Three brief examples illustrate the influence of networks upon patterns of USD.

First, the process of capital accumulation has long hinged upon networked relationships among firms. Although firms within the same sector aggressively compete for profit shares, others engage in cooperative relations through forms of subcontracting, information sharing, and diverse "untraded interdependencies" (Storper 1996). While the precise nature of such interconnections has evolved historically, they have powerfully intensified patterns of urban-regional agglomeration and, by implication, broader grids of place-based USD during the history of capitalist development (Scott 1988).

Second, the consolidation of the modern interstate system has likewise entailed various types of networked relationships within and among national state apparatuses. Through international organizations, international treaties, international agreements, and other types of informal regulatory and judicial agreements, networks have played an important mediating role in governing the global interstate system (Rosenau and Czempiel 1992). Networks have also long figured centrally in intergovernmental relations within each (national) state apparatus, where they have generally served to coordinate activities among diverse agencies, branches, and tiers of government. Insofar as these intergovernmental networks have influenced the geographies of capital investment, state activities, public service provision, and sociopolitical struggle, they have also necessarily impacted broader patterns of place- and territory-based USD.

Third, in addition to their place-based, territorially grounded, and scale-differentiated forms, social movements have deployed networked modes of organization in order to pursue their goals. From the international socialist movement to ACT UP and the global justice movement, the activities of social movements have depended upon networked ties as a basis for both communication and mobilization across places, scales, and territories. Social movement networks are generally embedded within, and intertwined with, places and territories, and they are always articulated in scale-differentiated forms. Yet, their geographies cannot be reduced to any of the latter dimensions of sociospatiality. Insofar as networking strategies impact the ability of social movements to influence ongoing processes of sociospatial change under capitalism, they also influence historically specific formations of USD.

In sum, networks may impact patterns of USD in at least two central ways. First, networks generally crosscut place-based, territorial, and scalar patterns of USD. In so doing, network formations may reinforce, interrupt, or destabilize intraplace divisions, spatial divisions of labour, territorial borders, interterritorial relations, or scalar hierarchies. Concomitantly, networks may also reinforce rather than alleviate extant geographies of sociospatial inequality, whether place-based, territorial, or scalar (Leitner and Sheppard 2002; Sheppard 2002).

Second, and contrary to popular representations of networks as non-hierarchical and democratic, many actually existing networks are internally stratified and externally exclusionary. They contain power hierarchies that marginalize some social forces at the expense of others, both within and beyond the network (Leitner and Sheppard 2002). They may be manifested through the differential abilities of participants to influence network operations; through the establishment of a division of labour within the network that differentially allocates resources, tasks, and burdens among participants; or through the establishment of distinctive rules of closure that limit participation within the network to particular individuals, groups, or organizational entities. While these network-based power relations may be expressed in variegated socio-organizational forms, they express USD insofar as they are articulated in distinctively geographical patterns.

The question of how network geographies are impacting contemporary patterns of USD is a matter of considerable scholarly contention. Many scholars of globalization have suggested that networks are today superseding the geographies of place, territory, and scale upon which the long-term geohistory of capitalism has been grounded. Alongside predictions that territoriality is being dissolved due to processes of deterritorialization (see, e.g., O'Brien 1990), this position has recently been articulated through several influential interventions, including Castells' (1996) notion of the "space of flows," Amin's (2002) arguments for a "non-scalar and topological" interpretation of globalization, and Marston, Jones, and Woodward's (2005) proposal for a "flat ontology." Of course, these authors' diverse intellectual and political concerns cannot be reduced to the specific theme of USD, but they do commonly imply that inherited formations of sociospatial inequality are now being transcended through a radically new form of sociospatiality, based upon an ontology of networks.

It is not possible to settle here the question of how inherited patterns of USD are being remoulded through emergent networks. Nonetheless, the arguments developed in the preceding pages are intended to underscore the limitations of any approach that privileges a singular dimension of sociospatiality. The observation that networked forms of sociospatial organization are gaining a renewed significance is potentially productive insofar as – much like Smith's (1984) initial reflections on scale over two decades ago – it directs attention to a previously neglected dimension of sociospatiality. However, this useful observation does not logically translate into the claim that places, territories, and scales no longer exist or no longer serve to mediate processes of USD. To proceed otherwise is to engage in the methodological fallacy of network-centrism: it entails a reduction of the *mille-feuille* of modern sociospatiality into a singular, totalized form, that of the network. The preceding analysis suggests that the key issue is not the *replacement* of places, territories, and scales by networked geographies but the co-constitutive *rearticulation* of each dimension of sociospatiality in relation to one another, through ongoing strategies and struggles over the present and future shape of USD.

Coda

By way of conclusion, it may be useful to comment on the concept of a "new political economy of scale" around which this book is organized. On my reading, this concept usefully underscores the increasingly reflexive ways in which scholars are analyzing the production and transformation of scalar arrangements within contemporary capitalism. At the same time, the preceding discussion suggests two specific modifications to this concept.

First, as understood here, scale cannot be the "object" of politicaleconomic analysis, for scales exist only insofar as key political-economic processes are scale-differentiated. From this point of view, it is more appropriate to speak of *scaled political economies* – that is, of the scaling and rescaling of distinctive political-economic processes – rather than of a political economy of scale per se.

Second, because of the endemically polymorphic character of sociospatiality, a scaled political economy is most powerful when it is reflexively linked to place-, territory-, and network-sensitive approaches to sociospatial theory. In other words, a scaled political economy can in itself depict no more than a silhouette of sociospatiality; it becomes most intellectually powerful when it is reflexively combined with studies of the political economies of place, territory, and networks.

2
Is Scale a Chaotic Concept?
Notes on Processes of Scale Production

Byron Miller

Since the publication of Andrew Herod's (1991) classic analysis of labour activism and "the production of scale," there has been an explosion of scholarship addressing the politics of scale. In recent years, however, a growing body of literature has begun to critique scalar concepts and analyses, arguing instead for a focus on networks. Indeed, several actor-network theorists see network analysis replacing much of the analysis currently conducted under the rubric of scale. Much of the recent fascination with networks stems from the work of Bruno Latour, who argues for a view of space and time rooted in actor-network topologies.[1] According to this view, actors gain power by drawing on fluid network relationships; indeed, power is about shaping and building networks. It is the "action in actor-networks [that configures] space ... These actions, and the relations in which they are conducted, are grounded; they never shift registers or scales but remain firmly within networks" (Murdoch 1998, 361). Actor-network theory and its conceptual cousins see spatiality in terms of translocal and transnational connectivity and absence.

While Marston, Jones, and Woodward (2005) and Thrift (1995) represent the most extreme positions in the scale debate, it is clear that a number of thoughtful critics have come to the conclusion that much scalar analysis is imprecise, attempts to subsume too much within its conceptual architecture, and yields little that could not be better understood in other terms. Howitt (2003, 138) has perhaps summed up the scale debate most succinctly, observing that, while "there is a wide consensus amongst human geographers that the social construction of scale affects cultural and political landscape," scale is a "troubling and even chaotic concept."

All of these critiques point, in one way or another, to a fundamental question: what is scale? Much of the debate over scale can be traced to the fact that definitions and understandings of scale are diverse and frequently ambiguous. Scholars conducting scalar analysis often do so without precisely defining scale or identifying the processes and technologies through which scale is constructed. Likewise, critics of scalar analysis frequently leap from identification of real shortcomings in the literature to sweeping generalizations that discard the baby with the bathwater. On both sides of the debate, far too little attention is paid to the specific processes and technologies that produce what we understand as "scale." My central aim in this chapter is to explore some of the key processes and technologies of scale production as they relate to the realms of the economy, state, and culture – the social production of scale and the scalar production of the social. In this exercise, I will also consider whether scale is – or is not – a chaotic concept.

What Is a Chaotic Concept?

The notion of "a chaotic concept" originally derives from Marx and has become widely known through the work of Andrew Sayer. As Sayer (1992) explains, a chaotic concept is one that is not rationally abstracted from objects and relations. It does not "isolate ... a significant element of the world which has some unity and autonomous force, such as a structure. A bad abstraction arbitrarily divides the indivisible and/or lumps together the unrelated and the inessential, thereby 'carving up' the object of study with little or no regard for its structure and form" (138). Like the notion of "services" in economics, chaotic concepts lump together a diverse range of objects and processes, many of them unrelated.

The notion of "scale," it seems, lumps together a number of different processes giving rise to differing conceptions of scale associated with size, level, and relation (see Howitt 2003). Whether the processes that produce scale are unrelated, thereby justifying the claim that scale is a chaotic concept, is another matter. The concept of scale may well subsume different processes, but they may be related in ways that warrant their consideration under a common umbrella term.[2] Any attempt to resolve the chaotic concept question requires, first and foremost, an understanding of the specific processes and technologies of power through which scale is produced. Only after we understand these processes and technologies can we begin to discuss whether scale is indeed a chaotic concept or whether it subsumes various processes that are nonetheless related.

Processes of Scale Production

Surprisingly, other than acknowledging that scale is socially constructed through struggle, the scale literature contains very little discussion of specific processes and technologies of scale production. In their critique of the scale literature Marston, Jones, and Woodward (2005) provide one of the few accounts of how scale is produced. They argue that scale is a form of bordering practice: "One encounters [scalar] 'structures' not at some level once removed, 'up there' in a vertical imaginary, but on the ground, in practice, the result of marking territories horizontally through boundaries and enclosures, documents and rules, enforcing agents and their authoritative resources. Geographies of extension highlight these geopolitical practices of space making" (420). Their discussion of scale as a bordering practice is a good place to start a discussion of scale production because it offers one of the very few accounts of a scale production technology. As they point out, the relationship between bordering practices and scale has not been comprehensively considered, yet, they are clearly related. "Scale as size," for instance, necessarily entails the delineation of territory, and territory requires boundaries. Yet, other technologies of scale production are critical as well, rendering their interpretation of scale as merely the "marking of territories horizontally" untenable. Technologies such as those relating to the assignment of responsibilities to, and the construction of capacities of, territorially constituted institutions play critical roles in the social construction of scale (Leitner and Miller 2007).

Boundaries delineate relationships of inclusion and exclusion across a wide range of social, cultural, economic, and political processes. Boundaries are integral to the definition and control of territorial space (Sibley 1995; Van Houtum, Kramsch, and Zierhofer 2005) yet never absolute or impermeable. Social space is replete with examples of ambiguous and fuzzy boundaries such as those between public space and private space. State space, to take a different example, may appear to be precisely bounded and indeed may be. But precisely specified boundaries can nonetheless be quite permeable, as demonstrated by a wide range of flows and connections across them (Adams 1996; Agnew 1994; Martin 1999). State territory, narrowly conceived, can never exhaust the range of sociospatial relationships that affect states, their actions, and their capacities. Indeed, the bounding of territory, such as scale as size, is shaped by forces both internal and external to a given territory as well as relationships and alliances across territorial boundaries. These forces are dynamic, meaning not only that the location of boundaries can shift but also that their permeability can change for particular actors or objects given the power geometry of specific struggles. Attempts to fix or change spatial relationships – including boundaries and scales – are part and parcel of sociospatial struggle.

Of course, scale as size cannot be simply reduced to a question of boundaries. Boundaries may have particular qualitative properties at given times and places, but of equal importance is what they encompass. Boundaries delimit territories that may range from very limited to very extensive. The question of the extensiveness of a territory is an extremely important one. Whether the issue is the number of people adopting a common territorial identity, the type and quantity of natural resources available, the size of internal markets, the number of actors involved in a network of solidarity, or the economic and political clout that an institution brings to a negotiation process, the extensiveness of a territory can play a crucial role in determining the balance of power among competing territorial groups and institutions.

It is not surprising that "scale jumping" or "scale shifting" is now widely recognized as one of a palette of strategies that social and political groups frequently employ in contentious politics. Shifting scale (as size) changes both quantitative and qualitative relationships of inclusion and exclusion, making it a critical technology of power in struggles to alter power geometries. In many conflicts, actors explicitly strive to shift scale in order to change the set of participants, relationships, and resources involved to their advantage. While actors often attempt to broaden the scale of conflict to attract more allies and resources, they may, alternatively, try to "scale down" to exclude allies and resources of an opponent and pursue an agenda under a more favourable, but locally specific, political opportunity structure (Leitner, Peck, and Sheppard 2007; Miller 1994, 2000).

While scale as size is constituted through the struggles of individual and collective agents, agents frequently operate from different structural positions. Contestants may not only struggle to shape scale as size but also attempt to shift to a different scalar "level" with different structural capacities and opportunities (Miller 1994; Peck and Tickell 1994). A wide variety of social, economic, and political organizations is commonly organized in a nested territorial manner, with different "levels" assigned different responsibilities and capacities. In the scale literature, the state is the most commonly discussed entity with a nested territorial structure, but it is by no means the only one. A variety of institutions, including labour unions, religious institutions, professional societies, and social movement organizations, is frequently organized on a nested territorial model. The responsibilities and capacities assigned to different territorial levels of these institutions are not fixed or rigid but reorganized on an ongoing basis through processes that involve both struggle and cooperation.

The rescaling of responsibilities and capacities not only alters power relationships but may also alter processes themselves. Not surprisingly, actors may attempt not only to gain standing and legitimacy at the scalar "level" that best suits their objectives but also to control the very processes by which responsibilities and capacities are rescaled. This rescaling can occur through a variety of means. Significant advantages accrue to actors that gain access to and control over higher-"level" institutions. These advantages are "most clearly exemplified by the power of state and parastatal institutions operating at the national and international levels ... [They have] the ability to shape those extralocal rule regimes that constrain and channel the strategic options and tactical behaviour of local actors" (Peck 2002b, 338).

Through the control of higher-level institutions – those that possess superior capacity with regard to resource authorization and allocation as well as the establishment and interpretation of laws and procedures – power can be exerted without necessarily having to gain broad-based support. Higher-level institutions often set the rule regimes for lower-level institutions. Through constitutional, legislative, judicial, administrative, and fiscal measures, higher-level institutions can establish and delimit the scope of policy and action at lower-level scales, enabling or preventing the implementation of democratically made decisions.

While more geographically extensive scales (e.g., national) are often the scales from which the assignment of structural responsibility and capacity emanate, many territorially nested institutions assign important responsibilities and capacities to less geographically extensive institutions within a scalar hierarchy. In the Canadian context, for example, provinces – not the central state – have jurisdiction over the development of natural resources; the central state has no standing in such matters. Likewise, health care is primarily a provincial, not central state, responsibility. In many countries, cities gain their authority and capacity to govern from provinces (or other subnational territorial entities) rather than the central state.

Moreover, many higher-level institutions exist only through the actions of lower-level entities. For example, while the popular mythology of globalization commonly attributes ultimate governance power to global regulatory institutions such as the IMF, WTO, and World Bank (and the "free" markets that they create), such institutions exist only through the decisions of national governments to create them and cede specific regulatory powers to them (Harvey 1989a; Peck and Tickell 1994). Indeed, these global institutions could be altered or dismantled if nation-states were to withdraw their legitimating and financial support.

In short, one must take care to avoid the intuitive but often incorrect assumption that institutions operating at more extensive geographical scales necessarily possess superior authority and capacity to govern. The authority and capacity to govern associated with "scale as level" are not necessarily congruent with the geographical extensiveness of "scale as size." Governance authority and capacity can be – and frequently are – shifted among different levels in a nested scalar hierarchy. Struggle shapes the powers associated with scale as level; these powers are just as subject to change as the characteristics of scale as size.[3]

Complicating the distinction between scale as level and scale as size is the fact that expanding the geographical extent of territory can, and frequently does, have implications for the capacity of territorially constituted institutions. By including more people, more natural resources, more economic activity, etc., within an expanded territory, territorial institutions expand the resources at their disposal and thereby their capacity to act.[4] Such is the logic behind a variety of territorially expansionist strategies ranging from territorial wars of nation-states attempting to control valuable natural resources, to corporations attempting to establish spatial monopolies, to municipalities attempting to annex lands that generate high property tax revenues. The capacity of territorial institutions to act is established both through rule regimes (legitimate authoritative and allocative powers) set through struggle at a variety of scalar levels and through the resource bases that they can lay claim to based on the extent of their territorial domain.[5] Scale as level and scale as size, then, are often related, but contingently.

In sum, at least three processes are implicated in the production of scale: constructing borders, establishing territorial extent, and determining the responsibilities and capacities of the various levels of territorially nested institutions. Constructing borders is by no means a straightforward matter. Borders may be precise or fuzzy, their locations may shift, and they may exhibit varying properties of permeability over time and space and with regard to specific categories of goods, services, capital, information, and people. The nature of borders clearly has important implications for the territories that they delineate, but territories are constituted by considerably more than their borders. Establishing territorial extent (scale as size) has critical implications, both qualitatively and quantitatively, for what is included within a territory. More extensive territory, all other things being equal, encompasses more people and resources, and displays greater diversity, than less extensive territory. Altering the set of resources, allies, opponents, etc., is a primary reason that contestants in a struggle may seek to scale "up" to a more extensive territory or scale "down" to a smaller one. But another reason that contestants may seek to shift scales has to do with the responsibilities and capacities of territorially nested institutions, including, but not limited to, the state. Responsibilities and capacities are unstable and can be shifted to different levels in a nested hierarchy. Such shifts can have major implications for the ability of agents working with or through such institutions to enact their agendae. Rescaling responsibilities and capacities can be a significant means of empowering, or disempowering, particular groups and classes.

Scaling the Economy, State, and Culture

The discussion of scaling processes and technologies has so far been posed in broad terms. A clearer understanding of the implications of scaling processes can be achieved through an examination of economic, state, and cultural scaling processes.

A number of authors have argued persuasively that capitalist economic activity tends to self-organize on a scalar basis. In one of the earliest accounts of the capitalist production of scale, Neil Smith (1984) identifies the urban, the global, and the nation-state as basic scales of capitalist economic organization. While few today would agree to a predetermined set of scales of capitalist activity, Smith does provide rationales for the scales that he identifies. According to him, "the geographical limits of the urban scale (not to be confused with the administrative boundaries of a city) are primarily determined by the local labour market and the limits to the daily commute" (136). The urban scale is, for Smith, the scale of agglomerated production activities and the labour force specific to them in a given metropolitan area. The global scale, on the other hand, is a product of capitalism's "tendency toward equalization" (139), its geographically limitless search for spatial fixes to its accumulation crises. In between these two extremes is the nation-state, the scale that provides for "the provision of various infrastructural supports and trade laws, the regulation of the reproduction of labour power, and support for the local money ... The state develops to fulfill these tasks, militarily where necessary. In addition, capital must defend itself against the working class" (142). Scholars writing on economies and scale today identify a much wider and more flexible set of scales of economic activity (as well as networked and other non-scalar ways of viewing the production of economic space), but Smith's account has the merit of conceiving of scale in a clearly relational fashion based on processes inherent to capitalist economies. The scales that Smith identifies have borders, territorial extent, and responsibilities and capacities associated with capitalist and state institutions.

Smith's borders vary considerably in their characteristics. The borders of the urban scale are extremely fuzzy and permeable. They essentially delimit commuting patterns rather than institutional/state jurisdiction. The global scale, as Smith defines it, is the scale of the planet. It is a scale of potential capitalist economic activity rather than truly global material practice. In between these scales are nation-states, entities with (mostly) clearly defined borders but with flexible properties of permeability relating to trade and labour mobility. The extent of the territories also varies widely; the urban scale is largely determined by the drain that commuting poses to the value of labour power. Nonetheless, the extent of city-specific labour sheds is shaped by local conditions. Nation-states can and do vary in their extensiveness. There are reasons to extend territorial domains to encompass expanding production complexes and relations of dependence, but, for the most part, territorial extent is seen as a product of "a series of historical deals, compromises, and wars" (Smith 1984, 143). The potential field of play of capital extends across the entire globe. The responsibilities and capacities of various levels of territorially nested institutions are only briefly considered in Smith's account. The role of the state/institutions at the urban scale is not clearly specified, although Smith recognizes that segregated urban spaces of production and reproduction must be integrated. The nation-state plays a more significant role in attempting to moderate capitalist tendencies towards differentiation and equalization by "establishing a hierarchy of nationally based laws of value more or less integrated within a larger international law of value" (142). Global institutions "fulfill some of the functions of an international state" (144). In this formulation, nested state institutions fulfill functions specific to the particular scalar dynamics of the capitalist economy.

Since Smith's early work on scale, several new conceptualizations of economic processes have come to the fore. A great deal of the economic geography literature has analyzed the changes in technology, production processes, corporate organization, command and control relationships, and spatial divisions of labour giving rise to new territorial, scalar, and network formations. Some of the most fundamental rethinking of economic geography, however, has come from labour geographers, such as Herod (1991, 1997, 2001), who have largely inverted the capital logic approach to the economy by focusing, instead, on the role of labour in constructing economies. Herod's work demonstrates the critical role that labour struggles play in the construction of economic landscapes, including scalar relationships. Herod focuses on labour unions, employer organizations, and the strategies that both have taken to shift the scales of bargaining to their advantage. His work shows the scalar dimensions of economic relationships to be highly fluid, with the boundaries, extent, responsibilities and powers of the different levels of conflicting institutions in nearly continuous flux.

While capital logic and labour-focused approaches to the analysis of capitalism's dynamics yield important insights, both operate with only a skeletal notion of the state and virtually no notion of culture. Over the past twenty years, regulation theory has addressed important aspects of these lacunae. Rather than viewing the economy as a separate realm with its own internal dynamics, regulation theory posits a strong role for the state in economic processes. Complex capitalist economies are seen as crisis prone, but, through state intervention, historically specific periods of relatively stable capital accumulation are frequently achieved (i.e., regimes of accumulation). This relative but geographically and historically uneven stability is achieved through largely ad hoc constellations of state institutions and policies, private institutions and practices, and consensual social norms (i.e., modes of regulation). Regimes of accumulation have been shown to have particular geographical characteristics (Peck 2002b; Peck and Tickell 1994, 2002), with the Fordist regime of accumulation organized first and foremost around the regulation of national economic spaces.

Peck and Tickell (1994, 282) find that "the crisis of Fordism and the search for a new institutional fix are both intrinsically geographical problems." Not surprisingly, their work has addressed a range of geographical dimensions, scale being the most prominent. In their classic 1994 work, they provide what is probably still the most detailed overview available on the rescaling of state responsibilities and capacities as they relate to the crisis of "*after*-Fordism." For them, the rescaling of responsibilities and capacities is part and parcel of the "liberalization (or constitution) of competitive market forces, the abandonment of demand-side intervention in favour of supply-side policy measures, and the rejection of both social partnership and welfarism" (292). The *after*-Fordist "hollowing out" of the nation-state has entailed not only the collapse of Keynesian macroeconomic management and draconian cuts to social programs but also the reassignment of nation-state responsibilities and capacities both up (to global or supranational bodies) and down (to local and regional bodies) the scalar spectrum. This reassignment has had the effect of setting local and regional states against each other in a zero sum competition for investment that undercuts the effectiveness of lower-level regulation. With local and regional states operating in a more competitive environment, state spending shifts away from social welfare and towards the creation of favourable business climates. Significantly, the rescaling of responsibilities and the rescaling of capacities need not go hand in hand. Responsibilities may be shifted to a different level – for example, the local state – without any change in the capacities of that level, producing a pattern of mismatched rescaling that nominally enhances local democratic control but, in practice eviscerates the capacity to enact democratic decisions (Miller 2007; Peck and Tickell 1994).

Peck and Tickell (1994) address borders, territorial extent, and responsibilities and capacities of state institutions in their analysis, but their emphasis is clearly on the rescaling of state responsibilities and capacities. For the purposes of their analysis, borders are mostly fixed, the exception being when a level of the state is created or abolished. The permeability of state borders, however, changes with regulatory regimes. Peck and Tickell are especially concerned with border permeability as it relates to flows of trade and flows of finance capital, two core aspects of regulation. Territorial extent is considered primarily as it relates to the formation of global regulatory agencies and supranational trading blocks and to the negative effects of downloading/regulatory fragmentation. The greater the territorial extent of trading blocks, the greater the potential to provide internally coherent regulation and some measure of insulation from global competitive pressures, although downloading and deregulation increase competitive pressures within many trading blocks as well. Peck (2002b) and Peck and Tickell (1994) provide especially nuanced accounts of the rescaling of responsibilities and capacities.

Another substantial body of literature, based primarily in cultural geography, analyzes the ways in which agents construct scalar and territorial identity and consciousness (e.g., Jones and MacLeod 2004; Martin 2003; Martin and Miller 2003; Miller 2000; Paasi 2002). Much of this literature focuses on the ways in which identity and consciousness are constructed through the entanglement of agents with complex structural and institutional forces. Paasi argues that an analytical distinction between the *identity of a region* and *regional identity* can help to clarify the links between identity and region. The identity of a region can be defined as "those features of nature, culture and inhabitants that distinguish or, in fact, can be *used* in the discourses of science, politics, cultural activism or economics to distinguish a region from others. This occurs in the construction of regional divisions, regional marketing, governance and political regionalization ... These classifications are inevitably based on choices, where some elements are included and others excluded. Thus they are expressions of power in delimiting, naming and symbolizing space and groups of people" (140). Paasi's notion of the identity of a region primarily pertains to the characteristics and qualities of subnational territory emphasized and codified by the state. But the identity of a region must be distinguished from regional identity. The latter can be equated with regional consciousness. By showing how the Finnish state has redefined and reconstituted subnational regions in the wake of Finland's entry into the European Union and how regional identity varies substantially among state-defined regions, Paasi demonstrates the complex and variable relationship between the identity of a region and regional identity. Paasi's analysis, moreover, shows how regional delimitation and the construction of regional consciousness is often a multiscalar process. In the Finnish case, the identification of regions involves not only the Finnish central state and subnational regions but also the policies of the European Union, which promotes a "Europe of regions." The regional policies of Finland and the European Union are intended to create not only functionally coherent regions but also regional identities that can be turned into "products" to be "exploited in business life and for attracting new residents (or for avoiding out-migration)" (142).

In Paasi's (2002) empirical example, the creation of new regional entities and, in turn, new patterns of regional consciousness begins with state action, followed by the proliferation of media narratives. In other empirical studies, the development of regional or other forms of territorial/scalar consciousness stems to a greater degree from individuals' time-space paths and the contacts and bonds that they develop through patterns of interaction as well as activists' deliberate attempts to frame territorial/scalar identities for strategic purposes. These collective identities commonly range from the neighbourhood to the transnational and can be employed in a variety of challenges to the state and other entities (e.g., Jones and MacLeod 2004; Martin 2003; Martin and Miller 2003).

Paasi's (2002) discussion of the production of the identity of regions and regional identities strongly emphasizes the construction of borders. Borders serve to include and exclude, thereby creating a territorial basis of common identity. With regard to the identity of a region, borders may be fairly precise though certainly not fixed. With regard to regional identity, borders tend to be permeable and fuzzy. Regional borders are highly permeable to migration from other regions, undermining efforts to construct strong regional consciousness as new migrants often identify with the regions from which they came. The construction of regional consciousness is shown to be a very complex matter involving the Finnish central state, the European Union, a variety of media narratives, and complex migration patterns across regional borders. Paasi addresses issues of territorial extent primarily with regard to the shift in Finnish policy from an emphasis on counties to an emphasis on provinces; the shift to new territorial units has implications for the construction of regional identity. The responsibilities and capacities of state institutions figure in Paasi's account in at least two ways. The entry of Finland into the European Union meant that Finland became subject to regional policy emanating from a new supranational-scale authority. Carrying out EU regional policy meant not only new responsibilities for the Finnish national state (to restructure the scalar hierarchy within Finland) but also new responsibilities and capacities for provinces, including direct connections to the EU Committee of Regions.

The preceding examples confirm that constructing borders, establishing territorial extent, and determining the responsibilities and capacities of different levels of territorially nested institutions are common to a wide range of scaling processes in the economy, state, and culture. While no claim is made that these examples represent a comprehensive account of scale production processes and technologies, they are undoubtedly among the most common. Specific processes and technologies take on different levels of importance depending upon the characteristics of each concrete case. In all cases, however, it is clear that scale production processes have direct implications for the constitution of social struggle, in terms of both setting the "rules of the game" and shaping the capacities of agents and institutions to effect change.

Conclusion: Scale, Networks, and Agency

Based on the preceding examples, we can define scale as *a set of territorially nested, malleable relationships among territorially embedded or constituted agents and institutions, shaping their responsibilities, capacities, opportunities, and constraints through territory-specific rule regimes, resources, and identities.* To understand how scale is produced, however, we must be prepared to examine the specific processes through which borders, territorial extent, and the responsibilities and capacities of territorial institutions are constructed. These processes are often, but not always, related. It is possible, for instance, to alter the permeability of borders without changing the territorial extent of territorially nested institutions. The configuration of responsibilities and capacities of territorially nested institutions can be changed without affecting the territorial extent of those institutions or the nature of their borders. But in a great many cases, changes in one process have significant and necessary implications for others. Changing the location of borders necessarily changes territorial extent; changes in territorial extent necessarily change relations of inclusion and exclusion as well as the resources available to, and the opportunities and constraints faced by, contestants in struggle. Likewise, rescaling responsibilities and capacities of territorially nested institutions changes the matrix of resources, opportunities, and constraints – as well as the dynamics of spatial competition and struggle among territorially constituted actors and institutions. Social movements may attempt to alter the dynamics of struggle through their own rescaling efforts, for example forming alliances over broader (or smaller) territories to bring in new (or exclude) contestants and resources or reframing the scalar extent of a struggle to legitimate (or delegitimate) other contestants. Relations among border construction, establishment of territorial extent, and determination of territorially nested institutions' responsibilities and capacities are sometimes contingent, sometimes necessary, sometimes symmetrical, sometimes asymmetrical.

Understanding the production of scale this way, is scale a chaotic concept? The answer is not straightforward. Clearly, scale is not reducible to a single necessary relation. The production of scale is attributable not to an arbitrary set of contingent relations but to a limited set of frequently intertwined necessary and contingent relations. The processes through which scale is produced hang together with considerable frequency. Rather than dismissing scale as chaotic, then, it would make more sense to think of it as an umbrella term for a set of commonly intertwined relations.

The relations that underlie the production of scale are ultimately important because they shape possibilities for human agency. One of the significant blind spots in recent arguments for an agency-focused network alternative to scalar analysis is that such arguments often ignore the processes through which agency is constituted. Agency is never free-floating; it is always constructed within a matrix of sociospatial relations that both enable and constrain. In much of the network literature, agents purportedly derive their capacity to act in direct relation to their level of network connectivity. Indeed, power is often portrayed as a matter of network presence and absence. But the constitution of agents' capacity is far more complex than mere network connectivity. The capacity to exercise agency depends on the quantity and quality of available resources, the legitimacy of actors' claims to authorize and allocate resources, the strength of collective identities as a means of mobilizing other agents to act, the number and strength of competing agents, the rules of interspatial competition, and much more. All of these factors are shaped, in some considerable measure, by scalar relationships.

The sweeping argument that network analysis is a preferable substitute for scalar analysis ignores the fact that scalar relationships affect network relationships and vice versa. In one of the most frequently cited examples of the relative merits of a network approach, Latour (1993, 117-19) asks whether a transcontinental railway is local or global. "Neither," he answers. "It is local at all points," but it is also global "since it takes you from Brest to Vladivostok." Latour essentially contends that the global-local scalar distinction is a red herring. What this transcontinental railway is, he asserts, is a network: "Networks are nets thrown over spaces ... They are connected lines, not surfaces." In this analysis, territory, region, and scale are downplayed, all subsumed by the network. But there is more to this example than Latour acknowledges, for a transcontinental railway is not merely a network. It is also the product of higher-order scalar decisions, including transnational agreements coordinating the laying of rail lines across several national territories, assuring that all links are built at the same gauge, and allowing for travel across national borders.

The scalar constitution of networks is, among other things, a means of regulating inclusivity and exclusivity. For example, the annual G8 meetings constitute networks of elite state actors who travel freely around the globe to discuss and set global economic and political policies. In contrast, antiglobalization activists constitute a mostly non-elite network of actors hostile to global neoliberalism. Not surprisingly, the governments of G8 states institute a variety of barriers to the global free travel of these activists, scaling the space of free travel back from the globe to the nation-state, thereby breaking transnational links in the network. Such action excludes many would-be members of the antiglobalization network, thereby weakening it (Miller 2004). The G6B meeting (the antiglobalization group of 6 billion) held parallel to the G8 meeting in Alberta was considerably weaker than it might have been, due in part to the fact that over forty key antiglobalization activists from around the world were denied entry visas into Canada. Networks are not free-floating alternatives to scalar arrangements. Rather, they are embedded in them. As

Leitner, Pavlik, and Sheppard (2002, 286-88) note, networks are themselves scaled.

Networks are embedded in, and may cut across, economic, political, or cultural territories and regions. These territories and regions are typically part of a scalar hierarchy and subject to rescaling through the actions of organized, networked actors (Leitner 2004). Conversely, territorially constituted actors, first and foremost state institutions, can have dramatic impacts on the capacity of networks to expand, contract, or even exist at all. It is reasonable to conclude – contrary to the claims of some scale critics – that the concepts of scale and networks do not stand in opposition to each other but are in fact co-implicated in a wide range of economic, political, and cultural processes. If we are serious about understanding the conditions under which agents are empowered or disempowered, we should begin to move away from stand-alone spatial concepts and either/or binaries. Instead, we need to focus more on the interrelations of diverse sociospatialities – and the implications of these interrelations for citizen empowerment.

NOTES

1   As Latham (2002, 131) summarizes, topology is the science of "nearness and rifts" in which "time-space consists of multiple pleats of relations stitched together, such that nearness and distance as measured in absolute space are not in themselves important."
2   Moreover, as Sayer (1992, 139) points out, "there are ... many situations both in everyday life and scientific practice where such chaotic conceptions can be used unproblematically as simple categories for descriptive purposes." But scalar analysis foregrounds process and struggle, not mere description.
3   One can imagine a critique of this conception of scale as level as "confounding the distinction between society and space," the critique that Collinge (2005, 189) levels against Swyngedouw's work on scale. It might be argued that defining scale as level in terms of the socially constructed responsibilities and capacities of nested-territorial institutions merely captures differences in institutional power. Yet, Collinge himself acknowledges that his critique of Swyngedouw "highlights the *necessity* of a division between society and space ... [and] the *impossibility* of such a division" (203). My own position is that all social processes must be considered inherently *sociospatial*. While the exercise of sociospatial power need not take scalar form, the scope and capacity of nested-territorial institutions to regulate and discipline actors at a given scale are established through struggles among agents at different levels in the territorial hierarchy. Scalar shifts in responsibilities and capacities can have significant effects on a wide range of spatial governance

practices. Understanding scale relationally, then, must include understanding how responsibilities and capacities can be altered and reconstituted both up and down a scalar hierarchy.
4 Territorial expansion can also increase demands for infrastructure and service provision, imposing, in some cases, a net drain on territorially constituted institutions.
5 Their capacity to act is also influenced by their ability to lay claim, both legitimately and illegitimately, to resources beyond their territorial domain.

3
Why the Urban Question Still Matters: Reflections on Rescaling and the Promise of the Urban

Stefan Kipfer

This chapter is an intervention into debates about the status of the "urban" in the scale debates and the wider theoretical implications of these debates for urban social theory. For this purpose, I would like to take up Neil Brenner's (2000) formative discussion of the relationship between the "urban question" and the "scale question" in the work of Henri Lefebvre. While Brenner's intervention underscored the importance of one relatively circumscribed notion in Lefebvre's work (*échelle*), I emphasize the continued relevance of Lefebvre's notion of the urban as mediating level (*niveau*) and form (centrality/difference). This notion of the urban is subject to (re)scaling but not a priori scale-dependent. Rather than supplanting the urban question by the scale question, I underline the importance of explicitly rescaling, yet retaining the urban as a multiscalar problematic with significant epistemological implications.

The purpose of my rereading of the relationship between urban and scale questions is theoretical, political, and analytical. A reading of Lefebvre's notion of the urban as level underlines the limits of political economies of scale. The effect of reading urban as *niveau* into scale *échelle* was to contribute to a sophisticated refinement of a form of *geographical political economy* shaped above all by David Harvey's powerful urban marxism, with which most political economies of scale share a rather particular reading of Lefebvre's theories of urbanization and the production of space. Most references to the urban in the scale debates are indebted to Harvey, who conceptualized the urban as a dialectical unity of "thing" (the spatial fix, the structured coherence of urban regions) and "process" (the urban process of investment in the built environment as an aspect of the laws of motion of capital). Other notions of the urban in the scale literature are less central. Marston's feminist intervention makes reference to Castells' early views of the urban as a produced, metropolitan space of collective consumption (Marston 2004, 171-72), while those emphasizing the importance of the urban as a multiscalar network borrow from Castells' later concept of space of flows (Sassen 2003; Taylor 2004).

In distinction to Harvey and Castells, Lefebvre understood the urban as a fleeting, produced form of centrality/difference. As such, the urban functions as a level of analysis mediating between macro- and microlevels of reality and possibility. In other words, the urban leads not only to an analysis of the macrorealities of state, capital, and empire but also to a differential and dialectical critique of everyday life. It also yields an insistence on the importance of negative and radical refusal (in relationship to positive reality) and a normative commitment to totality as open-ended possibility. A consequence of this conception of totality is a critique of the very categories of political economy (bourgeois and otherwise). To put it differently, Lefebvre saw the politically revolutionary and epistemologically crucial importance of the urban in the fact that it pointed to a *critique* of political economy. Given the heated debate between Marxist and feminist political economists on the role of social reproduction and the household as *scale* (Brenner 2001a; Marston 2000, 2004; Marston and Smith 2001), Lefebvre's reading of the urban appears to be additionally important. It may provide an alternative approximation between Marxist and feminist approaches *through* a scale-sensitive conception of *urban* research.

From the Urban to the Scale Question? Lefebvre in the Scale Debates

Brenner (2001a, 592, 604) suggests that Lefebvre's work provides a reasonably if incompletely solid foundation for a theory of the production of scale. Zeroing in on Lefebvre's fourth volume on the state, he argues that the "urban question is today increasingly assuming the form of what Lefebvre once aptly termed 'the scale question' (*La question d'échelle*)" (2000, 362). According to Brenner, Lefebvre's remarks about scale and state anticipated a shift from the urban question to the scale question in the 1990s. To mobilize Lefebvre for this broader shift, Brenner (2000, 368) foregrounds the notion of scale (*échelle*) in Lefebvre's tomes on the state at the expense of the notion of level (*niveau*), which was central to Lefebvre's earlier work on the urban. Extremely productive in its own right, this procedure has major consequences for urban theory. Instead of keeping to the notion of the urban as level, which allows one to retain the worldwide, multiscale notion of the urban revolution (Brenner 2000, 369-70, 374-75), Brenner proposes a research agenda that binds the urban to a scale that can be analyzed in relation to "supra-urban processes" and "inter-scalar networks" (366-67). In this project, elements of

Lefebvre's metaphilosophy get tied to an analytical research agenda to study the mesolevel of capitalist development (Brenner 2004, 21-22).

Brenner's mobilization of Lefebvre for a "new political economy of scale" (Jessop in Brenner 2004, 11) parallels Harvey's reading of Lefebvre in the 1970s. It may help to recall that Harvey's (1988) move from "liberal" to "socialist" formulations in urban theory was based in no small measure on a reading of Lefebvre's urban work that was enthusiastic but also strictly qualified by Harvey's attempt to make selective use of Lefebvre for the purpose of Marxist political economy of urban space. Harvey did not reject Lefebvre's urban writing as "ideological," as did Castells (1977, 86), who, in his Althusserian phase, considered Lefebvre to be on the wrong, non-scientific, or idealist side of the epistemological break in marxism. He took on board Lefebvre's suggestion that urbanization, land rent, and the transformation of city and countryside during industrial capitalism should not be seen as an afterthought in Marxist theory but as a process with real, relatively autonomous effects on capital accumulation. But for Harvey (1985, 62, 64, 82, 88; 1988, 303-12), the *Urban Revolution* underestimated the continued importance of the primary circuit of accumulation in the expanded reproduction of capital. Lefebvre's insights were too speculative to furnish an adequate basis for a sober, rigorous political economy of urbanization. To develop a Marxist urban *political economy*, Harvey (2000a, 82) preferred to "stick to Marx's own terms" and a classical marxism largely unmediated by debates in continental marxism (78-79, 93-94).

Neil Smith, who otherwise disagrees with Brenner's assessment of Lefebvre's work for the scale debates,[1] has also developed his thoughts on political economies of scale on the basis of Harvey's urban marxism. The urban appears in two distinct ways in this framework. First, the urban is described as an operational scale: that is, a set of substantive processes of land-rent-driven spatial differentiation that is typically bounded by the urban region as defined by the "daily sphere of the labour market" (Smith 1993, 107). In this vein, the urban is often simply described as a scale unto itself (Brenner 1997, 21; 2000, 363, 366-67; Harvey 2000b, 192, 196; Smith 1991, 172; 2003, xii, xiv; Swyngedouw 2000, 68-69, 141). In other instances, the urban appears at least implicitly as a multiscalar process and strategy (Brenner 1997, 9-12; 1998b; 2000, 362, 369-70, 374). This is particularly the case in Smith's (2002) view of gentrification as global urban strategy; Harvey's (1996, 379, 396, 429) term "global urbanization"; Swyngedouw, Moulaert, and Rodriguez's (2002) analysis of the transnational production of urban megaprojects; Swyngedouw and Baeten's (2001) study of "glocal" elites in "scaling the city"; and Swyngedouw and Kaika's (2003) idea of "glocal" urban modernities. The urban thus appears simultaneously as a *locally and regionally* bounded operational scale and a process that, though scaled, cuts across and articulates multiple spatial scales.

The ambiguity in the status of the urban in this subsegment of the scale debates may simply reflect a duality of process (urbanization) and thing (the city), as Harvey brilliantly suggested (1995, 50-54; 1996, 418, 421). The relationship between city as scale and urbanization as scaled process thus expresses nothing more than a dialectical unity of the *urban process* (as a particular moment in the crisis-ridden circuits of capital and periodic switching crises) and the "city" (understood as a contingent *spatial fix* of the built environment and the *"structured coherence"* of urban space) (Harvey 1982, 1985, 1989a, 2001). However, the tensions in this dual understanding of the urban in the production of scale are not often translated well. In the debates on local and regional regulation and state rescaling, which originally relied on Harvey's notion of structured coherence of space (Duncan and Goodwin 1988), the urban often simply appears *as scale* (MacLeod and Goodwin 1999, 515) synonymous with subnational, local, and regional scalar configurations of state intervention and coalition formation that regulate the structured coherence of urban space (Goodwin, Duncan, and Halford 1993, 85; Jessop 1997, 61-66, 69-70). Transferred into state theory, Harvey's rich if occasionally elusive twin notion of the urban as process and thing becomes a background category to the investigation of the local extended state. At least in this area of scaled state theory, which has produced its own share of brilliant insights, there is a danger that the urban shrinks to a *local* and *regional* application of political theory.

The dialectically linked dualities in these conceptions of the urban in scale theory point, perhaps inadvertently, to "the limits of scale," a perceived "slippage ... between notions of geographic scale and other core geographic concepts" (Brenner 2001a, 592; Schmid 2003). On the one hand, if a theory of the production of scale promises to be a theory of spatial differentiation, a theory of fixing social differences, regulating uneven development, and containing conflict within scalar configurations of struggle (Marston 2000; Smith 1993, 96-97; 2004, 196-97; Swyngedouw 2004b), then it must to some degree keep to a notion of "urban" scale as bounded spatial form, node, or arena (e.g., the local state or regional spatial fixes). On the other hand, the focus on processes that produce scale and the linkages that connect scalar units in relational fashion, which is by definition primary in a relational, social constructionist view of scale (Brenner 2001a; Howitt 1998, 2002b, 2003; McMaster and Sheppard 2004), suggests that these linkages and processes cannot be logically reduced to scale. They transcend porous scalar boundaries and cannot be permanently tied to an operational scale or ontology of scalar mosaics and hierarchies. This is true particularly for urban questions, which deal with both scalar fixities, or nodes, and trans-scalar processes and networks (Leitner 2004; Taylor 2004). The difficulty of scaling the urban indicates that, just as the notion of the production of space shows the limits of "spatial theory," the idea of the production of scale points to the limits of "scalar theory."

In the following, I will reexcavate Lefebvre's notion of the urban. I won't propose that Lefebvre provides a superior substitute to the political economy of scale developed within the lineage of Harvey's urban marxism. Lefebvre's work provides a series of orientations and sensibilities, not a fully fledged analytical model that can compete with a political economy of scale on the latter's terms. I insist on the importance of Lefebvre's notion of the urban as form and level of mediation, reality, and possibility in order to underscore some insights within scale debates and add a set of correctives to these debates. First, Lefebvre's notion of the urban, perhaps even more forcefully than Harvey's, is clearly not reducible to scale. Instead, one may see the scale question as a particular aspect of production of urban space (see also Schmid 2003). Second, and this follows logically from the previous point, the urban cannot be reduced to a question of local-regional research (as much as it should incorporate such questions). Rather, the urban represents, increasingly, the main mediation for critical knowledge in our world (Prigge 1995, 180-82; see also Cunningham 2005). Third, Lefebvre's notion of the urban as mediation *systematically* ties urban analysis to considerations of everyday life. As is acknowledged in recent contributions that complement Harvey's lineage with insights by Benjamin, Debord, and Lefebvre (Merrifield 2002, 2006; Swyngedouw and Kaika 2003), Lefebvre's understanding of the urban question does not exclude a political economy of scale but *must* transcend and subvert the latter.

Lefebvre and the Urban as Level and Mediation

Lefebvre (1970a, 1972, 1996, 2003c) argued that the industrial city signalled a historic break in patterns of urbanization. This break was consolidated under neocapitalism, which accelerated the expansion of the built environment of metropolitan regions, the industrialization of agriculture, and the integration of preexisting social spaces into urban networks. As a result, the age-old if historically malleable distinction between city and countryside as discrete sets of social relations was superseded: the city as a bounded social space disappeared, and the urban became the central form and mediation of social life (Lefebvre 2003c, 1-18). For Lefebvre, the urban question was a new way of developing "the critique of everyday life." In fact, everyday life established itself as a central problematic of critical theory through urbanization. Lefebvre's urban writings in the 1960s and early 1970s made it possible to reconfigure marxism through an integration of considerations of everyday life, urbanization, and the reproduction of capitalism into an explicit theory of the production of space and time (Hess 1988, 288). The general significance of Lefebvre's thesis of an urban revolution is related to the fact that urbanization escapes and reconfigures scalar boundaries such as those of the walled city, the industrial urban region, and the nation-state.

In *The Right to the City* and *The Urban Revolution*, Lefebvre described the urban as form and mediation. The urban is sociospatial form – centrality, encounter, discontinuous simultaneity (1996, 137-38, 168-74; 2003c, 115-27). As such, the urban mediates everyday life with the social order, links past, present, and future, and articulates multiple scales of multidimensional human activity. The urban is an intermediary level (M) between the "global" (general) level G and the "private" level (P). The urban, level M, connects the macrostructures and institutions of the "far" order (state and capital, patriarchy, institutional knowledge) (level G) to the "near" order of everyday life (level P) (1970a, 282; 1996, 111-14; 2003c, 77-91). Lefebvre argues that

> The city's transformations are not the passive outcomes of changes in the social whole. The city also depends as essentially on relations of immediacy, on direct relations between persons and groups which make up society (families, organized bodies, crafts and guilds, etc.). Furthermore, it is not reduced to the organization of these immediate and direct relations, nor its metamorphoses to its changes. The city is situated at an interface, half way between what one calls the near order [l'ordre proche] (relationships of individuals in groups of variable size, more or less organized and structured, and the relations among these groups) and the far order [l'ordre lointain], that of society, regulated by large and powerful institutions (Church and State), by a legal code, formalized or not by a "culture." (1996, 100-1)

Lefebvre did not treat the urban in reified ways as fixed, determining physical form, contrary to some assertions (Castells 1977, 86; Katznelson 1993, 101-2, 290, 306). Rather than a transhistorical spatial determinant of ways of life (as in the Chicago School of urban sociology), Lefebvre suggests that the urban is a dialectical mediation. As form, it is both product and oeuvre and thus related dialectically to its content.

Even though Lefebvre did not deliver an integrated political economic theory of spatial differentiation (Smith 2003, xiv), difference is central to his conception of the urban. The urban as fleeting form is not only centrality but also a point of convergence, an ensemble of differences (Lefebvre 2003c, 117-18, 126). Key here is Lefebvre's distinction between minimal and maximal difference. Not to be confused with the liberal *diversity* or the deconstructive *différance*, this distinction emerges from a differentialist understanding of marxism (Lefebvre 1970b). Lefebvre calls actually existing differences minimal or induced. They are alienated, isolated fragments that encapsulate difference-as-sameness, forms of repetition "that tend toward formal identity" (1991, 395). Exemplified by "diversity between villas in a suburb filled with villas" or "variations within a particular fashion in dress" (372), these differences embody formal logic. In turn, for Lefebvre, maximal difference is a category of dialectics; it implies a "shattering of a system," where a "given set gives rise, beyond its boundaries, to another, completely different set" (372). This latter, maximally different set gravitates towards festive, creative, unalienated, qualitative, use-value-oriented forms of plurality and individuality that are not bound by the grid of spatialized clock time and assume social relations unfettered by "indifference": individualism, pluralism, imitation, conformism, fragmentation, homogeneity (Lefebvre 1970b, 70, 134, 145-51).[2]

To work with and transform existing forms of maximal difference, which only exist in fragmented form, one must pursue a dialectical project that links the actual with the utopian and the immediacies of everyday life with the "global" order (Lefebvre 1970b, 186). This project Lefebvre (1979, 285) calls "the right to the city": claims by inhabitants to the social surplus and decision-making power that are tied to claims to spatial centrality. In his studies of Mourenx, the company town, and Paris in May 1968 (as well as the Commune in 1871), he asserted that claims to the right to the city take the form of a dialectic of centre and periphery. The promise of the city cannot be realized by defending the historic city (the Latin Quarter in Paris) or by retreating to the new suburbs (the rings of *banlieues* around Paris). It must be produced in a "new social, political and cultural sphere" – urban society – that may emerge through an interaction between centre and periphery (Lefebvre 1968, 136). In the fluid links between the Parisian periphery (Nanterre) and the old historic core (the Left Bank), an effective (if not necessarily explicit) attempt was made to overcome the dissociations of the postwar metropolis: the separations between centres of decision making and segregated suburban peripheries: factories, student dormitories, and housing projects (Lefebvre 1968, 100-10, 115-19, 129-30, 136-38, 148-49, 151-54).

In this spatial dialectic of centre and periphery through which the struggle for the right to the city is waged, the urban may function as a prism and mediating level through which alienated social differences are articulated and transformed. Calling for the right to difference (in the maximal sense) is thus the flip side of urban strategies to reclaim centrality. Out of the contradiction of abstract and minimally differential space, which is embodied in everyday life as well, "class struggle" and "political action of minorities" may assert (potentially maximal) rights to difference (Lefebvre 1991, 55, 64). May 1968 was promising insofar as it contained forms of differential space and cyclical time that were produced in a (fleeting) transformation of the relationship between centre and periphery in the Paris region, achieved by a spatial dialectic of mobilization: "The right to the city legitimizes the refusal to allow oneself to be removed from urban reality by a discriminatory and segregative organization ... [and] proclaims the inevitable crisis of city centers based upon segregation" (Lefebvre 1996, 195). Asserting a right to the city thus asserts a right to difference in two related ways. It represents claims to society's wealth and power as avenues towards a different, postcapitalist society, and it is an attempt to reclaim spatial centrality by those who struggle to dismantle the walls of separation of the exploding metropolis.

The Urban as Multiscalar Level

Lefebvre's theory of the production of space clarifies how a *particular* social space – the urban as shifting form – incorporates multiple (perceived, conceived, lived) dimensions and, as such, mediates macrological and micrological levels of social life. It is important to point out that this language of levels is not the same as the language of scale. For Lefebvre (2002, 118–25), levels refer to dialectically interrelated, mutually implicated aspects of reality or distinctions in a differentiated whole. The notion of level is related more to the distinction between micro- and macroaspects of life (122, 139-42) than to the notion of level in geographical research, where level (as scale) may refer to a hierarchy or pyramid of increasing complexity reaching from the local to the global (Howitt 1998, 51-52; 2002). Contrary to Smith's suggestion (2003, xiv), Lefebvre's levels are also theorized scales not under-theorized (understood as spatial differentiation). As Brenner (2000, 368) himself indicated, while level (*niveau*) points to different aspects of social reality in capitalist modernity, scale (*échelle*) "captures the notion of scale in its customary, territorial sense." Even so, Brenner, whose primary interests lie in the (highly pertinent and brilliant) project of scaling state theory, decided to focus "somewhat one-sidedly upon the territorial aspect of scale" (*échelle*) (368). In contrast, the following manoeuvre resists the containment of the urban within scaled political economies of state and uneven development by insisting on the relevance of the notion of the urban as level.

Analytically, each of Lefebvre's levels can itself be scaled. At first sight, it makes intuitive sense to suggest that the "global" level of social order is best studied at national and worldwide scales, while the "private" or "lived" level is most likely local in character (referring to body, household, neighbourhood) and "the urban" refers to the metropolitan region. None of Lefebvre's levels is strictly scale-dependent, however. "Large" categories of social order (empire, state, capital, etc.) are clearly subject to intense scaling. States, for example, have appeared in the form of city-states, nation-states, and multinational entities (Lefebvre 2003b). In turn, and given the complex, contradictory, and geographically stretched character of modern social relations, everyday life cannot be captured adequately as only locally bound routines. The same is, of course, true for the urban itself. Urbanization is of such consequence for Marxist theory precisely because of its capacity to undermine scalar boundaries of the historic city (locally bound, even walled settlements) and countryside (physically and socially distinct agricultural regions) – and thus a key problematic in revolutionary theory and the practice of state socialism. It is this aspect of Lefebvre's thesis about the urban revolution as a boundary-destroying process that both Castells (1977, 12, 23) and Harvey (1988) accepted in principle, even though they did not agree with the specific ways in which Lefebvre theorized the urban. Today, Lefebvre's urban revolution resonates with attempts to come to terms with the worldwide and transnational character of urbanization (Smith 2003, xx-xi).

The notion of the worldwide (*mondial*), increasingly important for Lefebvre since the mid-1960s, is central to thinking about scale in his work. Key here is that *mondial* as scale (*échelle*) is not to be confused with the *global* as level (*niveau*).[3] Brenner (1997, 2000) has argued convincingly that volumes three and four of *De l'état* provide a wealth of ammunition for a political economic project of scaling state and capital. Lefebvre's insistence on the globalization (not internationalization) of state, capital, labour, and neoimperialism (1977, 153-68; 1978, 282, 348-49) underlines the importance of scaling level G, the "far level" of society, and its role in producing conceived space (1978, 280-82). But Lefebvre's project to "spatialize political thought" (1978, 165) is systematically related to a scaling of levels M and P and, thus, quickly reaches the limits of political economy (1976, 307). In *De l'état*, Lefebvre (1978, 270-71) insists on the relationship of the state to the urban as level. The role of the state in this regard is, among other things, tied to the political organization of relations between dominant and dominated spaces at worldwide, interregional, and intraregional scales (173-86). Such a scaled analysis of the state in the "urban phase" of capitalist development alerts us to the "globalization of the everyday" itself (432) as well as to the worldwide as revolutionary possibility (414). Urban movements, for example, are of planetary significance in broadening the class struggle (163) and contributing to a potentially global front of peripheralized spaces against neoimperialism (247).

What Lefebvre's prototheoretical scaling and globalization of all levels of analysis corroborates is thus not only an analytically promising but also *politically* explosive multiscalar notion of the urban. Lefebvre developed interest in the urban not as a specialized field of research but as a linchpin in his broader concerns about theory, daily life, and political practice. As he clarified in *Du rural à l'urbain*, which traces the early development of his urban thinking, his interest in the urban was motivated by what he saw, in the 1960s, as a shift from the peasant to the urban question as a central, multiscale terrain of revolutionary theory and practice:

> Except in a few countries, agrarian reform has exhausted itself almost completely ... What is going to replace it? Urban reform. In my opinion, urban questions are no more than a chain-link and an aspect of the socialist revolution in the highly industrialized countries, but this chain-link is indispensable; we must think through what contribution and support urban problems can bring to the problems of the socialist revolution. Questions about the city, about urban planning, in short about urban society put in sharp relief and question a part of the fundamental structures of existing society ... We are not talking about fundamental themes of proletarian revolution, of socialist revolution at the global scale, but about an indispensable aspect of this revolution that has to be

rethought in its entirety today. The first wave of the world revolution has exhausted itself, ... and we are living it in its last traces. It was marked notably by agrarian reform ... The second wave of the world revolution, the contours of which can barely be sketched today, will in my opinion be defined by urban reform, one of its fundamental aspects, not its only, essential, or unique aspect, but one of its driving forces. (1970a, 218-19)[4]

Urban reform is interesting not only because it runs up to the limit of private property and asks for the socialization of land but also because it questions "society in its entirety" (225). A critique of postwar urbanism revealed the forces of the state, phallocentrism, and commodification that produced abstract space. In that sense, the urban is not only the setting of struggle but "also the stakes of that struggle." Engaging the urban, occupying space is to stop reducing politics to the reified "political sphere" and "reach for the places where power resides" (386-87).

Insisting on the urban as level (instead of containing it as a demarcated scale within wider scalar hierarchies) is, thus, the only way to uncover the hidden consequences of urban research. Although focused mostly on highly industrialized countries, Lefebvre saw the revolutionary relevance of the urban in worldwide terms. As Hess clarifies:

> The urban is a political stake. This stake can be worked out conceptually at a theoretical level. Lefebvre redeploys the concepts of alienation and the critique of everyday life. A strategy of knowledge (connaissance) must be developed to confront this theory constantly with experience, to usher in a general (global) praxis: that of urban society. The latter is to be conquered as a human appropriation of time and space, a superior modality of freedom. To be sure, politics controls this process with its technical mastery. But the role of contestation is to take on the task of dialectical analysis that would allow one to articulate the real, the possible, and the impossible and make possible what seemed impossible. The analysis becomes global (mondiale). The urban question does not pose itself the same way in South America ... as in North America, in Asia, and in Europe. Lefebvre establishes the principles of urban strategy, which should rest on (1) the introduction of the urban problematic into the forefront of political life; (2) a political

program with generalized self-management as its first article (this urban self-management should be conceptualized together with industrial self-management); and (3) recognition of the right to city: that is, the right not to be excluded from centrality and its movement. One senses how these propositions are pushed by real social movements, urban revolts that developed then in the whole world. (1988, 280)

Shaped by the moment of "1968" (which was worldwide in scope and effect), Lefebvre saw the urban question as a multiscale matter. A worldwide problematic, the urban is also not just a scale of human interaction but also a mediation of everyday life and social order that incorporates local, national, and global scales.

Lefebvre's emphasis on the urban as a mediation of revolution was intimately tied to *epistemological* concerns, not least those of totality. In the mid-1960s, Lefebvre stressed that the manifold crises of conventional philosophy required a *metaphilosophical* orientation. Among other things, metaphilosophy has to come to terms with the fact that in the modern capitalist world, "totality ... comes to us only in fragments" (Lefebvre 1997, 64). This shattering of totality is a result of, among other things, the "installation of the everyday" through urbanization (114-15). Metaphilosophical investigation must thus be more than an interdisciplinary strategy of analysis. Starting with a negative critique of positive totality, metaphilosophy is committed to open-ended strategies that reconnect the "broken, fragmented, contradictory" pieces of totality (53) and reassemble aspects of life residualized by the production of abstract space (275-76). This strategy of reconnecting residual fragments is necessary as a critique of totalizing strategies that work through separations (Lefebvre 2002, 180-93). It should not, however, take the forms of falsely authentic holism, metaphysical systematization, or "scientific" modelling of the city as an object-like positive totality (Lefebvre 1997, 189; 2003c, 57). Even though "the urban phenomenon can only be comprehended as a totality, its totality cannot be grasped" fully (Lefebvre 2003c, 186). The importance of dialectical urbanism thus lies less in its capacity to furnish sophisticated analytical models than in its radical, negative critique of totalization and its quest to reconstruct totality imperfectly as *virtuality* in situations where life lies in the ruins left by the explosive, boundary-destroying process of urbanization (Lefebvre 1997, 115; 2002, 183). Calls for the right to the city are prisms to refract postcapitalist possibilities from within the fragmented interstices of really existing urbanization. They represent aspirations for an open-ended and incomplete revolutionary totality (Lefebvre 1970b, 119).

Lefebvre's notion of the urban as mediation is thus tied to a skepticism about premature totalizations of positive reality as well as an unrelenting normative commitment to totality as the open-ended, utopian horizon of theory and practice.[5] Placing the urban at the interface of macrological and micrological aspects of life thus allows us to *partially* reconnect the fragmented (but also homogenized) world of the metropolis and the conurbation. It is no accident that the urban as level gives us a good sense of proportion of Lefebvre's work (which itself is an open, moving totality). As Kanishka Goonewardena (2005) has pointed out, the three levels of analysis (G, M, P) allow us to understand the dialectical interrelationship between key components of his work, from his urban and spatial writings to his work on the state and his most enduring concern of all: the critique of everyday life, to which Lefebvre returns in the final pages of *De l'état* (1978, 429-32) and in his late writing on everyday life and rhythmanalysis (1981, 1996). We ignore "the vitality of these 'levels' and their dialectical relations only at the risk of drastically reducing Lefebvre's thought to a mere caricature of its tremendous overall integrity and richness, while impoverishing our own politics" (Goonewardena 2005, 23-24). Scale and level must be distinguished because the latter forces one to maintain an integral perspective that ties particular aspects of social life to an open-ended horizon of totality *as possibility*. If only ephemerally, levels connect different aspects of reality to a less than rationalist openness to the unexpected.

It is true that a political economy of scale takes us beyond Lefebvre. Just as Harvey's neoclassical marxism redefined radical geography as we know it, contemporary political economic (and other) contributions to the production of scale, often indebted to Harvey, give us analytical tools that Lefebvre himself does not. However, it is important not to forget that for Lefebvre (1991, 148), the urban question is not disconnected from his enduring critique of everyday life and his notion of "marxism as a critical knowledge of everyday life." Such a marxism entails a critique of the easily reified categories of political economy: the economy, the political (Lefebvre 1972, 70). Dissolving the urban question into a political economy of rescaling thus may give us additional rigour but at a cost of introducing systematizations that shrink our sense of everyday life, difference, and political mobilization as a not fully determinable set of tensions and time-space contradictions (see also Castree 1995; Keil 1987; Schmid 2005; and Wright 2006). In other words, a political economy of scale, by prioritizing macrological forces of causation, may lead us to delink the urban from the level of everyday life (P) for the benefit of wedding it more closely to an analysis of the far order (G). The implication is that the urban is *determined* by G and transmits those determinations to everyday life. The production of urban space is then merely a two-dimensional process determined by conceived and perceived space. Lived space becomes a residual, passive site where "global" forces are inscribed or "habituated" from the outside (Harvey 1989b, 261).[6]

One may take these arguments in explicitly feminist directions. Within the scale debates, feminist arguments have been taken up through political geographies of social movements (Brown 1995; Staeheli 1994) and political economies of the household *as scale* (Marston 2000; Smith 1993). Mediated through Lefebvre's notion of the urban, considerations of everyday life may provide another avenue. As Frigga Haug (1994, 2003) has argued, the promise of Lefebvre's work lies precisely in its dialectical critique of everyday life as a particular level of analysis. For Haug, Lefebvre's reformulation of marxism as a critique of everyday life (alongside Gramsci's notion of marxism as philosophy of praxis) can be reoriented into a specifically feminist problematic of research into material gender relations as a set of normalized but *contradictory* experiences and ideologies. In this, Haug draws links between Gramsci and Lefebvre and Dorothy Smith's Marxist feminism. In a critique of falsely universal categories of research, Smith's (1987) *The Everyday World as Problematic* mobilized an antistructuralist Marxist method for a feminist analysis of the gendered links between two *levels* of reality: the everyday experience of embodied subjects and the relations and institutions of "ruling," defined more abstractly by the commodity form, bureaucracy, and written discourse.[7]

Lefebvre's work was infused with recurrent essentializing, gendered assumptions. But Lefebvre clearly underlined the privatized and patriarchal dimensions of the colonization of everyday life (1970a, 102; 1978, 184-86; 1991, 49-50, 302, 392; 2003a; McLeod 1997; Ross 1995). Seen from an *explicitly* feminist angle, Lefebvre's multiscalar understanding of the urban is crucial precisely because it allows us to highlight the gendered, "phallocentric" links between macrolevels of the social order and contradictory realities of everyday life. In this sense, his work resonates with that of Haug and Smith and other antiracist, Marxist, feminist approaches that eschew demarcations between "political economic" and "cultural" analyses and see microlevel experiences and macrolevel institutions of patriarchy as distinct, mediated aspects of totality (Bannerji 1995; Mohanty 2003). Extending Lefebvre, one may suggest that *all* of these levels of totality (including the microworlds of everyday life) are subject to scaling. One may also propose that the urban understood as middle level introduces an additional, strategically important mediation between micro- and macrolevels. With proper qualifications, potentially multiscalar calls for the right to the city may thus also refract antipatriarchal (and anticolonial) calls for the right to unalienated difference in postcapitalist worlds (Goonewardena and Kipfer 2005; Kipfer 2007; Kofman 1998).

Conclusion

> The urban became [Lefebvre's] *metaphilosophical* stomping ground, the contorted arena of new contestation and reinvented Marxist practice.
> – Andy Merrifield, *Henri Lefebvre: A Critical Introduction* (2006, 80)

Lefebvre's urban insights give us not a fully fledged political economy of scale but a theoretical orientation that has implications for contemporary scale debates. From a Lefebvrian perspective, debates on scale appear as particular moments *within* urbanized critical inquiry. Lefebvre's urban and spatial writing is not a priori scale-dependent but underscores the necessity of adopting a multiscale notion of urbanization. His concept of the urban as a mediation of everyday life and social order thus remains a vital component of critical urban research precisely because it is not restricted to local-regional considerations. Indeed, his dialectical understanding of the urban as mediating form embodies many aspects of his understanding of marxism not primarily as an alternative, antibourgeois conception of political economy but as an open-ended, integral, and differential engagement with life and the world as reality and potentiality. If Lefebvre's notion of radical critique is tied to a revolutionary commitment to totality, then this commitment is mediated politically and epistemologically through the urban. In our world, totality is knowable only *through* the fragments left by the exploding dynamics of urbanization. The epistemological promise of urban theory and practice thus lies in the notion of the urban as a possible prism to understand, connect, and act on the fragmented and homogenized aspects of the modern world, the contradictions and possibilities of everyday life. This has implications not only for specialized spatial disciplines but also for critical Marxist, feminist, anticolonial theory more generally.

NOTES

1. For Marston (2000) and Smith (1991, 2004), who otherwise acknowledge the richness of Lefebvre's work, his few comments about scale are too vague for a fully fledged theory of the production of scale (Marston and Smith 2001, 616-17). For them, Brenner was wrong to read scale theory back into Lefebvre. These particular disagreements notwithstanding, Smith and Brenner share a strongly contextual reading of Lefebvre. For Smith (2004, 210), Lefebvre's failure to flesh out a theory of the production of scale in part reflects the fact that Lefebvre could not have captured the full implications of capital's time-space compression during the 1980s and 1990s. For his part, Brenner (2001b, 798) insists that Lefebvre's writing on state and self-management/*autogestion*, which is written in the "theoretical grammar of Fordist Marxism," can only be rescued for a political economy of scale provided that one move from the urban question (which implies a critique of postwar capitalism) to a rigorous theory of territory and scale in state and globalization under neoliberalism. The sentiment expressed in Smith and Brenner parallels Harvey's earlier assessment precisely, if in a different context.
2. In *The Production of Space*, the distinction between minimal and maximal difference is taken up in the discussion of abstract and differential space. As a historical product of state, commodification, disciplinary, rationalist knowledge, and phallocentrism, abstract space incorporates the contradictions of the spatialized, linear time of modern capitalism: use and exchange value, homogenization and fragmentation, quantity and quality. Abstract space harbours fragments of differential space and cyclical time and thus the very tensions between minimal and maximal difference (Lefebvre 1991, 47-63, 234, 255, 268-90, 292-308, 352).
3. In French, *global* refers to a general level of analysis, and in Lefebvre it refers to a particular level, while *mondial* refers to the worldwide as scale. This does not mean that Lefebvre does not insist on the epistemological (rather than just analytical) implications of *mondial/mondialisation*. *Mondial* sometimes appears as a scaled substitute for totality (Lefebvre 1977, 133; 1978, 340-41; 1997, 65), while *mondialisation* occasionally refers to the multiplication of centres of knowledge formation, thus, epistemological multipolarity (Lefebvre 1978, 330). See also Elden (2004, 231-35).
4. Unless otherwise indicated, all Lefebvre quotes from original French texts are translated by the author.
5. The language of descriptive and normative conceptions of totality is borrowed from Martin Jay (1984).

6   As Alex Demirovic (1992) has argued in his pathbreaking Gramscian critique of regulation theory, grasping social reproduction and its regulation as habituation (Bourdieu) effectively grasps everyday life as a site where "external" pressures are "internalized" into popular culture and consciousness from the outside. As a result, notions of everyday life such as Lefebvre's (or Gramsci's) are read in a one-sided way, without the appropriate attention to internal tensions between good sense and common sense (Gramsci), everydayness and everyday life (Lefebvre). While Harvey (1996, 322; 2006a, 279) has qualified his earlier attempt to infuse Lefebvre's triadic conception of the production of space with a rigorous set of determinations, everyday life and lived space never became key categories for him.
7   Lefebvre and Smith are also connected loosely in Michael Gardiner's (2000) survey of "critiques of everyday life."

PART 2
Political Scales

4
Avoiding Traps, Rescaling States, Governing Europe

Bob Jessop

Lively debates over the future of the state resurfaced in the 1980s as scholars, critics, and politicians began to suggest that the scale of national states had become too small to solve the world's big problems and too big to solve its little ones. The most frequently cited problems included (1) the rise of an uncontrolled, possibly uncontrollable, process of capital accumulation that is increasingly and allegedly irreversibly integrated on a world scale; (2) the emergence of a global risk society; (3) the challenge to national politics from identity politics and new social movements based on local and/or transnational issues; (4) the difficulties facing national states in dealing with the particularities of local, metropolitan, or regional economic crises and challenges and overcoming uneven social development and new forms of social exclusion through customized solutions, local participation, and capacity building; and, more recently, (5) the threat, real or imagined, of new forms of protest, terrorism, and decentralized network warfare. Disputes continue about the impact of such "problems" on the future of the state, giving rise to a range of prognoses, all of which refer to various spatial dimensions of the state – political territoriality, place making and spatial planning, parallel power networks crosscutting administrative boundaries and territorial borders, and rescaling and changes in their overall articulation. This set of problems should provide a warning about reducing changes in the state to their scalar features and about the limits of scalar analysis. Such caution does not, however, justify calls to ignore or deny the role of scalar changes as opposed to putting scale "in its place" within a broader spatiotemporal perspective on the state and its embedding within the political order and its wider social context.

Accordingly, this chapter undertakes three successive tasks that reflect important concerns in the political economy of scale raised in the introduction to this volume. It first addresses the nature and limits of the scalar turn, identifies different scalar traps, and proposes some ways to reinvigorate scalar analysis within a broader concern with spatiality. It then presents a set of concepts for dealing with the scalar nature of the state in this broader context. In particular, it highlights the importance of focusing on the changing articulation of different dimensions of spatiality as one way to grasp, albeit incompletely, the historical specificity of different state forms.

I illustrate these arguments through a model of multiscalar metagovernance as an alternative interpretation of the changing forms of European statehood within the broader context of the world market, the global interstate system, and world society. Here I respond to the call in the introduction to explore the interconnection between scale and network rather than to treat them in isolation. In this context, I propose that scale and network have replaced place and territory as the primary axes around which state spatial strategies are developing (Mahon and Keil, this volume). Whereas the metatheoretical arguments about scale and spatiality have wide-ranging implications, the substantive focus of my analysis is more limited. Specifically, I focus on the implications for the national state of the rescaling of economic and political relations associated with (but not exclusively caused by) the increasing integration of the world market. Different conclusions might follow from focusing on other "problems" – although, on my reading, neoliberal globalization is currently the most powerful influence on global dynamics (Jessop 2001, 2002a).

Scalar Turns and Scalar Traps

The scalar turn takes three forms: thematic, methodological, and ontological. A thematic turn occurs when scale is recognized as an important but hitherto neglected analytical topic. In recent years, this thematic shift has been particularly associated with the alleged crisis of nationally scaled territorial states (see below). This crisis is reflected empirically in the relativization of scale, the recalibration and interweaving of scalar hierarchies, struggles over the scalar division of labour, and scale jumping. More generally, a thematic turn rejects "scalar indifference" and argues that, for some purposes, scale is a key category in spatiotemporal analysis. A methodological turn occurs when scale is deemed a fruitful entry point for social analysis. The recent scalar turn is partly a methodological response to the territorial trap, especially its "methodological nationalist" variant,[1] and partly a thematic as well as methodological response to the increasing importance of scalar issues.[2] Finally, a simple (non-essentialist) ontological turn occurs when scale is recognized as an important, unavoidable dimension of the natural and social worlds and hence as one that must be integrated sooner or later into any analysis of these worlds.

A major problem in recent debates on scale has been a failure to distinguish these turns and to consider whether and how far each might benefit social analysis. This failure is reflected in three fallacies.

1 *Scalar conflationism* occurs when analysts fail to distinguish among (a) scale as a relational property of social relations; (b) phenomena *conditioned* by scale in this sense, by its causal processes, and by its emergent effects on non-scalar aspects of the real world; and (c) non-scalar factors *relevant* or implicated in the production of scale. As Miller (this volume) suggests, scale becomes a chaotic conception and can be found anywhere and everywhere insofar as all phenomena are directly scalar, scale-conditioned, or scale-relevant.

2 *Scalar reductionism* occurs when only scale is included as a relevant causal factor in explaining the non-scalar features of a given explanandum. This fallacy involves a one-sided emphasis on scale to the detriment of concern with place, territory, network, or other spatial phenomena. It then concentrates on the relative importance of specific scales (cf. Leitner 2004; Wood 2005). At worst, it treats scales as ordered in a single, fixed, multilayered pyramid or cone with a rigid descending hierarchy of power with the processes on each scale operating separately and discretely from others (cf. Allen 2004; Wood 2005; see also Mahon and Keil, introduction this volume). Even relatively benign forms of scale-centrism overextend the scalar perspective, with the result that almost everything appears to be scalar in one sense or another and/or that other key spatial features and dynamics are ignored.

3 *Scalar essentialism* occurs when an ontological turn is taken to extremes. This can happen in three ways: (a) ideationally, when scale is taken as an a priori mental category or metric rather than an emergent effect of social imaginaries and processes; (b) materially, when scale is treated as *the primary aspect of all social relations* without regard to circumstances; and (c) fetishistically, when scale is considered as an ontologically distinct phenomenon that exists independently of its instantiation as a moment of natural and/or social relations. In the third case, scale is abstracted from its associated substantive content, with the result that the aggregate, cumulative causal powers of a given object are attributed to its scalar

properties alone (cf. Sayer 2000 on spatial fetishism). In each case, scholars tend to take given scalar categories and hierarchies for granted and to populate the relevant conceptual boxes with objects regardless of fit. This procedure is deeply problematic, of course, and has recently led to an antiscalar backlash in favour of a horizontal network topology (e.g., Amin 1998, 2002) or even a "flat ontology" (Marston, Jones, and Woodward, 2005) that denies the very existence of geographical scale (for responses, see Collinge 2006; Hoeflé 2006; and the editors' introduction to this volume).

Thus, while the scalar turn has a useful role to play in the logic of social scientific discovery and highlights real causal mechanisms and actual phenomena, it also has definite empirical limits and poses serious theoretical risks. Thematically, scale is only one dimension of spatiality; methodologically, it is not always the best entry point into spatial analysis, and, even where it is, it should not be the exclusive exit point; and, ontologically, there are real risks of scalar essentialism. There are clear "limits to scale," and a scalar perspective can only explain certain aspects of certain trends (Brenner 2001a; cf. Taylor 2004). Thus, it is important to note the ambivalences and difficulties produced by the overextension of scalar language while avoiding a *fourth fallacy*, "scalar rejectionism," which is based on the total rejection of scale. Elaborating a scalar and scaled political economy is only one possible approach to contemporary capitalism. Thus, if a scalar approach is adopted on thematic, methodological, or simple ontological grounds, it should be complemented by other types of spatial analysis in a consistent conceptual framework and more comprehensive investigation. One way forward is to explore the structural and strategic articulation of scale with other dimensions of spatiality, such as place, territory, and network. This is the path recommended in the editors' introduction and the one taken below.

To avoid these scalar traps, three steps are needed. The first step is to recognize all four types of fallacy as a necessary but by no means sufficient precondition of avoiding them. This step will enable observers and participants alike to explore the relevance and limits of scale theoretically and practically. The second and third steps will then highlight the potential of scale analysis.

The second step is to examine scale as a socially produced dimension of spatiality that is one among several dimensions. More precisely, scale is an emergent, divergent, spatiotemporal process that is a *relatum* of existing or emerging ensembles of social phenomena. As such, it involves many kinds of scalar phenomena that may be convergent/divergent, compossible or mutually exclusive, complementary/contradictory, etc. This is an important consideration because one factor leading to scalar rejectionism is the mistaken assumption that scalar theorists recognize only one nested hierarchy of scales that are identified in casually conventional terms (e.g., local, regional, national, and global). Yet, the existence of multiple scaling processes and scalar orders opens an important field of investigation into scaling, rescaling, and descaling processes, the factors that condition, enable, or generate these processes, and the effects of these processes in different conjunctures. A strategic-relational approach could be useful here on at least three grounds. It avoids the view that scale is an external material constraint and/or an a priori mental category; it interprets scale as an emergent constraint that results from social action and recognizes the variability of spatial horizons of action; and it allows for scalar selectivity and scalar-selective activities (cf. Jessop 2001).

It is important to develop a sufficiently rich set of concepts for each of the dimensions of spatiality and for their articulation to permit an adequate weighting and articulation of these dimensions. Whenever the conceptual and theoretical apparatus for exploring one aspect of a complex phenomenon is more differentiated and comprehensive than the apparatus(es) for other aspects, its relative descriptive and explanatory power could overwhelm mechanisms linked to other dimensions. Or, paradoxically, given the inadequacy of other sets of concepts, it could lead to simplistic analyses that nullify explanations in terms of the well-specified dimension(s), reducing them to mere details or mediations.[3] While simplistic scalar analysis supposedly justifies scalar rejectionism, scalar essentialism is the reciprocal temptation for those who ignore other spatial dimensions. Both are theoretically unacceptable. One solution is to develop appropriately rich[4] – and commensurable – vocabularies with a similar capacity to move from abstract to concrete analysis for each dimension of spatiality and then to combine them to produce concrete-complex analyses as appropriate and necessary for particular explananda.

This is a counsel of perfection, of course, that typically involves a broadly spiral movement as first one and then another moment of spatiality (or, better, spatiotemporality) is stressed thematically, methodologically, or ontologically. A spiral approach would enable investigators to explore the social world from different entry points while still ending with an equally complex-concrete analysis of the current conjuncture in which each aspect of spatiality finds its appropriate descriptive-cum-explanatory weight. Researchers could thereby overcome not only the three main scalar fallacies but also their equivalents for other moments of spatiality. Thus, a focus on territory (as the instantiation of territorialized political power) is associated with the territorial trap, especially, during the postwar period, with methodological nationalism (cf. the critique in Agnew 1994); a concern with place can lead to a place centrism that looks at places as distinct, discrete, institutionally thick, more or less self-contained, more or less self-identical ensembles of social-ecological relations (cf. the critique in Massey 1992, 1995) or to a network centrism that assumes "flat ontologies" that emphasize frictionless "spaces of flows," "topological spatiality," "new mobilities," or rhizomatic topographies of power (see, respectively, Castells 1996; Amin 2002;[5] Law and Urry 2004; Deleuze and Guattari 1988; Hardt and Negri 2000).

The relevance of the second step can be seen in the number and range of compound or hybrid concepts that are used to describe spatial phenomena – concepts that involve *relata* that refer to two or more dimensions of spatiality. Examples include glocalization, glurbanization,[6] federalism, neomedievalism, territorial networks, virtual regions, polynucleated cities, graduated sovereignty, network states, multilevel governance, global city hierarchies, "highly networked glocal enclaves,"[7] and "a network-archipelago of grand poles."[8] Indeed, it is difficult to imagine how one might define any given moment of spatiality without regard to at least one other moment. As one moves towards increasingly "thick description" and/or tries to provide spatially sensitive explanations of more concrete-complex phenomena, one's analyses should involve the dynamic articulation of two or more moments. This stipulation is illustrated in the recent emphasis on the dialectic of scales and networks (Castree 2000a; Leitner 2004; Wood 2005) or McDowell's (2001, 231) argument that the social relations associated with the space of flows can sediment into connections across and between scales in the form of a space of places. Consider, too, the suggestion that cities comprise "places of juxtaposed spaces and superimposed relational webs" (Amin and Graham 1999, 36). Work on the Europolity has examined not only the reterritorialization of political power but also the rise of functional networks and governance regimes that pay limited attention to political frontiers (e.g., Schmitter 1992). Paasi (2004, 529) argues that "the institutionalization/deinstitutionalization of region, place and scale are in fact inseparable elements in the perpetual process of regional transformation," while Jones (2005, 3) calls for a reorientation of regional research around the notion of "phase space," which highlights the spatiotemporal becoming of regions from a topological stance but insists on the compatibilities between networked and scalar/territorial perspectives on space.

The third step in breaking with our four problematic approaches to scale is to relate scale to structure, process, imaginaries, and agency in a comprehensive critical-realist, strategic-relational approach. This step should recognize not only the multidimensional nature of spatiality but also the necessary and inherently complex articulation of spatiality with temporality (Jessop 2001, 2002a). Against the temptation to see *space as static* and *time as dynamic* (Massey 1992) or, worse, to see both space and time as external parameters of social practices and processes, we must stress the dynamics of spatiotemporality as well as potential dislocations between emergent spatial and temporal properties. Key themes here are the dialectic of scaled structures and scalar imaginaries, scalar selectivities and scalar strategies, the making, unmaking, and remaking of scalar selectivities and strategic reflections on such selectivities, and the recursive selection and consolidation of structurally inscribed scalar selectivities and specific scalar horizons of action so that specific scalar fixes come to be stabilized for a time as part of more general spatiotemporal fixes (see Jessop 2001, 2002a). Here, too, appropriately balanced sets of concepts are required.

Key Categories of Space and Spatiality

Approached from a strategic-relational perspective, actually existing spatial configurations offer a whole series of different strategically selective possibilities to stretch, compress, and otherwise develop social relations over time as well as space. This section aims to put scale "in its place" within a broader set of spatial concepts and, for this purpose, treats "space" as the umbrella concept for analyzing spatial relations. A contested concept, space comprises socially produced grids and horizons of social action that divide the material, social, and imaginary world(s) and orient actions in terms of such divisions. Place, territory, scale, and network are important subordinate concepts that identify additional emergent properties of spatial organization. All four are temporal as well as spatial phenomena – they are linked to specific temporal metrics and intertemporal linkages, have their own discursive, strategic, and material temporalities, as well as their own horizons and expectations, and can become objects of governance and reflexive redesign in their own right in relation to the state and other organizational and institutional orders.

As a product of social practices that appropriate and transform physical and social phenomena and invest them with social significance, space can function as a site, an object, and a means of governance. Inherited spatial configurations and their opportunity structures are *sites* where governance may be established, contested, and modified. Space is an *object* of governance insofar as it results from the fixing, manipulating, and lifting of material, social, and symbolic borders, boundaries, and frontiers. Space can be a *means of governance* when it defines horizons of action in terms of "inside" and "outside" and configures possible connections among actors, actions, and events accordingly. Boundaries both contain and connect. They frame interactions selectively, privileging some identities and interests over others, and they structure possible connections to other places and spaces across different scales. While such spatial divisions may generate fundamental antagonisms, they may also facilitate coordination across spaces, places, and scales through solidarity, hierarchy, networks, markets, or other governance mechanisms. Which mechanisms, if any, dominate and their relative success or failure varies with the primary forms of sociospatial organization, ranging from simple nomadic bands and segmentary societies through centre/periphery relations to "world society" with its multiscalar functional differentiation and multiple bases of social fragmentation. The same arguments apply, a fortiori, to the various moments of spatiality. Thus, place, scale, territory, and network can also be viewed as sites, objects, and means of governance.

Space is constructed and governed at many scales, ranging from the corporeal to "outer space." Individuals create their own "personal space" materially and socially, with intimacy and distance varying by locale, type of social relation, and capacities for surveillance and/or intrusion. External efforts also occur to govern "bodies" (including "hearts and minds") and their interrelations in many ways. Thus, building on his classic study of punishment, Foucault (2004) analyzed the "anatomopolitical" (individual) and "biopolitical" (population-focused) practices of modern states and other "disciplinary" apparatuses. Other sites of spatial governance, involving great heterogeneity in objects, stakes, mechanisms, actors, and potential lines of conflict, include residential areas, markets, workplaces, schools, prisons, places of worship, (de)militarized zones, public spaces, private and common land, the built environment, air space and outer space, areas of outstanding natural beauty, and so on. Such complexity suggests that there is no "one best way" to govern time and space and that no actors are inherently privileged or powerful in this regard.

Place or *locale* is a more or less bounded site of face-to-face relationships among individuals and/or of other forms of direct interaction among social forces. As such, a locale will be more or less extensive depending on whether direct interactions require the co-presence of specific individuals or can be mediated through representative individuals. Place is generally closely tied to everyday life, has temporal depth, and is linked to collective memory and social identity. Places (or locales) provide strategically selective social and institutional settings for direct interactions and structure connections beyond that place to other places and spaces on a range of scales. Place making is an important process that enframes social relations within spaces of everyday, more or less proximate interactions; place differentiation refers in turn to the horizontal differentiation of various types of place in a variegated areal landscape. The naming, delimitation, and meaning of places in place making and differentiation are always contested and changeable, and the coordinates of any given physical space can be connected to multiple places with different identities, spatiotemporal boundaries, and social significance (cf. Massey 1992). Thus, we find significant shifts in the naming, delimitation, and meaning of the places in regard to which place-centred activities are undertaken and in the nature of their material connections.

Territory denotes segments of terrestrial space that have been demarcated and organized in terms of political power. Thus, territorialization refers to the segmentation and enclosure of social relations into relatively bounded, demarcated political units and/or the attempted reorganization of such units. It is a special case of the ordering of relations among places through their coordination and enclosure within territorial borders – from which comes the misleading idea of the state as a power container. The typical features of political territory are a *Staatsgebiet* (territory), *Staatsvolk* (population), and *Staatsapparat* (administrative apparatus). The national territorial sovereign state is only one form of demarcating and organizing political territory and is subject to counterprojects based on extraterritoriality rather than the redrawing of territorial boundaries, borders, or frontiers.

A third moment of spatiality is *networking* or *reticulation*. Like the other basic dimensions considered here, networking is a polyvalent term. It can refer to flat, decentred sets of social relations characterized by symmetrical connectivity as well as to centred ensembles of asymmetrical power relations organized on functional rather than territorial lines and operating in the shadow of hierarchy. There is a large literature on network typologies and the modus operandi of different network organizations, and this emphasis poses a major risk of neglect of the hierarchical relations that exist among networks. Even if power relations within all networks were egalitarian and symmetrical, inequality and asymmetry could still occur in network-network relations as expressed in differential capacities of networked agents to pursue their own distinctive strategies and realize their own interests. Such asymmetries and inequalities arise from where networks are grounded (global cities or marginal places), the different scales at and across which they operate (dominant, nodal, or marginal), the territorial interests with which they are linked (e.g., centre versus periphery, strong versus weak states, imperialism or empire). Thus, an adequate topography of networks depends on locating them within a broader spatiotemporal, strategic-relational analysis.

Finally, scale has been defined as the nested hierarchy of bounded spaces of differing size, such as local, regional, national, or global (Delaney and Leitner 1997; for a critique, see Howitt 2003). While this definition is a useful starting point, it does not indicate the polyvalence of scalar analysis. Scale sometimes refers to differences in areal scope (terrestrial or territorial), spans of organizational or administrative control in a vertical or horizontal division of labour, relative dominance in control over more or less significant resources, capacities, and competences, distinct levels of analysis that will typically vary by substantive focus, or, relatedly, the articulation of bounded spaces of differing size, for example local, regional, national, continental, global, and so on.[9] This heterogeneity in focus reinforces my call for a differentiated set of categories to support concrete-complex analyses. Even if we restrict scale to vertical hierarchies and ignore areal differentiation, far from there being some single, overarching peak at which multiple scalar hierarchies culminate (e.g., a sovereign world state), multiple scalar orders exist that are often individually tangled and mutually disconnected. The number of scales and temporalities of action that can be distinguished is immense, but relatively few (although still many) get explicitly institutionalized. How far this happens depends on the prevailing technologies of power that enable the identification and institutionalization of specific scales of action and temporalities.

Thus, how scales come to be defined and institutionalized is crucial. Given that natural and social worlds are too complex to be directly accessible to representation, a key concept for spatial horizons of action and spatial strategies is the spatial imaginary: that is, different ways of representing space that, inter alia, give more or less weight to place, scale, territory, or network in that representation. Spatial imaginaries are discursive phenomena (semiotic ensembles and associated semiotic practices) that distinguish specific places, scales, territories, networks, or spaces in general from the inherently unstructured complexity of a spatialized world. While many spatial imaginaries involve little more than alternative construals of that world, some have a performative impact through the discursive-material construction of spatiality. Yet, even spatial imaginaries that are not "arbitrary, rationalistic, and willed" and have been consolidated in specific spatial orders are prone to instability because no imaginary can be fully adequate to the complexities of the real world (cf. Jessop 2002a, 2004a). This is particularly the case because of the basic contradictions and strategic dilemmas of the underlying social formation and because of the inability of any imaginary and its associated behavioural repertoire to comprehend the full range of factors that bear on their successful realization.

Three further interrelated scalar concepts are especially useful: (a) the scalar division of labour, (b) scale jumping, and (c) the relativization of scale. For Collinge (1999), the scalar division of labour refers to the distribution of different tasks or functions to different scales within a vertical hierarchy of scales – as opposed to the spatial division of labour in which the same tasks or functions are divided among different places on the same spatial scale. An important aspect of recent rounds of economic and political restructuring is its concern with the most appropriate scales for different tasks. It does not follow that the most powerful institutions and actors are located at the peak of a hierarchy. This is why Collinge distinguishes dominant, nodal, and marginal scales.

Dominance concerns "the power which organizations at certain spatial scales are able to exercise over organizations at other, higher or lower scales" (Collinge 1999, 568). It can derive from the general relationship among different scales as strategically selective terrains and/or from the characteristics, capacities, and activities of organizations located at different scales. Together, these features often mean that one level of a scalar system gains special sociopolitical significance by becoming "dominant": that is, by playing the dominant role in the scalar division of labour and offering maximum power over rival apparatuses across several institutional orders (Collinge 1999). For example, in Western Europe, the national scale became dominant during the postwar economic boom thanks to a socially constructed coincidence of national economies, national states, and national citizenship regimes. As scale dominance depends on specific conditions and the possibilities opened by the politics of scale, it is always incomplete, provisional, and unstable. Nodal scales lack such dominance but have key roles in delivering certain activities in a spatiotemporal order. Thus, while the national scale was dominant in economic and social policy making in the Fordist period, the urban scale was nodal for collective consumption and social policy. More marginal or peripheral scales may become important as sites of problems or resistance and so get redefined as nodal sites in delivering solutions for old and/or new problems.

Scale jumping occurs when actors seek to make policy, resolve conflicts, exercise power, and so forth, at the scale that is most favourable to their values, identities, and interests. The motivation for scale jumping is to take advantage of the structurally inscribed scalar privileging of some forces, spatial horizons of action, strategies, policies, etc., over others. The scalar division of labour and scale jumping are linked to attempts to redefine and recalibrate that division, engage in interscalar articulation, institute new scales and/or abolish old ones, and redefine scalar selectivities in order to gain advantage in the jumping game. Scalar strategies are, nonetheless, just one set of possible spatial strategies. Others can target other spatial dimensions of social relations. For example, state spatial projects and strategies can seek to reorder the territorial matrix of political power through de- and reterritorialization based on new spatial imaginaries (on these terms, see Brenner 2004).

State spatial projects, strategies, and imaginaries can also focus on place making or new forms of reticulation or some combination of these approaches. European Spatial Development Planning Process is an impressive example of this compound approach, focusing as it does on territorial integration: creating infrastructural networks, promoting uneven development for the sake of increased competitiveness, and providing compensation for adversely affected places for the sake of social cohesion. It involves the creation of a new scalar division of labour in which European-level institutions become dominant in spatial planning, and national and regional institutions become nodal and consolidating centre/periphery relations at the heart of EU policy making (cf. Faludi and Waterhout 2002; Jensen and Richardson 2004).

The relativization of scale involves a major discontinuity in the scalar division of labour compared to the dominance of the national scale associated with the postwar period of Atlantic Fordism, import substitution industrialization, export-led growth, and state socialism. The current period of globalization involves a proliferation of spatial scales, their relative dissociation in complex tangled hierarchies (rather than a simple nesting of scales), and an increasingly convoluted mix of scale strategies as economic and political forces seek the most favourable conditions for insertion into a changing international order (Jessop 2002a). While the national scale has lost its postwar taken-for-granted dominance, no other scale of economic and political organization (whether "global" or "local," "urban" or "triadic") has acquired a similar dominance. Instead, different economic and political spaces and forces located at different scales are competing to become the primary or nodal point of accumulation and/or state power. The relativization of scale also offers important new opportunities for scale jumping and struggles over interscalar articulation. This raises the interesting question of whether a long-term solution requires a new dominant scale with a complementary set of nodal and marginal scales or whether the relativization of scale is the new norm, and the importance now attached to network forms of coordination is a viable strategic-relational response to this situation.

Multiscalar Metagovernance in the European Union and Beyond

How can a *methodological scalar turn* contribute to the analysis of the changing forms of European statehood, bearing in mind that this does not require that scale is the only spatial dimension to be considered or that spatiality is the only major feature of the changing configuration of statehood? I want to argue that a scalar entry point is useful insofar as the main axes of state reorganization today concern scale and networks rather than place and territory and that, in this sense, the scalar turn is justified not merely on thematic and methodological grounds but also on non-essentialist ontological grounds. More precisely, while place, territory, scale, and network are equally important *analytical* dimensions of state spatiality, their substantive articulation and relative weight in specific state formations (or ensembles involved in the territorialization of political power) can nonetheless vary significantly. In this context, I suggest that the relative primacy in state spatial projects and strategies of territory and place in the period of Atlantic Fordism has been replaced by a relative primacy of scale and networks. This argument develops a general issue alluded to by the editors in their introduction to this volume and relates it to changes in statehood in the European Union.

The spatiotemporal fix of the leading Atlantic Fordist economies rested on the primacy of national money over international currency and of the individual and social wage as a source of domestic demand rather than as a cost of international production, and these twin priorities were reflected in the primacy of national economies, national welfare states, and national societies managed by national states concerned to unify national territories and reduce uneven development. In this context, there was a relatively stable scalar division of labour in which the national was dominant, albeit embedded in a liberal international order and supported by the nodal role of local states in delivering certain complementary forms of economic and social policy, and networks were primarily corporatist and/or clientelist, operating within the national Atlantic Fordist economic and political matrix. The crisis of Atlantic Fordism and its Keynesian national welfare states has enhanced the power of international currency and capital flows over national monetary and fiscal policies and prioritized the individual and social wage as a cost of production and, concomitantly, undermined the complementarity of national economies, national welfare states, national societies, and national territorial states and intensified uneven development. These effects are reflected in the increased importance of competitiveness as the axis around which new modes of regulation in a globalizing knowledge-based economy are being organized and in a search for new forms and functions of statehood that can address the crisis of the national territorial state.

It is in this context that the relativization of scale has put scalar issues firmly on the agenda both theoretically and politically and that there is significant experimentation with network forms of organization that might contribute to the development of a stable, postnational state better able to steer the integration of changing economic and political spaces into a globalizing knowledge-based economy marked by increased uneven development. Let me stress that this is a working hypothesis concerning the changing spatialities of the state rather than an established fact and that further research is required to explore the "limits of scale and networks" as a methodological entry point into the analysis of the European Union as a state in the process of formation. But it is one based on prior research on the changing modes of growth and regulation associated with the crisis of Atlantic Fordism and its spatiotemporal fix and is consistent with these changes. The emergence of new theoretical paradigms concerned with multilevel governance and the network polity and, even more recently, the formal development of the Lisbon agenda with its commitment to a new policy paradigm based on the "open method of coordination" as a form of multiscalar metagovernance also lend prima facie credibility to this hypothesis.

This hypothesis reinforces the importance of going beyond what is conventionally termed "multilevel governance" to examine "multiscalar metagovernance" as an important feature of the emerging European political order. Development of the open method of coordination can be seen as part of continuing efforts (often at cross-purposes) by key economic and political actors to produce an appropriate balance between different modes of economic and political coordination across functional and territorial divides and to ensure, under the primacy of the political, a measure of apparatus unity and political legitimacy for the European Union. These efforts have taken different forms at different periods in the pursuit of the European project, especially as the latter has been shaped at different times by shifts in the relative weight of Atlantic and European economic and political strategies, by shifts in the relative weight of liberal and neoliberal *échangiste* ("money capital") perspectives and neocorporatist and neomercantilist productivist projects, and by the tendential shift from a Keynesian national welfare state approach concerned to create a single market to realize economies of scale to a Schumpeterian workfare postnational regime approach concerned to transform the European Union into the most competitive and dynamic knowledge-based economy and to "modernize" the European social model.

Of course, this Europe-wide, multiscalar, metagovernance project is being conducted in conditions of successive rounds of expansion (which have increased the heterogeneity of the growth dynamics and modes of regulation of different regional and national economies as well as the forms and extent of uneven development and inequalities) and in conditions under which national economies and national states have been subject to their own individual structural problems and crises as well as the shared crisis tendencies derived from their integration into the circuits of Atlantic Fordism and into the emerging globalizing knowledge-based economy. Finally, this multiscalar metagovernance project is part of a broader post-Westphalian "metaconstitutional conversation" occurring between non-state and state actors (including metastates such as the European Union) as they struggle to develop and institutionalize a new political order (Walker 2000).

New methods of multiscalar metagovernance are being developed and combined in a complex system of metagovernance (cf. Scott and Trubek 2002) that is "being made more precise and applied (with adaptations as for its intensity) to other fundamental policy fields, traditionally under the competence of national and sub-national authorities: education, structural reform and internal market, technological innovation and knowledge-based society, research and social protection" (Telò 2002, 253).[10] From a strategic-relational perspective, this clearly implies a shift in the strategic selectivities of the modes of governance and metagovernance in the European Union. While it builds on past patterns of liberal intergovernmentalism and neofunctionalist spillover, it has its own distinctive momentum and will weaken more hierarchical forms of coordination (whether intergovernmental or supranational). It also entails complementary changes in the strategic selectivities of national states and subordinate levels of government and governance, calling for new forms of strategic coordination and new forms of (meta) governance in and across a wide range of policy fields.

The pattern of multilevel metagovernance in the European Union is still evolving, and – given the inherent tendencies towards failure typical of all major forms of governance (market, hierarchy, network, etc.) as well as metagovernance itself (Jessop 2002a) – continuing experimentation, improvisation, and adaptation are only to be expected. Nonetheless, "the perspective would be that of a new system of democratic legitimacy and governance: multilevel (international, national, supranational, transnational), multifaceted (territorial, functional, modern, and post-modern) and with a multitude of actors (social, economic, political, and cultural; institutional and extra-institutional), rather than that of a classical democratic normative model – federal/constitutional or democrat/republican" (Telò 2002, 266; cf. Schmitter 1992).

This approach is also useful in interpreting the continuities and discontinuities in the development of the European Union as a moment in the structural transformation and strategic reorientation of statehood in a world of states that is not limited to Europe but extends to the global polity (cf. Hettne 1997; Shaw 2000; Sørensen 2001). The European Union can be seen as a major and, indeed, increasingly important supranational instance of *multiscalar metagovernance* in relation to a wide range of complex and interrelated problems. While the sources and reach of these problems go well beyond the territorial space occupied by its member states, the European Union is an important, if complex, point of intersection (or node) in the emerging, hypercomplex, and chaotic system of global governance (or, better, metagovernance) and is seeking to develop its own long-term "Grand Strategy" for Europe (Telò 2002, 266). It is still one node among several within this emerging system of global metagovernance and cannot be fully understood without taking account of its complex relations with other nodes located above, below, and transversal to the European Union. Indeed, while one might well hypothesize that the European scale is becoming increasingly dominant within the multiscalar metagovernance regime of the European Union, it is merely nodal in the emerging multiscalar metagovernance regimes that are developing on a global scale under the (increasingly crisis-prone) dominance of the United States.

Conclusion

This chapter has highlighted some key theoretical issues associated with the scalar turn: the always-contested social construction of scale orders; the relative stability of spatial categories such as place, space, and scale and their associated spatiotemporal properties; the politics of interscalar articulation and rescaling; and the politics of scale jumping rooted in differential capacities to switch scales. The chapter has also argued that scale is only one aspect of a broader spatiotemporal research agenda and that scale must be put in its place within this agenda. This said, it is possible that the scalar and network turns are not merely part of the normal intellectual fashion cycle but also reflect important changes in the organization of statehood. The final part of this chapter addressed this issue by reviewing alternative approaches to the European Union as a state in the process of formation and noting the heuristic value of a multiscalar methodological turn in addressing its novelty within a more general reorganization of statehood on a world scale. The key issue for a research agenda into this new form of statehood is the manner and extent to which the multiplying levels, arenas, and regimes of politics, policy making, and policy implementation can be endowed with a certain apparatus and operational unity horizontally and vertically and how this governance problem affects the overall operation of politics and the legitimacy of the new political arrangements. Many of these broader issues require us to look well beyond the scalar turn to include the analysis of the changing geography and political economic dynamic of contemporary capitalism and the other challenges that confront the modern state in a changing and increasingly crisis-prone global order.

NOTES

1. The territorial trap assumes "that states and their powers can for practical purposes be thought of as contained within the bounded territories over which they have formal sovereignty" (Glassman 1999, 670).
2. Dicken et al. (2001) advocate a methodological network turn on similar grounds.
3. Another illustration is Harvey's (2003) attempts to combine the territorial logic of statehood with the spatial logic of capital accumulation. Because his analysis of the former is insufficiently rich, conceptually, the explanatory logic of capitalism is far stronger. This strength is countered by crude geopolitical explanations that essentialize imperialism in terms of the primacy of political motives or the expansionist drive of states or state managers *qua* subjects (for a critique, see Jessop 2006).

4 This recommendation does not imply an equal number of concepts for each dimension – which would entail a numeric conceptual fetishism. It is simply a recommendation to develop a broad array of concepts of different degrees of abstraction/concreteness and simplicity/complexity to do some justice to the complexities of the real world (see Jessop 1982, 210-28).
5 "A topological sense of space and place, a sense of geographies constituted through the folds, undulations, and overlaps that natural and social practices normally assume, without any a priori assumption of geographies of relations nested in territorial or geometric space" (Amin 2002, 389).
6 Whereas glocalization refers to the spatial strategies of potentially mobile actors, glurbanization refers to place-making and place-marketing strategies that seek to fix potentially mobile actors in a given location.
7 Bunnell and Coe (2005, 834), paraphrasing Graham and Marvin (2001, 376), who actually refer to increasingly self-contained glocal enclaves.
8 The last phrase comes from Veltz (1996, 6).
9 To ensure adequate theoretical and empirical analyses, different scales must be properly specified rather than identified in casual, conventional terms.
10 Telò is commenting on the open method of coordination, but his comment can be generalized to other forms of metagovernance, including partnership, comitology, social dialogue, and so forth.

5
Scaling Government to Politics

Warren Magnusson

To ask for a political economy of scale is to suggest that we can locate ourselves politically by means of an analysis given by the science of political economy. I think that this suggestion is false: indeed, it is profoundly misleading. Perhaps everyone knows this – which is why there is so often a gesture towards an indeterminate and indeterminable politics that will take us out of the sorry passes in which the science of political economy shows us to have been caught. This sort of gesturing betrays what it is meant to conceal: namely, that we lack the science of politics that would tell us how to get out of such passes. In its original Aristotelian sense, political science was supposed to guide political action, not just explain what was given. The Marxian form of political economy – to which critical political economists have been responding ever since – had a similar purpose. Unfortunately, Marxian political economy is as defective as Aristotelian political science. If Aristotle makes the mistake of abstracting politics from the mode of production, Marx makes the opposite mistake of embedding it there. Now, more than ever, we should realize that the politics of material gain (the politics that is implicit in evolving relations of production) underdetermines the politics of security (how we deal with threats of violence) and the politics of identity (how we define who and what we are). Each of these politics has its own dynamic and hence its own scalar logic, which affects and is affected by the other scalar logics. The politics of "the politics of scale" is far more complicated than any political economy of scale could reveal, for much of what has to be understood falls outside the rubric of political economy.

What does political economy have to tell us about the implications of being Muslim or Christian or Canadian or American – or about the meaning of our claims to be civilized or modern? What are we supposed to be securing when we try to secure our future or our children's future? Who is this "we" that we are talking about? Indeed, who is this "I" that is asking this question? Marx, notoriously, tried to evade such questions. Most critical political economists have followed in Marx's footsteps in this respect or have resorted to the stereotypes on offer in what they take to be progressive political thinking. That is not good enough. If we want to deal seriously with contemporary politics, we have to confront these questions as seriously as the ones that flow from changes in the patterns of international finance and investment. The contours of political space are not fixed: we produce new political spaces through our own political activities (Magnusson 1996; 2000, 289-306). We scale politics to our purposes. This does not mean that we can do exactly what we want – just that the scales on which we act are relative to our own purposes as well as to the conditions we confront. Political economy can tell us much about those conditions. It cannot tell us what we are to make of them or how we are to respond to them.

The state is still the key problem that we have to contend with when we think politically. Modern politics is scaled to the state in two different ways. In the first and most obvious sense, the size of the polity is dictated by the size of the state. The development of transnational authorities such as the European Union has had little effect on this since these authorities are rooted in states. The presumption is that a state must be of a certain size (in terms of population and territory) if it is to be viable.[1] This is partly a matter of having the requisites for self-defence: a territory with defensible borders and the resources for a well-equipped modern army. It is also a matter of economic self-sufficiency: having an economy or economic agglomeration large enough to produce internally most of what is needed for modern life. In the latter regard, a capacity for social or cultural reproduction seems to be especially important. In other words, the state must be large enough for the ongoing reproduction of a self-sustaining modern population (Gellner 1983). Liberal democrats suppose that such a population will be capable of self-government and hence of the form of politics that has come to typify the modern state. The self-governing modern population is the living substance of the modern state, but we generally suppose that this population must be of a certain size and occupy territory of a certain size if it is to be viable as an autonomous political entity. The general view is that the scale envisioned by Aristotle is much too small now and that a viable state or polity must have a population in the millions (if not the tens or hundreds of millions) rather than in the low thousands, as he imagined.

There is a second sense in which modern politics is scaled to the state. A scale in music is a metric – a way of relating notes to one another in standardized measures. There are scales of many other sorts that we use to measure speed, distance, volume, statistical deviation, and so on. So scale in this sense is a question of the metric we use to determine the relation between things. A certain scale, measure, or standard of judgment is implicit in the idea of the state, and it is in relation to this scale, measure, or standard of judgment that modern politics is normally understood and evaluated. In the ideal, the state bespeaks a self-sufficient constitutional order at one remove from the cultural, social, and economic relations of everyday life (Vincent 1987). It somehow flows from but nonetheless begets and sustains the legal order that governs everyday life. The constitutional order regulates politics by establishing procedures for changing the law. It also establishes a procedure for changing the constitution itself. Politics is thus articulated with the form and disposition of the lawful (law-making, law-enforcing) state. Although, as noted, there is a presumption that a legally self-sufficient state must be of a certain size, in terms of population and territory, there is much more than this involved in scaling politics to the idea of the state. Hidden in modern thinking is a series of assumptions about the way people have to live if they are to *be* modern rather than traditional or primitive. To scale politics to the state is to force people to exist in a certain way and to adopt a particular scale to measure their own lives.

This is a situation that poses especially difficult problems for indigenous peoples; as a result, they pose especially difficult problems for the modern state and hence for modern politics. Think first of the question of size in relation to population and territory. Indigenous peoples organized themselves in many different ways in the premodern era. Although some of the so-called tribes were quite large (in terms of population and the territory occupied by that population), a small scale of sociopolitical organization was the norm. In any case, the peoples who now understand themselves as indigenous nations – distinguished by language, custom, history, and politics from other indigenous nations – are often small in population (often measuring themselves in the hundreds or low thousands) and have been displaced to a greater or lesser degree from their traditional territories (and suffered many unwanted incursions into those territories by outsiders). Canadian indigenous peoples are quite various; they are intermingled with one another as well as with those whose ancestors are from away; they live partly within and partly outside their traditional territories; but, as individual *nations*, they are generally quite small by any measure that we might associate with the logic of state organization. In the context of treaty negotiations in British Columbia, indigenous nations have been challenged by the need to document the extent of their traditional territories, provide evidence of traditional and ongoing land-use practices, and explain to outsiders their various houses and clans and their particular systems of property, methods of adjudication, and arrangements for law and treaty making and interpretation. Vexing as the demand has been for First Nations to explain their being and disposition to outsiders (to prove that they are whom they say they are), there have been certain benefits, in terms of an opportunity (and relevant resources), for First Nations to reflect upon what they want as a form of collective life that might be sustainable under current conditions (which, of course, are conditions that are not of their own choosing). Nevertheless, one of the troubling issues has been that the form of organization expected of First Nations presumes a scale that many First Nations would have trouble maintaining.

Discussions of local government organization are illuminating when juxtaposed with the problem of First Nations organization. In highly urbanized areas, the assumption has been that the optimal scale of local government organization is one that encompasses the metropolis as a whole or at least some significant portion of it. In terms of population, one talks in millions or at least in hundreds of thousands. Even in accounts that suppose multiple scales of organization within the metropolis, the tendency is to suppose that a neighbourhood or community would need to have a population in the thousands and a reasonably coherent territory to function as an autonomous entity within the larger whole. Among the considerations invoked in working out the minimum scale for political organization are the following: fiscal self-sufficiency, administrative self-sufficiency, shared territory, discernible boundaries, and a shared interest in services and facilities that can be organized efficiently on the scale imagined. There is, for instance, a long tradition of thinking of the catchment area of a public school or recreational centre as the minimum that one would need for the organization of an autonomous neighbourhood unit. The presumption is that a politically workable neighbourhood would need to have charge of *some* public services and facilities and that there is a certain population required to provide such services and facilities effectively and efficiently. Moreover, such a neighbourhood would have to generate a substantial proportion of the resources necessary for these facilities and services from within. Most importantly, it would have to generate its own political leadership and attract appropriate administrative cadres. All of this suggests a certain minimum scale: one that may be unattainable in rural areas but one that is always already available in urban areas.

Any analysis that follows along these lines will put the possibilities for First Nations self-government into question since many of the First Nations seem to lack one or more of the requisites, such as fiscal self-sufficiency or a cadre of professional administrators.[2] Such an analysis will reveal something else, however: the issue of "scale" is less a matter of size than a way of life. Think of traditional ways of life. It is obvious that those ways of life are on the scale appropriate to them, in the double sense of "size" and "measure." Each way of life has a measure or measures internal to it: at least one metric, if not more, that will enable the participants to judge their own lives. Are we living appropriately? Have we succeeded or failed in these endeavours? What is the significance of our success or failure? What is required of us now? How should we act in the future? Some degree of reflexivity is implicit in any way of life, but the matters on which one reflects and the mode of reflection are likely to vary with the form of life itself. Those of us who are schooled in statist ways of thinking – which is to say all of us – are inclined to think (at least some of the time) that a person should be a "good citizen" and comport herself accordingly. This standard of judgment involves a particular metric or scale that we impose on the people concerned (including ourselves): this scale is unintelligible except with reference to an assumed way of life. If one imposes that scale on the traditional ways of life of indigenous peoples, then the effect is to measure them by a standard that they could not possibly meet: one that is at several removes from the purposes implicit in the ways of life in question. To insist on such a scale is to devalue all forms of life that are not consistent with it. The arrogance of this is apparent. What may not be apparent is that the effort to impose a uniform scale is ultimately self-defeating, even for those of us who are not indigenous to the territories that we now inhabit.

What is involved in establishing a particular metric or scale for measuring a way of life? One of the common claims about modernity is that it entails reflexivity, carried to a degree previously unknown (Foucault 1997, 303-19; Kant 1991, 54-60). The principles of our way of life are made explicit and become the subject of ongoing debate. From such explicit reflection on explicitly stated principles comes a widely shared understanding that is subject to ongoing revision. To be modern is to be self-conscious, open to new and different alternatives, prepared to revise one's principles and hence one's way of life. To be modern is to put traditions in question, compare them with one another, and consider new alternatives. Modernity thus entails openness to the future and to other ways of life. Ironically, modernity also involves a series of closures in relation to forms of life that are deemed to be inconsistent with modernity itself. This is especially evident in the way that traditional forms of life are treated. We have a concept of the obsolescent – the family farm, the outport village, the ethnic neighbourhood, the Native reserve, the nomadic band – that we apply freely in judging ways of life. Often these ways of life are embraced freely by people who are fully conscious of the alternatives: the reflexivity that is supposed to characterize modernity is clearly present. Nevertheless, these ways of life are assigned to a past that somehow burdens the present and that must be eliminated to enable modern life to go forward. This sort of reaction reduces the diversity that modernity is supposed to allow as well as the differences that it is supposed to recognize and celebrate.

Aristotle insisted that the *polis* should be scaled to the requisites of the good life (1996, 73-75, 171-79). Military security and economic prosperity were important from his point of view but not so important as the possibility for self-government. A properly organized *polis* would be on the scale required for self-sufficiency, but the crucial dimension of self-sufficiency was political rather than economic or military. The citizens of the *polis* could not be so many that they had no chance of familiarizing themselves with one another or deliberating together. Nor could they be so few that they had no common life other than the familial or the parochial. The *polis* had to be big enough to support the full range of human activities and human possibilities, but it had to be small enough to enable people to consider these activities and possibilities collectively and to arrange their lives together in accordance with their sense of what was best. To the extent that there has been any argument on the matter in the modern era, the claim has been that Aristotle underestimated the scale necessary for the full range of human activities and possibilities and overestimated the enabling effects of intimacy (Dahl 1990; Held 1996). Modern means of communication are supposed to enable intimacy at a distance; in any case, the larger canvas of modern life is supposed to be required for the great spirited among us. Aristotle might not have minded these adjustments. He was little interested in the mass of ordinary people. Nevertheless, from a democratic perspective, the enlargement in scale from the *polis* to the state is clearly problematic because it puts the bulk of the population at a considerable distance from the venues in which mutual recognition and face-to-face deliberation might occur. Thus, there is the insistent suspicion among us moderns that politics is no longer scaled to the practices in which we must engage if we are to live the best lives of which we are capable.

While politics has been scaled to the state, this scale is less a matter of size than of disposition towards a constitutional-legal order at a distance from everyday life: that is, towards an order that is impersonal and perpetual. This order offers a form of rationality that springs from the very essence of humankind and thus (in Hegelian terms) "grounds and completes" human nature. The state is the imagined universal implicit in the particularities of human interaction. Politics has been scaled to this universal, which takes us outside of our particularities and replaces those particularities on a register between the permissible and the impermissible. The particular universal implicit in the imagined community of the state is one that creates distinctive zones of impermissibility. We can understand three of these zones in terms of the marker years of 1492, 1648, and 1789: 1492, marking the distinction between the modern civilization of the West and the barbarian peoples at its margins; 1648, marking the mutual limitations implicit in the system of states that enable particularities within a universal order; and 1789, marking the difference between a future of democratic self-government and a past of ancient traditions that limit people's freedom. Socialist politics long promised to bring everyone into the privileged zone, but the terms of entry have been improved, if at all, on liberal terms, which reify the original modern understandings of what it means to be human. Thus, the zones of permissibility and impermissibility in the original modern disposition of the state remain much as they have been. Indigenous peoples are in a zone of impermissibility because they embody possible ways of life that do not compute with – cannot be scaled to – the particular form of modernity that has been advanced under the aegis of the modern state.

Marx invoked notions of the primitive to conjure up an image of freedom in the communist future. That future would be one in which I could "hunt in the morning, fish in the afternoon, rear cattle in the evening, criticize after dinner, just as I have a mind, without ever becoming hunter, fisherman, cowherd, or critic" (Marx 1977, 169). This vision suggests that the zone of impermissibility associated with 1492 would be integrated with the zone of communist permissibility, as a consequence of the abolition of capitalism and the state with it. Marx's conception of the future underscores the exclusions implicit in the present, but it also highlights the way that his own thought (and socialist thought in general) is keyed to the scale of the modern state. The imagined future is reachable only *through* the state, conceived as an inevitable stage in human self-organization required for the organization of the forces of production in the last antagonistic social formation, capitalism. Since Marxian communism is not in our immediate future, it follows (from this analysis) that the state (and hence the state scale or metric) is an inevitably necessary form of organization in the present: not one from which we could hope to be free. So it follows that, for Marxists as for more conventional liberals, the zones of impermissibility remain much as they have been for hundreds of years. The permissible forms of governmental and political organization are keyed to the state form, which lays the ground for the next stage in the development of human life. The main difference between Marxists and liberals is that the former envisage a zone of indistinction, in which impermissible revolutionary activity becomes permissible by virtue of its progressive promise. Marxists agree with liberals that ways of life that do not compute with the state are obsolescent: they can be recovered, if at all, only in a poststatist future. For the present, the state remains the regulative ideal.

This binding of life's possibilities to the metric of the state has particular consequences for indigenous peoples, who are thought to be living archaically and hence impermissibly. We should not lose sight of this, but we should be careful about accepting the idea that indigenous peoples are peoples apart, fundamentally different from all other peoples. After all, the latter is the idea that has legitimated the ongoing marginalization of indigenous peoples. Although the claim that they are fundamentally different from other peoples has been turned around, so as to become a relatively effective *defensive* claim for those peoples, it has its origins in European claims about the difference between civilized and savage (or advanced and primitive) peoples. The latter claims were tied to a "stages" theory of history, which implied that some peoples were living in a past that the Europeans (and other "civilized" peoples) had long since left behind. As I have indicated, this theory assigns indigenous peoples to a zone of impermissibility: they may be permitted to remain there for a time, but they are doomed by history. To say that this theory is arrogant and insensitive is not to say anything that hasn't been said many times before, more effectively and knowledgeably than I ever could. What I want to suggest is that the difference implied – between the civilized and the savage, the modern and the traditional – is doubly misleading, in that it not only makes an invidious and misleading distinction between some ways of life and others but also incites us to believe that such a distinction is crucial to modernity. On this view, modernity is always about getting beyond ways of life that are tied to a past that we have (for better or worse) left behind. That leaving behind may sometimes be perceived as a tragedy (of lost innocence or simplicity), but the tragedy is always figured as a *necessity* with which we must all come to terms (Weber 2002). There is no way back, for us or them. The sense that modernization is a *tragic necessity* has structured Western thought since the eighteenth century, and it has provided the underlying rationale for many brutalities: brutalities of a scope and scale that non-Western peoples have scarcely ever matched. These brutalities are not an incidental effect. They are intrinsic to a way of thinking that forces us to expel a wide range of human possibilities from our present and imagined future.

The viability of a way of life depends on its internal vitality, the fit that it offers with the natural environment, and its relation to other ways of life that have the capacity to affect it. Indigenous peoples *were* living modern lives when the Europeans came along; they still *are* living modern lives; it's just that the conditions of possibility for indigenous ways of life have deteriorated as a result of Western incursions. There is an analogue here to the way in which so many other ways of life have been rendered "obsolescent" by the ongoing articulation of a particular way of life that passes itself off as uniquely modern. It is not an uncommon or incidental feature of modern thought and practice to say that this or that way of living – for instance, the life of an artist, writer, hunter, fisher, farmer, craft worker, villager, co-operant, or communard – is not (or is no longer) viable. Nor is the violence that flows from such a judgment incidental or uncommon. On the contrary, judgments of this sort structure the routine violence of life in the Western dominions (which is to say, now, in the world as a whole). We are not outside these judgments or the violence that accompanies them. We practise this violence on ourselves and our children as well as on others whom we deem to need our assistance in becoming modern in the appropriate way. We seek to scale ourselves as well as others to the metric of an imagined modernity, a metric that demands that we "live large" in a now globalized economy, participate in a globalized culture, and become good citizens of a state within a system of states. The demand upon indigenous peoples in Canada is that they become good Canadian citizens. This demand appears innocent to us – we frame it as an offer to include indigenous peoples in a multicultural society that has room for many differences – because it is a demand that we put upon ourselves and our own children.

At stake, then, is a range of impermissible possibilities that we *know* to be perfectly viable. We know them to be viable because people live them in our midst or at least stake the possibilities in a way that makes it obvious that these ways of life could be viable, but for socioeconomic and political arrangements that undermine them. It is not their *impossibility* that makes them frightening and disturbing. Their *possibility* is what frightens, because it calls attention to the narrowness, shallowness, and disciplinary single-mindedness of the particular way of being modern that we have been induced or forced to follow.

Marx made a crucial political move when he replaced the state with the mode of production as the main object of study. He suggested that we are actually *governed* by the mode of production and that the rest of what we do politically flows from that. If he is correct in this respect, then any analysis that focuses on the state in abstraction from the mode of production is bound to be misleading. Moreover, the most important practices of government may be the ones embedded in the economy or society, beyond the bounds of state regulation and hence of politics as it is normally conceived. If we are to contest these practices, then we have to open up the domain of the political. Unfortunately, Marx's approach commits us to a stages theory of history that suggests that we have no choice but to move towards a particular form of modernity. That commitment is bound up with another, more important, idea, however – that political economy determines politics. The latter idea (as well as the former) are secreted in the work of most critical political economists, who turn to political economy to reveal the forces that structure the political possibilities of the present. In making such a turn, political economists neglect the fact that the politics of identity – for instance, nationalism or religious commitment – often overrides political economy, in the sense that it changes the political stakes and rescales politics (in both senses) in ways that could hardly have been anticipated from the struggles implicit in the mode of production. Since the politics of identity is geared to questions about who we are and how we should live, it always is underdetermined by political economy, related as that is to material stakes. Both forms of politics raise security issues for which the state is supposed to be the solution (Campbell and Dillon 1993). Hobbes argued that political economy presupposes the effective resolution of the "security dilemma" and hence, he suggested, the prior establishment of the state.[3] A better way of putting it is that the politics of security, the politics of identity, and the politics of material gain (if that is what we want to call "political economy") are always in play simultaneously. None necessarily determines the others.

It follows that, if we look to the political economy of scale to reveal the political possibilities of the present, we are liable to be misled. There are always other things happening that rescale politics in different ways. Remember 9/11? We need not take that marker to indicate that the politics of the present is bleak. Rather, it is a reminder that unexpected and unpredictable things happen, for both good and ill. If we were to go by the "judgment of history," it would seem that Marxists (and others who have tried to imagine a future beyond capitalism) have been "condemned" in much the same way that indigenous peoples have. The period from 1917 to 1991 now appears like a phase in the *longue durée* of capitalist development, a time when certain difficult obstacles were overcome. The Communists were problematic, but so were the Indian chiefs, Oriental potentates, and feudal lords before them. All were swept aside as capitalism spread and developed in accordance with the logic of the mode of production. Are we to accept this judgment of history, or are we to put its metric into question by rethinking the relation between political economy and political possibility?

I want to suggest that we can do the latter but that in order to do so, we need to move away from sociological explanations of political possibility. The Indians are still with us, and the socialists will remain with us too, as witnesses, exemplars, and agents of possibilities concealed by accounts that embrace "actually existing modernity" (if I can adapt an old phrase to a new purpose) as a regulative ideal. To be put out of history, as Indians and socialists have been, is to be assigned to a vast zone of impermissibility, where much of contemporary life is actually lived in both aspiration and practice. How to understand that life *politically* rather than *sociologically* is the crucial task of our time. By a sociological understanding, I mean one that explains the present naturalistically and so presents current conditions as effects of forces, structures, struggles, or events that overdetermine current possibilities. The more complete the analysis, the tighter the space of present political possibility. In fact, to the extent that such sociological analyses actually work on their own terms, the political choices that we have to make fall out like solutions from mathematical equations.

Liberal economists, Marxist social scientists, and the realist analysts of power politics are sisters under the skin who share a common aspiration: to make political judgment irrelevant by scientizing its exercise. I want to suggest that the gap between social scientific and political understanding is unbridgeable. You/we cannot get to where we need to go by that route, because the political is not just across the other side of a chasm. The political is in another world, a world of action and human possibility, a world of imagination and desire, a world that articulates what we are striving to be or to remain in the face of another world that is always already imposed on us. The fact that this other world – the world analyzed by economists, sociologists, international relations scholars, and other social scientists – is more potent than the worlds that we would like to sustain or create is already known. We scarcely need to be told that. No doubt it can be helpful to understand the grip of that world better and to appreciate how a temporary loosening of the grip can be the prelude to a tighter hold. Nevertheless, what we need (now especially) is to see that the impermissible possibilities of the present – the ones that are out of scale with the particular version of modernity that has become dominant – *can* be nurtured, *can* be acted out, and not irrationally. *Pace* Marx, Weber, and Hayek, the human future is not given to us in a form to which we have to adhere. Other modernities may indeed emerge in a world where the chains of causation are non-linear and political action is always a matter of human freedom.

To speak of politics is to invoke the domain of human possibility: a world of judgment, choice, and action. The premise of politics is uncertainty: an uncertainty that provokes differing judgments and leads to courses of action that have indeterminate outcomes. Although there are always efforts to impose a fixed scale on politics, the scale of the political can never be fully determined in advance. With what reach and within which register people choose to act are always matters of uncertainty. New forms of the political can be developed with surprising speed, and their effectiveness can be extraordinary. We already know the effectiveness of the old forms of the political. The new forms surprise us. Even for the politically experienced, politics is a puzzle for which there are no easy answers. To put the point otherwise, our political possibilities are not sociologically or economically determined; there are always *other* ways of thinking and acting in the present; there are always other possibilities not foreseen by the analyses that we can develop on the basis of old ways of thinking.

We have been reminded of this by the revival of various forms of religious fundamentalism. This revival was about as unexpected as the collapse of the Berlin Wall. We can offer *ex post facto* explanations of evangelical Protestantism, religious Zionism, Islamism, Hindutva, and all the rest, but we do so in bad faith unless we acknowledge that social scientists did not expect things to go in these directions. Are we not dealing with the human capacity to articulate new understandings that posit new identities, new futures, and new scales of human interaction? Who, really, would have predicted the scales of struggle implicit in the post-9/11 war on terror or anticipated that this supposed war would be framed in religious terms? The measures that the US government and its allies have taken are a reminder that the political economy of scale is always overdetermined by the politics of security, a politics that is always related to basic existential questions.[4] Who is this "we" that wants to be secured? And for which purposes? Surely it is not just about protecting one's property within the existing mode of production. Nor is it just about positioning oneself in relation to the advance of capitalism. People really mean it when they talk about protecting the true faith or advancing the Second Coming. Their politics is not just a confused expression of their economic interests or social anxieties. The scales and boundaries of political action have been redefined by movement after movement in our time, and these movements simply refuse to accept the logic of political economy as the ground on which they must act.

In the Aristotelian view, the *polis* (and hence politics) were to be scaled to the requisites of self-government, understood as a crucial dimension of the good life for the best of men. This view has been maintained in contemporary understandings of liberal (and especially deliberative) democracy. Nevertheless, the presumption has always been that the *polis* has to be scaled to the requisites of government (e.g., military defence or economic prosperity or civil order) to be effective. The requisites of government are secreted into the requisites of politics by imagining good politics as a politics that generates effective government. Many assumptions about the nature of effective government are built into an analysis conducted at one remove from the analysis of politics itself. So, in the end, the form of the political is always already determined in large degree by the form of the governmental. Current trackings of the governmental point us up, out, and down: up to the global, out to civil society (or the economy), and down to the local (Brenner 2004). The privileged position of the nation-state is supposed to have been compromised by the requisites of a new governmentality keyed to globalized capital on the one hand and responsibilized individuals and communities on the other (Rose 1999). The conditions of possibility for this new governmentality are such that it depends on networked authority on a "glocal" scale: that is, on a scale that makes the global present in the local and the local present in the global in new ways. Glocal governmentality offers opportunities for political intervention at many sites, accessible to a variety of actors who have the capacity to move in and out of those sites. These mobile actors can operate on various scales, often simultaneously. No one site is necessarily favoured for global effectiveness. The privileged actors are the ones who can operate in many sites and in many scales simultaneously. Mobility is the key. Fixtures can be a burden. So, if we are to scale our politics to the current requisites of governmentality, we have to learn to be mobile, operate in many sites simultaneously, and avoid commitment to fixtures that we will not be able to maintain.

These prescriptions make many people uncomfortable, and not without reason. First, they seem to implicate us all in the neoliberal world – force us all to move in the direction in which we are already moving in order to become more modern (or postmodern). Second, they seem to pass much too quickly over the fixtures that have treated us well in the past. The state may be one of those fixtures, but I would say that the more important fixtures are those that stabilize ways of life that embody human possibilities now being ruled out of court. People can and do live otherwise, in ways that do not comport with the current requisites of governmentality. Are we, once again, to rule their lives out because they are insufficiently modern (or postmodern)? Is our task to make sure that everyone gets with the program?

I read the current situation doubly. To the extent that the new requisites of governmentality determine the conditions under which we have to act politically, the conditions for political action are more favourable than ever to glocal interventions from many sites accessible to actors with a strong sense of commitment but relatively few resources. This is a favourable situation. On the other hand, the requisites of governmentality are not politically determining in the strong sense to which I have been alluding. We have to deal with the world as it is, but the way the world is does not determine how we must respond to it; the future will depend on our various responses, the exact outcomes of which we can never quite predict. So there will always be political possibilities different from the ones that seem to flow from the current requisites of governmentality. In the end, we have to go back to what we *want* politically: what we want to achieve. It is *that* which should determine the scale of our politics: the reach to which we aspire and the register that we should use in measuring our activities. In this effort, we can all gain much inspiration from indigenous peoples, who have always resisted the pressure to give up their identities and surrender to the particular forms of modernity that have been forced on them. There are different ways of being modern, different scales by which we can judge ourselves, and different scales on which we can act.

Political economy developed in the eighteenth century as a science of the state. It posited an economy, at one remove from the rulers, governed by its own natural laws. The suggestion was that the rulers had to govern through people's economic freedoms if they were to achieve their own purposes. Political economy was the science of this. Since Marx's time, critical political economists have tried to liberate their science from the problematic of government and link it to the problematics of popular politics. They have not been very successful in this regard because the organizing assumptions of the original science linger in their analyses. The economy or capitalism or the sociospatial relations of the current mode of production are set out as objects for analysis, at one remove from the analyst in his guise as a potential ruler. This approach replicates the relationship implicit in government at a distance. The sovereign analyst, like the sovereign ruler, is always above politics even when he injects politics into the analysis. The injection is always in the nature of an arbitrary move. Genuine politicization involves something more difficult: putting political economy itself at risk by suggesting that it may be fundamentally inadequate as a science of politics. If there is an adequate science of politics, then it would have to encompass the politics of security, the politics of identity, and the politics of material gain. Political economy, identified as it is with the last of these three, is at best a partial science. Moreover, the relevant science of politics must be a guide to action and not just to explanation. This means that the politics we need to discover will not be revealed by the sort of analysis alone that a political economist can offer. We will have to discover the scales appropriate to politics by other means, ones premised on our ability to transcend political economy and become other than the subjects that we have allowed ourselves to be.

NOTES

1 This presumption is implicit in two key decisions of the Supreme Court of Canada that deal with the questions of Aboriginal self-government and Quebec independence, respectively: *Delgamuukw v. British Columbia* [1997] 3 S.C.R. 1010 and *Reference re Secession of Quebec* [1998] 2 S.C.R. 217. The court assumes, as almost everyone does, that Quebec has the requisites for independent statehood, whereas Aboriginal nations do not.

2 See the discussion in the 1996 *Report of the Royal Commission on Aboriginal Peoples* at http://www.ainc-inac.gc.ca/ch/rcap/index_e.html.
3 Thomas Hobbes, *Leviathan* (1651; repr., Cambridge, UK: Cambridge University Press, 1996).
4 Let me be clear: I recognize that the chain of determination can also go the other way.

6
Producing Nature, Scaling Environment: Water, Networks, and Territories in Fascist Spain

Erik Swyngedouw

Burying Francisco Franco's Water Dream (in 2004)
When on 14 March 2004, just a few days after the March 11th Madrid train massacre, José Luis Rodriguez Zapatero of the socialist Partido Socialista Obrero Español (PSOE – Spanish Socialist Workers' Party) unexpectedly won the elections, one of the first measures that his new government took was to scrap the most controversial parts of the Second National Hydraulic Plan that had been approved in 2001 by José María Aznar's conservative administration. The primary target of the discontent was on the plan to transfer large quantities of "surplus" water from the Ebro River basin to the "deficit" basins of the semi-arid southeastern regions of the Levant on the one hand and to Barcelona on the other. The national "disequilibrium" of Spain's water economy has been highly contested terrain since democracy was restored in Spain in 1978. Spain's "water fever," of course, goes back much further in history, and restoring the perturbed equilibrium of the Spanish erratic hydraulic landscape had been a key objective of Spain's fascist rulers throughout the twentieth century. Indeed, the current controversies over the future organization of the hydraulic landscape reflect the legacy of the radical technonatural and socioenvironmental transformations engineered during the long dictatorship that lasted from 1939 (the end of the Civil War) until Franco's death in 1975.

Under General Francisco Franco Behamonde, more than 600 dams, small and large, were constructed in Spain (Vallarino 1992, 67), leading to a complete reengineering of the ten continental river basins of mainland Spain. By the end of the dictatorship, the waters of the southern river basins were fully used as the water-intensive irrigation agriculture and tourist-based regional socioeconomic development model had developed, and a major interbasin transfer scheme – the backbone of a national water grid – from the river Tajo to the Segura was under construction. As Gómez De Pablos González (1973a,

242) puts it, "during the two decennia after the plan of 1940, the Spanish rivers were really 'created,' on which a nationally integrated water politics rested."[1] Under Franco's rule, Spain's hydraulic development reached its apogee, and its logic continued long after the transition to democracy.

In this chapter, I seek to document and substantiate the notion of the scalar production of socionatures by elaborating how Spain's modernization process after the Civil War became a deeply and very specific scalar geographical project. I will focus on the momentous transformation of the hydraulic environment during the Franco period (1939-75) and seek to reformulate Spain's sociohydraulic reconstruction in the context of a double and partly contradictory "scalar" politics. Two theoretically interrelated arguments guide this endeavour. On the one hand, Franco's ideological-political mission was predicated upon cultural and material national territorial integration and the eradication of regionalist or autonomist aspirations (Carr 1995). On the other, the implementation of this modernizing program was predicated upon rescaling the "networks of interest," on which Franco's power rested, from a national visionary to a geoeconomic and geopolitical integration in the US-led Western alliance that emerged during the Cold War politics of the second half of the twentieth century. This empirical account seeks to elucidate a series of more general interconnected arguments. First, I intend to show how every political project is necessarily also a project of the production of particular socioenvironmental scales. Second, this production of scale operates by assembling human and non-human actors in a more or less coherent but heterogeneous network that sustains the socioenvironmental transformation process. Third, the chapter shows how this scalar production proceeds through territorial and relational scalar processes. Before I dive into the intricacies of Franco's sociohydraulic dreams, I will first briefly situate the theoretical concerns that guide the subsequent analysis.

Producing Nature, Scaling Environments

There is a broad consensus in the literature that nature is socially and materially produced (Braun and Castree 1998; Castree 2000b, 2002; Demeritt 2002; Smith 1984; Swyngedouw 1996) through socioecological metabolic transformations (Swyngedouw 2006). Such "productions of socionature" are not socially or politically neutral but embed, express, and reconstitute physical, social, cultural, economic, or political power relations (Castree and Braun 2001; Desfor and Keil 2004; Harvey 1996; Heynen et al. 2006; Swyngedouw 2004c). In other words, social relations are organized in and through the sociometabolic transformation of socionature. In this chapter, I view Spain's fascist hydromodernization as a sociophysical process of producing new technonatures, through which symbolic formations are forged, social groups enrolled, natural processes and "things" entangled, and socionatural networks produced, solidified, and maintained (see Gandy 2002; Kaika 2005; and Löwy 1994). Parts of nature become enrolled in and reconstituted through the "networks of power" that animate this process (Kirsch and Mitchell 2004).

The second theoretical theme that runs through the argument focuses on the forging and mobilization of "scalar" strategies and arrangements and views the "production of nature" as part of a process of "producing scale" (Sneddon 2003; Swyngedouw 2004b). Notwithstanding the great theoretical controversies over scale that I cannot rehearse within the context of this chapter (see Chapter 1 for a review), I start from the view that scale is not ontologically given but socioenvironmentally mobilized in sociospatial power struggles, and these struggles, in turn, produce particular and significant scalar configurations. In other words, sociospatial relations have a "scalar" constitution as relational *networks* are forged producing spatial geometries that are more or less long, more or less extensive (Swyngedouw 2004b). Yet, at the same time, these relational scalar networks articulate with produced *territorial* or geographical configurations that also exhibit scalar dimensions (Natter and Zierhofer 2002; Zimmerer 2000). In the Spanish postwar context, the remaking of Spain's hydrosocial landscape produced a new sociophysical territoriality, centred on the creation of an integrated national scale that was trying to obliterate regionalist aspirations and desires and to reverse the prefascist attempts to create semi-autonomous regional scales. Yet, this nationalterritorial sociophysical remaking of Spain was predicated upon forging national sociopolitical, cultural, and, most importantly, international networked scalar arrangements.

Paco Rana's Water Dream for Spain, 1939-75

The hydraulic policies of Franco's regime paved the way for a scalar transformation of the sociohydrological structure of Spain. Originally structured around the river basin as the key geographical unit of hydraulic planning, Spain's water question was considered from a national perspective during the postwar period. This perspective aimed at "correcting the existing inequality in the distribution of water by means of a physical interconnection between river basins" (Melgarejo Moreno 2000, 273). The approval and construction of a large interbasin water transfer scheme, from the Tajo to the Segura basin, would become the pivotal linchpin that triggered the physical consolidation of the national scale as the central arena for hydrological planning (Melgarejo Moreno 2000, 276). Throughout the Franco years, water infrastructure and the transformation of the hydrotechnical edifice of Spain would be mobilized by the propaganda machinery to such an extent that the popular nickname for General Franco, still engrained in people's minds today, is Paco Rana (Frankie the Frog). Indeed, the most omnipresent image of Franco during this period is of him visiting and inaugurating yet another completed hydrotechnical project.

From the early twentieth century onward, the "natural" distribution of rainfall and water availability was increasingly decried as a "disequilibrium" that required "rectification" (Sánchez de Toca 1911, 299-300). And the means to achieve this was "to crisscross the country with an arterial hydraulic system, a national network of dams and reservoirs, and, by doing so, to create nature" (Costa, cited in Gómez Mendoza 1992, 241). An internal war against drought had to be fought so that "idle" rivers would provide "drink to the dry lands of Spain" by means of a "chirurgical remedy" to balance the socioecological matrix of the nation (Rodríguez Ferrero 2001, 126). The regions with water shortages suffered an "injustice of nature," which demanded that the state deal with this "discrimination." Water became scripted as a national distributional issue, resulting from the view that "Spain would never be rich as long as its rivers flowed into the sea" (Maluquer de Motes 1983, 96). Great symbolic value was assigned to the "mutilating loss of the soil of the Fatherland as a consequence of the 'nature' of the pluvio-fluvial regime" (Gómez Mendoza 1992, 240). The nationalist hydrosocial project indeed became formulated as a "hydrological correction of the national geographical problem" (Gómez Mendoza 1992, 236). By the late 1930s, this sociophysical construction of water as the source of Spain's precarious condition because of its erratic temporalities and uneven and almost unnatural spatial distribution, which could be "rectified" through appropriate technonatural structures, had become deeply engrained in the elites' imaginations of Spain's condition. This particular staging and mobilization of water was captured effectively by Franco and often repeated in his texts, discourses, inaugural speeches, and the like. The propaganda machinery effectively played on the constructed twin position of water: that is, as simultaneously the source of Spain's problems as well as the "thing" from which salvation could be wrought. The debate over water as well as water engineering became squarely structured around the desire to construct a nationally more equitable and just distribution of water resources by means of a grand geographical reorganization of the flows of water. Entangling water thus, rectifying this error made by nature, and restoring a national hydraulic balance demanded the upscaling of the management and planning of water resources from the scale of the river basin to the national scale, national integration, a centralized hydraulic administration, and a strong national state that has centralized and absolute power over the waters of the country, a mission that Franco successfully delivered.

Indeed, *Generalissimo* Franco clearly realized his water dream for Spain. Figure 6.1 summarizes the great expansion of dams and reservoirs, both in number and in capacity, during the Franco period, particularly in the second half of his dictatorship. Over the thirty-five years of Franco's rule, the number of dams grew from about 180 in 1939 to over 800, the reservoir capacity grew exponentially, and the backbone of a nationally integrated system for inter-river basin transfers, which would permit considering the hydrosocial cycle as an integral and unitary national cycle (Hernández 1994, 15), was under construction (the Tajo-Segura transfer) by the time that Franco died.

There are clearly two phases in the making of the fascist hydrosocial landscape. The first period, between 1939 and 1955, was characterized by a sustained rhetoric reiterating the urgent need for expanding irrigation through the construction of state-led grand hydraulic works, but with few real achievements. While 106 new dams were built between 1941 and 1955, the capacity of reservoir water rose only from about 4,000 cubic hectometres to 8,000 cubic hectometres. The disastrous financial and political economic conditions of autarchy during the early years of the Franco reign prevented, however, the massive sociohydrological revolution that had been envisaged and that continued to be presented as the salvation of the fatherland. There literally was not enough steel, concrete, money, and machinery available to make the waters flow uphill.

The acceleration of the scalar remaking of Spain as a hydrosocial network would have to wait until a repositioning of the geopolitical relations and their associated political economic networking and flows of capital, expertise, and steel would take a radical turn after 1953. This moment would prove to be a "watershed" in terms of permitting the realization of Paco Rana's hydro-vision for Spain. Indeed, the two periods coincided with major shifts that would prove vital in terms of turning the hydraulic fantasy into techno-natural reality. I will take up this theme in the last section below. Towards the end of his life, Franco was seen as the great master dam builder. Achieving this hydraulic "success" depended crucially on the loyal support of a

126 ERIK SWYNGEDOUW

FIGURE 6.1

Evolution of dams constructed and volume of reservoir water in Spain, 1910-2000

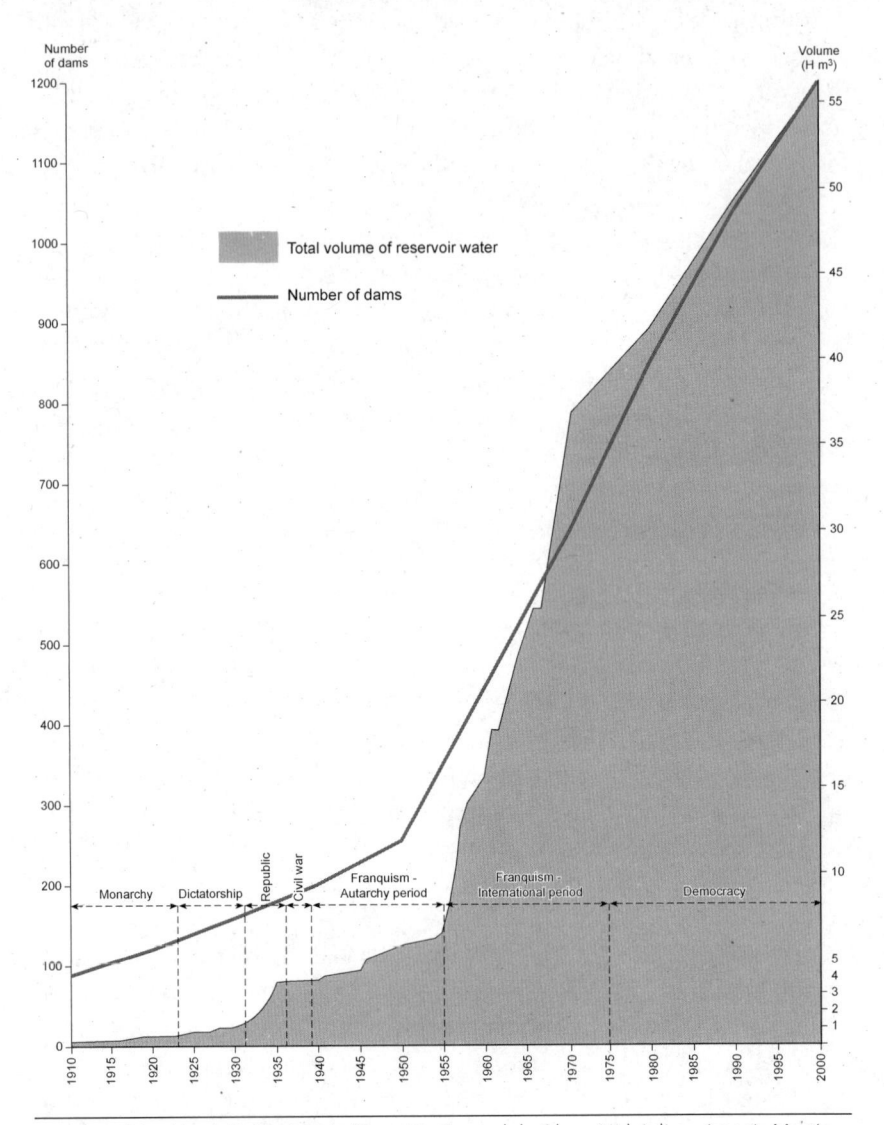

SOURCES: Díaz-Marta Pinilla (1997); Dirección General de Obras-Hidráulicas (1990); Martín-Mendiluce (1996); Ministerio de Medio Ambiente (2000); Torán and Herreras (1977).

series of powerful, interlocked national "networks of interest" and coalitions (Melgarejo Moreno 1995, 7). They often overlapped partially, were occasionally antagonistic, and required careful massaging and "managing" within an overall "Falangist" program and ideology. It is these national networks of interest that supported and consolidated the Franco regime and, together with the mobilization of water, produced the assemblages that would render the sociohydraulic edifice possible, which I will turn to next.

Producing Scalar (National) "Networks of Interest"

The socioeconomic alliances that were forged skilfully by Franco generated a labyrinthine network of power relations that supported the regime and assured its longevity. The civil war had of course eliminated, either physically or through imprisonment or exile, the most activist parts of the oppositional movements, both liberal and socialist-communist. In the process, Franco had assured himself of the loyalty of many royalists, nationalists, the large landowners, the Catholic hierarchy, the military, and significant parts of the national industrial bourgeoisie. The Falange was the only allowed political party and the conduit for Franco's political support. The strong state-economy linkages would cement a corporatist state structure that could count on an endogenous capitalist sector, whose success and profit were closely tied up with the state's investment flows (see Fusi and Palafox 1989; Preston 1990, 1995; and Preston and Lannon 1990). I will focus on the key ideologues and practitioners who provided the technical, scientific, and discursive-semiotic support that would build and maintain, both materially and symbolically, the expanding networks of dams, pipes, hydromachinery, and irrigation systems that would produce an integrated, unitary, unified, and solidarist-fascist Spain: the large landowners, the electricians, the engineers, the geographers, and the media.

The outcome of the Civil War, of course, solidified the interests of the large landowners (*latifundistas*) (Bernal 1990). With the victory of the fascists and the end of the Second Republic, hydraulic politics indeed took an important turn. In particular, the relationship between land and social reform and hydraulic infrastructure that had been part of the Republican agenda was broken, eliminating everything that could be a threat to the interests of large landowners (Del Moral Ituarte 1999). Attempts at land redistribution stopped. Indeed, the dictatorial regime transformed its sociohydraulic politics into an ultraprotectionism of the *latifundistas* (Acosta Bono et al. 2004, 112; Ortí 1984).

As Sánchez-Albornoz (2004, xxv) maintains, "the landowners received the double gain of both an increase in production from its irrigated lands as well as the revalorization of its lands, without much counterpart other than to support the regime, something they unfailingly offered." Indeed, the state covered the cost of infrastructure; the landowners reaped the benefits, with an estimated 1,200 to 2,000 percent improvement of their economic returns (Bernal 2004, xxxvi). As a group, large landowners would, not surprisingly, become one of the social pillars on which Franco's political edifice would rest.

Despite the great rhetorical attention paid to the irrigation "mission" of the state's hydraulic project and the emphasis on internal colonization, this served primarily as propaganda machinery to legitimize the continuing construction of grand hydraulic infrastructures (Díaz-Marta Pinilla 1997, 73). The greatest efforts went into securing the necessary energy resources for the self-reliant development of Spain (Gómez De Pablos González 1973b, 338; Simpson 1995, 261). Until the late 1950s, more than 75 percent of the energy needs of Spain were generated through hydroelectric power. Between 1939 and 1957, installed hydroelectric capacity increased from 1,400 megawatts to 5,200 megawatts, generating a total production of 2,844 million kilowatt hours in 1939, increasing to 18,790 million kilowatt hours in 1957. Here, too, the bulk of the expansion took place after the mid-1950s (see the last section below), representing a total investment of approximately US $458 million (1957 parity) (Garrido Morrión 1957). After 1964, the relationship between irrigation and hydraulic works was further severed in favour of hydroelectric developments. Of the dams constructed between 1964 and 1977, only ninety-six (38.2 percent) were destined for irrigation purposes, while 57.6 percent of the created capacity was earmarked for energy generation. In addition, twenty-nine hyperdams (of more than 1,000 cubic hectometres) were constructed, many of which were also vital for the regulation of electricity production (Vera Rebollo 1995, 313). By the end of Franco's rule, total energy capacity was over 25,000 megawatts, and production had reached 82,000 gigawatt hours (Antolín-Fargas 1997, 202).

The electricity production sector was closely allied with the networks of interest that produced the fascist polity (Núñez 2003). The immediate post-Civil War period saw an intense process of vertical and horizontal integration of electricity companies and an interlacing of the state with the oligopolistically organized electricity companies (Antolín-Fargas 1999; Buesa 1986). This national integration of capital and organizational structures was paralleled by a national territorial physical integration of the electricity network through the production of a national high-voltage grid (Puente Diaz 1949). The electricity companies (and their banking allies) were among the most profitable businesses in the country. The state's policies and interventions generated a significant transfer of state capital from the public to the private sector, either indirectly, through major hydraulic works that regulated the erratic flows of the rivers to permit continuous production, or directly, through subsidies, cheap loans, and cross-capitalizations (Antolín-Fargas 1997). A symbiotic relationship developed between the state and the energy producers, something openly presented as a mutually beneficial undertaking (Vicens Gómez-Tortosa 1961, 438-39).

The great transformation envisaged by the regime depended crucially on the loyal support of the Spanish Corps of Engineers. The civil engineers were the key protagonists of the implementation of the hydropolitical agenda and guaranteed continuity in the pursuit of Franco's water dream (Gil-Olcina 2003, 56). The engineers were, of course, traditionally closely associated with the state apparatus, but under Franco, the quest for a newly manufactured national hydraulic geography by means of the "rebirth of public works and the success of an efficient hydraulic politics" (Sánchez-Rey 2003, 26) propelled the engineering fraternity (they were all men) to the forefront of Spain's fascist modernizing project.

By early 1940, the engineering profession had fully embraced the new "visionary" politics embodied by the Franco regime. Never before had the engineers endorsed and unequivocally supported a political regime with such vigour and unmitigated enthusiasm. A special issue of the engineering journal *Revista de obras públicas* dedicated to the "Spanish Crusade – 1936-1939" contained a portrait of the Caudillo on its front page, subtitled "FRANCO! FRANCO! FRANCO!" It paid homage to colleagues who had fought and died during the "brilliant campaign of liberation" on the side of the *generalissimo* (1940a), celebrated the new regime, and pledged its unconditional support to the nationalist cause.

The Corps of Engineers would put their collective efforts into modernizing the country within the collective enterprise shaped by the new regime. Public works became one of the pillars of the regime, in Franco's words, "an excellent means of protection and stimulator of its prosperity" (cited in *Revista de obras públicas* 1940b, 2). Indeed, "the Corps of Engineers constituted consequently one of the most solid supports of the policies of the new regime" (Songel González 2003, 84). During the following thirty-five years, no explicit political statements were made by the Corps of Engineers, but its journal filled many pages with celebratory articles extolling the virtues of dam construction, recounting the technical details and achievements of newly built dams, providing annual summaries of dam construction and progress in the execution of grand hydraulic projects, and providing detailed celebratory and hagiographic reports of Franco or other government dignitaries visiting and inaugurating major water projects, extolling each time in hyperbolic terms the rapturous reception that Franco unfailingly received from the local people, praising the great progress that the Franco-engineering alliance was making. In 1971, the chairman of the Spanish Committee for Large Dams saluted, in front of Franco, the engineering contribution "of raising the flag, the Spanish flag of grand dams, sustained by twenty years of glorious history and adorned by the ribbons of the 360 battles [i.e., newly constructed dams] that your excellency succeeded in winning" (Torán 1971, 315). Garnering the loyal support of the elite intellectuals of the Corps of Engineers had been an easy task. It was now a matter of winning the hearts and minds of the masses.

While Spain's geography was undergoing the most momentous and spectacular sociophysical transformations in its history, academic and professional geography remained symptomatically silent about these changes. Instead, geography and geographers chose to play a pivotal role in creating and sustaining a patriotic vision of a mythical unitary Spain, a vision that complemented, at a representational/discursive and semiotic plane, the physical-geographical unification pursued by Franco's engineers. Indeed, in the transition from the civil war to the postwar Falangist "stabilization," a radical transformation swept through academic geography. A "fascist" geopolitical discourse thrived during the war, one that celebrated the nationalist-imperialist project with which Franco had aligned himself (see Vicens Vives 1940, 1941a, b) and modelled after the Nazi geopolitics and its materialist-ideological constructions of race, nation, and empire. The core themes of this "geographical" analysis focused on the indisputable unity of Spain as a vital (if not vitalist) national living space and explored its manifest "imperial" destiny.

However, after the war, the discredited geopolitical thought that had accompanied fascist geopolitics no longer served the interests of the now consolidating fascist regime, which preferred to see a much more depoliticized and less radical (at least explicitly) geography emerge (Gómez Mendoza 1997), one "that should lead to the aggrandizement of the fatherland" (Bullón 1941, 676). The state's vision advocated a depoliticized geography that would contribute to justifying the image of the "New Spain" as promoted by the new regime (Reguera-Rodríguez 1991, 52), one "that widens the horizon of our knowledge of the universe, the world, and the fatherland and that also increases our patriotism and our love for the highest creator" (Asían Peña 1941, 10). In practice, geographical research became the study of the regional and local landscape, one that would celebrate the unity of Spain through its diversity. Politics as such disappeared completely from the geographical agenda, yet the political-ideological role of geography remained, as ever, significant. This role was further consolidated by the official "national-Catholic" doctrine of education, the censure of books that did not "respond to the principles of religion and Christian morality and exalt patriotism" (Sánchez Pérez 1981, 10), the laws that repressed masonry or communism and raised regionalist aspirations or concerns, and strict state control over access to teaching and academic posts, including the exiling and deportation of those considered hostile to the regime.

This state-led educational propaganda system was paralleled by the growing self-censorship of intellectuals whose professional positions depended on their allegiance to the official doctrine (García Alvarez 2002). Being doubly blind (i.e., both to the geopolitical tactics of Franco's regime and to the actual geographical transformations that were actively producing a new Spanish landscape), geography in effect served as a legitimizing veil for the "patriotic" and unifying mission of Franco's regime. While the actual participation of geography and geographers in the planning and implementation of geographical projects was non-existent (Capel 1976, 30), the ideological role of geography in the "network of interests" (Sánchez-Recio 2003, 13) that supported *Franquismo* was nevertheless significant. Of course, the production of consent in academia was paralleled by that of the popular media, which would prove to be vital in securing and maintaining consent.

In Franco's Spain, sophisticated propaganda machinery was quickly put in place after the fascist victory. As soon as Franco had consolidated his position as head of state, an official state institute for documentary filmmaking was established, Noticiario Español Cinematográfico (NO-DO), in addition to the tried tactic of controlling and censuring the press. Grafted onto the popular cultural success of cinema, NO-DO produced "news" and general interest film reels that were to be projected in the country's cinemas and were sent abroad for screening. Highly subsidized, this propaganda instrument served to celebrate the regime personalized by Franco, to galvanize the enthusiasm of the people for the regime's efforts, to extol the virtues of Spanish traditional cultural values, and to mythologize the "crusade" for a new reinvigorated, conservative, and Catholic Spain. Between 1943 and 1981, when NO-DO was finally abolished, about 3,925 documentary reels were produced. Until 1956 (when television entered the scene), it was the main cinematographic information source available to the wider public. In analyzing the content of NO-DO's reels, Rodríguez (1999, 223-24) points out that, "above all, inaugurations" filled the screens. A symbiotic relationship was systematically instilled between Franco and the great national public hydroelectric and irrigation mission. Franco personally inaugurated hundreds of dams and other waterworks. Each time, the event was widely publicized by NO-DO and covered in great hagiographic detail in magazines and newspapers as well as in the specialist engineering and professional journals. On each occasion, Franco was welcomed by the "grateful and admiring masses" as "the victorious Caudillo of Spain," celebrating the "enormous social works of the country" and detailing the "great technical achievements" of the country.

Inaugurations, the deployment of the regime's activities, and the support of the popular masses fused together in NO-DO's reels, which became like a monographic documentary, a festival of laudatory images and commentaries. The image of inaugurated dams became the most iconic image of Franco – hence his nickname Franco Rana – who oversaw the new hydraulic landscape, listened to the adulations of his entourage, and received graciously the ovations of the grateful masses. These frequent visits suggested a Franco who was close to the pulse of the nation and attentive to the transformations taking place in the country, while emphasizing the transcendental role of himself and his state in galvanizing and producing the creative energies that made these transformations possible (Tranche and Sánchez-Biosca 2002, 215). The sites of inauguration became emblematic representational spaces, symbolically and materially conveyed through the newsreels. They became geographical symbols of, and material reference to, the unmitigated success of the Francoist national project, emblematically embodying a technocratic developmentalism while celebrating the beauty, unity, and traditions of the Spanish landscape. The images celebrated the solidaristic, spiritual, and moral values of traditional Spain, the tenacity of its workers, the power of the regime, and the virtues of technical modernization (see Kaika 2006; and Tranche and Sánchez-Biosca 2002).

Newspapers, of course, were equally marshalled to espouse the virtues of the regime and its achievements. On a daily basis, the press would report ecstatically about yet another great speech from the Caudillo as yet another sublime achievement was inaugurated. The reproduction of Franco's speeches in the newspapers was invariably accompanied by equally exalted, triumphant, and jubilant commentary by journalists. This heroic mission, thus visualized and narrated, was spread throughout the country; galvanizing the hearts and minds of the Spanish and urging them, like the grateful peasants, to embrace the remaking of the fatherland; and widening the networks of interest that would maintain loyalty to the Fascist modernizing cause. However, forging a series of national networks of interest is, in itself, not a sufficient condition for building the dams and pipes that would realize Spain's water dream. Another series of geopolitical scalar transformations was required to mobilize the necessary capital to achieve this grand mission.

Reworking the Nation, Rescaling the Networks of Interests

> Almost a quarter of a century has passed since a great and brave people began, under the leadership of a soldier-statesman, its heroic and successful campaign to repel for ever all the roots of communism. I am referring to Spain, our friend and ally, and its leader and Chief of State, *Generalissimo* Franco.
> – Senator Styles Bridges, *Diario ABC* (18 July 1959, 35)

A great dictator, political will, engineering plans, corporate support, God's will, and a hydraulic desire remained insufficient, of course, in the absence of concrete, steel, machinery, capital, and specialist know-how if the flow of water was going to be fused with technostructures that would achieve the restoration of a great Spain. The early Franco era (up to the mid-1950s) was economically one of relative paralysis, enduring shortages, untold misery for many, and sluggish growth. As Figure 6.1 shows, up to the mid-1950s, very little of what was promised rhetorically had actually been implemented, but this situation changed dramatically after the mid-1950s, as the reengineering of Spain's water flows really took off at an accelerated pace. This shift coincided with a profound scalar renetworking of the political economic networks on which Franco's stability rested.

The political economic vision of the elites during the early postwar period centred on self-generated national autarchic development, achieved through the mobilization of national resources. The enrolment of key elite groups and of a rhetoric of nationally integrated development were incorporated into what Raymond Carr called "the permanent ideal of autarchy" (2001, 156). A strictly controlled market, the freezing of wages, the control of the labour force, and an imposed international isolation because of Franco's wartime support for the Axis powers turned into an ideology of self-reliant development that was seen as the way to restore Spain's lost grandeur. The making of a nationally integrated economy, so the doctrinal argument went, should be based on mobilizing, almost exclusively, national resources and national capacities (MAPA 1990, 99). However, the absence of material, energy, equipment, and, above all, capital made progress in constructing the desired landscape excruciatingly slow. Electricity cuts were rampant until the mid-1950s, as hydroelectric power generation did not expand fast enough (but, as usual, the "persistent drought" was blamed [Pérez 1999, 649]). Madrid suffered from a disastrous water shortage in 1948-49, irrigation and colonization progressed slowly (Barciela López and López Ortiz 2000, 362), dam construction was far below expectations, food was rationed, peasants became even poorer and either flocked to the cities or emigrated to northern Europe to work as *"gastarbeiter"* (Reher 2003). The average income per capita fell from index 100 in 1935 to 82 in 1950 (Gallo 1974, 192-93).

However, cheap and docile workers were clearly not enough to relaunch Spain's modernizing desires. The country's autarchic political economic model just did not generate enough capital and equipment to move the earth and enrol the powers of its waters. For that, it had to turn elsewhere and re-arrange the coordinates of its geopolitical spatial imagination, its networks of interest, and its geoscalar articulation. In 1952, film director Luis García Berlanga made *Bienvenido Mr. Marshall!* a movie that caught the wrath of Franco but became a Spanish film classic (see Figure 6.2). The movie humorously captured both the desire and the enthusiasm of the Spanish people to be "developed" by Yankee dollars but also foretold how the promised capital would remain glued to the hands of the elites. The script, carefully navigating around the censor's scissors (which it did not fully succeed in doing), narrates how a small Castilian peasant village, after state dignitaries informed the mayor of the pending visit of a high-ranking US delegation, prepares to receive it festively in the hope and expectation that the villagers will benefit from generous aid dollars. The peasants draw up a list of desirables, ranging from a new bicycle to a sewing machine to a tractor, and prepare expectantly for the big event. When the great day finally arrives, the villagers gather in the square in their best outfits, the marching band is ready to play, and the mayor anxiously rehearses his speech. However, the shiny black sedans of

FIGURE 6.2

Movie poster for *Bienvenido Mister Marshall!* (1952)

the American delegation race through the village "in a cloud of dust, without stopping, leaving the village and its peasants as poor as ever" (Gallo 1974, 224). While the movie captures the mood and conditions of the time well, anticipating the inflow of US aid dollars and foreshadowing metaphorically the trail that this capital would walk, it is also a marked pointer of an immanent radical change in Spain's geopolitical networking.

Indeed, by the early 1950s, the rhetoric of national autarchy sounded increasingly hollow as socioeconomic conditions continued to deteriorate (Barciela López and López Ortiz 2003; Miranda Encarnación 2003). Spain's political and economic elites increasingly realized that opening up new spatial links and pursuing the geopolitical insertion of Spain into the Western alliance was vital in order to secure not only the modernization of Spain but also the longer-term sustainability of the dictatorial regime. Strategically extending the spatial reach of the networks of interest on which the regime rested was pivotal to pursuing the project envisaged for Spain. The Spanish ruling elites understood the realities of the emerging geopolitical order, choreographed by Cold War strategies, and eyed the United States, whose geopolitical gaze also started to turn to Spain as a possible ally in the new geopolitical cartography of the postwar order.

Between 1950 and 1953, the institutionalization of the Cold War permitted a rapprochement between the United States and Spain. The United States chose symptomatically to forget its earlier hostility towards fascism and would increasingly begin to play the role of Spain's ambassador in the newly established postwar international political organizations. In 1952, Spain scored its first victory when it was admitted to UNESCO. In December 1955, Spain entered the United Nations. The most significant moment was undoubtedly the signing of the secret "Pact of Madrid" in September 1953, by Alberto Martín Artajo, Spanish minister of foreign affairs, and James Dunn, US ambassador, in which Spain agreed to let the United States use parts of its territory for military bases in exchange for economic, military, and technical aid (Liedtke 1998; Viñas 1981).[2] US financial aid and investment would start to flow into Spain, and, together with the diplomatic and economic relations that came with the implementation of the aid program, these pacts would provide the (financial) bedrock for the years of rapid growth and modernization of the late 1950s and 1960s (Niño 2003). Indeed, while primary materials and industrial equipment were extremely scarce until the mid-1950s, the inflow of US aid permitted the rapid development of infrastructure.

Literally, the presence of US military bases in Spain was secured in exchange for dollars and equipment that would, among other things, realize Franco's water dream. The new scalar network in which the Spanish elites became inserted would, in turn, contribute to the hydraulic-geographical integration that the national blueprints of Franco and his engineers had envisaged.

The financial support of the United States was earmarked as follows: 10 percent for administrative expenses, 60 percent for the military bases, and 30 percent for financial aid. From 1958 onward, 90 percent of the funds would take the form of financial aid (Suárez-Fernandez 1984, 72-73; Termis-Soto 2005). Between 1951 and 1963, more than $1.3 billion were granted to Spain in the form of economic aid (Calvo 2001). The assistance of the United States provided Franco with support to muscle his way into the Western Atlantic alliances and networks, permitted him to modernize the country militarily, opened up the economy at the expense of the advocates of self-sufficiency, and consolidated the regime while demoralizing and further marginalizing internal opposition and the international antifascist movements (Niño 2003, 26-27). For the United States, the economic stabilization of Spain would further entrench the power of Franco and ensure the continuing anticommunist stance of Spain, erode the danger of left-wing insurgency, and provide a vital territorial military presence against the Eastern Bloc.

A large part of the financial aid went to agricultural machinery, steel, electrical equipment, and infrastructure. Of the Spanish counterpart funding, most investment was directed to agricultural irrigation projects, railways, and hydraulic works (Fernández de Valderrama 1964; Puig 2003, 114). Of the direct financial aid, almost a quarter was invested in capital goods and infrastructure. Through this, Americans and Spaniards "wove and strengthened social networks with local, national, and international reach" (Puig 2003, 117).

The scalar rearrangement of the networks that the dictatorship wrought proved vital in the process of fascist modernization (Puig and Álvaro 2002). The scalar extension of Spain's political and financial networks, in turn, facilitated and nurtured the hydrosocial transformation of Spain's physical and socioeconomic geography. In the process, Spain modernized extraordinarily quickly during the 1960s and early 1970s, a process that further ensured the longevity of the regime, until Franco's death in 1975 announced the end of what was one of the most repressive and lasting dictatorial-fascist regimes that Europe has known.

Socionatural Transformations and Scalar Dynamics: A Conclusion

The extraordinary technonatural reordering of Spain, achieved by remaking its socionatural hydraulic configuration, was based on a particular discursive, symbolic, and material enrolling of H_2O in the making of a series of interrelated and interconnected hydrosocial assemblages. They were made possible and held together through the construction of specific national and international scalar networks of power. These networks effectively marginalized or repressed those who dissented. Franco's project literally produced a unitary national territorial complex, a feat predicated on eliminating dissenting political voices, regionalist impulses, and alternative configurations. Yet, the remaking of Spain's hydraulic geography was also predicated on rearranging wider scalar networks. In particular, the insertion of the Spanish economic and political elites into the Western geopolitical alliance and geoeconomic flows of money was vital for the realization of Franco's desired national-geographical project.

These scalar configurations would both implode and explode after Franco's death. The hydraulic engineers and bureaucracy and the agricultural and southern elites wished to perfect the system initiated by Franco, but, of course, the voices, scales, and actors around the hydrosocial nexus began to multiply as democracy took root after 1978. The growing muscle of environmental movements, the demands of the autonomous regions, and the financial and political might of the European Union (rather than the United States) are increasingly entangled with newly enrolled actants such as birds, wetlands, sediments, and local cultural rights, demanding new and different scalar organizations and forcing new networked arrangements, around which radically different socioenvironmental and technonatural projects crystallize.

More importantly, perhaps, this chapter has attempted to bring together two hitherto disconnected theoretical perspectives. Relational and territorial notions of scale were mobilized in the context of an analysis that aimed at considering how nature is remade through the fusion of the social, the technical, and the physical. The historical-geographical reconstruction of the production of specific fascist technonatural assemblages, which fuses the mobilization of nature and technology with the social networks of power that shaped and maintained Franco's reign, shows not only how every political project is also an environmental project but also how such socioenvironmental projects are predicated on scalar tactics and strategies. The political and the technical, the social and the natural, thus become mobilized through and etched on spatial arrangements that shape distinct geographies and landscapes – landscapes that celebrate the visions of the elite networks, reveal the scars suffered by the disempowered, and nurture the possibilities for alternative visions. Spain's hydrosocial and technonatural landscapes are simultaneously heroic achievements expressing a modernizing desire, the legacy of a brutal authoritarian regime, the imprint of the elites' dream, and the pain and suffering of millions of unnamed workers and peasants. It is also on this edifice and in the interstices of often enduring power assemblages that a range of new socioecological movements, innovative political visions, new scalar arrangements, and alternative sociotechnical projects are debated, framed, envisaged, and contested.

NOTES

1   All quotations originally in Spanish have been translated by the author.
2   As today, the official US interpretation of these agreements very much follows the doctrine of the "manifest destiny" of the United States to redeem humanity from tyranny and dictatorship in whatever form they take historically. The 1953 pact is seen as such an initiative, which would eventually pave the way for development, freedom, and democracy. In 1993, for example, in an article dedicated to the fortieth anniversary of the Madrid agreement, Vernon Walters, who acted as interpreter between Franco and both Eisenhower and Nixon, stated, "los acuerdos firmados en septiembre de 1953 ... permitieron que el país se conviertiera en una de las principales economías mundiales en un ambiente de libertad y de democracia ... Me atraveso a pensar que sin los acuerdos entre España y los Estados Unidos la historia podría haber sido muy differente" (167). [The agreements signed in September 1953 allowed the country to change into one of the most important economies of the world in an environment of freedom and democracy ... It seems to me that without the agreements between Spain and the United States history might have been very different.]

7
Getting the Scale Right? A Relational Scale Politics of Native Title in Australia

Richard Howitt

Relationships between Indigenous peoples, colonial powers, settler populations, and postcolonial governments have always been spatialized by a complex politics of geographical scale. Geographical expansion of colonizing states into the territories of others constructed new geographical scales – new scales of power, governance, society, and economy. The Western imaginary of a singular, all-encompassing narrative of colonization reduces the pluralism of diverse Indigenous experiences to a simplified and singular-scale politics in which the local, Indigenous other is oppressed by a singular and powerful European colonizer. Whatever truth this dominant narrative captures, it is not particularly helpful in developing political, economic, and social strategies to reconfigure Indigenous realities and construct new social and political geographies rooted in the recognition and acceptance of Indigenous rights.

Using a relational approach to geographical scale, this chapter offers a reconsideration of these circumstances to provide new insights into the nature of the spatial politics of colonization – with implications for both theories and practices in relation to Indigenous rights as well as the dominant narratives of dispossession and marginalization of Indigenous peoples. Specifically, the chapter argues the following:

1 Processes of colonization of Indigenous domains involved forms of primitive accumulation that included erasure of the geographical scales constructed by Indigenous peoples as the basis for their social organization – and such colonization continues in contemporary situations.
2 Scale-literate social analysis and political action to construct new scales of action and governance (and sometimes the reconstruction of previously erased scales) provide opportunities for a rethinking of Indigenous peoples' circumstances and futures.

3   The success of new Indigenous-scale politics will rely heavily on getting the scale right in the reconstitution of relationships within and between Indigenous peoples as well as between Indigenous and non-Indigenous groups.

While I think that this argument may hold some broader relevance, the particular construction of the argument here relies specifically on my involvement in and analysis of the experience of Aboriginal groups in Australia.[1]

Political and judicial circumstances have left many Indigenous Australians deeply dissatisfied with the capacity of the Native title system to deliver any meaningful recognition to their people. Reconfiguring this situation to allow Indigenous initiatives to set a different sort of agenda for social transformation has not been easy, particularly given the level of hostility to a politics of recognition that has developed within the conservative parties at the national scale. A scale analysis of this situation, however, opens up new horizons.

Primitive Accumulation and Indigenous Australians

In contemporary political economy, the idea of primitive accumulation is easily relegated to the prehistory of modern capitalist accumulation and globalization. Yet, for many Indigenous peoples, it remains an insistent contemporary reality (Howitt 2001, 23-26). The most fundamental factors of industrial production – land, natural resources, labour – continue to be taken from Indigenous peoples' control by states and private interests. In earlier periods of European expansionism, industrialization and development were predicated on barbarous acts of theft (Blaut 1993; Chomsky 1993; Howitt 1993a; Wolf 1982), which delivered erasure or surrender of Indigenous rights or their conversion into forms recognizable by and acceptable to Eurocentric forms of authority, privilege, and power.

Indigenous systems of governance in Australia, like all systems of human governance, reflected (and continue to reflect) specific sets of people-people and people-environment relations – specifically scaled institutions and arrangements of governance. The well-documented systems of law that governed Indigenous Australian societies (see, e.g., Myers 1986; Rose 1992; Sharp 1993; Sutton 1995; Williams 1983, 1986), underpinned by the resources derived from control over various sorts of economic, cultural, and environmental capital, were constructed at scales that suited available technologies and social forms. The intrusion of European and, later, Australian state and national interests into the Indigenous homelands of Australia changed the scales at which things happened. New transport technologies allowed social groups to extend the range of their economic, social, and ceremonial interactions, and government and missionary methods of exercising social control centralized groups into less mobile settlement structures. The establishment of "communities" of "households" constructed new scales at which Aboriginal subjectivity and identity were constructed, administered, and governed.[2]

Contemporary forms of primitive accumulation juxtapose various scales in ways that construct complex and difficult scale politics. The local-national relation in Australian Indigenous issues, for example, continues to be dominated by discourses that emphasize Aboriginal community dependence on state welfare transfers and justify micromanagement by the state of various employment, training, education, enterprise, and capacity-building programs – although it is often Aboriginal people's capacity to fit into a non-Indigenous development trajectory that such programs seek to develop.[3] Simultaneously, however, the national government intervenes in international arenas to oppose the extension of the right of self-determination to Indigenous peoples and to repudiate the efforts of international agencies to criticize the racist implications of various state and national policies and acts of Parliament. The government also pursues detailed programs of institutional control and reform that have recently disestablished the national elected representative body for Aboriginal and Torres Strait Islander peoples – the Aboriginal and Torres Strait Islander Commission (ATSIC) – and prioritized "practical reconciliation" and "shared responsibility agreements" through detailed local activities overseen by formal agreements. Most recently, the shift to "coerced reconciliation" has undone locally constructed authority structures, permit systems, and land tenure arrangements on Aboriginal land in the Northern Territory.

Colonial "possession" of Australia, and the subsequent construction of both colonial and postcolonial forms of ownership and governance, depended on two crucial fictions. The legal fiction of *terra nullius* asserted the absence of Indigenous others from Australia's legal landscapes (e.g., Howitt 2002a, 2006; Mercer 1997; Pearson 1997). Even more pervasive and pernicious, however, has been the social fiction of Aboriginal absence from Australia's geographical landscapes (e.g., Howitt and Jackson 1998). These myths shape popular and legal imaginaries of possession, dispossession, and governance across Australia. The Crown was constructed as the institutional vehicle of possession of Australia. It embodied the scale at which governance was exercised. Thus, both the national and the provincial scales of governance are predicated precisely on the primitive accumulation of territory and its resources by the colonizing Crown. The Crown recognized no obligation in relation to existing systems of customary law and property, nor did it recognize the scales at which they were institutionalized and governed – although it was precisely this obligation that the 1991 *Mabo* decision found encumbered the Crown's relations with Indigenous Australians from the time of settlement. Even where land is returned to Indigenous "ownership," the Crown continues to claim the authority of "underlying title," and the rights provided to Indigenous owners are ultimately authorized by governments rather than deriving their status and authority from the law and custom of the land's traditional owners. In other words, even in those situations in which territory is apparently returned to Indigenous control, such return of territory is conditional upon an affirmation of the continuing absence of Indigenous governance.[4]

Yet, despite the legal façade of "dispossession" (and its inverse of non-Indigenous "possession"), customary law continues to create rights and responsibilities in the country. It continues to possess the people and their links to their territories and societies, to their country, and to each other. In other words, not only have Indigenous peoples never been absent from the cultural landscapes of Australia, but they have also been a concrete presence. This persistent presence in the landscape has haunted many aspects of Australian social and cultural relations, quietly mocking and parodying the dominant culture's querulous claims to the contrary. The High Court's sleight-of-hand ruling in the *Mabo* case addressed this paradox by introducing the slippery notion of "co-existence" (Howitt 2006). The legal system maintains the status quo, the dominance of the dominant culture, by asserting that the co-existence of Native title and competing Western tenures is possible because Native title is unequivocally extinguished to the extent of any inconsistency. In other words, no matter how persistent customary law is as a presence in the landscape, creating continuing interests in territory, it is rendered effectively absent from the *legal* landscape by any grant of an inconsistent title by the Crown or its agents.[5] The blatant injustice of this situation has required special legislation in the form of various Land Rights Acts, in which the state creates a set of rights and entitlements for Indigenous groups to return land to a form of Aboriginal ownership that is derived from and authorized by the state. In contrast, the significance of the Native title rulings of the High Court has been the implication that the rights recognized as Native title are derived from customary law and authorized by a self-governing collective with which the state is required to deal.

Native title, as a solution to the persistent "whispering in our hearts" arising from the injustices meted out to Indigenous Australians,[6] creates a complex challenge for Australian federalism. The scaled construction of governance within the federal system, for example, needs to acknowledge that some persistent Indigenous rights derive their authority from institutions that predate and survive the creation of the Crown in Australia. The coercive imposition of Australian federalism and the continuing erasure and denial of Indigenous scales of governance provide no secure foundation for the transformation of federalism in response to the challenges of republicanism and globalization. Political discourses that construct Indigenous peoples' place(s) in contemporary Australian federalism on the basis of historical injustice, rights derived from the authority of the state, contemporary needs, or reparations, risk falling into a quagmire of competing narratives and representations. In particular, they risk reconstituting Indigenous Australians as "special interest" groups, requiring the obliteration of an "Indigenous" right to self-determination as the precondition for extending the rights of national citizenship to this "special" group of citizens.[7] Developing a strategic analysis that considers scale as a key element provides a foundation for a very different understanding of the place(s) of Indigenous Australians in contemporary federalism and of the appropriate mechanisms for addressing historical and continuing injustices.

Recognizing the Erasure of Indigenous Scales of Governance

The extension of colonial administration into new territories inescapably involved the construction of new scales. Specifically, in Australia, it saw the initiation of the scale of the colonial governments, which became the states, and, from 1901, a national scale of federal administration. Underpinned by the Crown's claim of settlement by *terra nullius*, Australian governments disposed of Indigenous peoples' key assets through grants of land, the provision of mining and forestry rights, and the establishment of key resources (water, fisheries, minerals) as properties of the Crown. In a graphic physical metaphor, colonial and postcolonial administrations alike talked of "opening up" country for development – often requiring it to be euphemistically "emptied" as a precursor to the realization of its historic destiny in the heroic narratives of possession, settlement, and development. In creating a blank slate for occupation, however, it was not only crucial for new scales to be constructed to institutionalize and administer colonial power. It was also crucial that erasure of the scales that reflected, reinforced, and witnessed Indigenous Australians' possession, presence, and emplacement was also achieved. Such erasure required an extraordinarily detailed level of social control and micromanagement of "Native" administration across the continent, with the institution of strict controls over movement, association, property, suffrage, and basic social activities, including marriage, employment, parenting, and language. Frontier violence, which decimated traditional societies and economies, was followed by violent administrative controls that separated part-Aboriginal children from their families[8] and sought to erase the languages in which people spoke of their intimate presence in their landscapes and the ceremonies that affirmed their presence and the possession of self-governance that it implied. Material artifacts that attested to Indigenous peoples' presence were destroyed, and the social and economic institutions that enabled self-governance were similarly destroyed, belittled, and possessed for removal to collections that were represented as confirming Aboriginal peoples' place on the lowest rungs of the ladder of humanity (see, e.g., Anderson 2005, 2006) – and confirming the status of their systems of customary law and governance as uncivilized and beyond the scope of recognition by civilized international law.

So, while Australian Indigenous law continued to create relationships using the tools of Indigenous order, including the scales at which governance, territory (country), and accountability (law) were constructed, the new order of state, mission, and industry targeted specific activities for achieving the erasure and annihilation of precisely these relationships. In other jurisdictions, these scales were commandeered and manipulated rather than erased because the processes of primitive accumulation were able to secure value from the existing Indigenous economies. For example, the fur trade in the North American Arctic reconfigured the scale of Indigenous governance but required maintenance of Indigenous governance in areas where it was a product and surplus rather than only the land itself that was required for accumulation. In such territories, displacement and settlement were not the first priorities of colonization. In contrast, emptying Australia's landscapes for agricultural and pastoral settlement literally required the removal of Indigenous peoples and their institutions and the erasure of the institutions of governance that legitimated their ongoing presence in those landscapes.

Stanner (1979) referred to Australia's dominant culture of forgetting, in which undesirable elements of our cultural experience were simply forgotten – erased from the collective memory of the dominant culture as if they had never existed. This is precisely the relationship of many colonial and post-colonial policies regarding lands and resources to Indigenous Australians. It is also the relationship between many specific policies in Indigenous affairs and the scales of interaction and accountability that were established as the scales of governance in Indigenous Australian societies. Much academic and political attention has been placed on the impacts of these policies at the scale of the individual and the family. In the process, Indigenous societies seem to be less coherent, even less governable, than they actually are. In responding to the "problems" created by the reprehensible portfolio of colonial and more recent policies, this approach risks rendering policy solutions in terms of *more* government intervention, *more* support, and *more* welfare – rendering quite invisible the issue of self-governance. In the process, not only are certain policy options made more or less inaccessible, but also the scales at which Indigenous peoples themselves might organize or act to achieve different outcomes are treated as non-existent.[9]

This active erasure of the scales and institutions of Indigenous governance, in my judgment, has been a persistent policy target for most Australian governments over the totality of Australian settlement history. This is not just a question of rendering some scales invisible or leaving them missing from analyses (see Judd 1998). It is an active erasure that has been a crucial element in the scale politics of Indigenous rights in Australia, yet, it has not been subject to explicit consideration in academic commentary. On the one hand, geographers have paid more attention to contemporary issues of survival in matters such as land claims, land management, social impact assessment, and representation. On the other hand, legal scholars have largely treated issues such as sovereignty and self-determination as abstract legal concepts rather than in terms of relations between people and over places in the context of persistent legal traditions that establish ancient jurisdictions distinct from Western legal traditions. Yet, like so many elements of analysis that take scale seriously, once this issue is identified, it quickly becomes both obvious and powerful in terms of its relevance to strategic thinking about Indigenous rights.

This is not to say that governments explicitly or consciously adopt a scale-literate analysis and deliberately target the erasure of "Indigenous scales of governance." Rather, a scale analysis gives us tools with which to consider the situations experienced by (and currently facing) Indigenous groups from a new vantage point from which to rethink how to respond to those situations. Consider, for example, the conditional extension of recognition of some subset of Indigenous rights by some governments on the condition of surrender of other specific rights – Canada's insistence on the extinguishment of Aboriginal title as a condition for signing modern treaties or the United States' insistence on the acceptance of formal status under federal legislation as a condition for receiving so-called self-government funding or protection of intellectual property rights of Indian artists. In such situations, erasure of the institutional and procedural elements of customary law – including the relationships, values, and behaviours that constitute the scales of Indigenous governance – is an inevitable corollary of the practices of conditional recognition. In the process, the foundations of Indigenous governance and difference are undermined. If we take at face value national policy goals for Indigenous peoples within diverse, multicultural nations such as Australia, then erasure of the building blocks of cultural difference should not and, indeed, cannot possibly be a legitimate requirement of policy implementation.

Case Study: New Scales of Indigenous Governance in South Australia

My experience in working on state-wide negotiations for recognition of Native title in South Australia has brought home the practical value of a scale analysis in pursuing negotiated recognition without extinguishing Native title rights as a condition for recognition.[10] The process has effectively established a new scale of Indigenous governance, with an extraordinarily diverse group of Indigenous South Australians coming together to make decisions about how to negotiate and what to negotiate (Agius et al. 2002). When the discussions started in 1999, the South Australian government expected that any negotiated settlement would institutionalize the extinguishment of Native title. Preliminary discussions, however, indicated clearly that insisting on extinguishment as a condition for settlement would lead the parties back to a claim-by-claim war of attrition in the courts.

The details of the negotiations are beyond the scope of this chapter,[11] but the process illustrates the value and significance of a scaled analysis. One of the fundamental requirements of customary law was that decisions about country be made by those who were properly authorized to do so – specifically, local traditional owners needed to be the decision makers for their own affairs. This legal tradition within customary law is consistent with Western principles of self-determination and subsidiarity but inconsistent with conventional ideas of negotiation by delegated authority. Indeed, the idea of delegating authority to negotiate on matters of country is unthinkable in customary law. Meetings of the Native Title Management Committees (NTMCs), which embodied each of the twenty-three claimant groups involved, grappled with these challenges in a series of large meetings in 1999-2000. Consistent with customary law, each NTMC listened to and considered the whole discussion but then met separately to make its decisions and report them to the whole group. While this was time consuming, particularly as everything was translated into local languages, it ultimately produced a new organizational infrastructure for the negotiation process – which the NTMCs labelled a "congress" (Agius et al. 2004). The congress was, in effect, a new scale for making decisions that encompass both self-determination and developing self-governance (Agius et al. 2002).

The political process in South Australia, then, constructed authority within the structures of customary law rather than through the expected authorization of Indigenous processes by non-Indigenous agents. Because of the previous erasure of the institutions and scales of Indigenous governance in South Australia, and the failure of the state to recognize the scales of customary authority, the congress provided "a new scale for doing things":

> Through their action in setting up the Congress, the NTMCs have constructed two new scales for Aboriginal politics in South Australia. First, they have reasserted the primacy of their claim-based domains and organization. This is consistent with the basic principles of The Dreaming and ensures that local issues are dealt with locally. Local agreements, even if they are negotiated under principles and procedures which apply across the State, will still be negotiated by the locals for the locals ... Second, the NTMCs have constructed a new scale of Indigenous self-governance at the whole-of-state scale. This brings them into a negotiating relationship with the State and major industry groups in which they decide, they do the driving, and they see themselves as equals. (Agius et al. 2002, 10-11)

In tackling this task, recognizing the scale politics that influenced the interplay of local concerns within and between claimant groups, the communities that they were part of, their (sometimes competing) claims, and the drivers for various interests within the Indigenous domain (as well as non-Indigenous parties)[12] became an important element in thinking about what we were doing.[13] In discussions with the state negotiators, we emphasized the realities (rather than the technical legalities) of coexistence in the regions of South Australia – that legal extinguishment of Native title would not remove the Indigenous presence in these places and that legal defeat of the Native title claims would, in fact, remove a valuable political trigger for addressing the challenges of social transformation arising from the acknowledgment that Indigenous people did have status as prior owners of the state. In this sense, we also sought to rescale government and industry understandings of the problem, drawing them back to the scales at which the Native title claimant groups constructed their interests and emphasizing the need to avoid assuming that Indigenous South Australians would meet a statewide political or industry voice with a united voice of their own. In doing so, we confronted many of the hidden assumptions that arise from the taken-for-granted vantage point of the beneficiaries of colonization and the consequences of the previous erasure of Indigenous scales of law and governance in South Australia.

Getting the Scale Right: New Indigenous Geographies?

Our experience in South Australia, I hope, offers some demonstration of the value of a scale analysis as a practical tool for understanding and responding to the circumstances facing the Indigenous negotiators there. Our relational perspective on geographical scale provided a key reference point in dealing with procedural and structural issues thrown up by the negotiations.

Inevitably, my own developing thinking about scale influenced the way that the Indigenous parties thought about the scale politics.[14] In seeking to develop processes that were accountable within the governance framework of customary law, rather than imposing accountability to governments as a precondition for participating in the negotiations, we were always confronting the scale politics of the difference between customary law's idea of the primacy of the local and governments' constructions of geographical equity and the need for "solutions" that apply across the totality of their territorial domains, regardless of internal diversity.[15]

Getting the scale of the relations that structure the Indigenous politics right, then, becomes a central strategic challenge for organizing the Indigenous response to challenges such as "statewide negotiations" or "comprehensive claim settlements." In many previous situations, the automatic response has been to use existing organizations – even if they were a product of non-Indigenous legislation – or to create new alliances between existing organizations. In the first round of meetings in South Australia, we experienced directly the consequences of the historical erasure of the relationships, institutions, and practices that constituted the scales of Indigenous governance across the state – and the need to update and reconstruct them as a basis for informed, contestable, and accountable decision making about important issues and opportunities. In some meetings, internal disagreements became vehicles for reformulating self-authorized decision making at the emerging scale of the whole-of-group, a set of relationships and procedures that eventually emerged in institutional form as the scale of the congress. In these situations, there was no legal technical problem for expert resolution. Rather, it was issues within the Indigenous political domain that required properly authorized decisions. It was questions about the political construction of process and procedure within decision-making processes derived from customary law that needed scrutiny and debate. In ensuring that we did not repackage these issues as technical issues that could be resolved by reference to a lawyer or other non-Indigenous expert, we sought to facilitate the development of an internally robust political process that could tolerate difference and dissent and was not constrained to conform to an outsider's view of "Indigenous consensus decision making."

The need to meet the South Australian government's proposal to negotiate a comprehensive response to Native title across the state always pressured the Indigenous participants to rescale their relationships – to fit their "local" concerns into a set of relationships and issues at a wider scale – the whole-of-state scale. In this sense, getting the scale right was not so much an abstract or analytical challenge as a practical political challenge. Overcoming the historical erasure of Indigenous governance from the cultural and political landscape of South Australia was a practical necessity, not an idealized political ambition.

In this sense, then, we were confronting the need to reconceptualize geographical scale in a very practical way. Our work needed to rethink just what sort of thing scale is and which consequences it had for our political efforts on the ground. In my view, it was better to "conceptualise geographical scale as an event, a process, a relationship of movement and interaction rather than a discrete 'thing.' Despite its importance in the construction of influential things such as power, gender, being, identity and wealth (inter alia), it is unhelpful to think of scale as the sort of thing that has causal power in its own right" (Howitt 2002, 304). It was also necessary to recognize, following Ollman (1993), that scale,

> like any abstraction ... will demonstrate elements of "extension," "level of generality" and "vantage point". It reflects facets of space, time, culture and environment. It has dimensions of size, level and relation, and is paradoxically simultaneously hierarchical and non-hierarchical. If social relations are always spatial (e.g., Massey 1984), if we are always both "in place" and "in culture" (Entrikin 1991, 1), then social and environmental relations are also always scaled. Scale, in other words, is simultaneously metaphor, experience, event, moment, relation and process. It is implicated in, and simultaneously implicates other core concepts in geography such as space, place and time. It is also deeply implicated in core cultural concepts such as identity, subject and difference. (Howitt 2002, 306)

In reflecting on this experience, it seems to me that, in creating the new geographies that will reflect more equitable, just, and sustainable responses to Indigenous difference and diversity, a framework of analysis and practice that simultaneously gets the scale right and problematizes scale will be indispensable.

ACKNOWLEDGMENTS

Sherrie Cross, currently a PhD student at Macquarie University, is working on the scale politics of reconciliation, and it is from my discussions with her that the idea of erasure of specific scales of Indigenous governance arose. Bob Fagan, Sandie Suchet-Pearson, Robyn Dowling, and Kate Lloyd have also been part of a discursive community of "scale tragics" at Macquarie that has been both challenging and supportive over recent years. Parry Agius, my colleague and collaborator in the South Australian work reported here, has been an inspiration not just to me but also to many people around him.

NOTES

1 The relatively recent judicial, political, and social recognition of persistent Aboriginal and Torres Strait Islander interests in land as "Native title" in Australia provides an opportunity to reconsider the dominant narratives of dispossession from more Indigenous-centric perspectives. In the period since the judicial recognition of Native title in the High Court's *Mabo* decision in 1991, the politics of intercultural

relations has often focused on the urgent need to resolve the tension between systems of property rights that assumed the absence of actionable Indigenous rights and the legal obligation to recognize some of those rights as "Native title." The Native Title Act, 1993, provided a statutory framework for implementing recognition of Native title across the nation. Whatever the legislation's particular strengths and weaknesses, it demanded that Indigenous organizations pay close attention to the resolution of legal technicalities. This emphasis on legal technicalities empowered a judicial and bureaucratic system that disciplines Indigenous groups to marshal proper and acceptable "evidence" to support their claims before the courts and supports other parties (farmers, developers, miners, etc.) to oppose those claims (Agius et al. 2004). Empowering legal and bureaucratic stakeholders in the Native title system over Indigenous claimants ensures that for most Indigenous groups, the system's demand for sound evidence of "continuing connection" to lands in increasingly pedantic, complex, and demanding ways has been costly in terms of both financial and social costs arising from the frustrations of failure. This experience has left Indigenous groups marginalized, waiting for lawyers, courts, and politicians to authorize their status, and has configured lawyers and other technical experts as the front line of struggles for recognition and change in Indigenous domains.

2   It is worth noting, for example, that Rowse's (1988) analysis of the creation of households as a means of administering Aboriginal people in Central Australia parallels Marston's (2000) analysis of the social construction of the household as a scale in the United States.

3   This policy approach has culminated in mid-2007 with effective occupation of more than sixty Indigenous communities in the Northern Territory by federal government officials with a view to managing a response to a so-called "emergency" of widespread child abuse (see, e.g., Altman and Hinkson 2007).

4   In some jurisdictions, for example the United States and Canada, there is some ambiguity about the status of Indigenous governance. The situation in Australia is unequivocal: the Australian state assumes and reinforces the absence of Indigenous governance. Thus, while Silvern's (1999, 640) observation that Indian tribes in the United States "are semi-autonomous, retain powers of self-government and occupy a unique niche within the nested, hierarchically organized, political–geographical scale structure of American Federalism" opens some interesting prospects for rescaling the politics of self-determination in the United States, Aboriginal groups in Australia are neither semi-autonomous nor acknowledged as retaining any powers of self-government. Yet, in terms of social and political process, they also occupy a "unique niche" in Australian federalism.

5   Clearly, this is an oversimplification of a complex legal ruling, and there are some technical constraints and limitations on the power of the Crown to alienate land and other territories from traditional tenures (see, e.g., McHugh 1996), but the

legal system has consistently placed the onus on Indigenous claimants to establish their continuing presence in the landscape in technical legal terms, rendering as irrelevant to the legal situation their continuing presence in the real cultural landscapes of contemporary Australia.

6   Reynolds (1998) quotes a colonial observer as the title to his account of Australian dissent from the unjust treatment of Indigenous peoples since colonial times.

7   This is, in part, the critique of "sovereignty"-based arguments for Indigenous rights developed by Alfred (1999) in his brilliant book. It parallels an argument that is often constructed in environmental politics, where the resources required to secure environmental protection are available only on the basis of approving environmentally destructive "development" (see, e.g., Abayasekara 1999).

8   Again, detailed discussion of the "stolen generations" is beyond the scope of this chapter, but for an overview of the issues see, *inter alia*, Fraser (2000); HREOC (1997); and Manne (2001).

9   I am deeply grateful to Sherrie Cross, whose unpublished and ongoing work has been a major input to much of my thinking on this issue and the source of the idea of an erasure of scales of Indigenous governance as a product of existing policy settings.

10 I was employed as a consultant by the South Australian Aboriginal Legal Rights Movement (ALRM) in 1999 and have maintained a link to the processes in South Australia ever since. See, for example, Agius et al. (2002, 2004, 2007).

11 A detailed account of the first period of the negotiations (Morrison 2000) was commissioned by the ALRM and is available, along with other publications detailing the negotiations, online at http://www.iluasa.com/alrm.asp#Publications. A second review (2000-06) has recently been completed by Tom Jenkin and will be available from the ALRM in Adelaide and through the website http://www.iluasa.com.

12 The non-Aboriginal participants in the South Australian process are the government, Chamber of Mines and Energy, Farmers Federation, Fishing Industry Council, Seafood Industry Council, and Local Government Association. The National Native Title Tribunal has had official observer status in the process.

13 In referring to "we" here, I mean the group of Aboriginal leaders and non-Aboriginal advisers who constituted the Technical Advisory Group and ALRM Statewide Secretariat. Howitt, an academic geographer, led the strategic Technical Advisory Group. Andrew Collett provided legal advice, along with Malcolm Gray, QC, a former South Australian Solicitor General. Dr. Mike Metcalf, who had been a senior adviser to a previous state Treasurer, provided political and financial advice. Lesley Johns, a media consultant, provided media and communications advice, Rhian Williams provided advice on procedural matters, and Jo Fox and Venessa Kealy, young geographers from Macquarie University, provided research

and administrative support. Additional expert reports and advice were commissioned on specific topics from a number of fields, including environmental issues (Dr. Jocelyn Davies, Department of Geography, University of Adelaide), pastoral issues (Don Blesing), and others.

14 I hasten to add that the conceptual framework that I have developed about scale was not discussed explicitly in presentations about the practicalities of negotiations and that the idea of the process producing new scales of Aboriginal governance emerged in the discussions that Agius et al. (2002) had in writing that piece. For background of the development of my own thinking on the concept of scale, see Howitt (1993b, 1997, 1998, 2002b, 2003).

15 One of the key principles that is common in Aboriginal law across Australia is that people may only speak for and about their own country unless they are explicitly authorized by a local authority to speak on its behalf.

PART 3
Re/Productive Scales

8
The Cult of Urban Creativity

Jamie Peck

Creativity is, one might say, the new black. An increasingly fashionable urban development script has it that a historically distinctive "creative economy" – powered by raw human talent, as cool as it is competitive – is displacing sclerotic, organization-era capitalism. The prime movers in this *new* new economy are members of the so-called creative class, a mobile elite whose finicky lifestyle preferences increasingly shape the geographies of economic growth. We are told that cities – like corporations – have become embroiled in an endless "war for talent," as flows of creative individuals have become the fundamental vectors of innovation-rich growth. And lo, there is the man in black at the centre of this burgeoning creativity fad – Richard Florida, who makes frequent recourse to sartorial signifiers in his best-selling primers on the creative economy. As an architect and popularizer of the creative class thesis, Florida has been feted around the world as a cool-cities guru. While his catchy notions concerning the creative city and its inhabitants have certainly benefited from some savvy promotion, their apparent allure and salience arguably have little to do with the intrinsic explanatory power of the model of creative growth. Rather, the creative cities thesis has travelled so far so fast because it encodes an engaging "economic imaginary" based on a set of principles that combines cultural libertarianism and contemporary urban design motifs with neoliberal economic imperatives.

My argument in this chapter is that the discourses and practices of creative cities policy making are barely disruptive of the prevailing order of neoliberal urbanism, based *inter alia* on polarizing labour and housing markets, property and market-led development, retrenched public services and social programming, and accelerating intercity competition for jobs, investment, and assets (Brenner, Peck, and Theodore 2005). The creative cities thesis represents a "soft" scalar fix for this neoliberal urban conjuncture, making the case for modest and discretionary public spending on creative assets while raising a favoured bundle of middle-class lifestyles to the status of an urban development objective. This newly influential urban development script – which finds legitimacy in progressive circles for its social liberalism and its valuation of art and culture – is in fact completely enveloped in, and suffused with, market logics. *Homo creativus* trades on an especially atomized form of human capital ("talent"), while positively thriving on relentless competition and long hours of work; s/he ostensibly favours "plug-and-play communities" in which weak social attachments prevail and where social distinction is marked out in the sphere of consumption. (Collective commitments, together with social and job security are, in this context, seriously passé.)

Discursively downloading both risk and responsibility, the creative city concept is predicated on, presumes, and (re)produces the scale politics of the dominant market order. After experiencing successive phases of smokestack-chasing and convention centre building, cities again find themselves induced to do whatever it takes to secure mobile and scarce economic resources in a globalizing struggle against peer cities. New anxieties about creative flight are compounding the old fears of capital flight. Cities must now subsidize the talented, just as they have long subsidized corporations, on the fallacious reasoning that every place can win in the race to the creative peak. The creativity credo is a seductive imperative, in this sense, remobilizing cultural assets – like Motown and Eminem in Detroit – around the ostensibly shared endeavour of creative renewal, while canalizing policy options at the local scale. Urban leaders who don't buy the policy package, moreover, are not only failing to respond to a competitive threat but are fuddy-duddies too – they just don't "get it."

The craze for urban creativity strategies represents a manifestation of an elaborated (maybe even funky) form of neoliberal scale politics. The soft-focus creativity script is in fact the carrier of an insidious, if in many ways rather familiar, "scalar narrative" (after Swyngedouw 1997b), since the self-fulfilling story that it tells about contemporary urban policy amplifies and enervates market imperatives, while locating causality, agency, and responsibility at the local, if not bodily, scale. Creative subjects are celebrated for their hypermobility and for their strictly circumscribed, individualistic commitments to place. These economic hipsters thrive in buzzing 24/7 neighbourhoods where they can satisfy their craving for "heart-throbbingly real" experiences (Florida 2002a, 166), but, at the drop of a hat, may choose to relocate to an even more happening place. It follows that anything short of public pandering to the needs and desires of the restless creatives is practically guaranteed to secure their automatic "flight" (Florida 2005b). The creativity discourse amounts to a paean to the international talent market and its favoured agents, to which cities and regions must be performatively deferential. In this retread of the orthodox globalization script, the argument for decisive local action – featherbedding the creative supply side – is presented as no less than a new urban imperative. Cities must "attract the new 'creative class' with hip neighborhoods, an arts scene and a gay-friendly atmosphere – or they'll go the way of Detroit" (Dreher 2002, 1). Which way, then, to the creative city?

The Creativity Catechism ...

Routinely overstated and hyperbolic, Florida's essential argument is that human creativity has become the engine of early-twenty-first-century economic development, such that the competitiveness of nations and cities is increasingly rooted in the capacity to attract, retain, and "nurture" talented individuals – a newly dominant but unneveringly mobile factor of production. Florida (2002a, 21) explains that human creativity has become nothing less than the "defining feature of economic life ... [It] has come to be valued – and systems have evolved to encourage and harness it – because new technologies, new industries, new wealth and all other good economic things flow from it." What this account lacks in causal analysis it makes up for in alliterative chutzpah. Success in the new, creative economy is down to three *T*s – technology, talent, and tolerance. Technological capacity is a precondition for creative growth but on its own is insufficient. The gist, though, is that cities with a shot at the creative big time must have a strong cluster of high-tech companies and a good university. The lifeblood of the system is the flow of talented individuals, the second *T*, this restless but critical factor of production having become the carrier of creative potential. Productive capacity is therefore located not in institutional matrices or production systems but in the heads and hearts of creative individuals. Yet, a city's development strategies will add up to naught in the absence of the third *T*, tolerance – open, dynamic, and heterodox local cultures represent the supply-side foundations upon which creative clusters are built. A high-tech centre without a thriving music scene is merely a nerdistan; add in nightlife and a vibrant gay community and you have the secret ingredient of *Austinization*. As Florida (quoted in Dreher 2002, 4-5) informed the readers of *Salon* magazine,

In every economic measure, Detroit and Pittsburgh should be trouncing Austin. These are places that had probably two of the greatest technological powerhouses of their time – they were the Silicon Valleys of their day. Detroit in automotive, Pittsburgh in steel and chemicals ... What happened, however, was that both places fell victim to institutional and cultural sclerosis. They got trapped in the organizational age; they thought we really live in a patriarchal, white, corporate society and that the key to success was to strap on your tie, go to work 9 to 5, and behave yourself. There was no room for people with new ideas. People with new ideas in both Pittsburgh and Detroit were shunned. They were thought to be troublemakers, difficult, weirdos, wackos, eccentrics ... [In contrast, what] Austin did was they really hustled. In the 1980s and 1990s they said, 'We want to grab some of these high-tech companies,' so they did that ... And then, what I think is the key factor that distinguishes Austin from Pittsburgh and Detroit, was that in addition to doing all of that, they said, 'We're going to make this a fun place to live' ... They created a lifestyle mentality, where Pittsburgh and Detroit were still trapped in that Protestant-ethic/bohemian-ethic split, where people were saying, 'You can't have fun!' or 'What do you mean play in a rock band? Cut your hair and go to work, son. That's what's important.' Well, Austin was saying, 'No, no, no, you're a creative. You want to play in a rock band at night and do semiconductor work in the day? C'mon! And if you want to come in at 10 the next morning and you're a little hung over or you're smoking dope, that's cool' ... Austin saw this from day one.

Florida uses this kind of sophomoric sociology to make the argument that, riding the new wave of urban economic development, the creatives have inherited the Earth, and it is they who now make the rules. The logical, if stark, conclusion is that "the Creative Class has become the dominant class in society" (Florida 2002a, ix). Florida softens the edges of this millennial pronouncement with his own form of new-age atmospherics: he frequently declares that every human being has the capacity to be creative, just as every city has a shot at becoming a creative hot spot. Yes, the one-third or so of the population in the creative class is "doing well, and taking care of itself," but, ultimately, it is the moral duty of this dominant cadre to open up ports of entry to motivated members of the lumpen 70 percent, perhaps through occupations such as hairstyling, since they require "close physical proximity" to the creatives (Florida 2005b, 246-47). Awakening the creative spirit among those labouring in the service and working classes is ultimately the responsibility of the creatives themselves, assuming that they can transition from their current state of self-absorption to some kind of creative-class consciousness, since their "economic function makes them the natural – indeed the only possible – leaders of twenty-first century society" (Florida 2002a, 315).

Notwithstanding the libertarian universalism of such calls for creative-class consciousness, Florida's depiction of the real world of proto-creative capitalism bears little resemblance to this hipster utopia. In the here and now, the economics of creativity are rather more utilitarian: from the perspective of corporations and cities (the difference hardly seems to matter in this instance), talented workers are a scarce resource, yet, they are both highly mobile and discerning in their tastes; therefore, they must be given what they want or they will not come/stay; and without them, there is only creative disinvestment and economic decline. In the context of a persistent shortfall in the supply of talent, cities must learn what corporations before them have been forced to learn, that if they do not take steps to establish the right "people climate" for creative workers, if they are not appropriately welcoming, "they will wither and die" (Florida 2002a, 13). There are roles for government in this development vision, but they are safely located on the supply side of the creative economy: establishing the right kind of urban ambience becomes the key to "harnessing" creativity. (*Harnessing* is a favourite Florida word, used to denote the provisional bridling of an unruly or natural force.)

This can be seen as a supply-side version of the "capital flight" arguments of the early 1980s, which may have begun life in the form of legitimate concerns about "runaway shops" but later metastasized into a condition of generalized (even "global") insecurity: improvements in communications and logistics technologies, organizational innovations, and regulatory liberalization enabled increases in the rate of (relative/potential) corporate mobility, conditions that afforded corporations the benefit of "take it or leave it" bargaining positions with local actors (Bluestone and Harrison 1982; Peck 2002a). For cities, getting with this program entailed various forms of giving corporations what they wanted – tax breaks, development incentives and subsidies, less "red tape," flexible workers – while the price of failing to recognize the new imperatives would be counted in inexorable decline and disinvestment. Florida's argument mobilizes a similar underlying logic, working across the same neoliberalized terrain. Now the potential flight of *talented workers* is the new superscalar competitive threat, while the new urban imperative is framed in terms of giving the creatives what they want or else. Paradoxically, Florida seeks to celebrate certain "qualities of place," such as buzz and cosmopolitanism, while recirculating pernicious neoliberal narratives of external competitive threat/vulnerability to flight.

> The core of the challenge is what I've come to see as the new global competition for talent, a phenomenon that promises to radically reshape the world in the coming decades. No longer will economic might amass in countries according to their natural resources, manufacturing excellence, military dominance, or even scientific and technological prowess. Today, the terms of competition revolve around a central axis: a nation's ability to mobilize, attract, and retain human creative talent ... The global talent pool and the high-end, high-margin creative industries that used to be the sole province of the U.S. and the crucial source of its prosperity have begun to disperse around the globe. A host of countries – Ireland, Finland, Canada, Sweden, Australia, and New Zealand among them – are investing in higher education, producing creative people, and churning out cutting-edge products, from cellular phones to computer software to blockbuster movies. (Florida 2005b, 3-4)

It follows that no one and *nowhere* are safe from this new competitive threat. Even powerful economies can fall prey to new forms of creative competition, which (along with the hyperbole) is said to be "heating up" (Florida 2005b, 7). "The United States may well have been the Goliath of the twentieth-century global economy," Florida observes, "but it will take just a half dozen twenty-first century Davids to begin to wear it down" (2005b, 4). Reworking familiar motifs in neoliberal scale politics, he represents the global scale as the sphere of unmanageable forces and imperatives, while the local scale is reconstituted as a competitive node – the site of get-with-the-program-style adaptation and (induced) agency.

Help is at hand, however, since Florida's self-appointed role is not simply to disclose the new economic order. Florida is also a purveyor, conveniently, of winning urban strategies. Right along with the identification of policy imperatives comes a suite of new policy solutions, all designed to give the creatives what they want, while securing the position of cities within the evolving creative division of labour. Figuring out what the creatives want, and where they want to be, was a primary task of Florida's opening salvo in the creativity debate, *The Rise of the Creative Class: And How It's Transforming Work, Leisure, Community, and Everyday Life* (2002a). Here, Florida probed the locational proclivities of the creative class, using a combination of pop culture anecdotes, focus groups with young, restless, and talented people, insights into his own creative lifestyle, and supposedly suggestive spatial correlations, for instance between gays and growth. The results – sparsely documented from a social scientific perspective but nevertheless emphatically stated – indicated that the creative classes yearn, above all, to "validate their identities" (Florida 2002a, 304). Creatives seek out neighbourhoods amply endowed with the kinds of amenities that allow them to maintain an experientially intensive work-life balance. They are drawn to plug-and-play communities where social entry barriers are low, where heterogeneity is actively embraced, where loose ties prevail, where there is plenty of scope for creative commingling. These are communities that creatives "can move into and put together a life – or at least a facsimile of a life – in a week" (Florida 2002b, 20). Such diagnostically critical conditions are signalled by the conspicuous presence of gays and lesbians, designated here both as the "canaries of the creative economy" and as "harbingers of redevelopment and gentrification in distressed urban neighborhoods" (Florida 2005b, 131). Other more concrete indicators of urban edginess include "authentic" historical buildings, converted lofts, walkable streets, plenty of coffee shops, art and live music spaces, indigenous street culture, and a range of other typical features of gentrifying, mixed-use, inner urban neighbourhoods. In many respects, these kinds of inner urban environments represent the antithesis of the edge city and suburban generica, the social and cultural connotations of which have not been lost on conservative commentators in particular (see Malanga 2004).

But Florida's point here is not simply to send a countercultural message about funky forms of urban economic development or, indeed, to signal a preference for the kinds of urban design features typical of artsy neighbourhoods at the cusp of gentrification. Florida is advancing the much bolder claim that such environments serve as creative incubators. *Homo creativus* thrives on weak attachments and non-committal relationships, most often mediated through the market. These atomized actors seem to lack families and non-market support systems, revelling instead in long hours of work and individualistic competition. This twenty-first-century version of economic man may have a better social life, but he is still economic man. As a member of the creative class, Florida (2002a, 115) understands that "there is no corporation or other large institution that will take care of us – that we are truly on our own." The edgy urban neighbourhood facilitates and enables this *productive* lifestyle, allowing the creatives to plug into the new economy and play as hard as they like. The defining characteristics of this new urban überclass are all framed in competitive terms. They are, one might say, neoliberals *dressed in black*. It takes no effort at all, as Table 8.1 shows, to translate the founding principles of the creative doctrine into just such terms.

Since it is the creatives who are the favoured actors in Florida's account, it is ultimately their choices – writ large – that make the spatial division of creative labour, the creative urban hierarchy, and the parameters of the interurban talent war. And, "when it comes down to it, creative people choose *regions*," Florida explains. "They think of Silicon Valley versus Cambridge, Stockholm versus Vancouver, or Sydney versus Copenhagen. The fact that many regions around the world are cultivating the attributes necessary to become creative centers makes this competition even fiercer" (2005b, 10). Just like the wave of entrepreneurial urban strategies that preceded it, this form of creative interurban competition is both self-fulfilling and self-perpetuating: establishing open, plug-and-play communities that are welcoming of restive creative types becomes tantamount to both enabling and *subsidizing* the very forms of mobility that were the source of competitive anxiety in the first place. But since there is (again) only one game in town, cities had better make sure that they are ready to participate, to do what is necessary, or they will certainly lose out. This is a variant of the "do it or else" style of neoliberal urban policy making in which favoured strategies are translated into economic imperatives (see Peck and Tickell 2002), another urban cargo cult, "a successor to previous single-minded fixations on docklands redevelopment, high-tech parks, convention centers, and the like" (Berry 2005, 386). Again, cities must be reflexively responsive to a hypercompetitive external environment comprising "liberalized" flows of capital, public investment, consumer dollars ... and now talent workers.

The role for government, in this context, is to featherbed the creative supply side, Florida's chameleon-like position being to sanction discretionary, pink-tinged interventions at the local scale while demanding that big government get out of the way. "Where I share common ground with some Republicans and libertarians [is] that old-style government programs have become

TABLE 8.1

The creativity credo ... and its neoliberal translations

Creative principles ... *	... and their neoliberal translations
Cultivate and reward creativity; everyone is part of the value chain of creativity ...	... put creatives first; support creative growth as a universal strategy; back winners
Invest in the creative ecosystem, including arts and culture, nightlife, the music scene, restaurants, artists and designers, innovators, entrepreneurs ...	... subsidize yuppie culture
Embrace diversity; it gives birth to creativity, innovation and positive economic impact ...	... get cozy with libertarian individualism; value cultural liberalism as an economic asset
Nurture the creatives ...	.. genuflect to and pamper the creative overclass
Value risk-taking; convert a "no" climate into a "yes" climate ...	... entrepreneurialize and devolve risk; ignore dissenters and naysayers; boost your place
Be authentic; identify the value you add and focus on those assets where you can be unique; every community can be the right community ...	... valorize culture as a competitive asset; rest assured, every place can win
Invest in and build on quality of place, making communities more competitive than ever ...	... gentrify, subsidize, and hawk your artsy neighborhoods (no need to be concerned with the "uncompetitive" parts of town)
Remove barriers to creativity, such as mediocrity, intolerance ...	... liberalize and deregulate markets for creativity; spurn big government solutions
Take personal responsibility; improvise; make things happen; development is a "do it yourself" enterprise	... pull on those creative bootstraps; creative failures have no-one, and nowhere, to blame but themselves
Honor the creativity in every person; extend the right to creativity ...	... use universalist rhetoric

* As derived from the Memphis Manifesto at www.memphismanifesto.com.

a huge impediment to leveraging the creative age and allowing it to emerge," Florida explains, the more limited function of the state being to "set up the parameters in which market-based actions take place" (quoted in Steigerwald 2004, 2). Priming the creative pump therefore becomes a task for *urban* leaders; the way forward is with "grassroots initiatives" and "community-oriented efforts." Step forward the street-level activists of the creative age.

... and Its Converts

The response to the creative cities thesis among urban policy-making communities around the world has been nothing less than remarkable. Florida's ideas have been picked up by mayors, regional development agencies, policy entrepreneurs, advisers, and consultants across the United States, Europe, Australasia, and parts of Asia, both in wannabe locations at the bottom of his creative league tables (which are now available in numerous countries) and in established centres such as London, Toronto, and Melbourne. While Florida's argument has certainly benefited from relentless promotion, this alone surely cannot account for the rapid diffusion of the creativity credo. In fact, this "fast policy" success story may be attributable less to the revolutionary or transformative nature of the Florida thesis itself and more to its character as a minimally disruptive "soft neoliberal" scalar fix. The story is, in many ways, a familiar one, though the cast of characters has changed. National governments just have to get out of the way, deregulating talent flows, for the creative economy to flourish; effective urban responses call for bold leadership and vision, but some kind of response is essential for any city that wants to stay in the game; self-managing and hyperactive creatives, as bearers of creative market forces, will look after the rest, so earning their status as privileged urban subjects. These are the new rules. And they come with only the most elusive of libertarian-utilitarian consolations: there seems to be only limited scope for "trickle down" from the creative class to the majority class and no real prospect of "trickle out" from the urban talent hubs; less creative people and places must pull themselves up by their (handmade Italian) bootstraps.

In this neoliberalized global-urban terrain, a receptive and wide audience has effectively been preconstituted for the kinds of market-reinforcing, property- and promotion-based, growth-oriented, and gentrification-friendly policies that have been repackaged under the creativity rubric. The creative cities policy fix can be deployed to accessorize extant, market-based urban development agendas, with the minimum of interference to established interests and constituencies. At root, it simply adds a livability-lifestyle component to the established urban competitiveness stance (McCann 2007). The typical mayor is likely to see few downsides to making the city safe for the creative class. Establishment power elites have little to fear from conspicuous urban consumption, gen-x marketing campaigns, key-worker attraction strategies, and gentrification with public art. A creativity strategy can therefore be easily sutured to business-as-usual urban development policies while providing additional ideological cover for market-driven or state-assisted programs of gentrification. Inner-city *embourgeoisement*, in the creativity script, is represented as a necessary prerequisite for economic development: *hey presto*, thorny political problem becomes competitive asset!

Far from presenting an alternative to the prevailing package of neoliberal urban development policies, the creativity fix enables their augmentation and relegitimation. The creative cities strategy is a low-cost but high-visibility program, with outcomes that are politically legible in the short term. And it is conveniently consistent with the ongoing neoliberalization of housing, labour, and consumption markets: the strategy handily prerationalizes uneven outcomes (as consequences of the distribution of creative capital) while justifying policies favouring the creative "winners." Creative cities policies, of course, would hardly be spreading like wildfire if they represented a revolutionary challenge to the neoliberal status quo. In fact, they are being stamped out cookie-cutter style across the urban landscape, spanning a remarkable range of settings (see Berry 2005; Gibson and Klocker 2005; Krätke 2004; and Peck 2005), having become policies of choice, in particular, for those left-leaning mayors who have learned to live with, if not love, the market order. Nominally bespoke creativity strategies can be purchased from consultants in practically any mid-sized city these days, or they can be lifted off the shelf from countless websites and urban regeneration conferences.

To take just one of dozens of (very) similar examples, Michigan's Cool Cities program, derived directly from the creativity playbook, retasks state funds to the goal of localized gentrification, hipster style, in the hope that this will attract the creative class. Beneath the rhetoric of avant-garde economic development, the program entails the public subsidy of various kinds of "creative" collective goods and infrastructure projects, focused exclusively on locations with *demonstrated* development potential (a.k.a. "happening," gentrifying neighbourhoods). Making Michigan's cities attractive to the creative class has entailed a youth-oriented marketing program; extensive learning from other cities and from creative citizens themselves (given that "government cannot create 'cool'"); and a bundle of mostly repackaged policies aimed at the rehabilitation of historic buildings (specifically theatres, galleries, mixed-use housing), farmers' markets, streetscaping and public art, physical infrastructure development, façade improvements, outdoor recreation facilities, greenspace, parks, pavilions, and, if necessary, demolition (see Cool Cities Initiative 2004).

Posing in fashionable shades to launch the program, Michigan's governor, Jennifer Granholm, insisted that it was essential that this struggling, auto-industry state catch the *next* wave of economic development. Since the old "new" economy, which stalled with the millennial dot-com crash (see Frank 2000; and Peck 2001a), did little to help Michigan, maybe rounds of creative investment would be more accommodating. And the pop cultural symbolism would not hurt either, since Michigan has been experiencing an "exodus" of young, highly educated people in recent years as "large numbers of talented workers have fled the state in search of employment" (Cool Cities Initiative 2004, 3). According to the creativity script, the way to alleviate Michigan's economic decline is to reverse this critical flow of talent, since, in the new knowledge economy, jobs follow workers, not the other way around. The target demographic for the Cool Cities program is defined as college-educated young professionals in core fields such as science and engineering, art and design, entertainment, computing, and the media, whose defining characteristics include a "preference for lifestyle," distinctive purchasing patterns (reflecting individuality and self-statement), and above all *mobility*: "Today's young professional workforce is more interested in working as a means of experiencing and enjoying their lifestyle than their counterparts in decades past. This group is increasingly mobile, and in order to attract and retain them, cities have to change their paradigm of physical and social development. The city itself has to be attractive, not only to business, but also to the workforce" (Cool Cities Initiative 2004, 13).

Curiously, even though Michigan's creative class decamped "in search of employment," we are expected to believe that they will be attracted *back* by enhanced urban environments, and *then* the state's economy will revive: "Given the right mix of services and amenities, this group will 'vote with their feet' and relocate to vibrant, walkable, mixed-use communities. Attracted by a talented, diverse workforce, business will follow" (Cool Cities Initiative 2004, 4). A leap of faith is required for this strategy to be effective. Will young Michiganders, who left the state in search of better career opportunities (apparently having had their fill of the lifestyle options of Flint, Kalamazoo, and

Saginaw), now be tempted back by the policy-induced trendification of their old neighbourhoods? Furthermore, these investments will only generate economic development if Florida's (unsubstantiated and untested) causal arguments about creative growth transpire to be true. Even if the goal of "making Michigan the 'coolest' state in the nation" (Cool Cities Initiative 2004, 3) is a realistic one, it sits rather awkwardly with the sobering realities of structural economic decline and public sector downsizing in a state hardly renowned as a hipster haven. Michigan has one of the highest unemployment rates in the nation, the auto industry has entered a(nother) major phase of restructuring, and the rate of job loss in the state has been characterized by local commentators as "staggering" (Aguilar 2005; Valcourt and Aguilar 2006). Languishing for years in a single-state recession, business groups recognize that this is more than a cyclical downturn: "This is a structural crisis that is permanent" (Crain 2007). In the fall of 2007, the state narrowly averted a government shutdown due to its $1.75 billion budget deficit. Dumping fiscal burdens on municipal governments and other local agencies seems to be one of the longer-term outcomes, though the $4 million Cool Cities Initiative has been protected. As the Michigan Municipal League has complained, however, there comes a point when even "cool cities need cold cash" (Summer Minnick, quoted in Lane 2007).

An inhospitable climate for further rounds of "creative" policy making? Apparently not. In some respects, the level of enthusiasm for creativity makeovers may be inversely proportional to the scale of the economic challenge confronting local policy makers. In Detroit, for example, where the economic trajectory has been described by David Littman, chief economist at Comerica Bank, as a "graveyard spiral" (quoted in Wilgoren 2005), the creativity cult has been recruiting new members. CreateDetroit, an offshoot of the state's Cool Cities program established in 2003, characteristically self-describes as a "grassroots organization" despite sponsorship from the Detroit Regional Chamber of Commerce, the Governor's Office, the City of Detroit, Wayne State University, Detroit Renaissance, the Detroit Economic Growth Corporation, and corporations such as Apple and SBC Communications. CreateDetroit has been striving to turn around the flagging fortunes of Motown by making it a "destination city" for the creative class. Detroit was ranked thirty-ninth of forty-nine major cities in Florida's original "creativity index," but, as the creative economist himself has pointed out, this means that the city has more creative *potential* than almost any other city in the nation (see Klein 2004b). CreateDetroit is pursuing strategies similar to those of a range of other (newly designated) creative bottomfeeders, such as Memphis and Tampa Bay, which were similarly spurred to action by their lowly rankings in Florida's widely publicized league tables (see Peck 2005). These strategies include periodic events that splice the arts and urban development; creatively themed marketing and promotion activities; initiatives such as "free-agent Fridays" for independent entrepreneurs in the creative economy and "Connect Four," where artists, writers, designers, and media types can "meet, mingle, hunt, gather, network, and play"; and lobbying for creative investment. There are also plans to establish a downtown networking space, "like Starbucks on steroids," with conference rooms and lounges, which creatives will support through membership fees (*Crain's Detroit Business* 2006).

"The idea behind CreateDetroit," a founding member explained, "is to create a long-range plan, focused on making the Detroit region a magnet for new economy talent. The stakes are high. Those regions that do not flourish in the new creative economy will fail, according to Carnegie Mellon University professor Richard Florida" (Erickson 2003). A formative early step for CreateDetroit was to invest in one of the professor's two-day "regional transformation" workshops, photographs from which adorn the group's website. Following a well-established methodology, the event featured a range of local performance artists, plenty of feel-good provincial pride (along with *I Am Detroit* T-shirts), and a 350-person audience heavily tilted towards the arts and cultural communities, together with local policy makers and advocates. Florida's polished performance was greeted with enthusiasm, and there was widespread support for his populist message of "pro-people" economic development. His energetically delivered message, that Detroit was a deficit city in the balance of creative trade, focused attention on the out-migration of "talented" individuals while validating a distinctive set of arts-intensive investments in the city. Unfortunately, an irreparable failure of the computer system (and its backup) marred the audience participation segment of the workshop, in which attendees were invited to vote on their city's creative strengths and weaknesses prior to revelations of the "actual data" ... perhaps calling attention to some of Detroit's deficits on the first *T*, technology. But most of the participants, especially those in the (previously neglected) arts and cultural communities, seem to have left invigorated by Florida's "call to arms to take themselves seriously as an economic force" (Sousanis 2004, 4).

"The purpose of the event," Florida insisted, was not for "me and my team to come to Detroit and prescribe fixes. What will help Detroit is for swelling grassroots efforts like CreateDetroit to say, 'This is where we want to be in the future. This is what we plan to do to get there'" (quoted in Wallace 2004). Others were left wondering whether the creative backwash, should it ever reach the shores of Lake Michigan, would really lift all boats. Buzz aside, most recognized that this was in many respects a canned presentation and that Florida's troupe would soon be pulling "up their tent stakes, and mov[ing] on to their next destination" (Sousanis 2004, 3). "Florida had the air of a motivational speaker, claiming that Detroit has more raw potential than any other city in the nation. He gave a brief synopsis of his concept of what makes a city a livable, vibrant place – but other than the obligatory White Stripes and Eminem references, the speech could have been delivered in Anyville, USA" (Klein 2004a). In a sense, of course, the speech had been delivered in Anyville, a generic location for which it was carefully crafted. Scores of cities have heard, and often responded to, the same basic message, with each being urged to value – and valorize – whatever creative assets it might have on hand. According to Florida's prescription, practically any city can respond to the creativity treatment, at least as long as its civic leaders "get it" (Florida 2002a, 302-3).

On the face of it, Detroit's "hip hop mayor," Kwame Kilpatrick, still under forty and the proud wearer of a diamond ear stud, got it. The mayor offered a fulsome introduction to Florida when he came to Detroit with his promises of regional transformation, while the city endorses the work of CreateDetroit. (On this occasion, the mayor chose not to mention his opposition to same-sex marriage, which would not earn him high marks on the tolerance scorecard.) While the realistic prospects of a creativity-fuelled economic turn-around in Detroit may be remote, the city can hardly be faulted for its willingness to give anything a try. Its population has fallen by half since the mid-1950s; its unemployment rate is twice the state's average and getting close to three times the national average; 72 percent of the city's public school children receive free school meals (up from 61 percent in 2001); and "white flight has become bright fright, with families and people earning more than $50,000 a year leading the way out of town" (Wilgoren 2005; see also Sugrue 2005). For the city's government, sustained population loss, coupled with a declining tax base, has been fuelling an unprecedented and unresolved fiscal crisis: Mayor Kilpatrick's administration hovered on the brink of receivership, having cut bus services, closed the city zoo and thirty-four schools, and shed one in ten of the municipal workforce. The city has also been considering closing "non-essential departments," including – note the unfortunate inconsistencies – the Department of Culture, Art, and Tourism, and turning off streetlights. Its paralyzing three-year deficit amounts to just under one-quarter of annual general fund revenues (see Kaffer 2005). Yet, local assessments are that even the first round of serious cuts allegedly runs the risk of generating "a vicious cycle for a city already on the edge" (Bello 2005). Nevertheless, the city is targeting precious resources on a "creativity zone," upgrading the enterprise zone concept of the 1980s, with the active support of the business community (Detroit Renaissance 2006).

A recent convert to the cult of creativity, Detroit Renaissance has been striving, since the early 1970s, to turn the tide of long-run economic decline in the city, apparently without much success. Most of the conventional post-Keynesian policy remedies have also been applied to Motown, again to little avail (see Lawless 2002; and McCarthy 2002). Compared to the usual package of corporate tax breaks and big-box development subsidies, Cool Cities policies certainly look like a break with the past. But while there may be novelty in urban policy makers and business elites sharing the stage with fashion designers and hip hop artists, none of this makes the causal relationships between buzz and economic growth any less elusive. More sobering still, perhaps, is the absence of any extant compelling examples of *policy-led* creative growth, for all the hype around the efforts of creative wannabes (see Next American City 2004a, 2004b). But none of this will prevent cities, with few other realistic options, from trying. Recall, however, how entrepreneurial urban strategies proliferated during the 1980s and 1990s, facilitated by competitive leverage and the weak emulation of "winning" formulas, quickly stacking the odds against even the most enthusiastic of converts (Harvey 1989b). Coming on the heels of this experience, the creativity fix also seduces local actors with the no-less-false promise that any *and every* city can win in the battle for talent. Under such circumstances, the first-mover advantages for a few quickly descend into zero or negative sum games: more players pursue the same mobile resources, the price of "success" rises, the chances of positive outcomes fall. In cities like Detroit, the odds look daunting. This said, there remains plenty of enthusiasm among the activists at CreateDetroit for what they are calling "Plan B ... [making] sure the talent comes here" (Klein 2004b). Plan A was automobile manufacturing.

The Cool Cities program may indeed be an "economic development strategy that puts 'creative people' first" (Michigan 2003, 3), but in cities like Detroit, these look like perversely indulgent priorities. Should the Motor City really be investing its dwindling tax revenues in a market-following strategy for underwriting middle-class house prices and consumption desires, with distributional consequences that seem certain to be socially and spatially regressive? Entrenched problems such as structural unemployment, residential inequality, working poverty, and racialized exclusion are barely even addressed by this form of cappuccino urban politics. According to urban historian Matt Lassiter (quoted in Paul 2005, 19), "the Rust Belt capital of Detroit has basically adopted the Sunbelt strategy of Atlanta and Los Angeles: ignore social problems of segregation and poverty, and instead try to transform the image rather than the reality of the central city." Creativity strategies have been crafted to *coexist* with these problems, not to solve them. It should come as no surprise, then, that the creative capitals exhibit higher rates of socioeconomic inequality than other cities, as has been belatedly acknowledged by Florida himself (2005a). This awkward correlation is consistent, of course, with the argument that creativity strategies are predicated upon, and constitutively realized in the context of, uneven modes of urban growth and neoliberal scale politics. For his part, Florida (2005b, 246) has taken to issuing plaintive calls for the creative class *itself* to develop some kind of post hoc response to the "growing class divide" in and between cities, lest it should trigger "widespread social unrest." In this light, the creativity fix begins to look less like a solution to, and more like a symptom of, Detroit's problems.

Conclusion: Creativity Redux

As a discourse and as a set of policy practices, the creative cities strategy resonates with and reinforces a soft neoliberal form of scale politics. Risk and responsibility are downloaded to the lowest scales that can bear them. Only vaguely alluding to the presence of a (distant and dysfunctional) national state, creativity discourses amplify external competitive threats, privileging the local and bodily scales as the locations of both determinate processes and meaningful social action. Insisting that creative "environments cannot be planned from above," Florida (2004, iii) denudes the scope of governmental intervention to that of local lifestyle facilitation: get the urban preconditions right, and the creative economy will do the rest.

Practically all of the action in Florida's creative economy is likewise located at the very local scale. While Florida typically presents data for entire metro areas (including suburbs!), there is no doubt that it is central-city neighbourhoods that are where the creative economy is really supposed to *happen* (see Malanga 2005; and McCann 2007). These thickly described and causally fecund places represent the creatives' preferred habitat; this is where the powers of heterogeneous association are ostensibly realized. The world outside, in contrast, is a zone of barely bridled market forces; of Castellsian flows of creative capital, personally transported; of tight networks between the transnationally integrated creative hubs; of intense, competitive pressures; and of often wrong-headed governments. Creative individuals have the option of international mobility, but they move only when they feel like it, and then only between one creative hub and another, barely noticing the unfashionable hinterlands in between. The creatives value place – so long as it facilitates their self-actualization – but there is very little inertia in the world of the supercreative core. They constantly reevaluate place in cosmopolitan, comparative terms and may choose to move on at any time. It is this fear of creative flight that galvanizes urban policy makers, just like the fear of capital flight captured the attention of the entrepreneurial cities.

The pervasive "scalar narrative" of the creative city is performing powerful ideological work in defining privileged scales, spaces, sites, and subjects for new kinds of "intervention," just as it reformulates questions of urban economic and cultural development in significant ways. Creativity strategies presume, work with, and subtly remake the entrepreneurialized terrain of urban politics, placing commodified assets such as the arts and street culture into the sphere of interurban competition, enabling the formation of new local political channels and constituencies, and constituting new objects and subjects of urban governance. Creativity strategies work upon, indeed celebrate, mobile and adaptive creative subjects, making the case for public investment in their preferred local milieu while shifting the primary focus of proactive governance towards the "needs" of a technobohemian slice of the middle class. Taking the flexible/insecure/unequal economy as given, these postprogressive urban strategies lionize a creative elite while offering the residualized majority the meagre consolation of crumbs from the creative table. They enforce soft disciplinary modes of creative governmentality based on mandatory individualism, relentless innovation, and 24/7 productivity. And they do this within the framework of an inherited complex of new urban "realities" that variously contextualize, channel, and constrain "creative" urban politics. Say what you will about the fuzzy causality in Florida's model; its central message has certainly struck a chord. But as Detroit writer Carey Wallace (2004), among others, has begun to wonder, does the creativity craze represent "a new truth, or something people want very much to believe?"

9
State Spaces of "After Neoliberalism": Co-Constituting the New Zealand Designer Fashion Industry

Wendy Larner, Nick Lewis, and Richard Le Heron

Debates about new geographies of political economic space often attribute the rise of new state spaces to changing forms of governance associated with neoliberal globalization. The parameters of these debates are now well known; some governmental functions are being drawn into the realm of supranational institutions, whereas others are being devolved to regional and local governments. The assumed result is the multiscalar politics discussed by many of the contributors to this collection and elsewhere (see, for notable examples, Brenner 2004; and Jessop 2002a). This chapter takes a different approach to the analysis of new state spatialities. Rather than assuming that new spaces of governance reflect coherent and unified political rationalities, and so are made manifest in singular and coherent spatial imaginaries, we are concerned to show that state spaces emerge out of and imply distinct territorializations, and are co-constituted by multiple and unevenly developed political projects. These projects are premised on distinctive understandings of the problems of the current context, engage diverse governmental and political actors, operate at multiple spatialities and temporalities, and differentially constitute the spaces and subjects of governance. Consequently, rather than enter into the debate as to whether scales or networks are the dominant spatiality of the contemporary period, we would claim that it is important to focus on multiple spatial imaginaries that are helping to constitute multiple objects and subjects of governance. Our interest, then, is in exploring nameable on-the-ground political projects with a view to disclosing that the new spaces of governance are not pregiven – they are constantly in-the-making and under review.

We develop this argument through an account of the New Zealand experience of "neoliberalization" (Peck and Tickell 2002). Rather than a concerted state strategy, or an orchestrated political economic process, neoliberalization in the New Zealand experience is more usefully understood as involving ad hoc, *post facto* rationalizations in which connections are made across political projects that were initially quite discrete and even contradictory. Elsewhere we have called the New Zealand experience of this political process "after neoliberalism" to highlight the tenuous, multiple, competing, and sometimes contrary aspects of its constitution and reconstitution (Larner, Le Heron, and Lewis 2007). In this chapter, we further these claims by examining the implications of after neoliberalism for analyses of state spaces. Our argument pivots on two critical distinctions. First, what we are examining is not all neoliberal or indeed state. In the neoliberal-plus and state-plus world, we are sensitive to the mix of processes and their interdependencies and effects. Second, we contend that the constitutive effects of politics more than shape the economic; they also influence the political. To aid inquiry into these dimensions, we explore constitutive effects of politics through the lens of the "political project." We emphasize the spatial imaginaries explicit and implicit in particular political projects. Doing so enables us to reveal the diversity of claims, behaviours, and trajectories that are implicated in and through investment decisions connected with the designer fashion industry.

We explore in detail the ways in which four of the political projects that are part of this political process – globalization, the knowledge economy, creative cities, and social development – have understood and engaged with the newly fledged New Zealand designer fashion industry.

Our aim is to show that each of the political projects imagines the spaces of the designer fashion industry in a distinctive way. The globalization project, for example, sees designer fashion as an exemplar of a global production network (Henderson et al. 2002) in which New Zealand designers are able to access export markets through complex networks made up of designers, retailers, agents, public relations experts, marketing specialists, and expatriate consumers. In contrast, the knowledge economy project imagines the designer fashion industry as an "enabling sector." This spatial imaginary focuses on the national economy, seeing creative industries as playing a key role in reinventing national economic spaces and subjects in innovative, entrepreneurial, and value-added forms. The project of urban regeneration imagines the industry at the subnational level – cities, clusters, and regions – while the social development project privileges the social spaces of community and locality.

Scale theorists would see these diverse state spaces as global, national, urban, and local scales. While it is true that each project seems to take a distinct "scale" as its focus, our approach highlights the distinctiveness of each of these political projects as they have emerged in New Zealand by identifying the state agencies involved, the spatial imaginaries that they make manifest, and the objects and subjects of governance on which they focus. Networks, sectors, clusters, and communities are not component parts of a unified scalar imaginary or even the primary scalar horizons for each project; rather, they are co-constituted state spatialities. They are the governmental objects of different state agencies, they have different characteristics, and they are imagined as doing different work for the overall project of after neoliberalism. They can also work in different directions, creating tensions for those involved. As a result, the New Zealand designer fashion industry has found itself the bearer of disproportionate, often contradictory, and changing state expectations and is being co-constituted in multiple forms.

After Neoliberalism and the Designer Fashion Industry

Like other so-called third way governments, New Zealand's fifth Labour government has eased away from the ideological and political certainties of the "more market" approaches that characterized the 1980s and 1990s and has begun to carve out a new, but as yet poorly understood, political terrain in an attempt to overcome the failures of market-led neoliberalism, which has proven ineffective, politically unpalatable, and costly in social terms. The elements of the new terrain include an emphasis on the opportunities provided by globalization, the reembedding of economic and social relations, a new emphasis on innovation and creativity, and a reengagement with communities in the name of collaboration and partnership. The overall aim is to build new institutions and develop political strategies that will facilitate economic and social development.

A variety of labels has been used to describe this new variant of neoliberalism: roll-out neoliberalism (Peck and Tickell 2002), social neoliberalism (Cerny 2004), and inclusive neoliberalism (Craig and Porter 2004). We use the term "after neoliberalism" for two reasons, one theoretical and the other concrete. First, we argue that this new political formulation represents the conjunction of political projects that may or may not coalesce into a coherent "spatio-temporal fix" or an integrated "mode of regulation" (Jessop 2002a). While globalization has become the prevailing governmental rationality, we dispute the claim that this rationality has been able to impose unity on the various activities of the different state agencies. Nor, as we show, are the activities of the state agencies, their diverse political projects, and the spatialities that they constitute usefully captured by the concept of "scalar multiplicity" (Brenner 2004, 99). Instead, we are concerned to highlight the distinctiveness of the various state spatialities associated with this new political formation.

Second, our use of this term explicitly interrogates the current New Zealand government's claim that neoliberalism is over (Clark 2002), even though there is clear evidence of the continued use of discourses and techniques associated with neoliberalism. In this context, the term "after neoliberalism" highlights both the incomplete nature of the rupture with earlier forms of neoliberalism and the absence of a definitively new governmental formation. It also reflects our ongoing commitment to developing theoretical arguments through situated knowledges (Larner and Le Heron 2002). Not only does after neoliberalism clearly mark the antipodean origins of our work, but it also signals an intention to make intellectual interventions that are constitutive rather than reflective (Gibson-Graham 1994, 220). Rather than working from universalizing claims based on the identification of ideal types, we are concerned to highlight the ways in which political economic processes involve specific imaginaries, inventions, and forms of experimentation that actively reconstitute the economic, political, and social spaces in which interactions take place. In doing so, we use detailed interrogations of the New Zealand experience to make visible the contingent and indeterminate aspects of our political economic present.

While the New Zealand designer fashion industry may seem like a strange topic for a book such as this, as economic geographers, we have long been interested in the implications of neoliberalism for economic and industrial forms (see, e.g., Larner 2001; Larner and Le Heron 2004, 2005; Le Heron 2003; and Lewis 2004). Moreover, our research on the New Zealand designer fashion industry[1] was in part prompted by the rapidly increasing profile of this industry. Since the unexpected success of the NZ Four show at London Fashion Week in 1999, designer fashion has become the focus of an enormous amount of government and media attention in New Zealand, with designers achieving, locally at any rate, pop star status. Now presented as a successful export industry offering new opportunities for both economic growth and cultural rebranding, New Zealand designer fashion attracts attention not only from middle-class consumers and the media but also from the national government, corporate New Zealand, would-be creative cities, regional and community development agencies, and even schools.

On the face of it, this attention seems to be disproportionate to the activities involved. In New Zealand, designer fashion is a relatively new industry, emerging out of the deregulated ruins of the once highly protected clothing industry in the late 1980s and early 1900s (Larner and Molloy with Goodrum 2007). A 2002 scoping report showed that two-thirds of New Zealand designer fashion firms had been established in the 1990s, and another 13 percent had been set up since 2000 (Blomfield 2002). It is also made up of small businesses; in 2001, most had fewer than ten full-time staff, and nearly three-quarters had a turnover of less than $2 million. While the industry has grown significantly since, with the author of the scoping report claiming that turnover increased at least fivefold in the three years that followed his report (Blomfield, personal communication, March 2005), designer fashion continues to make a relatively modest contribution to the economy as a whole and pales in comparison with the traditional agricultural commodities and tourism, which remain New Zealand's largest export earners.

Why, then, has the New Zealand designer fashion industry recently become the target of heightened expectations among diverse political, economic, and social actors? One explanation for the burgeoning profile of the New Zealand designer fashion industry is that it has become decisively implicated in at least four of the political projects that have come together as part of after neoliberalism: globalization, the knowledge economy, urban regeneration, and social development. These political projects are widely reported in the media, and their naming makes them amenable to multiple political deployment as their potentialities are more systematically imagined. The designer fashion industry has proved to be both attractive and highly imaginable when considered from the premises of differing political projects. We are not suggesting that the successes of the designer fashion industry are the straightforward products of the interests of state agencies. There can be no doubt about either the merits of the individual designers or the efforts of key policy makers and cultural intermediaries. Rather, our aim is to show that the New Zealand designer fashion industry has become attached to these political projects in multidimensional ways that have helped to constitute the political economic spaces of this industry in particular forms. Each of the four political projects knows the designer fashion industry in distinctive ways; each gives us specific narratives of the industry and harnesses it to do particular work. In doing so, each of these four political projects (re)constitutes the designer fashion industry as a particular object of governance and contributes to the emergence of a distinctive state spatiality.

The Globalization Project

Globalization is not a new project; New Zealand governments first began to adopt proactive globalization strategies in the early 1990s. Yet, while the globalization project was initially understood in terms of increasing exports and encouraging direct foreign investment (Larner 1998), today globalization is a more expansive project in which many aspects of economic and social policy are framed in terms of increasing "global connectedness." The availability of this rationalization has conferred a new basis for spatial imaginaries of the industry. In the globalization project, the designer fashion industry has become a means of repositioning New Zealand materially and symbolically in global flows and networks. This project imagined designer fashion, initially, as part of a traditional commodity chain, then as a global production network made up of designers, policy makers, industry proponents, and cultural intermediaries, and most recently, as part of an image-based globalizing cultural economy that is drawing in new economic actors, the international media, and global consumers.

The first version of this spatial imaginary – the traditional textile and clothing commodity chain – can be seen in the earliest government engagements with the designer fashion industry. By the late 1990s, the then embryonic designer fashion industry had come to the attention of policy makers within the export promotions agency Trade New Zealand. For these policy makers, interventions in the fashion industry were seen as a means of bolstering clothing and textile exports rather than supporting designer fashion as an export industry in and of its own right. For example, in one of the earliest state interventions in the industry, Trade New Zealand supported selected designers to attend Australian Fashion Weeks in 1997 and 1998. The aim was to use the presence of international buyers in Australia to promote New Zealand clothing and apparel.

It was the success of the Australian initiative that encouraged Trade New Zealand's sponsorship success of the NZ Four designers to London in 1999. This sponsorship was premised on a revised understanding of the role that designer fashion might play in the globalization project. Admittedly, there was an ongoing emphasis on designer fashion as the top-end activity in a traditional commodity chain, marked most notably by the co-sponsorship arrangement with Wools of NZ, for which the venture was about selling New Zealand wools and wool products. For Trade New Zealand, however, the global (in Europe) positioning of the designer fashion industry was now to be a catalyst for other (more serious) industries, a platform for selling other New Zealand products, and an opportunity for augmenting Brand New Zealand. This marked a shift away from the more market approach that had dominated during the 1980s and early 1990s and towards the new after neoliberal approach in which the state would take on a more proactive and facilitative role in relation to the globalizing economy. More specifically, Trade New Zealand's profiling of the designer fashion industry sought to add sophisticated, creative, and cosmopolitan nuances to the rural and green images used routinely to promote New Zealand's export industries. In this context, the designers were essential to the London Fashion Week venture but were not themselves central to its rationale. Indeed, the success of the venture was gauged in terms of the amount of broader media and public relations material generated for New Zealand as a whole as much as by the number of designer garments sold.

By the inception of New Zealand Fashion Week in 2001, designer fashion was beginning to be understood as a successful export industry in its own right in addition to being a flagship for the "new" New Zealand economy. As a trade show geared to generating new export markets for designer fashion, New Zealand Fashion Week both reflects and supports the globalization project. Trade New Zealand joined with the then domestic economic development agency Industry New Zealand[2] and significant private sponsorship. The aim of this initiative was to bring international buyers to New Zealand, give both fashion designers and Brand New Zealand international media coverage, and construct new markets both internationally and domestically. Seen in this context, designer fashion is part of a global production network that draws in a range of cultural intermediaries – marketing specialists, public relations agents, fashion journalists, photographers – as well as the designers of the garments themselves and the models, hairdressers, makeup artists, and musicians involved in staging the show.

Today, the designer fashion industry performs multiple tasks for the globalization project. Most immediately, designer fashion is understood in the context of the global networks through which the garments themselves are produced, marketed, and consumed. More generally, however, the success of designer fashion is now used by a wide range of state agencies and corporate New Zealand to sell to New Zealanders the idea that they are "making it" in the world. Fashion designers are cast as vibrant, niche-oriented providers of internationally marketable creative products and as models for an innovative, design-based, entrepreneurial New Zealand export identity (Ryan 2001). Success stories of New Zealand fashion mix supercelebrity with glitz and photographic opportunities and now consistently grace, for example, airline magazines alongside similar stories about wineries, athletes, and musicians. Designer fashion contributes several stars to the galaxy of New Zealand celebrities and promotes a national imaginary in which New Zealanders are successful, globalizing cosmopolitans.

The globalization project has thus enabled significant extensions to the profile of designer fashion in the context of after neoliberalism, but it has also saddled it with multiple expectations that come from assessing the now much more visible and "important" industry against established measures – increasing exports of clothing and textiles, earning foreign exchange, and rebranding New Zealand as vibrant, creative, cultured, and urbane. For our purposes, the crucial characteristic of the globalization project is the way in which it imagines designer fashion primarily as a new means of accessing globalizing processes. Initially as part of a traditional commodity chain focused on textiles and clothing, then as a successful export industry that formed the basis for a global production network, and finally as part of a new "image-based" globalized cultural economy that draws in a wide range of new economic actors and cultural intermediaries, the spatial imaginary of the globalization project is firmly oriented towards integrating New Zealand-based activities into global flows and networks.

The Knowledge Economy

The knowledge economy project is of more recent provenance. It emerges explicitly from the fifth Labour government's ambition to create a new economic base from which to achieve its broader political, social, and cultural goals. This after neoliberal project marks a major reworking of national economic strategies that followed the wide-scale departure of major New Zealand corporations offshore during the 1980s and 1990s. Rather than continuing to try to retain a New Zealand base for large corporate actors, the new aim was to move New Zealand away from economic dependence on traditional resource-based and import-substitution manufacturing activities and towards niche "knowledge-based" export industries that would create new economic and employment opportunities for New Zealanders.

Whereas the globalization project was driven by Trade New Zealand, the knowledge economy project was initially the preserve of the national economic development agency Industry New Zealand and so was clearly focused on domestic activities. Designer fashion featured prominently in the early discussions about the need to rethink national economic development strategies. In keeping with new policies designed to promote knowledge-based industries, in 2001, Industry New Zealand named "fashion, apparel, and textiles" as one of five industries to be targeted as part of its regional development strategy. These industries collectively were described as exemplars of the "job-rich, high-skill, high-value export industries" (Burleigh Evatt and New Zealand Institute of Economic Research 2001, 1) that would underpin the new economic approach.

The knowledge economy project has been heavily involved in institutionalizing the designer fashion industry in New Zealand. Following comparable initiatives in the United Kingdom, Ireland, and Finland, the first move was to isolate and measure the "creative industries" and, in more traditional industries such as clothing and textiles, to highlight the designer/creative elements (NZIER 2002). It was the Burleigh Evatt Report (2001) that highlighted the different trajectories and fortunes of designer fashion (sunrise) and clothing (sunset), allowing the excision of the healthy organ of designer fashion from the textile and clothing industries more generally. The Blomfield (2002) scoping report referred to previously was also part of this project, explicitly scoping and measuring the activities within the newly identified designer fashion industry. It was followed in mid-2002 by the establishment of FINZ as an industry representative organization to give designer fashion a distinctive "voice" through which to engage with governmental processes.[3]

The prominence of designer fashion in the government's ambitions to create a knowledge economy was subsequently consolidated by the Growth and Innovation Framework launched in 2003.[4] In this high-level strategy document, designer fashion industry serves as an exemplar (along with film and music) of what the newly forming "creative industries" can do for the New Zealand economy. The creative industries are seen as one of the three "enabling sectors" – along with biotechnology and Information and Communications Technologies (ICTs) – that offer the greatest potential for growth and wealth creation in a knowledge economy (Office of the Prime Minister 2002). In reproducing arts and cultural activities as consumption goods, the creative industries are understood to be examples of successful, innovative, and entrepreneurial enterprises. Not only do these design-led activities offer creative and other employment opportunities, but they also offer the opportunity to reorient the economy as a whole by encouraging design-led innovation in more traditional manufacturing activities.

This vision of an enabling sector can be seen clearly in relation to the broader clothing industry. After having successfully distinguished designer fashion from the textile and clothing industry as a whole, the former is now seen as a catalyst to reinvent the broader clothing industry, which is understood to have far greater employment and export-earning potential than designer fashion per se (Martin 2002). In its publicity magazine *Venture*, Industry New Zealand frequently uses designer fashion as a role model for inspiring other niche clothing and related fashion enterprises (see Gale 2001; Leslie 2003; Martin 2002; and Ryan 2001). In reconstituting the wider clothing and apparel industry as innovative and design led, designer fashion does the work envisaged by the term "enabling sector."

The knowledge economy project is more explicitly after neoliberal and nationally focused than the globalization project. It has helped to make designer fashion amenable to a particular form of rule by forming the industry apparatus needed for remotely directed self-regulation and new relationships with the state. Industry associations fit neatly into the neoliberal language of private authority, market, enterprise, and self-regulation and the after neoliberal language of partnership, joint action, and consortia. The knowledge economy project is also premised on a distinctive understanding of designer fashion. Imagined as both a successful industry and an enabling sector, designer fashion is to help create the entrepreneurial, innovative, design-led small businesses that, it is hoped, will generate new forms of economic growth and employment.

Creative Cities

The designer fashion industry has also been harnessed to major urban regeneration projects in New Zealand's major cities. These cities are all encouraging "fashion districts" akin to those found in European and North American cities (Crewe and Beaverstock 1998; Scott 2000) – although they are working with much younger fashion quarters that are overwhelmingly about consumption rather than long histories of production. Unlike the nationally focused knowledge economy project, urban regeneration projects are localized initiatives that articulate emerging forms of urban governance with new aesthetics and landscapes of consumption. They seek to re-create cultural and economic vibrancy and relate them to the imaginaries of the "creative city"

(Florida 2002a; Hall 2000; Landry 2000). New state agencies also become visible when attention is turned to this political project; while national government agencies remain involved, the urban regeneration strategies of after neoliberalism are largely the domain of urban and regional governments.

Auckland's High Street was an early exemplar of these processes. Fashion designers had been resident in this area from the early to mid-1980s, reflecting both low rentals and long-standing fashion retailing in this part of the city (Lloyd-Jenkins 2003). In 1999, the redevelopment of the adjacent Chancery area sought to capitalize on the presence of the designers, with the developers aiming to "extend the area's reputation as Auckland's mecca for high fashion and café society" (Kroon, cited in Anderson 1999). While they had in mind Versace, Hugo Boss, and Esprit rather than New Zealand designers, the Auckland City Council later saw an opportunity to reconstitute the High Street precinct as an integrated "fashion district." Eighteen months later, citing the increasing international profile of New Zealand designers and its tourism potential, the council upgraded the streets in the area, installed signs that delineated this area from the rest of the inner city, and deliberately fostered both designer fashion and cognate activities in the area. Today the precinct is explicitly marketed as the "fashion capital of New Zealand" (Larner and Molloy with Goodrum 2007).

Following Auckland's lead, economic development agencies in Wellington, Christchurch, and Dunedin have also sought to develop new urban landscapes based on the small owner-operator-retailers who dominate New Zealand designer fashion. Wellington features a fashion precinct in a redeveloped bank building, while Dunedin has included fashion in its entrepreneurial, creative city approach to economic development. Christchurch uses the presence of a well-respected design course at the local polytechnic, encouraging new designers to take up low-rent premises in its own High Street area proximate to this educational institution. In all these efforts, designer fashion is explicitly linked to the rise of intense forms of urban living and associated aesthetics of consumption (high-density apartments, cafés, other high-status consumption spaces). The clustering of such activities, and the density of consumption activity that they foster, are understood as key to the success of these creative city strategies.

The emphasis on geographical proximity and clustering can also be seen in the designer fashion industry incubator schemes that have emerged as a key instrument in these urban regeneration strategies. Incubators have been established to bridge the gap between aspirant students and successful designers (see Bill 2003) by developing small-business capabilities, nurturing entrepreneurial impulses, and providing a supportive infrastructure in which targeted creative talents can be refined (Hodgson 2001). They have also come to express the urban regeneration aspirations of local governments as different cities have recognized their varied potential.

For example, the Dunedin Incubator is a local government-initiated partnership between local and central government agencies, local capital and educational institutions, and local fashion and business people, who volunteer as mentors and lend equipment.[5] The Dunedin City Council regards designer fashion as having great "potential" in a city with a prior reputation for its creative industries (McCarthy 2003). The incubator aims to guide young designers through the problems of establishing and nurturing a small-business venture. If accepted as "tenants," designers locate their businesses on the incubator premises, pay a subsidized monthly rental, and receive facilities and services, including studio space, administrative support, business and design mentoring, retail space in the incubator's outlet, and public relations support and media exposure.

Christchurch's fashion cluster initiative, run by the region's economic development agency Canterbury Development Corporation (CDC), has similar aims but takes a different form. The CDC is highly active in employment creation and vocational training. Its cluster initiatives provide a range of free information and support services designed to support and develop small- and medium-scale businesses (90 percent of Canterbury's 32,000 workers are in companies of fewer than 10 workers). These services are complemented by varied employment services, from educational initiatives to community employment schemes and unemployment assistance. The fashion cluster is seen as an attractive vocational education prospect for the city's young people and is inspired by the city's history as a leading centre of sportswear and textile manufacturing.

In these urban regeneration strategies and the incubators that they have spawned, we see a third spatial imaginary. In both creative city and regional development discourses, geographical proximity is key. The ambition of both urban and regional governments is to co-locate key activities in ways that will foster the sharing of industry activity and infrastructure, cultural capital, and tacit knowledge. Thus, whereas the globalization project privileges the global production network and the knowledge economy project, the enabling sector, urban regeneration strategies are supported by notions of clustering and industrial districts. As after neoliberal strategies, they are explicitly regionalized

– located to take advantage of, and add growth potential to, local resources, networks, and development trajectories (Martin 2002).

Social Development

The fourth, and most recent, project in which designer fashion features is that of social development. This is the after neoliberal political project that has received the bulk of attention in broader discussions of "neoliberalization." Analysts have focused their attention on the recent proliferation of community- and locality-based approaches to policy development and social service provision. It is argued that these initiatives are part of "roll-out neoliberalism" (Peck and Tickell 2002) – the contested processes of experimentation through which various state agencies are trying to distance themselves from the more market approaches of "roll-back neoliberalism" and re-create conditions for social integration around markets.

In this political project, designer fashion is deployed as a means of building social capital and encouraging cultural diversity. In the loose ensemble of initiatives that we label the social development project, designer fashion presents opportunities to build on the regional development discourses, developing locality and community capacity by entrepreneurializing and productively occupying the young and marginalized. While the national state is a key player here, these initiatives are neither bureaucratized nor driven exclusively from the top, as are the globalization and knowledge economy projects. Rather, social development projects are positioned in spheres where particular community groups have established social and cultural expertise. Indeed, the examples presented here illustrate the potential of designer fashion as an activity around which new relationships between government departments, local authorities, and community organizations are being forged in a distinctive collaborative partnering governmentality (Larner and Craig 2005).

Thus, in contrast to its counterparts in Dunedin and Christchurch, Auckland's Fashion Incubator of New Zealand (FASHINZ) was inspired by a model of employment creation and community development assistance. It was explicitly targeted at young Maori and Pacific people, who experience high levels of unemployment. Organized as a charitable trust and funded by the Community Employment Group of the Department of Labour, which ran a series of cooperative, mentor-centred, and vocational ventures at the community scale, FASHINZ began with three resident designers on the premises of the Waipareira Trust, a high-profile urban Maori social service organization.

After receiving additional funding from INZ and Auckland City Council, and an unsuccessful period in High Street, it is now located well beyond the central city within Auckland University of Technology's (AUT) Technology Park. While its new location and links with AUT's School of Fashion recognize its wider agenda as an incubator for more mainstream aspirant designers, as discussed above, FASHINZ retains an accent on Pacific and Maori arts and community development. Indeed, its failure on High Street and return to a student setting highlight the significance of the gap between visions of designer fashion as successfully globalizing industry and designer fashion as community development.

In a parallel initiative, the Creative Communities Scheme, under which Creative New Zealand co-funds community-based art projects on a per capita basis with local authorities, seeks to use designer fashion as a means of building locally based community capacity. It recognizes the links between fashion as a globally positioned economic enterprise and fashion as a place-influenced creative art, and it has a mandate to promote the contribution of designer fashion as creative industry to Brand New Zealand and as cultural expression to community cultures. Thus, under the Creative Communities Scheme, the small Waikato port town-cum-surfing mecca Raglan has stitched a thriving, small-scale, lifestyle fashion industry into its alternative culture. Similarly, until recently, the Wearable Arts Awards in Nelson allowed this small town to link the long-established alternative lifestyles of the local area to a highly successful venture into regional and national tourism. The recent relocation of the actual Wearable Arts Awards ceremony to Wellington only serves to underscore the tensions between fashion as enabling new forms of globalizing economic development and the emphasis on locally based social capital integral to the social development project.

The social development project privileges New Zealand's Maori and Pacific communities. While currently underrepresented as fashion designers, members of Maori and Pacific communities are intimately involved in urban cultural activities. Creative New Zealand has sought to commercialize these activities as creative industries. The idea is to "industrialize" activities such as those that underpin Style Pasifika – an annual celebration of Pacific Island visual arts fusing traditional and contemporary art forms in fashion – now in its tenth year and timed before Fashion Week. In 2005, highlights from this show were allocated a catwalk slot in the Fashion Week program. One of the highlights of this performance was the presentation of clothing by

Charmaine Love, a young Maori designer who has supplied clothing with Maori motifs to celebrated international popular music stars (Robbie Williams, 50 Cent, and the female vocalist from The Black Eyed Peas) and whose business partner, Maori golfer Michael Campbell, wore a shirt of her design when he won the US Open earlier in 2005. Seen in this context, designer fashion holds out the potential not only to promote social inclusion but also to actively encourage and support cultural diversity.

The diverse initiatives happening under the umbrella of social development focus on the spaces of community and locality. In these initiatives, designer fashion is not so much an economic enterprise as it is a means of building the networks of trust and affinity that underpin "social capital." It thus contributes to the building of community capacity. The targeting of young and/or problematic groups/people through creative activities such as designing fashion generates inclusive effects while stimulating entrepreneurialism and business subjectivities in marginalized groups. In this way, government support for designer fashion becomes both legitimation and legitimate welfare targeting. Moreover, whereas the targets of the earlier political projects are the actual fashion designers and cognate activities, herein the emphasis is on fashion as a means of accessing marginalized people and places and drawing them into broader economic and social processes.

After Neoliberalism, Designer Fashion, and the Political Economy of Scale

In this chapter, we have represented New Zealand designer fashion as a globalizing export industry in and of itself as well as a key instrument in projects of national economic growth, urban regeneration, and social development. It would be easy to interpret the four political projects as representing the gradual emergence of a competition state: going global, picking winners, revitalizing cities and regions, and building social capital. Yet, although there is a certain chronology to these projects, we think it premature to see them as component parts of an overall political rationality. "Built" (to use Jessop's language) explicitly from the mid-1990s in New Zealand, the economic and social configurations that characterize after neoliberalism are emerging out of a range of political projects that are only now being consciously aligned into a new stance on how to participate in the globalizing economy. Each of these projects constitutes its objects and subjects of governance in distinctive ways. Moreover, while there are many conjunctures between them, the ambitions of these projects may work, if not in opposition then at least tangentially to each other – global versus domestic orientations, elitist versus democratic impulses, national versus regional economic ambitions, economic versus social capital. The designer fashion industry is thus expected to perform multiple tasks in after neoliberalism – to earn foreign exchange, produce a particular image of New Zealand, generate employment, contribute to a national development project centred on creativity, and distribute its gains widely. We conclude by using this material to make a series of claims about scale theory and the nature of the state spatialities that come together in the new political formation that we label after neoliberalism.

First, we should be wary of treating any state, let alone that regulating the instability of after neoliberalism, as coherent and unified. This is not a novel observation; it is very familiar to political economists in general and scale theorists in particular. However, it has slipped from prominence in a literature concerned with the overall rationality of neoliberalism(s) and the discussions of the implications for state spatialities. Our work reemphasizes the fragmented nature of the contemporary state power in which there are non-orchestrated and often competing configurations of authority and expertise. Not only are political projects multiple, but they also involve the multiple performances of diverse state and other agencies. Thus, Trade New Zealand provided financial assistance in establishing export markets. It has also acted as the guardian of Brand New Zealand, establishing a proprietary interest for the state and in return attaching the brand and state credibility directly to the product and the company. Industry New Zealand has supported designer fashion by providing infrastructural support and sponsoring regional development initiatives in an effort to foster growth in domestic labour markets. Although the recent amalgamation of these two agencies into Trade and Enterprise New Zealand signals a renewed effort to achieve a more integrated and rational bureaucratization of economic development, there is still a dual aspect to their operations. Smaller but critical roles have been played by the Department of Labour, city councils, and regional development agencies. There are other state initiatives that we haven't discussed in as much detail. For example, in addition to the Creative Communities Scheme, the arts funding body Creative New Zealand has become centrally involved in constituting the vision of a future national prosperity built on the creative industries via the notion of an "imagination economy." Each of these arms of the state has played a distinctive, albeit shifting and sometimes contradictory, part in efforts to use designer fashion as a means of articulating nation, industries, cities, regions, and communities in after neoliberalism.

Second, globalization is becoming the taken-for-granted "context" in which these diverse political projects are situated. Seen in this light, it is clear that globalization is indeed a governmental rationality (Larner and Walters 2004). Our analysis highlights the multiple ways in which fashion is being used as a way of articulating New Zealanders into global flows and networks economically and culturally, revealing the increasing depth of the vision encompassed by this term. It is not only the export-oriented industries that fall under Trade New Zealand's purview that are to be the objects and subjects of globalization; so, too, are regions, cities, and communities. Hence Jessop's (2002a) observation that the state is playing a major role in the material and discursive constitution of the globalizing, networked, knowledge-based economy that its activities are seeking to govern. This approach is helpful because it directs attention to the *post facto* emergence of an overall political rationality and the attempts to impose a relative internal unity on the varied activities that make up contemporary forms of governance. However, in the determination to identify a coherent sociopolitical formation, assumed to be necessary to underwriting a new period of accumulation, scale theorists tend to emphasize the preconstituted at the expense of the constituted nature of governmental formations. We agree that the apparently incommensurate political projects of after neoliberalism can be related to enduring problems of the state but would argue that this *raison d'etat* emerges as much out of these diverse projects and experiments as it does out of any prior ideological or structural-functional coherence.

Third, just as after neoliberalism is not a singular state project, neither is a single state spatiality being constituted. In our account of the New Zealand designer fashion industry, we have shown how these political projects have given rise to multiple "institutional-geographical" (Brenner 2004) configurations that have distinctive spatialities. While it may be tempting to think of these various configurations – global production networks, creative cities, clusters, and communities – as scales, to do so would obscure the fact that they reflect quite different spatial imaginaries that have given rise to specific political arrangements. Nor would we suggest that, in the context of this small globalizing nation-state, the predominant spatial imaginary is that of the network. Rather, we would stress the diversity of state spatialities being constituted in the contemporary period. Close inspection is needed to explore exactly the processes by which particular spatial imaginaries are made material and distinctive state spatialities are being assembled in particular spheres.

Fourth, as we have also shown, industry, state, and nation are being remade as the New Zealand designer fashion industry has been identified, carved out, measured, and mobilized through these diverse political projects. In this context, we would emphasize the co-constitutive aspects of these processes. Our analysis has not simply shown how the designer fashion industry and fashion designers have been constituted as objects and subjects of governance; it has also shown how the processes associated with the reconfiguration of designer fashion have given rise to new and multiple state spatialities. These different state spatialities have not only helped to fracture coterminous understandings of nation, state, and economy but have also placed pressure on extant economic, social, and cultural identities. Globalizing New Zealanders, entrepreneurial New Zealanders, creative New Zealanders, and socially connected New Zealanders all read and engage with the designer fashion industry in different ways.

NOTES

1. The University of Auckland Fashion Project is a multidisciplinary project involving scholars in geography, women's studies, and sociology, including two postdoctoral fellows and three graduate students. Research to date has included interviews with established designers and/or their assistants, the "new generation" designers who participated in 2002 Fashion Week, industry specialists, and government officials. We also draw on commissioned reports, government and firm websites, media reports and interviews, and observations at New Zealand Fashion Weeks.
2. Trade New Zealand and Industry New Zealand have since been restructured into a single government agency, a move that underlines our broader argument.
3. See http://www.finz.co.nz.
4. See http://www.gif.med.govt.nz.
5. See http://www.dfi.co.nz/news.cfm.

10
Public Health and the Political Economy of Scale: Implications for Understanding the Response to the 2003 Severe Acute Respiratory Syndrome (SARS) Outbreak in Toronto

S. Harris Ali and Roger Keil

The movement of infectious disease pathogens between locations can be influenced by a myriad of social and political factors. Following the register proposed by Jessop, Brenner, and Jones (2008), territory, place, scale, and network are various sociospatial dimensions to be taken into account when analyzing how human societies are affected by the movement of pathogens. A large geographical literature has examined the relationships of contagion and cities in particular (for a review, see Ali and Keil 2008). In this chapter, we concentrate on the role of scale in particular. What implications do scale-based considerations have for the politics of place, given the neoliberal reforms that have so dramatically influenced the character of the public health sector in localities throughout Canada? The key question – not frequently asked within conventional epidemiological accounts of pathogen tracking – of how social and political conditions influence the transmission of disease is particularly pertinent since we exist in a "globalized world." How do globalizing sociopolitical forces affect the dynamics of infectious disease diffusion? How do these global forces affect the ability of local public agencies to respond to outbreaks within their jurisdictions?

In addressing such questions, the issue of scale becomes critical. In the highly connected network society (Castells 1996), a pathogen such as the SARS coronavirus, which infected more than 8,000 and killed more than 700 worldwide in 2003, can easily traverse the globe in record time. In the process, the virus can effectively "jump scales" of various sorts – geographical, temporal, political – demanding a response not only by agencies at the local, regional, national, international, and global scales but also by individuals. Of particular importance is the issue of how the governance and sovereignty of the urban and national jurisdictions are influenced by the policies of supranational agencies and agreements such as the EU, NAFTA, WTO, World Bank, and IMF, which now exert new and significant influences in the international economy through the regulation of global competition, international trade, and foreign direct investment (Amin 2002; Brenner 2000; Lefebvre 1979). The emerging relationships between the local/national and the supranational jurisdictions highlight the importance of what Jessop (2000) refers to as the "politics of interscalar contestation." Here we focus on the way in which various scales of governance intersect to produce a specific global city governance of health and emerging infectious disease (EID).

At all scales, institutional (e.g., hospitals) and procedural (e.g., quarantines), interactions occur and topological fixings (e.g., airport screenings) take place to create a layered complex of policies, actions, and (non-)decisions. The mobility of the virus also creates significant difficulties in pathogen tracking and by extension makes responses at all levels challenging, particularly in light of the need for trans-scalar coordination to ensure that effective measures are taken to contain the disease threat. The latter is particularly problematic because the jumping of viruses between localities has important implications for jurisdictional capabilities in terms of outbreak response and raises issues of sovereignty – the right of governments to respond to public health threats in an autonomous manner free from "external" political influences, particularly the influences of other nation-states and international bodies. Is a particular threat of infectious disease defined as a localized, contained outbreak, which would require local public health actions adopted at the discretion of local officials? Or is it defined as a global pandemic, necessitating the concerted and coordinated involvement of supranational actors, such as the World Health Organization, in the name of global public health security? As we will see in the SARS case, defining the scale of the risk of infectious disease outbreak has important political and governance implications for the nature of the response to the disease threat.

Public Health Governance

Let us begin with a sketch of what the governance of public health looked like before the SARS crisis hit. Since the nineteenth century, the Westphalian world of nation-states constituted the political scaffolding for the development of a global public health governance system. The Westphalian world was predicated on the notion of national sovereignty, non-interference, and legal contractual relations between nation-states. For global public health governance, there was the added reality of the principle of weighing global health concerns against the economic and political interests of nation-states (Fidler 2004a, b). The Canadian situation has largely reflected this scalar architecture of global health governance, as can be seen in this description of the Institute on Governance: "In Canada, the governance of health care is built on intergovernmental cooperation, reflecting a formal division of powers regarding health care as outlined in the Canadian Constitution and the Charter of Rights and Freedoms. In addition, governance of health care also takes place outside the governmental sphere. This complexity requires organizations, sectors, regions, First Nations communities and governments to forge capacities to govern" (Institute on Governance).

The role of urban governance in the management of societal matters in a post-Westphalian world is often underestimated. As we have shown elsewhere (Keil and Ali, 2008) in greater detail, this traditional distribution of responsibilities is lopsided. While the bulk of public health work is performed at the local level, there is a distinct absence of any reference to the role of cities in health governance. This omission can be partly credited to the traditional obscurity that municipal politics suffers in the Canadian state architecture. Still, urban public health authorities and their associates in local hospitals, urban non-state actors in the health field, as well as workers in urban medical settings have played an important role in the detection, identification, and monitoring of, and the fight against, EIDs in particular. In Canada, as elsewhere, they have provided the core responsibilities of public health – assessment, policy development, assurance – often without support and sometimes in conflict with and contradistinction to higher-level health authorities (Rodwin and Gusmano 2002, 446). This all occurred in a climate in which downloading and neoliberal state restructuring stacked the cards against local health authorities. Lim et al. (2004, 697) have said about the Ontario situation during SARS that "the province of Ontario was ill-prepared to deal with an infectious disease threat on such a scale. In Canada, the provision of health care, including public health, is a provincial responsibility. However, *the financial and operational responsibility for public health had increasingly been shifted to municipalities* such that, at the time of the SARS outbreak, funding was shared equally between the two levels of government. This funding shift created a decentralised public-health system, with the province's 37 public-health units operating quite independently of each other" (emphasis added).

Public health has, indeed, traditionally focused on the municipal level, with local boards of health connecting into a hierarchically structured system of ascending responsibility, which ends in the sovereign government and bureaucracy of the nation-state. One consequence has been that information on the state of health in cities is hard to come by for the metropolitan scale: statistics mostly use the national or substate scale as the area of reference (Rodwin 2008). Over the past decade, even before the SARS crisis hit, urban health had become subject to intense scrutiny, triggered partly by the AIDS pandemic and partly by reemerging diseases such as TB (Gandy and Zumla 2002). One inconclusive debate is whether there is a health penalty attached to living in cities or whether there is an urban health advantage.

In a longitudinal study of four of the largest cities in the OECD – London, Paris, New York, and Tokyo – Victor Rodwin and his co-researchers examined the preparedness of metropolitan health systems to deal with the specific problems associated with life in large cities. There are many differences in which health policies are scaled in the United States, the United Kingdom, France, and Japan, and there are differences in the socioeconomic and sociospatial distribution in all four global cities. How and at what scale strategic public health interventions take place varies significantly. In all cases but New York, national governments play a large role in governing health issues in their respective cities. Yet, Rodwin (2008, 44) concludes that "what is perhaps most striking is the emergence of convergent trends in public health intervention. Among all four cities, there is increasing awareness, among public health leaders, that the neighborhood is a critical spatial unit for targeted interventions to protect against risk factors for disease and to promote health."

While the strategic locus of intervention seems to have moved to the scale of the neighbourhood, it remains unresolved whether the new attention to metropolitan health has also shifted the scales of governance. Until recently, the interactive, multiscalar regulation of public health-related matters was fairly invisible in this governance network. While it was not the first such case, SARS changed this feature of invisibility rather drastically and rapidly, at least in the cities where outbreaks occurred. The outbreaks laid open, with deadly precision, the interconnectivity of places that were affected and bodies that were infected, necessitating a rethinking of previously rather hermetically sealed – or rather siloed, vertically hierarchized – systems of local health governance. New horizontal, urban-to-urban and urban-to-global, institutional connections across all scales were made visible. A new network of actors poured global activities against EIDs into a new mould. Instead of the previously highly centralized and industrialized nationally based efforts of the post-World War II years, this "involved a decentralized, horizontally integrated network of small projects – academic researchers, private vaccine and drug developers, epidemiologic surveillance projects and field laboratories – whose coordination is made possible by information-processing and communications technology" (King 2004, 70).

Thus, the rescaling of global health governance added up to a strengthening of the American position in a post-Westphalian world order under American hegemony, where global health issues where "framed" in ways compatible with internal US concerns. As King observed, "in contrast to Roemer's idealistic vision of global health, the emerging diseases campaign presented a set of scalar tools for reframing 'international' problems in language palatable to American interests" (2004, 76). At the same time, it strengthened the hand of the World Health Organization in dealing with future outbreaks. In the process, the WHO changed the substance and scalar reach of its policies significantly. According to Fidler (2004a, b), the WHO's response to the SARS outbreak was radical because it broke with the tradition of minimizing its influence on matters of international trade and travel. The WHO constitution and the 1951 International Health Regulations (IHR) did not grant the WHO independent authority to make travel recommendations. In fact, one of the stated objectives of the IHR was to "ensure the maximum security against the international spread of diseases *with minimum interference with world trade and travel* ... [it] identified specific diseases (e.g. cholera, plague, and yellow fever) and required WHO Member States to report outbreaks of these diseases and to limit trade- and travel-restricting health measures taken in response to outbreaks in other countries" (Fidler 2004a). In the wake of the SARS outbreaks, this principle of minimum interference in world trade and travel was overturned. In May 2003, the WHO modified the regulations so that it could be formally empowered to make travel alerts, advisories, and recommendations when needed in the future. By making recommendations directly to non-state actors (i.e., travellers), the WHO exercised power against its member states. We will come back to the travel advisory below.

In fact, globally active research networks have long subverted the national boundaries and hierarchies of health governance and have created a complex web of knowledge production and dissemination, which links observers in rural Chinese areas to the most sophisticated health labs around the world (Abraham 2004; Reynolds 2004; York 2005). On the basis of the existing – competitive yet interdependent – networks of EID research that span the globe, the 2003 SARS crisis led to an unprecedented level of cooperation among the world's best research virologists (Abraham 2004; Heyman 2005). Coordinated by the WHO's Klaus Stöhr, this cooperation led to the quick identification of the SARS coronavirus by Malik Peiris in a Hong Kong reference laboratory. This cooperation was short-lived as the race for publication of the results ensued shortly after the collective work. It was marred by an attempt by the American CDC to claim discovery of the elusive virus. Nevertheless, "this novel approach to science was a definitive improvement on the earlier patterns of laboratories working in isolation" (Abraham 2004, 95).

To some degree, this global cooperation of specialized laboratory actors amounts to a depoliticization of governance as subpolitical spaces of scientific inquiry replace and supplement the traditional hierarchy of public health and virological and epidemiological governance. The direct link between the global health problems "out there" and the specialized space of the laboratory, where solutions are to be found "in here," simplified the complexities of what led to disease in the first place and abstracted from the scales in between that are the subject of this chapter. Similarly, the new focus on the global scale (beyond the international) of a post-Westphalian world of governance tends to lead to disregard for subnational and civil society-based (non-state) forms of health governance. In this "new" world, nation-states face competing claims for public authority and power not just from global state institutions and global capitalist corporations but also from subnational state structures, non-state agencies, and organized civil society. Against this background, we look specifically at the metropolitan scale as both a receptacle and a switching station of EIDs and as a level of governance at which complex, politically produced (rather than laboratory-made) forms of health governance are being forged in more or less democratic processes of governance.[1]

The growing awareness of the interlocking health governance scales is linked to the realization that emerging diseases are embedded in a politics of scale (King 2004). Garrett (1996), Preston (1989), and others forcefully made the point more than a decade ago that diseases and the regulation of the national body by the national body politic were now being reregulated in a newly globalized system of health governance. As King shows, the notion of "(re)emerging" infectious diseases was itself a specific historical product and project of social forces in public health and beyond. Much more, after a decade of AIDS research and action, and the growing concern with exotic diseases such as ebola in the early 1990s, policy makers in national public health administrations became acutely aware of what they considered new global-local interplays in the outbreak and treatment of emerging infectious diseases. Furthermore, "the concept of emerging diseases offered journalists a powerful scalar resource for characterizing individual outbreaks as incidents of global significance" (King 2004, 70; see also Buell 2004, 129-42; Davis 2005; Garrett 2005; Gillmor 2004; and Specter 2005). For actors as diverse as military planners and community health advocates, the link of infectious disease to globalization provided a new plane on which health policies could be reevaluated and revamped.

Microbial Traffic and the Global Flow of Human Contacts

Morse (1993) has introduced the notion of "viral traffic" as a conceptualization of the movement and interaction of pathogens. The concept can be applied to all infectious disease microorganisms, employing the term "microbial traffic." Mayer (2000) identifies several dimensions of microbial traffic: (a) cross-species transfer; (b) spatial diffusion; (c) changes in the human-environment relationship; and (d) the pathogenic evolution or change in the structure and immunogenicity of earlier pathogens. The first three dimensions have particular relevance to the "scale jumping" of the SARS virus.

The SARS coronavirus is believed to have emanated from civet cats or raccoon dogs that populated the live animal markets in Guangdong Province, China (Naylor 2003, 23; Peiris et al. 2003). Such "exotic" animal species are used in both food and traditional medicine in southern China, but contact with these species in live animal markets facilitated the cross-species transfer of pathogens from animals to humans. The unsanitary conditions commonly found within these types of marketplaces are particularly conducive to the crossover because they provide a breeding ground for new flu strains (CIA 2003, 7), thus increasing the probability of zoonotic transmission.

The spatial diffusion of the SARS coronavirus has been well documented (Naylor 2003). In February 2003, a physician treating SARS patients in southern China travelled to Hong Kong, where he infected as many as eleven hotel guests, including an elderly woman from Toronto. These infected guests continued on their travels to different parts of the world, spreading the disease globally (WHO 2004). The Canadian index patient returned to Toronto on 23 February 2003, where she later died at home. Her son (the primary case) died shortly thereafter in a Toronto hospital. Secondary and tertiary cases were developed after sharing a room with the primary case, and the disease quickly spread to at least thirty-eight others, including hospital workers and visitors (Low 2003). Unlike the first outbreak, a second SARS outbreak in May 2003 in Toronto was limited to one hospital.

Both outbreaks reveal the extent to which the flow of human contacts was crucial to the microbial traffic flow, and they highlight the importance of the human-built environment relationship of hospitals in disease transmission. The "flow of human contacts" (Affonso, Andrews, and Jeffs 2004) refers to the configurations of spatial movements made by individuals within and between various *health care* and *community spaces* – a flow pattern in which health care workers became facilitators of microbial traffic not only within but also between hospitals.

The flow of human contacts was also crucial to disease transmission between cities (i.e., community spaces). These processes of human interaction across transnational communities occurred in the scaled realities of a world economy characterized by increasingly free trade and liberalized markets on the one hand and severe controls and regulation of human migration on the other. States and borders mean very much on both sides of the diasporic reality: the sender and recipient states and cities. Often cast away in a sea of economic and human insecurity, pawns on the chessboard of international investments and labour market structuration, migrants are also active participants in the construction of new transnational worlds in which even the most vulnerable, disenfranchised migrant contributes to the making of a new multifaceted global reality, in which proximities and distances are redefined along many scaled lines. Yet, this reality also highlights the importance of a topological view of space in an analysis of disease diffusion. It is possible to argue that the virus exposed the rigidities that sometimes hamper scalar thinking when it is tied too closely to the logic of the state and underestimates the multifarious connectivities inherent in sociospatial relations that make up the city (Amin 2002; Amin and Thrift 2002).

Microbial Traffic and the Flow of Human Contacts within the Global Cities Network

One scale that is distinctly influential in a rescaled, post-Westphalian world of health governance is the network of global cities in general and individual global city-regions in particular. The "global cities" perspective describes the emergence of a dynamic interconnected network of a relatively small number of very large metropolitan areas, which exercise a disproportionate amount of political and economic power in the transnationalized context (Sassen 1991, 2000; see Brenner and Keil 2006 for an overview). With reference to the microbial traffic and flow of human contacts involved in the SARS outbreak, a key question is how the nature of the threat of infectious disease outbreaks has changed with the alteration of patterns in microbial traffic vis-à-vis the global city network (Ali and Keil 2006). From the vantage point of the global cities hypothesis, globalization is seen as producing new linkages among corporations, international organizations, governments, communities, families, and particularly cities (Waters 2001) – linkages facilitated through the technological connectivity available through new communication technologies (Graham and Marvin 2001).

In the study of Toronto as a "global" city lies an important key to understanding the social, cultural, and geographical dimensions of a public health threat that involved 438 probable and suspected SARS cases, including 44 deaths (Naylor 2003). Furthermore, the fact that SARS outbreaks occurred in Asian global cities such as Beijing, Hong Kong, Singapore, and Taipei (WHO 2004) brings to the fore the question of how the links between Toronto and other global cities influenced the transmission of the SARS virus. This is particularly important in light of Yulong and Hamnett's (2001) finding that rapid economic development in the Asian cities of Beijing, Shanghai, and Hong Kong has led to their increased importance in the global cities network – a development bolstered by the strong and conscious efforts of the Chinese state to integrate these cities into the globalized economy (see also Ng and Hills 2003). In such circumstances, the relationship between Toronto and Asian global cities is noteworthy because of the increased prospects of networked trade between Toronto and China's emerging global cities. Bolstered by the large Chinese Canadian community in Toronto – Canadian citizens of Chinese origin comprise about 8.7 percent (410,000) of the 4.7 million people living in the Toronto metropolitan area, and the city is the preferred destination of most immigrants from Asian countries to Canada (Li 1998) – increased trade and interaction between Toronto's Asian diasporic community and the newly opened Chinese cities would not be unexpected.

The microbial traffic and flow of human contacts involved in the SARS outbreaks did indeed seem to reflect the patterned network of the global cities. First, it has been noted that overall population travel flux and the international movements of passengers have accelerated over the past few decades, and global cities have served as nodes in this network of travel (Keeling 1995; Smith and Timberlake 2001). These routinized networks of travel patterns in turn have made global cities particularly vulnerable to infectious disease threats over the long term, particularly in relation to the lateral scale jumping of pathogens (i.e., from one global city to another). Thus, not only do global cities serve as nodal points for the flow of information, commodities, financial transactions, and cultural goods that are commonly associated with global city functions, but they also serve as nodal points for the transmission of disease.

Second, the mechanism of disease transmission via global cities becomes even more significant when one considers the phenomenon of "superspreaders" – individuals who are especially infectious (for reasons currently unknown) (Gostin, Bayer, and Fairchild 2003). Thus, although it was commonly thought that the most at risk were individuals with close contacts to SARS victims – family members and health care workers – the transmission to many patrons at one hotel in Hong Kong and the SARS outbreak affecting over 200 residents in a single Hong Kong apartment complex bring to the fore the significance of superspreaders. The presence of a superspreader in an aircraft or in the crowded urban area of a global city is therefore quite disturbing.

Third, as Canada's global city, Toronto shares certain attributes associated with other global cities, such as an increase in large-scale immigration (Samers 2002; Sassen 1991). Indeed, Toronto is known as one of the most multicultural cities in the world and is home to many different diasporic groups (Balakrishnan and Selvanathan 1990; Driedger 2003). Thus, the relationship between Toronto and other global cities in the network is not based purely on economic, communication, and resource flows but also on cultural and familial linkages between Toronto's diasporic communities and their respective ancestral communities. In this context, Urry (2004) observes that a critically important aspect of the social life of members of diasporic communities occurs during "occasioned encounters" in which individuals travel in order to be physically co-present with one or more others for specific periods of time and in specific places (Boden and Molotch 1994).

These types of ethnocultural linkages, provided by occasioned encounters, also have implications for the microbial traffic of the SARS virus – in relation to both the lateral jumping of scales between global cities and the lateral spread of the disease within particular local diasporic communities commonly nestled within global cities.

The WHO and the Global City: A Multiscalar Conflict over Health Governance

In the past decade, metropolitan governance has begun to locate itself self-consciously in a context of global interurban competition (Keil and Boudreau

2005; Olds and Yeung 2005; Shen 2004). Whether it was high-end business services, high culture and spectacle, or tourism, or now "creativity" (Peck, this volume) global city-regions have now made their weight felt by acting, ostensibly autonomously, in a globalized frame of reference in which nation-states often play the role of enabler and observer rather than direct actor. Inversely, global-scale institutions have begun to recognize and deal directly with municipal and regional jurisdictions. In the SARS case, the WHO was one such global actor, which implemented a policy that directly affected (global) cities. An important interscalar conflict thus arose between the City of Toronto and the World Health Organization – a conflict that raises questions about the ability of a municipal body to govern public health within its own jurisdiction.

In the third week of April 2003, the WHO took the unprecedented step of issuing a travel advisory to Toronto and other areas such as China's Guangdong and Shanxi Provinces as well as the cities of Beijing and Hong Kong – recommending that visitors postpone all but essential trips to these areas. The WHO's warnings represented "the toughest travel advisories in its 55-year history" (Gostin, Bayer, and Fairchild 2003, 3231). One week later, a delegation that included Toronto public health officials, the provincial health minister, and the public health commissioner visited the WHO headquarters in Geneva. In response to the delegation's request, the travel advisory to Toronto was lifted after the WHO was given assurances that the city would intensify the screening of travellers to and from Canada.

This episode raises important issues concerning the governance aspects of public health in the globalized context. The WHO has a mandate to regulate international health matters, including the prioritization of various global health initiatives, the international coordination of health surveillance systems, and emergency responses to outbreaks (Price-Smith 2002, 134). At the same time, the WHO faces certain restrictions in the exercise of its power as it must deal with the sensitive area of national sovereignty within the international context. For example, it cannot intercede in an epidemic without first receiving consent from the afflicted nation-state (Garrett 1996). Furthermore, until very recently, only three diseases – cholera, plague, and yellow fever – have been subject to international regulation wherein the WHO has the power to dispatch United Nations officials to help regulate the movement of goods and people in an effort to limit cross-border epidemics (Garrett 1996). Although historically the WHO did not directly involve itself in the governance of a sovereign state, as doing so would have been in violation of the right to national sovereignty, the case of SARS in Toronto demonstrates that the international body can in fact influence domestic actions by using the threat of a travel advisory as leverage, in essence, imposing the threat of economic consequences. As early as 26 April 2003, before the second wave of infections hit the city, it was estimated that Toronto lost about CDN $2.1 billion due to the SARS outbreak (Ferguson 2003; Van Rijn 2003).

It was clear that the delegation sent to Geneva by the City of Toronto was intended to counter the consequences of lost revenue in the hospitality/tourism and other economic sectors within the city. The WHO rescinded the travel advisory on the condition that the city would increase the level of monitoring of passengers at its major airport (as well as at other major airports in the country). In response, the City of Toronto acquired several expensive thermal scanning monitors to detect elevated body temperatures. By August 2003, over 5,232,000 inbound and outbound persons were screened at the six major international airports, with approximately 8,700 referred to the screening nurses (St. John 2003). The number of SARS cases identified by such means was nil, thus leading some to question the efficacy of such surveillance techniques (Garrett 1996; Naylor 2003; Walker 2003). This was not an unexpected result, because screening fails to detect those who may be incubating the disease but who may not exhibit any of the symptoms (Naylor 2003). It seems, therefore, that Toronto officials were forced to adopt rather misguided and costly surveillance techniques in order to satisfy an external international body.

On a related note, the director of Health Canada's Centre for Emergency Preparedness and Response remarked that, since all SARS-infected patients in Toronto became ill only after arrival and sought help in the city's hospital emergency rooms, the new "border" for infectious diseases should be the hospital doors of the city and not the airport (St. John 2003) – an observation that highlights the increasing importance of studying the role of hospitals in the globalized context.

SARS and the Transition from "International Health" to "Global Health"

The response of both the WHO and the City of Toronto to the SARS outbreaks reflects the changing nature of infectious disease threats in the contemporary globalized world. The nature of the infectious disease threat has changed because the increasing mobility of individuals in the contemporary world, coupled with the ability to traverse vast distances over increasingly shorter time periods, has meant that microbes can no longer be viewed as "biologically stationary targets" that can be "geographically sequestered" through quarantine at a port, as was done in an earlier age of less mobility and slower travel times (Garrett 1996, 67). The changing character of the infectious disease threat also implies a transition from what was in the past considered "international health" to what can now be conceptualized as "global health." Lee, Fustukian, and Buse (2002) distinguish between the two, noting that international health refers to health matters involving two or more countries in which state actors hold primacy (e.g., in situations involving the quarantine of ships or the management of the threat of food-borne diseases from increased international trade by improving national, regional, and multilateral regulation of food production and trade). International health becomes global health, however, when the causes or consequences of a health issue circumvent, undermine, or are oblivious to the territorial boundaries of states and extend beyond the capacity of states to effectively address the causes and consequences through state institutions alone. Thus, in dealing with the transboundary global public health issue embodied in the SARS outbreak, the City of Toronto was forced to go beyond its formal jurisdiction to engage in dialogue with the supranational agency of the World Health Organization. Similarly, in dealing with a global health problem, the WHO had to reach beyond its conventional jurisdiction and intervene in domestic matters. The response to the SARS outbreak by Canada and the WHO represents one instance of a more general trend that is occurring with increasing globalization and the transition from international health to global health.

We have moved from a period of relative symmetry between the territorial boundaries of the state and its capacity to exert sovereign authority over its domestic population to a time in which the increasing porousness of national boundaries is eroding the power of the state – a porosity that is exemplified by the emerging network of global cities. According to Reinicke and Witte (2000), the impact of this trend has not been felt so much on formal or external sovereignty (i.e., the entitlement to rule over a defined territory) as internal sovereignty (i.e., the ability to articulate and pursue domestic policy). Although the global shift towards a world economy has perhaps been the leading driver of this redefinition of state capacities, the SARS outbreak demonstrated that this limiting of state power over domestic matters extends beyond governance over economic issues to include the field of health governance.

As such, the response to the SARS outbreak brought to the fore a general trend that was already under way: namely, the relative decline in the capacity of national policy makers to control health determinants of domestic populations because globalization, by its very nature, involves processes that transcend state boundaries.

Conclusion

Social and political conditions thus influence the transmission of disease in a manner that is expressive both of scalar hierarchies and of topological, networked relationships. In fact, the nested scales of health governance inside and among nation-states, as well as globally, are one important spatial framework for the spread of as well as the fight against infectious disease. Some flows of people, capital, knowledge, viruses, etc., among global cities violate these hierarchies as the scaffolding of the Westphalian system is tested through new topological relationships. The ability of local public agencies to respond to outbreaks in situ is compromised by the increased vulnerability brought on by globalization, on the one hand, and by the incursion into existing sovereignties by higher-level agencies, on the other. In both cases, such post-Westphalian insecurity has also led to interesting new discussions about the role of state and non-state actors in the global governance system. Finally, the implications for Toronto of the rescaling of the global governance of health in the face of EIDs have to be viewed in the context of neoliberal reforms that have changed the character of the public health sector in Canada.

ACKNOWLEDGMENTS

Research for this chapter was supported by a Social Sciences and Humanities Research Council Standard Grant.

NOTES

1   The latter focus on the urban scale and urban governance is based on the normative notion that urbanization as a social process (Lefebvre 2003a) strengthens our capacities as human beings to deal with risk and is fundamentally opposed to an antimodernist position taken in much of the literature reviewed by King – namely, "the idea of civilization as risk" (Rosenberg, cited in King 2004, 65).

11
Of Scalar Hierarchies and Welfare Redesign: Child Care in Four Canadian Cities

Rianne Mahon

The politics of scale continues to offer important insights into the restructuring of governance in the age of "glocalization." In particular, it provides a way of thinking about the changing place of national states that avoids the kind of zero sum thinking that often characterizes much of the globalization debate. Recently, however, scalar theory has come under attack by previous practitioners, especially for its emphasis on hierarchy. Yet, the notion of scalar hierarchies cannot be abandoned if we want to understand actually existing social relations and the governance structures in which they are enmeshed. The conception of hierarchy employed by political economists is also more complex than that suggested by the "Russian dolls" metaphor. It is not a question of a simple, singular hierarchy structuring interscalar arrangements and the social relations embedded therein. Rather, there is a multiplicity of diversely structured, overlapping interscalar rule regimes operative in and across diverse policy fields. While these arrangements clearly influence what happens at the local scale, sufficient room often exists for local actors to modify the effects.

It is not enough to assert that hierarchy, as used in the political economy of scale, is more complex and mutable than its critics would admit. The proof of the pudding is in the eating. In this chapter, therefore, the claim is supported by an analysis of the governance of child care provision in four Canadian cities.

Child care arrangements form an important part of welfare state redesign in many, if not all, OECD countries. They are becoming integral to social reproduction in postindustrial economies, where women form an increasingly important part of the labour force (Michel and Mahon 2002). The extent and form of provision are likely to be affected by national (and/or provincial) regulatory and funding regimes. In Canada, both the federal and the provincial governments are involved, with the key role being played by the provinces. Unlike social transfers, however, which national states can distribute directly to individuals, child care is a service produced and delivered at the local scale. Moreover, the impact of postindustrialism on labour markets, and, thus, the intensity and extent to which the need for non-parental child care is experienced, are likely to be greatest in major urban areas. The chapter accordingly focuses on child care in four of Canada's largest cities – Vancouver, Calgary, Toronto, and Montreal – each of which is subject to a distinct provincial regime through which federal contributions are filtered. Yet, as we shall see, these cities are more than "puppets on a string."

Welfare Redesign and Rescaling: Child Care in Four Canadian Cities

The literature that looks at the intersection of welfare state restructuring and rescaling tends to focus on the impact of neoliberalism. Thus, Swyngedouw (2004a, 41) suggests that "the restructuring and often outright attack on national welfare regimes ... leads to a downscaling (in size and space) of public money transfers, while privatisation permits a socially exclusive form of protection, shielding the bodies of the powerful, while leaving the bodies of the poor to their own devices." For Marston (2004, 174), too, neoliberalism has resulted in social reproduction being seen as of "decreasing salience in state practices." Peck and Tickell (2002), however, argue that neoliberalization involves a "rolling out" as well as a "rolling back" of the welfare state, giving it a more pronounced "disciplinary" profile. More specifically, Peck's (2001b) earlier work analyzed the turn from welfare to workfare and its intersection with rescaling processes in Canada, the United Kingdom, and the United States, as well as "the fast policy transfers" linking these three countries. This chapter focuses on another, explicitly gendered, aspect of welfare redesign – child care – in four Canadian cities.

This section accordingly examines the governance of child care in Vancouver, Calgary, Toronto, and Montreal. Women's labour force participation rates are high in all four cities: approximately 80 percent of women between the ages of twenty-five and forty-four are in the labour force (Mahon 2006a, Table 1). The financing and regulation of child care involve scalar hierarchies, and, as the analysis shows, they are indeed "tangled" and contested. One challenge to the liberal bias embedded in federal policy comes at the provincial scale: since 1997, Quebec has been moving towards a "social democratic"[1] model of child care provision. This is visible at the municipal scale: Montreal is able to boast the availability of spaces for 50 percent of preschool children and for 40 percent of school-age children, in marked contrast to Vancouver (11.1 percent) and Toronto (13.6 percent) (Mahon 2006a, Table 2). This is not surprising, as long-standing interscalar arrangements characteristic of Canada's federal state have meant that cities have not had the kind of revenue base required to ensure the provision of quality child care for all who want and need it.[2]

Yet, the analysis also shows that, even within the hierarchies established by the federal-provincial interscalar rule regime, cities can be more than puppets on a string. As Leibovitz (1999, 207) has argued, "the availability of local resources, the existence of effective political leadership, the degree of cooperation between locally based agents, the level of political mobilisation, the influence of local elites and changing external economic circumstances may all influence the direction of local policy." While Montreal's child care system largely reflects provincial policy, the Toronto and Vancouver stories lend support to this thesis. Despite the lack of provincial support, both cities have worked to lay the foundations for an affordable, high-quality child care system, accessible to all denizens. The Calgary story highlights the way in which earlier province-initiated changes to interscalar arrangements intersected with local politics to permit a certain centralization, while the current reconfiguration is opening new spaces.

Child Care at the Federal Scale

Federal policies have left an imprint on child care provision across the country, but they have reflected not only the liberal[3] character of the wider welfare regime but also an interscalar rule regime that centred on federal-provincial cost-sharing arrangements associated with executive federalism (Jenson 1989). Initially, that impact was limited, confined to Toronto and Montreal, as the federal government temporarily contributed to the financing of child care for mothers working in industries considered critical to the war effort. After the war, however, the federal government withdrew, not to return to the field until the passage of the Canada Assistance Plan (CAP) in 1966 as part of Canada's "war on poverty." Its liberal earmarks were apparent from the start, as CAP bundled together programs that had previously targeted various groups "in need." Thus, CAP made federal funds available for the first time for the support of lone mothers. In recognizing their "right to care," it also nodded in the direction of their "right to choose" employment, in the form of federal preparedness to cost-share, on a "fifty-fifty" basis, child care subsidies for those in need.

CAP was consistent with the broad pattern of federal-provincial arrangements initially imagined by the Rowell-Sirois Royal Commission as a solution to the increasingly visible "imbalance" between federal spending powers and provincial responsibilities in the growing fields of education, health, and welfare.[4] Yet, it also contributed to the consolidation of an interscalar rule regime whose aim it was to achieve pan-Canadian equity. Thus, one of CAP's key objectives was to support the development of effective welfare administration at the provincial scale. Aware of moves in several provinces to assume control of "community services," such as child care, demand for which was exceeding the capacity of municipalities and local charities, CAP aimed to enable all provinces to develop the capacity to support such services.

CAP funds did not mark the start of a truly national child care program, however. CAP entailed no obligation on the provinces to develop child care programs, which meant that levels of regulated child care provision varied substantially across the country. It did provide some broad regulations should a province decide to participate, which included a slight bias in favour of non-profit provision. Nevertheless, the regulations reinforced the view that child care was a "welfare service," targeted at those in financial or "moral" need. It also left to the provinces to determine eligibility rules and levels of subsidy. In fact, a largely unintended consequence of CAP's province building, in most provinces, was the centralization of social services to the provincial scale, at the expense of cities.

The elimination of CAP in 1996 occurred at a high point of neoliberal restructuring, reflecting precisely the kind of downloading and abandonment of equity concerns at the national scale suggested by Brenner (2004) and Peck (2001b). CAP was rolled into the new (and reduced) Canada Health and Social Transfer fund, which meant that child care was forced to compete for fewer dollars with entrenched heavy spenders such as education and health. At the same time, the federal government signalled that it would no longer use its spending power to initiate new social programs. It was also in this period that federal support for child care, via the National Child Benefit, became part of the turn to workfare, as Bashevkin's (2002) analysis suggests.

Yet, these initiatives were followed by a succession of others that drew from a different (albeit still liberal) paradigm (Mahon 2006b). Associated with this turn was an attempt to construct new interscalar arrangements – the Social Union Framework Agreement (SUFA) – through which the federal and provincial governments might work to address pressing social concerns. While the "workfarist" National Child Benefit was ostensibly the first program sanctioned by SUFA, subsequent policies were marked by an inclusive liberalism (Mahon and Macdonald 2006). Thus, the Early Child Development Initiative, introduced in 2000, included child care as one of four areas in which the provinces *could* spend federal money. The 2003 Multilateral Framework Agreement on Early Childhood Learning and Care focused directly on preschool child care, with the provinces left to select from a broad menu of options, including how to fund – demand-side measures such as information or subsidies versus investment on the supply s;ide such as operating grants, wage subsidies, and training – and whether to include commercial providers.

In 2005, the federal government moved beyond the SUFA framework, which had never managed to include Quebec, to negotiate bilateral agreements with all ten provinces to put $5 billion into registered early learning and care programs for preschool children over a five-year period. While flawed, these agreements might have made a real difference in the level and quality of provision across the country. Unfortunately, a neoliberal government was elected in January 2006. Its first act was to serve notice that it would withdraw from the agreements in a year's time.

Despite these changes, there are two consistent elements in federal policy from CAP to the present that reflect a certain path dependency. First, the federal government has never deviated from a liberal policy path, and this liberal bias has, until recently, been reflected in provincial policies. Second, it is the provinces that occupy the key place within the hierarchies governing social policy, including child care. In many provinces, control was centralized at the provincial scale at the expense of municipalities. Of our four cities, only Toronto is located in a province that left a greater or lesser role for municipalities. The others – Calgary, Vancouver, and Montreal – are in provinces that opted for the more typical pattern of centralization. Vancouver, however, has come to play an important role despite the lack of provincial mandate in this field, in contrast to Montreal, where the city has no role. Centralization in Alberta was only partial, as municipalities retained a role in organizing and financing care for school-aged children, and recent provincial initiatives have resulted in a certain decentralization to the local scale, which has facilitated the emergence of new "partnership" arrangements linking local agents of the province, municipalities, and civil society.

Toronto/Ontario
In Ontario, provincially generated interscalar arrangements meant that municipalities retained a welfare services role even after the passage of CAP. Until

the late 1990s, they were not required to develop a child care plan, but Toronto has had a child care policy since the 1940s. It was forged out of the ashes of the temporary wartime intergovernmental arrangement that saw federal funds supporting the establishment and operation of municipally run day nurseries. When the federal government withdrew funding after the war, parent groups, city councillors, and child development experts succeeded in getting the province to pass the Day Nursery Act (DNA) of 1946, which established the (then optional) provincial-municipal cost-sharing arrangement that has lasted to this day (Prentice 1993). The DNA marked the first provincial initiative to regulate child care in Canada, and it remained the only provincial legislation for several decades. As part of the broader trend towards the professionalization of social services, the DNA established high standards for the province – though Toronto set and maintained even higher standards. At the same time, the DNA strongly favoured the liberal view that day nurseries were a service for the poor or those "at risk" – in other words, not a public service for those who wanted and needed it.

For several decades, Toronto's child care policy continued to look very much like Ontario's. With provincial support, twelve of the eighteen municipal centres established during the war were reopened but only as a "welfare service." To eliminate mothers "working from choice," fees were doubled and a tough means test imposed (Prentice 1988). When the metropolitan government[5] assumed responsibility for welfare services in 1967, it inherited a child care system built on these liberal welfare principles. In the 1970s, however, the new policy beginning to take shape in Toronto began to break with the liberal orientation of not only its own policy legacies but also those established at the provincial and federal scales.

There is not the space here to detail the steps in this process or the politics attending them. Elsewhere, I have shown how feminist child care advocates, city officials, and municipal councillors forged a network of support behind a vision of quality child care as a citizen right, provided in public or non-profit auspices by child care providers receiving fair wages (Mahon 2005a). The breakthrough was facilitated by a favourable political opportunity structure – the emergence of a broad reform coalition "that welded social democratic currents with a strong urbanist orientation to a liberal and 'Red-Tory' ... constituency" (Kipfer and Keil 2002, 239).

In the mid-1980s, it looked as if this model would get much-needed financial support from higher scales, but when the federal Conservative government did not pass its Child Care Act, the province curtailed its spending plans. The local network of child care advocates was strong enough to induce Metro Toronto to fill the gap, thus assuming more than its 20 percent share of the costs. The network's strength was tested again in the 1990s, especially after the election of a neoliberal government in Ontario. Toronto Children's Services developed new ways to expand the local pool of funds, however, while the newly created children's advocate and her advisory committee kept the issue high on the municipal agenda. Despite the fact that the first mayor of the newly amalgamated Toronto was markedly pro-business, the new municipal government supported the "children's strategy" developed by the Metro Toronto Task Force on Services to Young Children and Families. The Council's support reflects not only the effectiveness of the alliance between progressive councillors, city bureaucrats, and parents but also the attitudes of the business elite, who had become convinced that Toronto's competitiveness depended on social investment. As Hamel, Boudreau, and Keil (2005, 24) found, "issues such as transportation, the tax burden, recreation facilities, safe communities, friendliness, *access to early child development and care facilities,* a very good public education system, a vibrant city core that is safe, clean and has many parks, were raised in many interviews as essential elements for generating growth and for transnational business" (emphasis added).

The political mobilizations of the 1970s and 1980s thus left an important legacy in the form of a high degree of cooperation among local agents. Municipal politicians and bureaucrats, local school boards, child advocates, and leading elements of the Toronto-based bourgeoisie had come to support the common vision. As a result, Toronto has the largest child care system in Canada outside Quebec. To achieve this, the municipality has worked with local school boards and others to establish the foundations for a high-quality early learning and care system delivered largely by non-profit providers. Its standards consistently exceed provincial guidelines – standards that an earlier provincial government tried to get it to abandon in the interests of "economy." Most recently, the city developed a set of operating criteria built on the values of quality, respect for diversity, and parental involvement. The quality of care is also dependent on the ability to attract and retain qualified care providers, and this, in turn, depends on wages and working conditions. Toronto not only offered decent wages and conditions to those working in municipal centres. It also pioneered the development of a wage enhancement policy designed to provide fair wages without sacrificing affordability. Toronto has also been a key driver of innovative pilot projects, including the development of an integrated set of children's services. In all of this, the municipality has come to operate as a "spider in the web" linking child care operators (mainly non-profit), school boards, providers of other children's services, and advocacy groups.

Toronto has not been able to realize its vision to the full, however. Although it has laid the foundations for a child care system based on "social democratic" principles, it still is only able to provide spaces for one-fifth of preschool children and as little as 7 percent of school-aged children. Its financial dependence on higher scales was made all the clearer when the federal government announced its intention to withdraw from the new agreements in January 2006. Toronto had planned to add 6,000 new spaces, with one-third of them targeted at poorer, underserviced communities. Many of these spaces are unlikely to see the light of day – unless the province proves willing and able to extract equivalent resources. The city has no (direct) say in these negotiations.

Vancouver/British Columbia

Unlike municipalities in Ontario, those in British Columbia have no official role in the provincial child care system. To be sure, unlike other municipalities, since 1953, Vancouver has been governed through its own charter, which "gave the city much greater powers of self government than other British Columbian or Canadian cities, which remain subservient to provincial municipal acts" (Punter 2003, 13). Yet, the charter neither indicated that "social services" such as child care should be part of the city's mandate nor provided the resources to finance them. What makes the Vancouver story so interesting, therefore, is that the city did come to play a very active role despite this limitation. It provides perhaps an even more telling illustration of the thesis of Leibovitz (1999) than does Toronto: the provision of child care may be governed by a hierarchy in which the province occupies the key position, but local resources can be mobilized to increase the room for manoeuvring.

In Vancouver, economic restructuring created the need for, and the possibility of, developing a child care policy, yet, needs do not speak for themselves. It took the emergence of local parties capable of challenging the business and social elite who had governed the city since the 1930s. The new parties opened the way to a new civic activism, reminiscent of McQuirk's (2003, 217) description of Sydney, as a "relatively open and participatory political culture in which business bargaining powers compete with the demands of community based non-government organizations." As we will see, in Vancouver, there were similarly fertile conditions that child care advocates were quick to exploit. Like their Toronto counterparts, they were able to break with the liberal model dominant at the provincial and national scales. In this, they could rely only intermittently on provincial support.

British Columbia began to assume control of child care later than Ontario or Alberta. The province was not involved in the wartime day nurseries program. Although it had begun to license child care in the 1930s, many providers remained outside the system (McDonell 1992). It was not until the passage of CAP that the province began to provide any funding, and even then it was slow to start. Only when a social democratic government was elected in 1972 was overall funding increased, ceilings raised on eligibility for subsidies, and funds made available for launching new activities. What funding the province has subsequently been prepared to provide – and this funding has varied significantly as governments shifted between the right and the left – went directly to providers, however. Moreover, although control was centralized to the provincial scale, jurisdiction has long remained divided among provincial ministries (McDonell 1992, 32).

The city showed an interest in child care already in the 1970s when, under the leadership of a reform council,[6] it provided funding for the Coalition for Improved Day Care Services, many of whose members would later go on to found the British Columbia Action Coalition in 1981. While formation of a new coalition helped child care advocates to develop a common voice, as in Toronto, it was the development of a favourable political opportunity structure – marked by the emergence of TEAM and its left-wing counterpart, COPE – that ultimately paved the way for the adoption of Vancouver's child care policy in 1991. As Hutton (2004, 1956) notes, the appearance of new political forces at the municipal scale laid the foundation for the city's proactive role: "Local policy and planning powers have been deployed in the interests of reproducing Vancouver's central area via dialectical relations with market actors and with certain social groups. In practice, this has meant accommodating the profit-seeking imperatives of capital ... and facilitating the emergence of ascendant social contingents, but has also incorporated the insertion of broader public values and needs, including social housing and public amenity." One example is the 1987 planning exercise designed to provide a policy framework for the central area, which included improved "livability" – understood to involve "adequate parks, accessible retail and commercial services, a well-designed public realm, and child care and community facilities" (Punter 2003, 107) – among its priority goals.

In the context of these planning debates, three important breakthroughs occurred. First, the mayor's 1988 Task Force on Children resulted in the establishment of a Vancouver children's advocate. The advocate, long involved in struggles for child care, produced a "civic child care strategy" based on the principles of quality, accessibility, and affordability. The strategy was endorsed by council in 1990. Among other things, the strategy committed Vancouver to being "an active partner with senior levels of government, parents, the private sector and the community in the development and maintenance of a comprehensive child care system in Vancouver" (Griffen 1992, 97). This would have meant little, however, without the second breakthrough – the appointment of a child care coordinator as part of the social planning department. The coordinator developed the detailed plans supporting municipal action in five key areas: capital programs, child care planning, operating funds and program support, development, and administrative support and advocacy.

Vancouver was able to follow through on these commitments in part because of the third innovation – the invention of cost levies and community amenity contributions. Although they were introduced by a pro-business mayor and council, the presence of a strong left contributed to the outcome. As Punter (2003, 109) argues, "with all the opposition coming from the political left, he [the mayor] was able to finesse right-wing cuts and convince developers that they had to accept development levies, selective changes to zoning, master planning of major redevelopment and elaborate participatory planning processes in return for large-scale projects and development certainty." The development cost levies and community amenity contributions have played an important role in strengthening the foundations of Vancouver's child care system. Through the amenity bonuses, developers receive extra density permits *if* they deliver to the city a child care facility built to the city's standards. The Vancouver Society of Children's Centres was created to operate these centres. The city has also supported Westcoast Child Care Resource Centre, an invaluable resource for the local child care community, and has launched several projects to further strengthen local child care infrastructure. Finally, following the adoption of the new child care plan (see City of Vancouver 2002), the city, the Vancouver School Board, and the Parks Board signed a child care protocol that established a framework for the three to work together to build a comprehensive range of childhood education and care services, with equal access across the city.[7]

Vancouver has thus been able to establish the foundation for the kind of child care system envisaged in the 1991 plan. The impact of its policies is visible in the high percentage of spaces – 84.2 percent of all spaces – under non-profit auspices. Vancouver has also done somewhat better than either Toronto or Calgary in providing out-of-school-hours care (8.6 percent). More broadly, like Toronto, the city has come to operate as the spider in a densely woven web of children's service providers and advocates. These achievements, as in Toronto, came as a result of child care advocates' ability to seize a favourable municipal political and economic opportunity structure. In the 1970s and 1980s, the city was being transformed from a centre for processing resources to a postindustrial economy. Socio-economic transformation generated the need for child care, the physical space to build it, and the political will in the form of reform-oriented parties ready to take a proactive stance. Child care activists were able to convince them that children (and working mothers) had a place in this "livable" city.

Nevertheless, the limits imposed by interscalar arrangements are also apparent. Despite considerable effort, the low overall levels of coverage – 11 percent of zero to twelve year olds, 10 percent of preschool children – remain low. Moreover, reliance on the community contributions and development cost levy instruments may have exacerbated a problem common to many child care systems where demand clearly outpaces supply – concentration of spaces in the new developments that cater primarily, though not exclusively, to the "postindustrial" urban middle class highlighted in Hutton's (2004) analysis. As Hertzman (2004) found, there is a tenfold difference in neighbourhood access rates, with the largely working-class east side markedly underserviced. The city's plan aims to address these rates, but without the financial resources only obtainable from higher levels of government, this will be difficult to do.

Montreal/Quebec

Of all the provinces considered here, Quebec currently exercises the most control over the development of child care and, since 1997, has offered the most extensive support, breaking with the liberal pattern that otherwise prevails across Canada. This has not always been the case. In fact, although daycare centres in Montreal received federal funding during the war, the conservative Union National provincial government was not prepared to fund them when the war ended, and there was little local opposition to this decision. For the most part, support was limited to the small working-class anglophone community, as the francophone community continued to rely primarily on family networks for care during the war. Despite the emergence of a strong Quebec feminist movement in the 1960s, child care was not incorporated into the vision of a modern Quebec, supported by an active state that characterized the Quiet Revolution. The provincial government ignored the 1968 brief demanding provincial support for a tax-financed non-denominational child care system, which was backed by over 100 associations (Desjardins 1992).

For a while, grassroots organizations were able to get access to federal funds through programs such as Opportunities for Youth and the Local Initiative Projects. Through them, over thirty centres had been established in Montreal by 1972, mainly in poorer, working-class areas. These experiments established some core features that would later become part of what is now known as the "Quebec model," notably the emphasis on parent involvement in decision making in non-profit, community-based centres and organizations at the submunicipal scale. That model was long in the making, however. The province only began to draw on CAP funds for child care in 1974. As it chose to make subsidies available to low-income parents (and the eligibility ceiling was low), not to centres, this did little to establish a viable child care infrastructure.

An important breakthrough occurred in 1979, when child care got its own Office de services de garde à l'enfance (OSGE). As Desjardins (1992, 39) argues, the new structure was given a wide mandate:

> Apart from ensuring that quality child care services are available, it also plans the implementation of services in relation to other family policies. Moreover, it is in charge of formulating an annual development plan that takes into consideration the extent of the demand for and the viability of the projects submitted. All these tasks must be accomplished while maintaining close contact with the network [of child care providers], since the OSGE must also provide technical and financial support for child care services, centralize information on the issue and circulate that information, provide better staff training, ensure compliance with health and safety rules, and so on.

At the neighbourhood scale, another provincial body – the Centres locales des services communautaire (CLSCs) – played an important role, working closely with the child care units in their catchment areas (Jenson 2002, 315). Yet, the OSGE lacked the political backing to develop a comprehensive plan prior to the passage of the 1997 policy. Thus, there was inadequate support for the expansion of the non-profit centres to match demand. This inadequacy of support was reflected in the uneven access to child care that Rose and Chicoine found in their 1991 study of access to school child care services in Montreal inner-city neighbourhoods. It was also reflected in the growth of a substantial commercial sector.

The implementation of the Parti Québécois government's 1997 five dollars a day[8] child care program has had a substantial impact on the number of spaces available for preschool children, just as the earlier decision by the Ministry of Education substantially improved access to Out-of-School-Hours (OSH) care for school-aged children. Montreal now has spaces in registered child care for 50 percent of its preschool children and for 40 percent of school-aged children (Mahon 2006a, Table 3). Provision of OSH space for children has allowed Montreal to stand out among the cities under consideration and shows the positive impact that a strong provincial policy can have. In addition, the core of the program is consistent with the 1970s experiments, as a key role was allocated to the non-profit, community-based Centres de la petite enfance (CEPs), responsible to elected boards. The share of non-profits in preschool provision is, however, lower than in Toronto and Vancouver, an artifact of previous years of underfunding and that sector's political clout.[9]

In addition, despite Quebec's substantial commitment to affordable, accessible, quality child care, equitable access remains an elusive goal. Thus, Japel, Tremblay, and Coté (2005) found that children from middle- and upper-class families were more likely to have a space, and in better-quality settings, than were children from working-class families. The latter are often forced to rely on inferior for-profit centres, lower-quality family daycare, or unlicensed care. This pattern is visible in Montreal, where the Conseil régional de développement (CRD) documented the difficulty of establishing good-quality family child care in poor neighbourhoods. These results follow in part from the way that Quebec planned the implementation of its 1997 policy. It was a "bottom-up" process in which proposals for a centre had to be generated at the community level. While funds were made available for groups interested in developing a proposal, and the CRDs were able to work with them on this, it was not sufficient to ensure that enough proposals came forward from poorer communities.

More broadly, there is no municipal role, nor has there been one. This is not to suggest that the local level is of no importance: the *centres de la petite enfance* are located in neighbourhoods and run by elected boards, with a majority of parents. There is thus local involvement, albeit at a submunicipal scale. The CEPs, working in tandem with the community-based CLSCs, provide opportunities for local input – but again, not on the municipal or the metropolitan scale. As in Toronto and Vancouver, the school boards form part of the local child care system, but whereas in the latter cities this is the result of local initiatives, in Quebec, it is the provincial Ministry of Education that has made them responsible for providing OSH care whenever there is a demonstrated need.

The Montreal case raises a broader question: clearly, strong provincial commitment to establishing an accessible, affordable, high-quality child care system province-wide makes a difference. Yet, there is also a valuable role for city-wide structures that have the authority to develop and implement an equitable local plan. The CRDs lacked such authority. While the territory covered by locally elected school boards is less than metro-wide, the boards are at least required to develop plans for ensuring equitable educational services across their jurisdictions (Mahon 2000).

Responsibility for this weakness in an otherwise impressive system cannot be laid entirely at the feet of the provincial government. It can also be seen as a reflection of the particular legacy of Montreal's urban reform wave. As Hamel, Boudreau, and Keil (2005, 12) note, "while urban social movements were numerous in Montreal and were responsible for the election of the Montreal Citizen's Movement (MCM) to City Hall in 1986 ... they were unable to secure new alliances on a metropolitan scale (beyond their neighbourhood scale of action)." More broadly, equating democracy with decentralization to the neighbourhood scale, reform movements in Montreal have not tried to establish a strong role for municipal-scale institutions. This local political culture subsequently came to be reflected in Montreal's new governance structure, in which the boroughs were given a critical role in community service provision (Hamel, Boudreau, and Keil 2005). Thus, recreational services, which form an important part of the child care system, especially during vacation, reflect the same uneven distribution found in the CEP-based system.

Calgary/Alberta

Calgary's story may be the most interesting of all. Calgary initially developed a child care program by making use of a provincial program that, like Ontario's, involved municipalities in cost-sharing arrangements. Although the province gradually assumed control over the financing and regulation of child care for preschool children, there was room for municipalities to maintain their distinctive programs, which Calgary did until the local balance of forces shifted. More recently, provincial moves to decentralize operations – part of a broader trend especially marked in Alberta – have created new spaces for the emergence of local partnerships. Unlike the Toronto and Vancouver cases, however, it is a civil society organization that seems to be playing a critical role.

Alberta, and Calgary as one of its largest cities, almost signed on to participate in the temporary wartime intergovernmental accords to finance the establishment and operation of day nurseries, as Langford (2003) has documented. The province's failure to do so meant that higher scales of the state did not become involved until the 1960s. With the passage of Alberta's Preventive Social Services Act (now Family and Community Support Services or FCSS) in 1964, however, Alberta was better prepared than most provinces to take advantage of new federal funding for child care when CAP came into effect. This also meant that, as in Ontario, municipalities in Alberta were directly involved in these interscalar arrangements, with municipalities ultimately covering 20 percent of the costs of programs such as child care. These arrangements also gave the municipalities considerable latitude to develop innovative programs. Although all projects had to be approved by the province, and the province expressed a clear preference for provision by private social agencies in order to contain costs (Masson and LeSage 1994, 389), Calgary established a municipal child care system that was to operate as a "lighthouse" in the field. By the end of the 1970s, it had established fifteen municipal centres and six family child care programs linked to these centres. Like Edmonton, its sister city, Calgary was recognized at that time for its innovative, high-quality programs and decent staff salaries.

Underpinning its growth was a pattern of alliances similar to those found in Toronto and Vancouver. The city had appointed a daycare counsellor as early as 1969. This appointment established a voice for child care within the municipal bureaucracy, one that was actively supported by both traditional women's groups, such as the Calgary Local Council of Women, and a new generation of "women's liberation" activists, centred at the University of Calgary (Langford 2006, Chapter 5). Despite the city's impressive effort, however, the supply of municipal child care services did not manage to keep up with the rapidly growing demand. As a result, by the end of the 1970s, Calgary had developed the largest commercial child care sector in the province, and it had organized to represent its interests at both local and provincial scales. The presence and organization of a strong commercial sector had an impact on municipal policy. Thus, when the province adopted a new child care policy in 1978, which involved a turn to portable subsidies tenable at *any* licensed centre, including commercially operated ones, Calgary was the first municipality to sign on (Langford 2003, 70).

Nevertheless, the city's social planning department remained strongly committed to its "lighthouse" child care centres. Thus, when the province moved to centralize control over preschool child care, while leaving municipalities a role in organizing after-school care, Calgary continued to back its original centres. To finance the original centres, it negotiated an innovative "flow through" arrangement that allowed it (and other Alberta municipalities) to get access to CAP funds, even though the province had withdrawn its support for the preschool programs (Jenson and Mahon 2002). Calgary's eventual abandonment of the municipal program for preschool children cannot therefore be attributed to provincial dictates. While the province made it more difficult for the system to survive, strong support from the municipal social services department and parent users enabled it to hang on for a decade, despite increasingly fierce attacks from a powerful city councillor and long-standing member of the city's Community Services Committee. The city abandoned its preschool program only when those opposing the policy managed to push the department's director into retirement. The opponents were able to do so, moreover, because the civil society organizations that had come to its aid in the 1970s and early 1980s were silent (Langford 2006, Chapter 10).

At the provincial scale, the 1990s were a period marked by substantial cutbacks and restructuring. With the election of Klein's Conservatives, the budget of municipal affairs was cut in half, as was funding for kindergarten (Miller and Martin 2005, 26). Provincial allocations for regulated child care fell from a high of $67.6 million in 1995 to $54.3 million three years later and have yet to recover (Friendly and Beach 2005, Table 28). At the same time, however, the province moved to decentralize the administration of social programs in community services and health care. Child care is thus now handled by regional branches of the Child and Family Services Authority (CFSA). The CFSAs report to boards appointed by the province. Although the members are selected from the region, they enjoy a limited degree of autonomy from the provincial government. Under the Klein government, the province made clear its authority over "decentralized" regional bodies by terminating the election of regional health authorities and firing a medical officer of health for criticizing the provincial government's environmental stance (Miller and Martin 2005, 28).

Nevertheless, the Calgary CFSA does have enough leeway to participate in local networks. It has developed connections with its municipal counterpart, which remains in charge of child care for school-aged children. Both organizations work with the voluntary sector, especially the Calgary Children's Initiative, which the United Way has taken a lead role in organizing. This initiative, which brings together various levels of government, community groups, businesses, labour, and researchers, has supported some innovative programs aimed at developing a supportive environment for children and youth. One of these programs is focused on raising the quality of preschool care, long a problem in the now commercially dominated system.[10] It is interesting to note, however, that unlike in Toronto or Vancouver, in Calgary, it is not the municipality that plays the leading role in establishing a network of children's services, nor has that role been taken up by the CFSA. Instead, it is the voluntary sector that operates as the "spider in the web" (Mahon 2006a). The limited role for municipalities partly reflects the long-standing provincial bias in favour of the voluntary sector, but it is also testimony to the vitality of what Miller and Martin (2007) call "a place-based ... moral community," one that may have the potential to regenerate support for a different model than that on offer at the provincial scale.

Conclusion

Although some former contributors to scale theory would now argue for a "flat ontology," we need to recognize that (1) hierarchies do exist and cannot be wished away and that (2) hierarchy is theorized in the political economy of scale literature in quite a different way from the manner alleged by these critics. As Peck (2002b, 333) suggests, however, "it is one thing to say that scales are relationally and socially constituted and that cross-scalar relations matter; it is another thing to demonstrate how this process works in more concrete and institutionally specific contexts." By sketching the elaboration of an (uneven) set of interrelated scalar hierarchies or funding arrangements, this chapter has tried to show that historically generated scalar hierarchies shape but do not determine possibilities for action.

The arrangements established by CAP formed part of the wider interscalar rule regime that constituted the scaffolding of Canada's liberal version of the Keynesian welfare state. These interscalar arrangements allowed the federal government to construct a pan-Canadian welfare state in the postwar years. In this set of tangled hierarchies, however, it was the provinces, not the federal government, that occupied the decisive position. Cities had no official place in these arrangements. This province-centred interscalar regime resulted in a "patchwork of provision" in child care as well as other parts of the welfare state (Boychuk 1998). What the analysis of child care politics in the four cities shows, however, is that, while provincial policies clearly had an impact on what could be done at the local scale, these arrangements did not completely determine what happened on the ground. Although variably constructed, the scalar hierarchies left room for local forces to manoeuvre, and in three of the cities, local actors forged networks that supported the development of alternative models of care. In Toronto and Vancouver, moreover, municipalities operated as "spiders" building a web of children's services. Calgary's history has been more checkered. Nevertheless, there, too, what happened on the ground was not simply dictated by the province but also reflected changes in the local balance of forces.

At the same time, the analysis supports the historical instinct of labour and other social movements to jump to or create higher scales. As the limited provision in Toronto and Vancouver shows, in Canada, cities lack the financial resources to achieve their alternative visions on their own. Thus, Montreal's superior level of provision underlines the importance of adequate provincial support for a community-based, democratically governed system. The weakness of Montreal/Quebec's system lies in the urban reform movements' failure to develop the capacity for social policy coordination at the municipal scale. In other words, the kind of scalar hierarchy that is most likely to promote equality and democracy is one in which a "social democratic" policy regime operating at the national/provincial scale is supplemented by institutions of democratic control at the neighbourhood level and by a planning structure capable of working towards equity at the municipal scale.

The analysis also suggests that, whatever the impact of neoliberalism, social reproduction remains very much on the contemporary agenda. The political economy of scale thus cannot remain preoccupied with capital's search for a new "scalar fix" or the disciplinary aspects of the current "rolling out" of the state. To be sure, some variants of the "farewell to maternalism" (Orloff 2004) involve the rolling out of coercive workfare programs (Bashevkin 2002), but more is involved than this. The generalization of the "adult earner" family form, pushed at the transnational scale by organizations such as the OECD and the EU (Mahon 2006b), is generating the need for alternative care arrangements. In other words, the end of maternalism has given rise to pressures for new initiatives such as public support for non-parental child care and leaves to care for infants, the sick, and the dying. Scalar arrangements play a part here – from "fast policy transfers" that identify the "new needs" and prescribe how they might be met to the kinds of interscalar arrangement analyzed above.

ACKNOWLEDGMENTS

This chapter comes out of a longer study, involving eleven Canadian cities, commissioned by the Cities of Toronto and Vancouver. I would like to thank Julie Mathien, Petr Varmuza, Jane Jenson, and Katherine Mortimer for their help on that study.

NOTES

1 For purposes of simplicity, I follow Esping-Andersen's (1990) well-known classification of welfare regimes. According to this system, social democratic regimes provide high-quality, publicly financed (and often publicly run) social services, available to all who want and need them.
2 See Bradford (2002) for an incisive analysis of the mix of change and continuity in interscalar arrangements that marked the transition to a Keynesian welfare state combined with a reflection on the current push to reconfigure those arrangements to give more weight to cities.
3 Liberal regimes tend to leave families to fend for themselves on the market, stepping in primarily to support those considered unable to manage (Esping-Andersen 1990).
4 The Royal Commission on Dominion-Provincial Relations (1937-40) recommended federal responsibility for unemployment insurance and the establishment of equalization grants to enable all provinces to provide a similar level of service, both of which were adopted. While other recommendations were initially blocked by the provinces, Canada's Keynesian welfare state was ultimately achieved through the negotiation of a series of cost-sharing arrangements.
5 A new scale – or two-tier municipal governance – was introduced in the early 1950s, but social services were scaled up to the metropolitan level only in the mid-1960s.
6 The Electors Action Movement (TEAM), described by Punter (2003, 14) as being committed to "more participatory planning practices and a more inclusive vision for the future of the city, which appealed to the younger, better educated, more urbane and environmentally conscious electorate." The left-wing Confederation of Progressive Electors (COPE) has remained an important force in city politics.

7 City of Vancouver, administrative report to Vancouver City Council from the director of Social Planning, "The 2005 Civic Child Care Grant Report – Allocation One of Three," 24 May 2005.
8 Now seven dollars a day.
9 Under the original plan, the commercial sector was gradually to be eliminated, but the moratorium was lifted in 2002, and this sector grew rapidly under the Liberal government elected in 2003 (Jenson 2006).
10 In Calgary, just over a quarter of the child care spaces for preschool children are non-profit. This percentage stands in marked contrast to the pattern in what remains of the old FCSS-financed sector, where over half of the spaces are in the non-profit sector.

PART 4
The Scale of Movements

12
The Spatiality of Contentious Politics: More than a Politics of Scale

Helga Leitner and Eric Sheppard

Over the past decade, the politics of scale has become a popular way of conceptualizing the spatiality of politics, in both human geography and other disciplines. Theorists of the politics of scale have shown that scale is a relational, power-laden, and contested construction that actors strategically engage with in order to legitimize or challenge existing power relations. In the course of these struggles, new scales are constructed, and the relative importance of different scales is reconfigured. Central to the politics of scale is the manipulation of relations of power and authority. This process is highly contested, involving numerous negotiations and struggles between different actors as they attempt to reshape the spatiality of power and authority (Leitner 1997). In this chapter, we review the utility of the politics of scale for conceptualizing the spatiality of contentious politics, which, for the purposes of this chapter, we define as "concerted social action that has the goal of overcoming deeply rooted structural disadvantage" (Sewell 2001, 55).

While geographical scale has become influential in conceptualizing the spatiality of politics for good reason, we are concerned that the attention paid to scale has had the effect of marginalizing other spatialities associated with political struggles – spatialities that play an important role in the practice of contentious politics.[1] We are not the first to express concern about the danger of overlooking the limits of scalar thinking. Neil Brenner has attempted to place some limits on what counts as a politics of scale by stressing the necessity of a multiscalar, relational approach to scale, which we endorse: "In the absence of an explicit causal argument linking the substantive social content of the spatial unit in question to its *embeddedness* or *positionality* within a broader social hierarchy, there is little reason to theorize the issues connoted by the singular usage of the 'politics of scale' in a scalar terminology rather than through an alternative geographical lexicon, such as that of place, locality, territoriality, or networks" (2001a, 601).

As the introduction to this volume notes, others have argued that scale should be jettisoned. By contrast, we argue in this chapter that the spatiality of politics entails the co-implication of a variety of spatialities, including scale, that shape and are shaped by political struggle.

Although scale remains relevant in contentious politics, it is insufficient to account for the variety of ways in which social movements draw on and shape the spatiality and temporality of society. We begin by noting the ways in which scale remains important to contentious politics. We then discuss problems associated with "scale centrism," in which the hypercomplexity of spatiality is collapsed into the master concept of scale. Rejecting proposals to discard scale altogether, we identify other spatialities – place, mobility, and networks of spatial connectivity – highlighting their importance to both the practice and theorization of contentious politics. We argue that these other spatialities do not simply exist alongside, but are also co-implicated with, scale. Finally, we propose the concept of sociospatial positionality as a gateway into comprehending both how various spatialities are co-implicated with one another and how the social and the spatial co-evolve in contentious politics.

Scale and Contentious Politics

There is no question that the politics of scale is important to contentious politics. First, much contentious politics takes on state institutions, whose spatiality has traditionally been dominated by nested scales, ranging from the national to the regional and local (Brenner 2004; Ferguson and Gupta 2002; Swyngedouw 1997a).[2] This scalar spatiality is reconfigured by state and non-state practices in ways that shift the relative importance of different scales, occasionally even resulting in the construction of new scales. For example, local legal aid organizations in the United States have had to adjust to funding restrictions stemming from the devolution of legal aid funding from federal to state governments, accompanied by federal recommendations that local legal aid organizations should be consolidated into state-wide organizations. A supportive state bar association, state supreme court, and state political environment may be crucial to the ability of such local organizations to survive the transition away from federal to state and private sector resources, as has been the case in Minnesota (Laws 2004). To the extent that contentious politics engages the state, therefore, the strategies available will be shaped by state-constructed scalar configurations and the different conditions of possibility within local places.

Second, social movements' scalar strategies have received much attention in the discussion of the geography and outcomes of contentious politics. Some scholars have shown how social movements can overcome limitations of localness through scale jumping: turning local into regional, national, and global movements to expand their power. Movements ranging from the Zapatistas to labour unions, indigenous peoples' organizations, feminism, environmental justice, and the living wage campaign have benefited from devising strategies for jumping from local to broader scales to advance their causes (Froehling 1999; Herod 1997; Miller 2000; Smith 1992b; Swyngedouw 1997b). Others have argued that social movements can gain strength by being kept local. In this view, resistance draws its strength from local particularity. Such strategies of localization often rely on attachments to territory and culture and attempt to reaffirm the importance of local particularity as necessary to successful broader-scale strategies (Cresswell 2002, 20). For example, Escobar (2001) suggests that place-based cultural, ecological, and economic practices are important sources of alternative visions and strategies for reconstructing local and regional worlds, no matter how produced by the global they might also be (see also Boudreau and Keil 2001). Many social movements have used multiscalar strategies, simultaneously broadening the scale of their action while drawing strength from reinforcing the local scale. As Harvey (2000b, 51) observes, "the choice of spatial scale is not 'either/or' but 'both/and' even though the latter means confronting serious contradictions."

Third, scalar strategies entail the development and deployment of scale frames by social movements and their opponents in struggles over relations of power (Jung 2004; Kurtz 2003, 2004). For example, opposition to the concentration of power over immigration policy at the supranational scale of the European Union has come from both nationalist right-wing political parties and transnational non-governmental human/immigrant rights organizations, each employing different scale frames (Leitner 1997). Nationalist right-wing political parties framed their opposition to the development of a supranational migration regime as a defence of the national scale, presenting themselves as guardians of the national interest and of a national identity and cultural/racial distinctiveness that is in danger of being obliterated by European integration and foreigners. In contrast, non-governmental human/immigrant rights organizations framed their grievances within a universal/global human rights framework that would require Europe to fulfill its human rights obligations towards economic migrants and political refugees and grant equality of treatment to all legal residents within its territory.

Fourth, an as yet underexamined aspect of scale in contentious politics involves the difficulties faced when conflicting scale frames and scalar strategies coexist within social movement alliances, potentially undermining their cohesion and shaping their strategies. For example, in the Minneapolis-St. Paul metropolitan area, the Alliance for Metropolitan Stability has been advocating metropolitan scale solutions to address sociospatial inequities within the metropolitan area. Yet, its coherence has been partially undermined by the different scale frames of Alliance members (Walling 2004). The metropolitan scale is of particular importance to middle-class white participants in the Alliance, such as Myron Orfield's advocacy of metropolitan-wide fair housing, but this does not extend to members from communities of colour. The Just Equity Caucus, advocating on behalf of people of colour, eschewed the regional or metropolitan designation entirely, framing sociospatial inequities at both the neighbourhood and the national scales. Differences in the spatial scales at which problems are framed also influence the scale envisioned for action. In the case of the Alliance for Metropolitan Stability, disparities in scale frames of the problem/grievance resulted in conflicts over the scale at which Alliance action should be focused. Eventually, a compromise was forged in the form of a multiscalar strategy, with the Alliance combining a focus on the metropolitan scale, for data analysis, with localized actions in particular minority neighbourhoods.

Problems with Scale Centrism

Despite the continued relevance of scale, an exclusive focus on scale for conceptualizing the spatiality of politics is problematic. First, a focus on scale presumes that vertical, interscalar relations dominate the spatiality of politics (Sheppard 2002). Conventionally, geographical scale is thought of in terms of territorially bounded political entities, in which lower scales are nested within larger scales (from the body to the globe). Scalar thinking is pushed to its limit in trying to incorporate relations between territories at the same scale but widely separated in space. For example, when Swyngedouw (1997b, 142) refers to scale jumping as "stretching and contracting objects across space," he implies that the fortunes of places located in different regions of the same nation-state are connected vertically, via processes operating at the larger (national) scale within which each is embedded.

Yet, the spatiality of contested politics often connects people and places horizontally. When activists, travelling from localities around the world, gathered at a World Social Forum (WSF) meeting in Porto Alegre or Mumbai, they were not being brought together via some larger spatial scale that each is embedded within (see Conway 2005). Rather, cybernetworks established among activists allowed them to link up with each other and plan the events. They travelled to these events on their own initiative, and their co-presence and face-to-face deliberations in the space of the WSF meetings allowed for the further development of common agendas and strategies and strengthened networks among activists from different parts of the globe. Such networks and deliberations and co-presence in place cannot simply be subsumed under a scalar politics but are suggestive of other aspects of spatiality not readily reducible to scale: sociospatial connectivities through translocal networks, mobility across space, and the building of social relations in place. Whereas scale is associated with vertical relations among spatially bounded and nested entities, networks span space without covering it (Leitner 2004). Furthermore, co-presence in place matters, even in the absence of interscalar relations.

Second, the verticality entailed in any nested set of territorially bounded political entities is suggestive of hierarchical power relations. Some have taken this to imply a top-down power hierarchy, whereby geographically more extensive scales dominate lower ones. In ecology and physical geography, scales are often thought of in exactly this way (Sheppard and McMaster 2004a). According to what is known as hierarchy theory, slower-moving, larger-scale processes operate as constraints, limiting the operation of smaller-scale, faster-moving processes (Wu 1999). Under these conditions, broader scales shape conditions of possibility at local scales, making local agency subservient to macrologics of structural power. Such a top-down power hierarchy has been roundly and appropriately criticized by feminist and poststructuralist theorists for its neglect of the potential transformative power of the local (Freeman 2001). It relies on the assumption that smaller-scale entities are not directly interconnected horizontally in any significant way and, thus, are dependent on larger scales.

It is important to note, however, that many scale theorists reject the assumption that scalar power operates through a top-down hierarchy (Delaney and Leitner 1997; Herod 1991, 1997; Miller 1997; Sheppard and McMaster 2004b). Jessop (this volume), drawing on Collinge (1999), argues that while power hierarchies always exist, with dominant, nodal, and marginal scales, the largest scales need not dominate such hierarchies. Rather, a periodic reconfiguration of scale occurs, during which other scales become dominant. Swyngedouw (1997b) rejects any necessary existence of top-down power hierarchies linking scales, and Leitner (1997) suggests that power asymmetries between different scales are always contested. Indeed, as Sayre (2005, 286) notes, "this is, in fact, what much of the recent literature on geographical scale is concerned to show and understand."

Third, scale theorists typically pose a nested sequence of scaled, materially bounded entities, from the home to the globe, at the centre of their analysis. Place theorists have called attention, however, to the fact that places are open and heterogeneous. Places are complexly interpenetrated by both vertical and horizontal connectivities, which shape their heterogeneity and political dynamics (Massey 1991; Verstraete and Cresswell 2002). Within any territory, "different social groups have distinct relationships to this anyway-differentiated mobility: some are more in charge of it than others; some initiate flows and movement, others don't; some are more on the receiving end of it than others; some are effectively imprisoned by it" (Massey 1991, 149). In this way, place theorists highlight the mutually constitutive nature of the heterogeneity, openness, and interpenetration of places. Indeed, social groups within a territory may have more in common with similar groups in other distant places than with co-residents of the same territory.[3] This has been widely documented for political elites (Castells 1996; Galtung 1971) and for transnational migrants (Ong 1999).

This critique calls into question the coherence of any territorially bounded political entity, as differently positioned agents with different and often conflicting worldviews, agendas, and subjectivities are co-present. Indeed, it is well known that territorial political identities are difficult to maintain, which is why territorial states continually resort to a variety of technologies of rule to elicit consent, in turn contested by other groups within or entering that territory.

More than a Politics of Scale

The limitations of scale do not mean that we should throw the baby out with the bathwater (Leitner and Miller 2007; Mahon 2006c). As we argue here and illustrate below, contentious politics works through a variety of co-implicated spatialities, including scale, whose complex intertwining cannot adequately be captured by forcing a choice between supposedly distinct spatial ontologies. In order to illustrate how the spatiality of contentious politics involves more than a politics of scale, in this section we explore three other spatialities that have been important to the practice of contentious politics. We want to emphasize, however, that they do not simply coexist side by side with scale and one another (Howitt 2002b). Rather, as we will go on to exemplify through a case study of the Immigrant Workers Freedom Ride, they are co-implicated in and co-constitutive of the practice of political struggle.

Consider, first, the *politics of place*. Places are sites where people live, work, and move and where they form attachments, practise their relations with each other, and relate to the rest of the world (Massey 1994). Everyday spaces within the city – streets, places of work, residence, consumption, and worship – become important sites and anchors in social movement struggles and contentious politics, in both the physical and the metaphorical senses, as the literature on geographies of resistance and urban activism has repeatedly shown (Brown 1997; Keil 2002; Leitner, Peck, and Sheppard 2007; Martin 2003; Pile and Keith 1997). Social movements often seek to strategically manipulate, subvert, and resignify places that symbolize priorities and imaginaries that they are contesting; to defend places that stand for their own priorities and imaginaries; and to produce new spaces where such visions can be practised, within the city and beyond.

For example, Sziarto (2003) showed that the manipulation of microspaces within the city was an important component in the repertoire of the tactics of progressive religion-labour alliances in Minneapolis-St. Paul, advocating for workers' and immigrants' rights. One of their spatial tactics of protest was transporting their grievances into the workplace – for example, a group of clergy moving into a hotel lobby in downtown Minneapolis and praying in support of the hotel workers before joining the workers on the picket line. By employing religious modes of expression and transporting them into the secular space of the hotel, activists were resignifying the meaning of these spaces of consumption as spaces of contention. Another tactic of these alliances has been to take messages of organized labour, their grievances and imaginaries, into religious spaces through so-called "Labor in the Pulpits" annual events. Murphy (2004) describes a similar resignification of corporate places. In 1999, a national movement of gay, lesbian, bisexual, and transgender employees of United Airlines (UA), in cooperation with community activists in San Francisco, campaigned to demand that UA extend its employer-paid benefits to employees' domestic partners. Much of this successful campaign was staged outside the confines of corporate and political offices:

> A multiplicity of actions that drew on the political history and social networks of San Francisco's queer community immediately confronted the airline on the streets of its largest Pacific gateway. High-visibility disobedience actions regularly occurred. For these events the activists adopted a spatial strategy, bringing queer comedy, theatrics, and irreverence into United's ticket offices, places coded in the airline's image as a highly regulated, sterile, and conservative Fortune 500 multinational corporation. The ironies and dissonances of United Airlines ticket offices becoming centers of queer performance brought unprecedented visibility to the campaign against the airline. After it came out that United was working in concert with the American Center for Law and Justice, a right-wing think tank funded by Christian evangelist Pat Robertson who had bizarrely lambasted the purple British Teletubby TV character for being "gay," local activist Gilbert Baker, who had been instrumental in designing the AIDS quilt, sewed several purple Tinky Winky costumes. Tinky Winky-clad demonstrators then shut down United's California Street ticket office, and were hauled away to jail in front of a wildly amused public and press. In a similarly striking disturbance, queer activists collected dozens of old suitcases and decorated each one with details of a different discrimination lawsuit against United filed by employees. They then barricaded shut the doors to the Geary Street ticket office, publicly demanding that United "Get Rid of Its Tired Old Baggage" before making headlines with another comedic arrest. (Murphy 2004, 11)

Second is the politics of *networking*. Recent work on geographies of resistance has shown the importance of dynamic translocal networks connecting individuals, institutions, and activists from different places for shaping the development of strategies and tactics of social movement politics. Rather than covering space, they create translocal social spaces transcending the boundaries that separate them and challenging scalar hierarchies. Keck and Sikkink (1998, 2) argue that "transnational advocacy networks, such as human rights and environmental networks are proliferating, with the goal to change the behavior of the state and international organizations." Leitner (1997) shows how transnational networks of human rights and immigrant activists have been challenging the sovereignty of European nation-states and the European Union. Through a discursive strategy that redefines citizenship rights as universal human rights, these transnational networks attempted to reconfigure nation-states' and the European Union's ability to territorialize their authority and to stake claims to superior generality and universality.

Third is the politics of *mobility*. Social movements have long relied on physical movement in and between places, such as mass demonstrations, rallies, pickets in public spaces, and bike and bus rides traversing and transgressing space, to transform their spatiotemporal conditions of possibility. Indeed, the ability of social activists to appear unexpectedly in certain places, ahead of those seeking to contain their actions, has been an effective tactic at scales ranging from street demonstrations to national revolutionary movements. The shared experience of such groups in motion, as well as their co-presence in particular spaces, not only allows them to negotiate differences within the movement but also helps to create shared understandings, visions, strategies, and tactics that are essential for the mobilization of collective action.

The scholarly literature on geographies of resistance and social movements has produced valuable insights into these various spatialities – scale, place, networks of spatial connectivity, and mobility – and their roles in mobilization and the efficacy of urban activism (Knopp 1997; Martin and Miller 2003; Miller 2000; Moore 1997; Rose 1997a; Rose 2002; Routledge 2003; Slater 1997; Wainwright 2007; Wainwright, Prudham, and Glassman 2000). Yet, the question of co-implication of diverse spatialities at times remains underexposed, and there exists a tendency in some geographical scholarship to either privilege one type of spatiality or subsume diverse spatialities under a single master concept such as place or scale. For example, Glassman's (2001) insightful analysis of resistance movements to neoliberal globalization discusses multiple spatial practices but frames this discussion around scale and scale jumping by local activists. Similarly, in analyzing black social movements in Colombia, Oslender (2004) subsumes scale, networks of spatial connectivity, and mobility under the concept of place.

We suggest that privileging any one spatiality, or subsuming their multiplicity under one master concept, is problematic and insufficient. Multiple spatialities are co-implicated and co-constitutive in complex ways during social movement struggles, with unpredictable consequences. The Immigrant Workers Freedom Ride illustrates the complexity of these interrelations, and their effects on movement mobilization and efficacy, underlining the importance of empirically investigating social movement practices. Yet, they must also be theorized, and we will turn to the idea of sociospatial positionality for this purpose.

Co-Implication in Practice: The Immigrant Workers Freedom Ride[4]

In 2003, an alliance between organized labour, community groups, and immigrant workers staged the Immigrant Workers Freedom Ride (IWFR) in the United States to publicize a broad agenda for, and to build a national movement in support of, immigrants' rights and national immigration policy reform – with the longer-term goal of changing US federal policy. Specifically, the alliance was advocating the granting of legal status to working and tax-paying immigrants, easing access for the acquisition of citizenship, restoring rights on the job, reunifying families separated by immigration laws, and respecting and upholding civil rights and liberties for all. In September 2003, eighteen buses with nearly 1,000 immigrant workers and activists set out from ten different cities in the United States for a week's journey across the country, bound for Washington, DC, with stops in 103 cities and towns.

The idea of the freedom ride originated in 2001 with a staff person of the Hotel Employees and Restaurant Employees International Union (HERE) Local 11 in Los Angeles. The then president of HERE in Los Angeles, Maria Elena Durazo, took up the idea with HERE's national leadership. The national leaders were receptive to the idea and announced their intention to organize an "immigrant freedom ride" in cooperation with civil rights leaders and immigrant rights activists. Besides achieving visibility for unions' support of immigrants' rights and communities of colour, this alliance allowed the union to both draw on the resources of a broad activist base across different places and strengthen local labour-community coalitions. In planning the stops, local coalitions were formed among union locals, community organizing networks (e.g., the Association of Community Organizations for Reform Now (ACORN) and Jobs with Justice), local churches and local chapters of faith-based organizing networks (e.g., Southern Christian Leadership Conference and Interfaith Worker Justice), local chapters of United Students against Sweatshops, and locally based immigrant organizations. Thus, the IWFR mobilized locally through a wide range of secular and religious organizations in order to build a national movement for immigrants' rights, workers' rights, and racial justice.

The choice of a bus ride, traversing the country towards the centre of national political power, was simultaneously symbolic and strategic. It was designed as a reenactment and commemoration of the freedom rides of the civil rights movement of the 1960s. This symbolic connection was reinforced by the participation of activists from the civil rights movement, by drawing on civil rights movement tactics (see below), and by stopping at civil rights movement memorial sites.

Participants in the freedom ride engaged in a multiplicity of practices at the stops along the route, which drew upon the different identities of participating groups, including union rallies, pickets, marches, prayer breakfasts or lunches, and worship services. The sharing of lived experiences and visions of social justice was central to many of these events in the cities and towns but also on the buses. The spaces of the buses, in particular, became sites where riders shared their stories and articulated visions of citizenship rights as human rights ("no human being is illegal") – thereby constructing community and enabling practices of solidarity. For example, civil disobedience was practised on the buses from Los Angeles when they were stopped by the border patrol outside El Paso, Texas. Anticipating this action, riders on the bus had packed away their legal identification and wore only IWFR identification cards with their first names. They presented these identifications to border patrol agents, who had boarded the bus and demanded identification from all riders of colour. In response, border patrol agents ordered all riders off the bus, separated them into small detention cells in the checkpoint station, and threatened them with arrest unless they divulged their names and citizenship. None of the riders acquiesced, and those in the cells kept singing "We Shall Overcome," a song that they had started on the bus. For the brief time of the interrogation (about four hours), all riders were neither immigrants nor citizens but stateless human beings without papers, challenging successfully the authority of the nation-state.[5]

This case study of the IWFR shows how different spatialities are co-implicated in practice without being reducible to one another. By moving bodies across national space, activists attempted to carry alternative messages about the impact of immigrants, and demands for immigrants' and workers' rights more generally, across the US territory, gradually scaling up their messages to the national scale (symbolized by arrival in Washington, DC, where they gained some national media attention). At the same time, the IWFR mobilized locally in order to build a national movement for immigrants' rights, workers' rights, and racial justice. Stops along the route, where riders joined local workers and community activists, allowed activists of different backgrounds and from different places to link up with each other, helping to construct translocal networks connecting disparate people and groups in different places in support of immigrants' and workers' rights. Thus, it was also an exercise in the politics of networking, highlighting that spatiality is not simply territorial (Massey 2005). The material space of the bus itself became an important place for the construction of community and solidarity among riders, allowing face-to-face interaction among activists and providing a safe space for learning, alternative modes of communication, and articulation of imaginaries.

The fluid way in which the IWFR drew on and interleaved diverse spatialities was crucial for sustained mobilization in support of workers' and immigrants' rights, at multiple scales. The local coalitions formed among diverse activist groups have subsequently established connections across the United States through which immigrants' and workers' rights are actively being promoted. They have also been brought together into a national-scale coalition, the New American Opportunity Campaign (NAOC), which is mobilizing and lobbying for a comprehensive national immigration reform.

Yet, even as social movements pursue complex sociospatial strategies and shape space to advance their agendas, they must also come to terms with already existing spatialities. In the case of the IWFR, the micropublic – a subaltern counterpublic – constructed during the course of the ride, on the bus and at stops along the way, faced its final and most pronounced test as the buses entered Washington, DC, and the ride culminated with a rally of 150,000 people in New York City. It was here, in the centres of political and corporate power, that the difficulties posed by the embeddedness of this micropublic in broader-scale processes and asymmetric power relations re-emerged. In order to gain access to the sanitary confines of the congressional offices of national politicians, discourses were adjusted to align with dominant discourses about immigrants. Thus, when buses arrived in Washington, DC, claims about immigrant rights shifted from a human rights discourse ("no human being is illegal") to one of "hard-working, tax-paying, play-by-the-rules" immigrants, in line with discourses framing two proposed immigration reform bills, the Craig-Kennedy farmworkers' bill, and the McCain-Kennedy immigration bill. Many riders found these strategic shifts to be problematic.

Sociospatial Positionality

We propose the concept of sociospatial positionality as a gateway into comprehending both how the social and the spatial co-evolve (Collinge 2005;

Soja 1980) and how various spatialities are co-implicated with one another (Sheppard 2006). Positionality, in feminist theory, was developed to describe the social situatedness, "in terms of gender, race, class, sexuality and other axes of social difference" (Nagar and Geiger 2007, 267), shaping a subject's understanding of and engagement with the world – her subjectivities, imaginaries, interests, and knowledge (Haraway 1988). In describing both social position as an outcome of social, political, and economic processes and social positioning as a trajectory of practices, positionality occupies a liminal position between structure and agency (Anthias 2002). It frames a subject's ontological and epistemological stance and her starting point for action (Kline 2006). Positionality highlights difference, the situated understandings of subjects, groups, and institutions, but also inequality and, thereby, always power relations. Yet, a subject's (institution's) positionality cannot simply be read off from her (its) social situatedness, because the social and the spatial are mutually constitutive. Space is always already implicated in positionality, as when Chandra Mohanty (2003) chides Western feminists for their blindness to the distinct experiences and positionalities of Third World women, and we use the adjective *sociospatial* to mark positionality as always simultaneously social and spatial.

Sociospatial positionality is also not fixed. It is reenacted on a daily basis, in ways that simultaneously reproduce and challenge positionalities – a process that Judith Butler (1990) has dubbed "citation." On the one hand, everyday actions routinely reproduce preexisting positionalities, giving them a durability that seemingly naturalizes them. Yet, they remain social constructs, always subject to the possibility of transformation. Through subjects' practices, relations of power and situated understandings are contested and renegotiated, as are sociospatial relations, thereby potentially transforming sociospatial positionalities (Rose 19b; Valentine 2002).

In the case of contentious politics, different actors and institutions are differently situated in political struggles and spaces: they bring distinct identities, interests, and imaginaries and differential powers to the boardrooms, workplaces, offices, and streets, in multiple places and at multiple scales. By traversing national space towards the centres of political power and media, and by lobbying political representatives in Washington, DC, the freedom riders inserted their alternative understanding and voice, or positionality, into dominant contemporary US immigration and citizenship debates. Key to the articulation of this shared positionality were both the stops along the route, in diverse localities, strengthening local mobilization in support of these alternative understandings, and the interlocal networking among activists that was facilitated by the IWFR.

To make possible and sustain collective action, the IWFR, in turn, needed to actively negotiate differences in positionality among participants – along lines of gender, class, legal and citizenship status, place of residence, and culture/religion. Much of this occurred in the face-to-face interactions between riders and local activists, both in the cities and towns and in the space-time of the bus rides. Counterhegemonic discourses were constructed and strengthened by getting acquainted, sharing lived experiences, and learning songs together.

Sociospatial positionality is not fixed, however. The shared positionalities that emerged during the IWFR were disrupted when it encountered the preexisting spatialities at its destination. As the IWFR entered Washington, DC, as noted above, discourses were adjusted to be more in line with the national orthodoxy. While this might be interpreted as a purely strategic move, it also brought preexisting power asymmetries between differently positioned IWFR participants to the fore. In the final mass rally in New York, it was not the voices of the riders that were heard but mostly those of white male union organizers and politicians familiar with this context.

Conclusion

In this chapter, we have sought to make two major conceptual arguments. First, we argue that, whereas scale is an important spatiality to contentious politics, particularly given the scaled nature of political and economic structures, other spatialities (place, networks of spatial connectivity, and mobility) are also important – and cannot and should not be reduced to scale or any other spatial "master concept." In contentious politics, each of these spatialities is co-implicated with the others rather than simply existing alongside the others.

Second, emphasizing the co-evolution of the social and the spatial, we highlight the sociospatiality of contentious politics. On the one hand, the already existing sociospatialities of society (both hegemonic sociospatial orders and alternative sociospatialities of grassroots movements) form the context of and thus shape the conditions of possibility for contentious politics. On the other hand, contentious politics seeks to transform existing sociospatialities through sociospatial struggles. We suggest the concept of sociospatial positionality not as a new master concept but simply as a starting point for making sense of these interrelated complexities. If there is an ontological conclusion to be drawn, it is that spatialities, in all their complexity, matter to the evolution of sociospatial relations.

These conceptual arguments are grounded in practice rather than philosophy. As we have sought to show through case study vignettes, actually existing social movements exemplify, in their imaginaries, strategies, and tactics, this co-implication of various spatialities with one another and with society.

ACKNOWLEDGMENTS

This chapter could not have been written without the intellectual contribution of the students in our two "Contested Urban Futures" seminars, in spring 2003 and fall 2004. In particular, we draw on research undertaken during the seminars by Kristin Sziarto, Serena Laws, Ryan Murphy, and Dayne Walling.

NOTES

1. We use the term "spatiality" to refer to any aspect of the socially produced geographical organization of society, shaping material conditions of life, power-knowledge, and subjectivities.
2. Indeed, one prominent definition puts states at the centre of contentious politics, defining the latter as "public, collective and episodic interactions among makers of claims when a) at least some of the interaction adopts noninstitutional forms, b) at least one government is a claimant, an object of claims, or a party to the claims, and c) the claims would, if realized, affect the interests of at least one of the claimants" (Tarrow 2001, 7).
3. Cindi Katz (2001a) has sought to capture such locale-transcending affinities, and contestations of them, through the idea of social topography and countertopographies.
4. The materials presented here are excerpted from Sziarto and Leitner (2006).
5. This civil disobedience replicated a strategy of the civil rights movement in which jailed protesters refused to communicate with police, instead singing "We Shall Overcome."

13
Regional Resistances in an Exurban Region: Intersections of the Politics of Place and the Politics of Scale

Gerda R. Wekerle, L. Anders Sandberg, and Liette Gilbert

On the fringes of cities in Canada and the United States, in the places where the rural, suburban, and urban are interleaved with designated ecological areas, agricultural uses, and extractive industries, resistance is forming to the pressures of urbanization and growth. Anti-sprawl and pro-environment campaigns have emerged in response to accelerated environmental degradation of exurban areas in Oregon, California (Walker 2003), and the United Kingdom (Murdoch and Day 1998), among many other places. In Ontario, more than ten years of struggle against urbanization and sprawl on the Oak Ridges Moraine and, more recently, support for a greenbelt around the Golden Horseshoe in the Greater Toronto Area exemplify these movements of resistance against sprawl and the destruction of nature in a fast-growing urban region.

The Oak Ridges Moraine is characterized by glacial sediments, rolling hills, kettle lakes formed thousands of years ago, and small towns and villages established in the nineteenth century. It extends 160 kilometres in length from the Niagara Escarpment to the Trent River and is on average 13 kilometres wide (and 150 metres deep). It crosses thirty-two municipalities and three administrative regions. The moraine is also located directly in the path of urban growth. Over the past fifty years, the urbanized fabric of the Toronto region has grown six to seven times as a result of a suburbanization process driven by increases in income, land consumption per capita, and pro-development agendas (Bourne 2000; Desfor et al. 2005).

The literature on region and scale tends to address the macrolevel issues of economic and political restructuring (Haughton and Counsell 2004; Paasi 2004). Less attention is paid to "the missing regional scale of politics" (Judd 1998, 33). The actions of environmental movements on the moraine challenge hierarchical and linear scale analyses. We suggest an analysis that draws

FIGURE 13.1

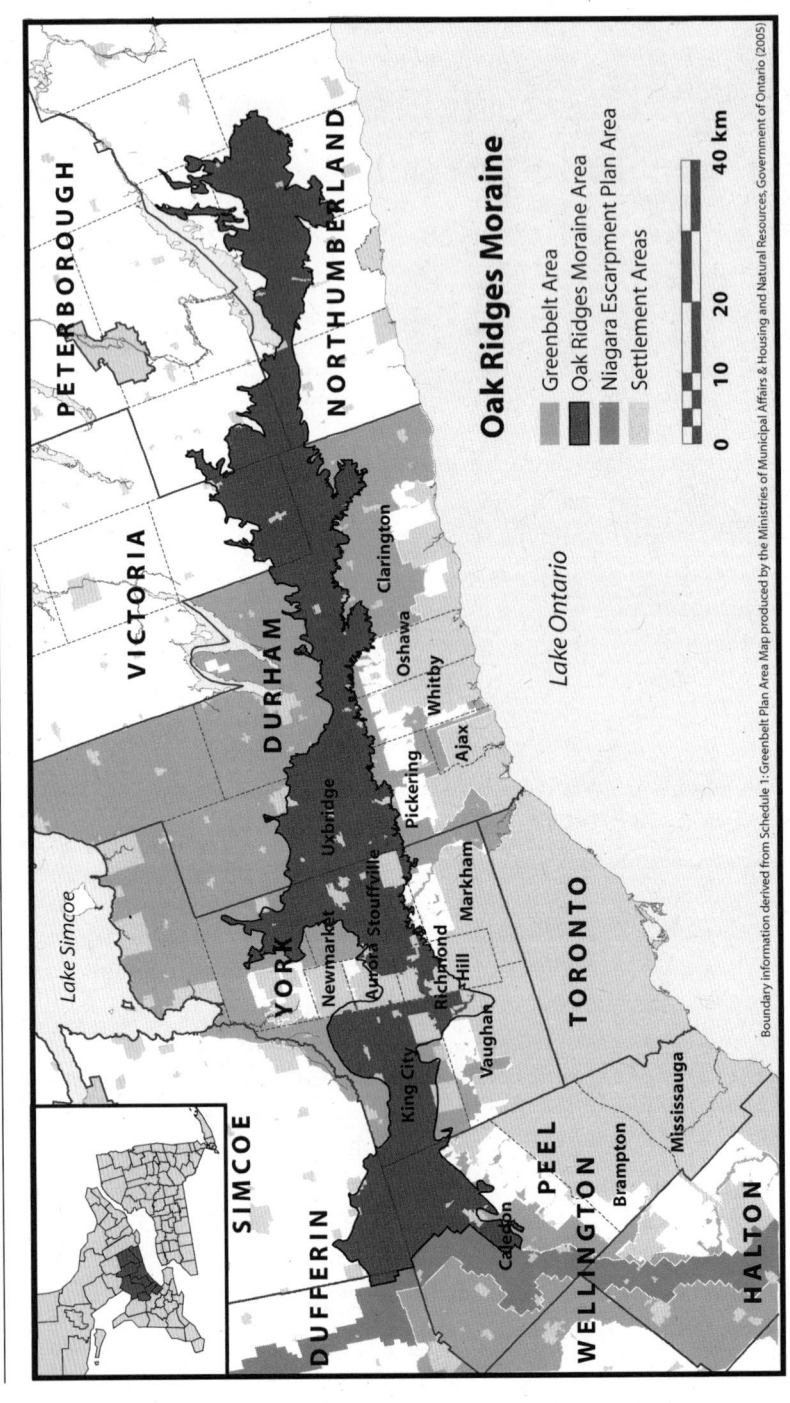

SOURCE: Adapted from Schedule 1: Greenbelt Plan Area Map produced by the Ministries of Municipal Affairs & Housing and Natural Resources, Government of Ontario (2005).

on social movements' imaginaries of place and ecosystem in forging multiscale, networked interactions. They represent a scaled politics of place that articulates a bioregional vision by which environmental movements strategically utilize discourses of bioregionalism and ecosystem management to mobilize resistance to development. By linking people and place, they engage in a scaled environmental politics that operates both vertically and horizontally across space, through bioregions, watersheds, and local, regional, national, and transnational networks. The moraine and the greenbelt examples in Ontario show both the significance and the limitations of this scaled politics of place advocated by social movements. On the one hand, environmental movements on the Oak Ridges Moraine have strategically constructed discourses of bioregionalism and ecosystem management to mobilize resistance to development and to pressure the provincial government to enact legislation to preserve nature and countryside and control sprawl. By linking places and movements across the region, they have engaged in a multiscalar politics that incorporates the interests of the core city and its peripheries. On the other hand, they have been met by state and industry discourses and scale narratives that similarly use ecology to construct win-win scenarios in which growth and ecological concerns can both be accommodated.

Our research suggests a tempered and interactive politics of scale that constructs networks of scaled politics in the urban and ex-urban regions. Such a meshwork emanates from traditionally dominant actors – global, national, and regional capital and state supporters – as well as the social movements operating at multiple scales. In situating our analyses on the exurban fringe of a growing urban region, we attempt to respond to Paul Robbins' (2004, 213) challenge to focus on "how these urban ecologies are produced and why these ecological networks look the way they do."

Narratives of Scale and Place
The geographical literature on scale has tended to focus on the processes of economic globalization. The preferred scale for this analysis tends to be the newly formed regional scales in the European Union and the nation-state and its interrelationships to flows of money, information, and power at larger transnational scales (Leitner, Pavlik, and Sheppard 2002; Swyngedouw 1992). In this chapter, we examine the ways in which social movements strategically and discursively construct and reframe scales and redefine political opportunities in a multiscalar politics. The concept of the politics of scale has come to be utilized to analyze a wide range of sociopolitical struggles as well as

socioeconomic processes. We focus specifically on "the political work that scale can perform" (McCann 2003, 160): that is, the ways in which scale is a discursive frame used by competing interests to define or redefine the locations of political power. The starting point for analysis is social actors rather than structures or restructuring. The focus is on social movement strategies, including the strategic uses of scale; the networks created over space and time; the dance of political opportunities opening up and closing down; the initiation of change; and the interplay between movement actors and state agents. Instead of "scale," it is useful to think of active verbs, such as *scaling* and *rescaling*, that denote dynamic processes. In the urban context, social movements, and particularly environmental movements, play the scales of space and time in their invocations of nature's place in a timeline of millennia.

Bringing a scalar dimension to social movements, one cannot avoid the importance of place and its constructions. As Smith, Light, and Roberts (1998, 4) argue, places are carved out by several interconnected processes, marking the place, naming the place to give it significance and identity, and intentionally reorganizing "the physical world" – the landscape. All of these processes of place making have been at work in the Oak Ridges Moraine struggles. The movements to preserve the moraine illustrate Manuel Castells' (1997) findings that the environmental groups growing fastest in number are grassroots, locality-based, and stewardship groups that focus on place and identity, the protection of natural features, and the linkage of issues such as pesticides, habitat destruction, and wetland preservation.

There is a long history of scholarship on regional development and the political struggles over the commodification of place (Haughton and Counsell 2004; Logan and Molotch 1987). Citizen resistances to sprawl are also prevalent in exurban places across Canada and the United States as formerly rural areas and areas of ecological significance are threatened by development pressures. What is significant about the resistance to development on the Oak Ridges Moraine is the creation of a regional citizens' movement focused on the concept of a bioregion (Gilbert, Sandberg, and Wekerle 2008; forthcoming).

Bioregionalism has been described as an environmental movement and social philosophy that evolved along ecological, anthropological, and spiritual lines (Taylor 2000). These approaches shared the idea of a region as "home," as "living in place" (Berg and Dasmann 1977), as "life place" (Thayer 2004) and its biophysical equivalent ecosystems. A bioregion is, therefore, more than biogeographical. As Aberley (1999, 34) argues, "bioregionalism supports place-based cultural transformations ... [and thus] the bioregion could become the political arena within which resistance against ecological and social exploitation could be produced." Some scholars, focusing on ecological scales, view ecosystems as specific places defined by natural boundaries such as drainage patterns. However, as Sayre (2005, 279) notes, focusing on the boundaries of ecosystems runs counter to the notion that "natural systems are determined by multiple processes operating simultaneously on numerous spatial scales." In this sense, "ecological scales are no less produced than geographical scales" (Sayre 2005, 287).

Regional Resistances: The Scaled Politics of Place

The politics of place and the politics of scale in the exurban regions of the Greater Toronto Area intersect in the regional resistances to urban sprawl over the Oak Ridges Moraine, to the north, and in the greenbelt in the Golden Horseshoe, stretching from Peterborough in the east to Niagara in the west (Wekerle, Sandberg, and Gilbert 2009, forthcoming; Wekerle et al. 2007).

Before 1999, citizens fought local place-based battles to preserve the moraine. In 1995, after the election of a pro-growth, neoliberal provincial government that relaxed environmental and planning controls, some hamlets and towns were faced with the prospect of new development proposals that would double and even quadruple their populations (Gilbert, Wekerle, and Sandberg 2005). These pressures came to a head in 2000, when development proposals to build 30,000 housing units on the edges of kettle lakes and wetlands in Richmond Hill (fifteen miles north of Toronto) threatened to split the moraine in half. One February evening, 1,600 angry exurban residents faced Richmond Hill's pro-development council and demanded a freeze on development.

This action was followed by several years of concerted organizing and citizen resistance, across the region, to development proposals for housing, golf courses, resorts, and road construction, all coordinated through coalitions and alliances that involved homeowners and naturalist groups, environmental organizations, and national and global organizations (Wekerle and Abbruzzese 2009). These groups forged a moraine-wide movement of resistance that emphasized common themes of water and ecosystem integrity that overrode the images of middle-class exurban homeowners solely protecting their own privilege against newcomers. The constant barrage of public protests, media events, legal challenges, and planning hearings eventually led the provincial government to initiate a region-wide consultation planning process. It resulted in the passage of the Oak Ridges Moraine Conservation Act in 2001 and the Conservation Plan in 2002 (Province of Ontario 2001, 2002). In keeping with the principles of ecosystem management, natural core areas and natural linkage areas were designated, as were areas where settlement was permitted. The many developments already under way were, however, allowed to proceed.

A change in the provincial government in 2003 resulted in proposals for a greenbelt. The 2005 Greenbelt Plan emphasized countryside protection, including natural heritage systems, the headwaters of major watersheds, and some of Ontario's best agricultural lands (Province of Ontario 2005). The aim of both the Oak Ridges Moraine Conservation Plan and the subsequent Greenbelt Plan is to reorganize conservation policy at a regional scale and increase the scale of land preservation to match species' habitats, thereby creating "natural regions" (Geisler and Benford 1998, 35). The Greenbelt Plan seeks to curb sprawl by targeting specific satellite towns and cities for growth while freezing growth in other areas. In the lead-up to this legislation, provincial government public consultation processes opened up new political opportunities for environmental movements to actively and strategically construct the moraine and the greenbelt as place, scale, and nature.

Social Movements Construct Scale

The moraine is both socially and politically constructed. The environmental movements and networks that came together around the preservation of the Oak Ridges Moraine and the establishment of a greenbelt have displayed substantial and extensive "scale capabilities." They have mobilized resources and supporters, created networks, taken advantage of political opportunities, and framed a credible discourse that challenges dominant growth discourses. As a primarily white, middle-class, and politically connected movement, it has succeeded in mobilizing counterpublics to pressure two different governments to preserve a large part of the moraine and pass greenbelt legislation that extends the bioregional agenda to protect natural systems and preserve farmland over a much larger scale. How has this come about?

We suggest that social movement strategies have transformed a politics of place focused on "hotspots" of environmental conflict across a broad region into a rescaled regional politics that networks environmental organizations operating at multiple scales (Wekerle, Sandberg, and Gilbert 2009). For more than fifteen years, environmental activists have been laying the groundwork for this struggle, beginning with the Save the Oak Ridges Moraine (STORM) coalition, founded in 1989, to coordinate the efforts of various small homeowner and naturalist organizations challenging development proposals. Many of these groups relied on the knowledge of other residents of the moraine – planners, landscape architects, and engineers – to interpret land use plans, critique developers' studies of environmental impacts, and assist in mounting legal challenges at a provincial planning appeal board – the Ontario Municipal Board. They also relied on the support from groups on other parts of the moraine to come out to public meetings, to send letters to councillors, mayors, and newspapers, and to share strategies. Local homeowner associations solicited the expertise of environmental groups for the scientific arguments for preserving the moraine, advice on how to make legal challenges to development, and training in new organizing tactics.

STORM, the Federation of Ontario Naturalists, and Earthroots called GTA-wide meetings in 2001 (in downtown Toronto) that linked both exurban and downtown Toronto environmental non-governmental organizations (NGOs). They developed a common analysis of problems on the moraine and created a website (www.oakridgesmoraine.com) with links to every group involved in fighting developments. STORM's map of "hotspots" of environmental threat across the moraine visually highlighted the region-wide nature of the problem. These actions attracted the attention of national and international environmental organizations such as the Nature Conservancy of Canada and the World Wildlife Fund, which linked their existing campaigns to the issues of sprawl and exurban nature at the same time as they attempted to piggyback on the visibility of the moraine campaign for their own organizations. With all of these diverse groups with different histories and scalar politics attempting to participate, environmental groups not only cooperated but also competed with one another for credit, air time, funding, and legitimacy.

Figure 13.2 illustrates two different and interrelated constructions of scale by social movement actors on the moraine. Environmental actors, including social movement organizations and the state, operating at different scales to preserve the Oak Ridges Moraine are presented in the left-hand column, linked to their constructions of nature at various scales in the right-hand column. While such a typology might create a somewhat illusory image of a hierarchy of scales with divisions between them, key actors are networked both vertically and horizontally across the region. Actors at each scale move across scales as issues are reframed and political moments appear and disappear.

Figure 13.2

ORM/greenbelt: Scales and actors

Environmental actors	Environment/Nature
Local/place	
Local naturalist groups	Species at risk: Jefferson salamander
Homeowners associations	Hotspots: e.g., Lake Wilcox
Municipal governments/villages	Environmental amenities: trails, parks
Regional: Identity and bioregionalism	
STORM	Oak Ridges Moraine
Save the Rouge Valley System	Rouge Valley, Oak Ridges Moraine
Greenbelt Alliance	Environmental hotspots
Ontario Nature	Watersheds: Humber, Credit, Rouge Rivers
Ontario Federation of Agriculture	Farmlands
Regional governments	Green space
Conservation authorities	Floodplains, watersheds
City of Toronto: ORM Committee	Headwaters
Provincial government	Environmentally sensitive areas
National: ENGOs and the state	
Environmental Defence Canada	Kyoto Accord targets; local hotspots
Nature Conservancy of Canada	Environmentally sensitive lands
Federal government	Federal lands, Endangered Species Act, fisheries
	Rouge Valley; rivers
Transnational/global	
Sierra Club	Ecological corridors and cores; global warming
World Wildlife Fund	Ecological corridors and cores

Supporting the provincial government's proposal for a greenbelt in the Greater Golden Horseshoe, a new organization, the Ontario Greenbelt Alliance, created a website (www.greenbelt.ca) that identifies the "hotspots" of environmental degradation across the region, leaving out political boundaries and jurisdictions. This strategy sought to expand attachment and mobilization beyond specific localities to encompass threats posed across the region by aggregate extraction, new roads, housing development on farmlands, and waterways contamination.

Environmental coalitions interlinked with regional organizations, such as the conservation authorities, regional governments, and the provincial government on specific issues or sites. Public meetings often included a mix of these key actors. Leaders and activists of certain environmental organizations were appointed by the provincial government as representatives of civil society to participate in advisory and consultative processes on the moraine and the subsequent greenbelt. Others were left out because they were deemed too radical or strident. After passage of the legislation, the provincial government established an Oak Ridges Moraine Foundation and Trust and a Greenbelt Foundation and appointed leaders of key environmental organizations to the boards. These quasi-autonomous agencies, reliant on state funding, reflected new models of environmental governance and ecosystem management based on partnership and the participation of multiple stakeholders that have become commonplace in environmental conservation (Cortner and Moote 1999). At the same time, such partnerships have also been criticized for pulling environmental leaders out of the movement and for potentially dulling the watchdog role of environmental organizations.

The City of Toronto has been a strategic actor in this regional conflict outside its boundaries. Framing its concerns for the watershed's streams that run through the city to Lake Ontario, the city established an Oak Ridges Moraine Committee that allocated over $1 million to the Toronto Region and Conservation Authority and Save the Rouge Valley System. These groups represented the city's interests at the Ontario Municipal Board hearings on development proposals in Richmond Hill when the board ruled that the City of Toronto did not have standing, as the city's boundaries did not extend into the area. Subsequently, the city allocated funding to another environmental group on the moraine to challenge a new regional sewer pipe that would open land for development and bring sewage from new residential developments to a waste treatment plant on the shores of Lake Ontario. In both instances, the City of Toronto utilized its financial and political resources to assert its interests in the environmental impacts on the city of new infrastructure and residential developments springing up on the periphery and outside the political boundaries of the city.

National environmental NGOs, such as Environmental Defence Canada, have also allocated substantial resources to research, advocacy, and litigation in the moraine battles, as have national think tanks such as the Pembina Institute. A scalar argument links global warming to sprawl and the pollution caused by the fossil fuel consumption of cars. The federal government became involved when environmental groups brought legal suits charging that the Fisheries Act is violated in the impacts of development on streams. Similarly, transnational ENGOs such as the Sierra Club and World Wildlife Fund have taken a strong interest in the regional battles over the Oak Ridges Moraine, linking them to their own campaigns on sprawl and global warming.

Strong interpersonal and political networks linking individuals from small residents' groups with long-standing environmental organizations headquartered in the City of Toronto, the links to municipal and provincial governments, and the movements back and forth from advocacy group to ENGOs to the state cannot be captured by a table. A landscape architect active in the work on the moraine and the city's waterfront commented that as few as twelve key people made a difference as they circulated in various agencies at different levels of government, operated as consultants, or were appointed to advisory panels and foundations. The connections suggest the construction of what Wendy Harcourt and Arturo Escobar (2002) refer to as "meshworks." Meshworks are woven by interlocking oppositional, non-hierarchical, and diverse actions brought together by complementarity or common experiences. They involve "two parallel dynamics, strategies of localization and of interweaving," that place and link together various sites (Harcourt and Escobar 2002). These meshworks are particularly well expressed in the common scalar notion of the bioregion and its implementation through ecosystem conservation.

Putting the Ecosystem Scale into Practice

How did the language of bioregions and ecosystems come to figure so prominently in the campaigns to preserve the moraine and to establish a greenbelt? Ecosystem management is recognized as including not just science but also values of social and political change. It integrates scientific knowledge of ecological relationships with a sociopolitical and values framework focused on the long-term protection of native ecosystem integrity (Grumbine 1994). The scale of management for biodiversity has increasingly been redefined to include not just islands of conservation surrounded by development but also entire bioregions of thousands of acres directed at long-term ecological change on the order of centuries (Cortner and Moote 1999).

Ecosystem concepts initially gained public attention in the Greater Toronto Area in the report of the Royal Commission on the Future of the Toronto Waterfront, *Regeneration: Toronto's Waterfront and Sustainable City* (1992). It outlined the fundamental themes of the ecosystem approach: the ecosystem as home; the entire web of links among and between ecosystems; sustainability; understanding places as interconnected scales, and integrating processes;

and the focus on watersheds. Environmental activists working for the Waterfront Regeneration Trust went on to play leading roles in regional ENGOs such as the Federation of Ontario Naturalists (now Ontario Nature), in the conservation authorities, in provincial ministries such as the Ministry of Natural Resources, and in the newly created Oak Ridges Moraine Foundation and Greenbelt Foundation. In this way, an organization located and focused on Toronto's waterfront became an important seedbed for the development of a new discourse of bioregionalism and supported the emergence of policy entrepreneurs who spread out into the region to promote regional innovation in ecosystem planning.

Initially, conservation discourse focused on watersheds. The headwaters of sixty-five streams and rivers are located on the moraine. Environmentalists on the moraine pictured the water we drink today as deposited thousands of years ago through glacial formations. This prehistoric water and the watersheds through which it flowed were linked to each household and body by domestic images, such as those invoked by calling the Oak Ridges Moraine "the rain barrel" of Ontario (Bocking 2005). This analysis of the moraine as the place of watersheds was further linked to the depletion of the rain barrel by bottling companies and a big sewer pipe through York Region to the lake that will open up greenfield development to more sprawling communities.

Over time, the prevailing discourse became that of ecosystem preservation and bioregionalism, which included watersheds within a large construct. An emphasis on watersheds provided rhetorical support for ecosystem approaches to land use planning on the moraine (Wekerle 2000, 2001). For example, in January 2001, Environmental Defence Canada and Save the Rouge Valley System invited an American conservation biologist, Reed Noss, to appear as an expert witness on their behalf at an Ontario Municipal Board hearing. Noss (2001) assisted the Oak Ridges Moraine activists in constructing a bigger picture of ecosystem integrity beyond the moraine – the Niagara Escarpment-Oak Ridges-Algonquin to Adirondacks Heritage (NOAH) project, moving it beyond the regional to the continental scale. Such a project does not seek to breach the borders of the security state that constrains the movement of people and goods, but by creating a connected system of green spaces NOAH would allow the free movement of animals, species, and genetic flows.

The language of ecosystems and bioregions also predominates in the public debates over both the Oak Ridges Moraine Act and the Greenbelt Act. Drawing on the bioregional imaginary of home, flyers from various environmental groups demanding moraine protection legislation have emphasized the interconnections between the habitats of humans in cities, towns, and rural estate developments and the habitats of animals, birds, and amphibians. Emotional appeals often connect habitat conservation to images of home. In a four-page colour flyer inserted in a major newspaper, Save the Rouge Valley System played on the sympathies of approximately 500,000 readers for a defenceless fawn (perhaps evoking their childhood recollections of the Walt Disney movie *Bambi*) in a poster that decried its homelessness. This flyer's images and text highlight the ways in which environmental campaigns on the moraine tend to emphasize the home place of nature while paying significantly less attention, rhetorically and in terms of social movement tactics, to the cultures of human residents on the moraine and the loss of cultural heritage in places at risk of being changed forever by development.

Time as Scale

In the resistance to development on the moraine and greenbelt, social movements simultaneously construct time and scale. One image that has often been used is a cross-section of the moraine with water coming in as rain and seeping through the sediments of sand and gravel to become deep aquifers. Environmentalists argue that water drawn from deep aquifers on the moraine may have been deposited there thousands of years before. Such constructions of time are often utilized in the moraine battles. In the focus on hydrogeology, environmental groups have framed their appeals in terms of nature's time, particularly in the narrative of how the ice age deposited sediment that allowed for the storage of ground water as aquifers. They also invoke ecosystem time when they argue that it takes fifty years to restore sand and gravel pits on the moraine or that streams that are degraded will take decades to restore. When arguments are made about species at risk, they are framed in terms of species time – the timeline on Earth of a whole species and the risks of extinction. Beatley and Manning (1997, 34) note that the notion of planning for enduring value over a time span of hundreds or thousands of years evokes "a moral time frame."

Residents often make generational claims, pleading that preserving nature occurs on behalf of their children and grandchildren (Richmond Hill Council Public Hearing 2000). Farmers challenging the greenbelt legislation argue that they have a right to be heard as their families have farmed the same place for five generations or that they live on a "century farm." The provincial government also strategically manipulates time: first in studying, shelving, and delaying decisions on the preservation of the moraine for almost thirty years and then in compressing public consultations on both the moraine and the greenbelt into two-week periods in the late summer and early fall, timed to coincide with vacation periods when citizens are least available for consultation or mobilization. Similarly, the provision for reviewing the Oak Ridges Moraine legislation after ten years scales time in such a way that existing politicians may no longer be in power when the debates on growth and conservation are reopened. For environmental movements mobilized around the struggles to preserve the moraine and institute a greenbelt, the emphasis is on long-term solutions, such as a commitment to an agricultural preserve on the moraine in perpetuity. The movement activists' emphasis on a long timeline is contrasted with the short-term time frames of politicians who are elected for four-year terms and the more medium-term scaling of time of developers who may own land for a decade or more. On the moraine, the scaled politics of time intersects with a politics of place to shape both the strategies of social movements and the policy outcomes.

The Politics of Scale, Place, and Global Capitalism

In observing the sociopolitical changes on the Oak Ridges Moraine and the greenbelt in Ontario's Greater Golden Horseshoe, the scalar and place politics of social movements have figured prominently in the debate over land use change. But how effective have they been? Social movements on the moraine have actively and strategically constructed the moraine, despite its variety of habitats, as one regional entity at risk and in need of saving – a tactic that makes it more difficult to accuse these activists of protecting their own privilege. A discourse of bioregionalism and ecosystems has drawn in state agents operating at local, regional, provincial, and national scales. The intensity and visibility of these environmental struggles have engaged the attention and resources of national and global environmental organizations that link these place-based struggles to similar campaigns elsewhere and to global environmental issues such as climate change.

Yet, social movements and citizen activism can only do so much. Inevitably, they come up against the scaled politics of global capitalism as represented by developers, the aggregate industry, and recreational industries that also construct the moraine as prime real estate. These moraine actors are in tune with state agencies and municipal governments that promote population growth through investment in infrastructure (Wekerle et al. 2007). These intersections and "the active way in which the property capital and land development process have propelled suburban decentralization" (Walker 1986, 402) have been underexamined.

The environmental movements on the moraine see themselves as engaged in land-based activism that intervenes in these property circuits through engaging in the land use planning process and envisioning alternative uses for the land. Instead of viewing the moraine land as waste land, or even as wilderness, they strategically construct the land as providing essential ecosystem services in storing and cleaning drinking water, providing habitat for endangered species, and offering a respite for urban dwellers. The slogan of the campaign, "SAVE DON'T PAVE," succinctly captures their vision. This view of land as productive ecosystems is meant to clash fundamentally with the belief that greenfield lands are primarily a commodity for exchange and profit, to be warehoused until the demand emerges for new development. At the same time, this view buys into a managerialist approach that emphasizes the services that nature provides rather than any inherent rights of nature.

The dynamics of growth and change in the Greater Toronto Area and pressures on the land base are linked to the global economy. Social conflicts around property rights arise when states attempt to intervene to manage growth. Ecosystem management proposals institutionalized in the Oak Ridges Moraine Conservation Plan and the Greenbelt Act in some instances appear revolutionary in their challenge of private property regimes and zoning that fixes rights in property. Reorganizing conservation policy on a regional scale has fundamental impacts on property rights. The large reserves required of the ecosystem approach cross boundaries of ownership and jurisdiction. This has been described as a move to "ecocentric land planning" (Geisler and Benford 1998, 132). It introduces "an ecological view of property" (Sax 1993), whereby land use is governed by ecological needs rather than being solely the owner's property to dispose of in the marketplace (Logan and Wekerle 2008).

In consultations on the greenbelt, environmentalists and the provincial government miscalculated and were taken by surprise by the opposition of farmers. In addressing primarily issues of ecological integrity and connectivity, and the concentration of growth in specific nodes, environmentalists created an opening for landowners to challenge an underlying principle of the greenbelt – that long-term public goals supersede private property relations. The bioregional vision of environmentalists had not addressed the survival and livelihood concerns of farmers. Over the past ten years, the decline in commodity prices for soybeans and corn has put Ontario farmers in direct competition with farmers in Argentina and elsewhere. Farmers bring the global economy "home" in their stories of bodies subjected to long hours of hard labour, work well beyond retirement age, and the stress of being unable to make a living after five generations have cultivated a family farm. They argue that economic growth strategies in the GTA put pressures on the farm infrastructure and on farmland. The analysis of farmers is that international and national economic policies impact their lives and livelihood. Their solution is the "last harvest" – selling out to developers who will pave over the farmlands for residential and industrial uses to feed capital accumulation. This response conflicts with provincial, regional, and municipal land use policies designed to manage growth and protect threatened countryside in a fast-growing region.

Farmers have argued that you cannot preserve farmlands without preserving farmers, which requires attention to the political economy of agricultural production, the impacts of capital flows, and the expansion of urban infrastructures on the land base. It requires greater attention to the social and political constructions of place, particularly as they are expressed in land conflicts and property rights. Throughout the process of implementing the greenbelt legislation, positions hardened. A radical fringe of farmers, with ties to Alberta and US-based "wise use movements," printed up red-and-white protest signs, "This land is ours. Back off government" (Forsey 2005, 21). Their claims are rooted in a view of land that is commodified, bought, and sold to the highest bidder. In contrast, environmentalists argue that "this land is *all ours,*" laying the groundwork for a stewardship ideology within a bioregion. Indeed, this claim has prevailed as farmers have not received compensation for land that was frozen from development.

However, the property rights of developers have been more readily respected. A land swap (whose terms have yet to be made public) gave major developers who lost land to parkland on the central part of the moraine properties of comparable or greater value on the eastern edge of the moraine (from provincially owned lands). On the greenbelt, a project of the provincial Liberal government, developers' interests were protected by drawing the boundaries of the greenbelt in such a way that sufficient land to the south, outside the boundaries of the urbanized area, was left to accommodate population growth for the next thirty years. In some towns on the moraine, 60 to 80 percent of remaining greenfields are already owned by developers intent on obtaining rezoning and development approvals in order to cash in on high demand for housing and other urban uses in the region. These actors, most of them regional developers, with a few multinational corporations, have the resources and connections to fight the greenbelt's freeze on development through private meetings with the minister of municipal affairs and housing, through their formal representation on advisory panels and in strategic stakeholder meetings, and in organized lobbying by their well-funded trade organizations, the Toronto Homebuilders Association and the Urban Development Institute.

The greenbelt boundaries also meant that farmland outside the boundaries, which had previously been protected by municipal plans was now subject to greater pressures for development. Furthermore, developers had already bought land or sought development approvals for lands that leap-frogged the greenbelt boundaries and put pressures on rural lands farther north (Wekerle 2008).

Developers and extractive industries construct their own scale narratives based on ecological and environmental concerns. Hydrogeological consultants for developers have challenged the moraine as a water filter, claiming that the majority of the water infiltration occurs outside the moraine. They also argue that, if proper care is taken, residential subdivisions can accommodate adequate infiltration (Swainson 2000). Sand and gravel producers similarly argue that their operations on the moraine contribute to lower carbon emissions because their trucks travel shorter distances to the local market. They also claim that sand and gravel pit rehabilitation measures can improve local ecologies (Chambers and Sandberg 2007; Patano and Sandberg 2005).

Conclusion

The long campaign to save the Oak Ridges Moraine and create a greenbelt represents an exurban movement that utilized a politics of place at a regional scale. This case study contributes to our understanding of a largely under-studied regional scale of politics. The moraine struggles reveal that place can be constructed at the scale of a regional ecological feature; attachment can be to an imaginary of home for human and non-human natures; and defence of privilege and generation of alternative visions may go hand in hand. Throughout various campaigns, the moraine was constructed as a place through the interconnected processes outlined by Smith, Light, and Roberts (1998). Boundaries were established (although not universally agreed upon), and the moraine was shown on maps of both environmental groups and government agencies. Stories were told about the origins of the moraine and changes over time. New narratives were generated, based on struggles over preserving specific streams, forests, or species, giving the moraine and its protectors significance and identity.

Our analysis outlines how these ecological networks came to be and how scale was actively constructed and deftly manipulated for political ends, incorporating contestations over local environmental hotspots, watersheds, and the bioregion as a whole. In support of Aberley's (1999) claims that bioregionalism provides a frame for both cultural transformation and political resistance to ecological and social exploitation, we found that exurban residents and environmental activists constructed a bioregional identity and transformed exurban politics by utilizing a bioregional frame to resist ecological degradation through continuing urban development. At the same time, they engaged in a scalar reframing of political networks and coalitions that brought together social movement actors operating at local, regional, national, and international scales. By linking places and movements across the region, the result was a multiscalar politics that incorporates the interests of the core city and its surrounding region while engaging movements operating at a broader scale in localized ecological struggles that reflect wider societal contestations over growth, sprawl, preservation of nature, and practices of democracy.

From the perspective of the outcomes – provincial legislation to preserve sensitive ecological systems and threatened countryside through regional plans – this may be viewed as another example among many of a top-down, state-centric attempt to politically construct a region to manage urban growth. Yet, our narrative suggests that the singularity of this case revolves around the construction of a regionalism from below that is based on the imaginary of a bioregion that is actively constructed by civil society actors in resistance to the notion of a region that is primarily constructed in terms of economic growth. Our narrative delineates how environmental non-governmental organizations operating at a range of scales devised multiscalar strategies to scale nature preservation as a regional issue requiring regional policy changes. These insights into the ways in which scale is discursively produced and strategically utilized deepen our understanding of scaling processes in regions undergoing economic and political restructuring.

This chapter also examines the intersections of the production of regional scale and identities and the processes of place making. Through political contention over saving the Oak Ridges Moraine from development and instituting a greenbelt, the region was socially and politically constructed.

Imaginaries of place and ecosystems came together in the articulation of bioregion. A bioregionally based movement sought to move beyond the limitations of defensive localism that is often attached to place-based movements by creating networks across the region and scaling up movement linkages and demands for change. Instead of separating critical analyses of scale and place, our study suggests that a closer examination of the ways in which political actors mutually construct scale and place may further illuminate the dynamic processes of change in urban regions.

ACKNOWLEDGMENTS

We thank Stephanie Rutherford, a PhD candidate in the Faculty of Environmental Studies, York University, for her assistance in researching timelines and environmental organizations.

14
Revolutionary Cooks in the Hungry Ghetto: The Black Panther Party's Biopolitics of Scale from Below

Nik Heynen

> Don't you know
> That for you
> And for me
> The world is a ghetto
> – War (1972)

In a fiery polemic on 18 November 1970, Huey P. Newton, co-founder of the Black Panther Party (BPP), addressed a large crowd at Boston College. Newton's revolutionary message was delivered to hundreds of people frustrated with the oppression of millions within the ghettos of American cities, in the United States as a whole, and throughout the world. Central to his message was a simple point: in order to fight these struggles at all scales, in order to ameliorate oppression within both US ghettos and other countries throughout the world, people must survive. This message – that human life is the foundation of emancipatory politics – set the tone for Newton's (2002a, 160-61) dramatic speech: "We, the people, are threatened with genocide because racism and fascism are rampant in the country and throughout the world. And the ruling circle in North America is responsible. We intend to change all of that, and in order to change it, there must be a total transformation. But until we can achieve that total transformation, we must exist. In order to exist, we must survive. It is necessary for our children to grow up healthy with functional and creative minds ... That is why we have a breakfast program for children."

The BPP's Free Breakfast for Children Program can be read as passive and reformist, as it was by former BPP minister of information Eldridge Cleaver when he suggested that "Babylon is quiet. Pigs are comfortable. Why? Because the vanguard is cooking fucking breakfasts instead of drawing guns!" (quoted in Brown 1992, 221). Alternatively, the breakfast program can be seen as providing a hopeful example of grassroots efforts to subvert biopolitics or engage in "biopolitics from below" for the sake of engaging with empire, whose power over local populations has long been at the seat of its political economic dominance. As Agamben (1998, 120) suggests in *Homo Sacer: Sovereign Power and Bare Life*, "in the notion of bare life the interlacing of politics and life has become so tight that it cannot easily be analyzed." In this chapter, I want to use the BPP's politics of scale as they unfolded through its radical anti-hunger politics, and specifically its Free Breakfast for Children Program, for the sake of drawing our attention to the potential for bare life, naked survival, and social reproduction as the keys to radical politics.

In focusing on bare life, social reproduction, and survival within the context of the BPP's radical anti-hunger politics, discussing US ghettos as distinct socially produced scales embedded within myriad other scalar configurations central to US political economy is key. Because the notion is so central to understanding the BPP's radical anti-hunger politics of scale, I want to clarify that I am using "ghetto" as a spatial scale in line with BPP political discourse. I argue that it is related to common discussions of the "inner city" urban scale but with greater specification in order to better grasp efforts to mobilize the political power within those local residents frustrated with the material inequality explicitly thrust upon them in US inner cities. Related to this, in 1969, BPP member Landon Williams, in an article in the party's newspaper *The Black Panther*, wrote about "black capitalism and what it means." The article discussed the disadvantages that inner-city African American communities faced as a result of their role within US political economy. Williams suggested that

> the crime rate and prostitution rate in our communities is due directly to poor education, poor housing, poor clothing, no jobs, and an ever present hungry stomach. These things again are directly attributed to capitalism and exploitation. The ghettos in this country are not here by accident. They're a place where a readily available source of cheap manpower can be dumped and stored until it is needed and as a market place for dumping billions of dollars worth of inferior goods and corrupt services. So the ghettos here in America are not here by accident. They're set up and maintained by capitalists in this country for a specific purpose and design. (2; emphasis added)

In an effort to reproduce ghetto spaces in response to these social power relations that Williams refers to, the social history of the BPP's political engagement with both grassroots supporters and the US government illustrates the degree to which the party's treatment of social reproduction has innumerable ramifications for better "unlacing" life from political economy for the sake of reorienting biopolitics. While the details of BPP history have increasingly been presented through biographical projects (see Abu-Jamal 2004; Brown 1992; Newton 1972, 1973; Seale 1978, 1991; and Shakur 1987) and related edited collections (Cleaver and Katsiaficas 2001; Hilliard and Cole 1993; Hilliard and Weise 2002; Jones 1998), there has yet to be substantial theorization about the ramifications of its radical anti-hunger politics for reproducing life and urban space. Engaging these politics presents hopeful insights into the theoretical power of the politics of scale but also, more importantly, serves to illustrate the degree to which the interrelated and independent processes of social reproduction are *always* embedded within *all* spatial scales *simultaneously all the time.*

Biopolitics from Below

At the conference where I first presented this chapter,[1] Neil Smith spoke about the potential blunting of political interventions that in one way or another engage scalar theory. He suggested that, despite the intellectual and political insights gained through scalar perspectives, these gains have come at some cost. More specifically, Smith said that, "Where everything is scale, scale becomes nothing theoretically, and it is vital to keep the theoretical edge of scale research moving forward." He then asked, "How does scale theory now help us rethink questions of uneven geographical development, and how do the experiences of global and local change help us rework the politics of scale?" I read Smith's question as referring to not just the politics of scale but also politics more generally. I would argue that, in order to keep the notion of politics of scale sharp, we must take several steps back and ground these politics, and all other politics, in the processes of social reproduction, material inequality, corporal survival, and naked life. In taking a step backward, we can hopefully remind ourselves that, in order to produce human history, humans must first live (see Marx and Engels 1998, 36). If we can manage to take this step back in a sincere, theoretically robust way, then I suspect that there will be much less need for concern about our sociospatial theorizing becoming dull.

While there has been a small group of scholars of all stripes, especially feminists, who have argued for more attention to these fundamental notions relating to social reproduction, for the most part, political economists still take many of these essentially material/biological processes for granted (for exemplary treatments, see Katz 2004; Marston 2000; McDowell 1999; Mitchell, Marston, and Katz 2004; and Pred 1981). In an attempt to highlight the significance of survival and social reproduction to other political economic processes of production, consumption, etc., I would like to suggest revisiting biopolitics as discussed by Foucault in such a way that we conceptualize the power of/control over life more in line with attempts to resist/topple empire.

Foucault's (1994) historicizing and theorizing of the "birth of biopolitics" present a useful concept to illuminate the connections between social reproduction and the politics of scale. Foucault's notion of "biopolitics" refers to attempts by liberal governments to rationalize the problems presented by sustaining human populations, including health, sanitation, birth rate, etc. According to Foucault, these issues became especially problematic for liberal forms of government when they began to struggle with which rules should be applied for managing biopolitics. Foucault (1990, 136) discussed how in ancient times *the sovereign* exercised the "right of life only by exercising his right to kill." This power has been turned on its head regarding the right of the social body for the sake of ensuring, developing, and sustaining its life. To this end, Hardt and Negri (2000, 24) suggest that "biopower is a form of power that regulates social life from its interior, following it, interpreting it, absorbing it, and rearticulating it." Because of its overwhelming capacity to command life, Foucault (1990, 141) suggests that these "naked questions of survival," and the biopower that resulted, were a necessary factor for the development of capitalism, since without controlling the social reproduction of bodies they could not have been inserted into the "machinery of production."

To understand the BPP's radical anti-hunger politics of survival as also necessarily a politics of scale against empire requires engagement with the generally "vexing" nature of social reproduction. It also necessitates underscoring how, because social reproduction serves as a foundation of capitalist political economy, there is the potential to thwart capitalism through the facilitation of biopolitics from below. Katz (2001b) helps to elucidate what makes social reproduction so easily taken for granted from a theoretical perspective. First, she suggests that, since social reproduction must be completed in order for society to persist, when the state, capital, or society fails to contribute to the processes inherent in social reproduction, increased pressures shift to individuals, households, and families. Because the state, capitalists, and different elements within civil society too often recognize this material priority, individuals are often pushed to their limits of survival. Second, Katz (2001b, 717) suggests that, by definition, "it [social reproduction] is focused on reproducing the very social relations and material forms that *are* so problematic." Like Huey Newton, Katz goes on to discuss the contradictory importance of theorizing social reproduction in revolutionary ways when "social reproduction is precisely not 'revolutionary,' and yet so much rests on its accomplishments, including – perhaps paradoxically – oppositional politics" (717).

Rianne Mahon (2005b) provides one of the best framings of the tensions within the politics of scale literature regarding the role of social reproduction through the context of welfare state restructuring. Mahon argues that feminist scholars have been critical of representations of shifts within the structure of the welfare state. In the past, "while the Keynesian welfare state focused on the risks faced by male breadwinners, as Peck suggests, it also assumed that mother-housewife-daughters were in the household, to provide primary care for the very young" (343). Regarding a shift towards neoliberal globalization, Mahon highlights downloading welfare provision responsibilities to subnational governments and off-loading responsibilities via privatization to families and markets. Drawing on Peck's (2001b) discussion of these transitions within the context of workfare, Mahon also locates this rescaling of welfare via the "internationalization of policy ... in the shift from 'passive' social assistance to 'activation' processes" (342).

The precursors of these shifts can be seen earlier in US ghettos that had long been ignored by US welfare provision. As Mettler (1998) argues, the formation of the US welfare state at the national scale treated both women and African Americans as secondary citizens. Particular to the connections between the failures of the US welfare state around food provision, the contradictions that Mahon discusses were made more desperate given the lack of employment/breadwinning by African American men. The inability for collective consumption of sufficient food that resulted from staggering unemployment within US inner-city ghettos in the late 1960s and early 1970s provides a crucial link to understanding the connections between social reproduction and the politics of scale.

Related to the core socionatural mechanisms that facilitate these interconnections, in *The Labour Standard* newspaper Engels (1881) suggested that "the Capitalist, if he cannot agree with the Labourer, can afford to wait, and live upon his capital ... The workman has no fair start. He is fearfully handicapped by hunger. Yet, according to the political economy of the Capitalist class, that is the very pink of fairness." It is this contradictory notion of "capitalist *fairness*" underwritten within capitalism that contributes to the production of material inequality and is paramount in articulating the interrelated and interconnected processes inherent in the contradictions of urban poverty, hunger, and how both impede social reproduction at myriad scales.

Marx's (1964, 181) notion that "it [hunger] therefore needs a nature outside itself, an object outside itself, in order to satisfy itself" has myriad scalar ramifications for understanding the lack of collective consumption and social reproduction by connecting bodily scales with extrabodily political economic socionatural scalar relations and processes. Related to Marx's conception is the fact that socionaturally nested scales of food production and distribution explicitly link the essence of human life and social reproduction (eating and food) through the everyday lives of those who do, and do not, have access to food and to the extrabodily scales at which the needs of hunger can be met. Thus, the interrelated power relations inherent in ghetto, urban, regional, and national food systems cannot be divorced from the political ecological/economic systems within which they operate. Nor can these food systems be considered as only bodily processes. They must also be thought of as interrelated local and global via the construction ghettos for social reproduction.

Marxist traditions for excavating scalar dialectics as necessarily relational processes help to illustrate how, in order to understand the political economy of hunger, we must also consider material, ideological, and social-ecological/metabolic processes that connect bodies to households to cities to states, etc. Herein rests the genius, and obviousness, of Swyngedouw's (1997a, c) notion that no particular geographical scale commands theoretical or political priority; instead, the social processes through which particular scales become (re)constituted are the most important aspect in considering scalar relations. Swyngedouw's (and Smith's [1992a]) deliberative focus on sociospatial processes is necessary since, in fact, all processes occur at the same scales at the same times. As such, prioritizing scale over process means that we miss most of the related processes that have an impact on the socionatural production of time and space. So I suggest that, as an alternative approach, if we focus first on the politics of social reproduction, then the politics of scale should follow if we are thorough, given the spatial/scalar unevenness inherent in political economy.

The Black Panther Party's Biopolitics from Below

With its formation in Oakland in 1966, the BPP evolved into one of the most important radical political movements in the United States, fighting to establish its own form of revolutionary socialism through mass organizing and the implementation of its community-based "survival programs." The BPP's self-help programs were seen as necessary because of the failure of the "war on poverty" to provide a safety net for many poor African Americans and other minorities. The BPP's survival programs served to provide the necessary social infrastructure for facilitating social reproduction within many inner-city areas across the United States. In light of the country's failure, members of the BPP literally took up arms first in efforts to defend themselves from the Oakland Police Department and then for the sake of creating a viable black national welfare state as articulated in the first point of their Ten Point Political Platform: "We want freedom. We want power to determine the destiny of our Black Community."

At the heart of the success of the Free Breakfast for Children Program was a set of interrelated scalar politics tied to social reproduction and played out as a result of (1) the failures of the US national welfare state, (2) the BPP's evolving vision of black nationalism, and (3) the local technologies employed to serve the poor through the mobilization of ghetto spaces and social infrastructures. All of these processes exploded outward towards an international audience of revolutionaries that led the BPP to have not only many local/bodily ramifications but also global social movement importance. We need to think about these politics as they played out between the material reality of bodily inequality (this inequality being most dominant within the discourse of oppression in segregated US ghettos), the imagined formation of a black national welfare state as an initial way to facilitate social reproduction, but then, ultimately, the combination of global working-class and postcolonial struggles feeding into the BPP's vision of revolutionary intercommunalism.

The BPP's survival programs consisted of everyday political strategies for meeting the community's day-to-day needs by providing food, health care, education, and other welfare services. The popularity of the BPP's ideology and spatial practices, as manifested especially within its survival programs, resulted in approximately 5,000 active party members in over forty-five chapters and branches across the country.[2] Paralleling Peter Kropotkin's (1995) revolutionary attention to the political power of food provision, the Free Breakfast for Children Program gained the most support from the African American community and the most attention from J. Edgar Hoover's FBI. Perhaps most pertinent to recognizing the importance of this particular survival program (one of over twenty different survival programs) is that it was both the model and the impetus for all federally funded school breakfast programs in existence within the United States today. It was through this co-optation of the BPP's political power through state-funded breakfast programming that the BPP has so dramatically shaped the politics of hunger in the United States.

The BPP's first Free Breakfast for Children Program was initiated at St. Augustine's Church in Oakland. About this, Bobby Seale[3] told me, "We started the Free Breakfast for Children Program in 1968, and in the spring of 1969 we were feeding 250,000 kids all across the country. You know, J. Edgar Hoover is denouncing the program. Well, we must be being effective or something, you know, and then the polls came out with 90 percent of the people in the black community supporting the BPP because of things like the breakfast program, sickle cell anemia testing, and preventative health care clinics." To Seale and his comrades, this logic was similar to the analysis that Engels (1958) made in *The Condition of the Working Class in England* about the physical basis for revolutionary work, and the parallels between the two arguments quite powerfully demonstrate the material reality underpinning the politics of hunger and social reproduction.

The social processes and spatial forms inherent in social reproduction, as represented within the evolution/transformation of the BPP's breakfast program, help to exemplify the politics of scale that link the material needs of human bodies to communities, cities, nations, etc., within the context of urban hunger. Seale told me that "We realized that, regarding hunger, the bread crumbs they [the US Keynesian welfare state] were throwing at us was only to pacify us, to keep us quiet. It wasn't to sustain us." As such, the BPP's survival programs were initiated to both sustain the social reproduction of the black community and build a political base that could be used to resist the hegemonic repression of the US government and capitalist interests. Seale also illustrated how the BPP realized the scalar importance of the breakfast program early on when he suggested that, while in the first instance, feeding individual bodies was required for them to survive, in the second and third scalar instances, these individual bodies together provide the political basis for cities, counties, states, regions, nations, etc., through their different organizing capacities. Seale, while not using the word *scale*, told me how the scalar relations inherent in hunger are a result of the universality of human needs, and looking at different scalar configurations of these needs presents new forms of political insight that can be marshalled for continued revolutionary action.

Because working to provide basic material needs related to the facilitation of social reproduction has historically been so difficult in US inner-city ghettos, revolutionary efforts by the BPP included paying special attention to the political structures of urban political economy. In fact, despite having been so successful at providing for, and working with, folks in the black community, these efforts were often recognized as reformist, not revolutionary. Nevertheless, they were also recognized as the most important building block for revolutionary praxis or to facilitate "survival pending revolution." To this end, Newton (2002a, 161) suggested that "we must not regard our survival programs as an answer to the whole problem of oppression. We don't even claim it to be a revolutionary program. Revolutions are made of sterner stuff. We do say that if the people are not here the revolution cannot be achieved, for the people and only the people make revolutions."

While simultaneously working to sustain its community, the BPP also worked to make it more politically powerful. In so doing in many cities across the United States, the BPP recognized and articulated structural contradictions that further impeded community economic development, which it recognized had everything to do with impeding social reproduction. The BPP theorized in great detail the same sociospatial configurations that led James Blaut (1974) to theorize "the ghetto as an internal neo-colony." He suggested that "neo-colonialism is fundamentally an economic process, supported by social and political institutions, and enforced by violence. Its purpose is to extract the maximum amount of wealth from every Third-World space, and channel that wealth ... to First-World corporations ... Neo-colonialism is supported, enabled, by a network of formal institutions" (39-40). Blaut's notions had long been recognized by the BPP, as illustrated by both Williams (1969) and other community members when they spoke of "defending the ghetto" against continued community imperialism. An undated BPP pamphlet stated that, "in our struggle for national liberation, we are now in the phase of community liberation, to free our black communities from the imperialistic control exercised over them by the racist exploiting cliques within white communities. Ours is a struggle against community imperialism. Our black communities are colonized and controlled from outside, and it is this control that has to be smashed, broken, shattered, by whatever means possible."

The scalar contours of the local community struggles against community imperialism, and for national liberation, were filled with many dramatic episodes; however, few received as much attention as the murder of Fred Hampton. On 27 April 1969, Hampton, who had co-founded the Chicago Chapter of the Black Panther Party, gave a moving address that embodied "what the Black Panther Party is about." His speech began with a discussion of the BPP's breakfast program and linked the starvation of children in inner cities across the United States to the destructive contradictions inherent in capitalism and the uneven development that it produces. Hampton discussed the revolutionary steps that the BPP was taking to ensure that poor children had enough food to meet their basic material requirements for social reproduction and survival. In so doing, Hampton articulated the ideological conflict that had materialized between the BPP and the US government. A month after Hampton's speech, on 27 May 1969, a memo signed by the FBI's director, J. Edgar Hoover, though actually written by Domestic Intelligence Chief William C. Sullivan, was sent to Charles Bates, the special agent in charge (SAC) of the San Francisco branch of the FBI. The memo, emblematic of the degree to which the United States saw the BPP as a threat to its notion of empire, declared, "You state that the bureau should not attack programs of community interest such as the BPP 'Breakfast for Children Program' ... You have obviously missed the point. The BPP is not engaged in the program for humanitarian reasons. This program was formed by the BPP ... to create an image of civility, assume community control of Negroes, and fill adolescent children with their insidious poison" (see Churchill and Vander Wall 2002, 145).

The murder of Fred Hampton and Mark Clark by police agents on 4 December 1969 galvanized local efforts in Chicago while sending shock waves of anger, frustration, and determination through other US cities as well as increasing international solidarity with the BPP by other revolutionary groups. The message by the BPP leadership both nationally and locally in Chicago was that people had to work to take community control of the public institutions and infrastructures that had been created for the people. The emphasis of community control was best illustrated through a continued effort within Chicago to transfer the power of supervising and administering the Chicago police to a citizen's council. At an even more local level within each of Chicago's twenty-one police districts, the BPP demanded that citizen police boards be established comprising nine elected citizens who represented the general demographic makeup of each district, thereby creating a network to administer the city's police affairs (see The Black Panther 1973). Theorizing and politically engaging locally to obtain community control were simultaneously occurring in ghettos throughout the United States in impressive ways. By the early 1970s, the BPP's revolutionary praxis began to take a more global scope, thus transforming the party's emerging scalar political strategies.

Revolutionary Intercommunalism

Huey Newton, as chief theoretician of the BPP, began to discuss the scalar interconnectedness of the oppression of individuals in Oakland, Chicago, and other US ghettos with the oppression of collective communities within which those individuals lived.[4] While the BPP had long framed their struggles across the urban/national scale, through Newton, the party was beginning to think of other ways to "jump scale" to achieve its political goals. These were the earliest notions of what would be a short-lived endorsement of black nationalism. The connections that Newton discussed were based on both the lack of basic welfare provision and the disciplinary tactics initiated by local/state/federal law enforcement agencies. Newton associated these local processes with the need for oppressed people in the United States to form their own national identity and to collectively support each other. Notions of the welfare state became explicitly concretized within the everyday discussions of "survival" and of how the United States was not concerned with the survival of inner-city minority residents. In order for people to survive and ensure social reproduction at a community scale and to begin building a political base, the survival programs were initiated within an explicitly scalar context. However, as an impetus for thinking about these issues but also relating back to them through praxis in solidarity, Newton later argued the need to engage in global liberation and working-class struggles. His scalar theorizations initially laid out a politics of scale that paralleled what I will refer to as a generic scalar continuum (community, nation, globe).

While in prison, Newton theorized many notions of the BPP emancipatory politics. These efforts included thinking about the scalar foundations of the BPP's revolutionary praxis. His theorization evolved into what would remain one of his most provocative and politically problematic notions, that of revolutionary intercommunalism. Newton argued that the United States was no longer a nation-state but had been transformed into a boundless empire controlling the world's lands and people. This made theorizing resistance to the United States more problematic. Because people and economies had become so integrated within the imperialist power relations of the US empire, Newton (2002b, 236) suggested that it was impossible for them to "decolonize": that is, to return to former conditions of existence. "The present fact is that we cannot ask our grandparents to teach us some 'native' tongue, or dance or point out our 'homeland' on a map. Certainly, we are not citizens of the United States. Our hopes for freedom then lie in the future, a future which may hold a positive elimination of national boundaries and ties; a future of the world, where a human world society may be so structured as to benefit all the earth's people (not peoples)." Newton's ideas would later be echoed in Hardt and Negri's (2000, 187) discussion of the lack of distinction between inside and outside of empire.

Because of these organizing problems, Newton suggested that new scalar formulations and strategies were necessary. The oppressed people of the world, since they were spatially diffused through a dispersed collection of communities, each with its own set of institutions geared towards serving the people, had to struggle collectively in a globally revolutionary way to take back control of economic, political, and cultural institutions. David Hilliard, former chief of staff for the BPP, summarized Newton's notions of revolutionary intercommunalism:

> In prison, Huey has developed an analysis of the present political movement. Nation-states, he argues are things of the past. Nationalist struggles, even revolutionary ones, are besides the point. Capital dominates the world; ignoring borders, international finance has transformed the world into communities rather than nations. Some of the communities are under siege – like Vietnam – and others conduct the siege, like the United States Government. The people of the world are united in their desire to run their own communities, the black people in Oakland and the Vietnamese. We need to band together as communities, create a revolutionary intercommunalism that will resist capital's reactionary intercommunalism. (Hilliard and Cole 1993, 319)

As Newton laid out an idealized spatial framework for a politics of scale, the amended formulation resulted in the splicing of global and national scales via the hegemony of the US Empire. This scalar compression bolstered the BPP's revolutionary praxis by situating *communities*, which it had already been fighting to command, as the highest-order site of struggle.

Newton's conception of a global network of interrelated communities struggling against the oppression of the US Empire is extraordinary. Beyond the importance of his political thinking about scale are the material foundations and praxis upon which his thoughts were based in the production of nature and space as they were all historically linked to processes of social reproduction via the BPP's survival programs, especially its breakfast program.

The spatial practices inherent in Newton's ideas provide a useful historical precursor to Smith's (1991) notion of "jumping scale" and the parallel, albeit unconnected, notions of "scale shifts" as explained by McAdam, Tarrow, and Tilly (2001). While notions of scale jumping have been an axiomatic foundation within scale theory, because McAdam, Tarrow, and Tilly are social movement theorists, their notions provide a useful entry point for considering how the BPP framed its radical anti-hunger politics of scale. They define scale shift as "a change in the number and level of coordinated contentious actions leading to broader contention involving a wider range of actors and bridging their claims and identities" (331). Thus understood, scale shifts refer to the institutional dynamics through which social movement forces can mobilize over larger spatial areas and increase their share of power. This happens through two sometimes linked sets of institutional dynamics, *diffusion/ emulation* and *brokerage/coalition formation*. McAdam, Tarrow, and Tilly suggest that *diffusion* involves flows of information along established lines of interaction, while *brokerage* entails connecting multiple unconnected social sites. The result of these processes, and why they lead to scale shifts, or scale jumping, are what McAdam, Tarrow, and Tilly refer to as the *attribution of similarity*, which simply means that information alone does not tend to lead individuals/ groups to adopt new ideas/strategies. It depends on a minimal identification between innovator and adapter.

Central to the BPP's history and theoretical ideas is the way in which its political struggles and social reconfigurations led to interactions over higher-level scales and, thus, over a wider terrain – that of the global – through the diffusion and brokerage of its ideas, largely via the success of its radical anti-hunger politics. This politics of scale of course worked because fundamental issues of social reproduction were being neglected by the state. Collective identification with childhood hunger allowed the BPP to gain widespread political appeal via the *attribution of similarity*. Interestingly, though, as shifting/jumping from an unconsolidated power base and instead collectively attempting to expand its territorial domain through many locally dispersed power structures, all working together, meant that, before a political, ideological, or material "shift/jump up" in scale could occur, a slide back down to the rearticulation of the local via communities had to occur. It was through this rearticulation of locally isolated ghettos, and their related spatial/social infrastructures, that diffusion/brokerage led to increased political/revolutionary power.

This process laid out by Newton and acted upon by many Panthers also provides a different context through which to understand Brenner's (1999) discussion of globalization as reterritorialization. One of Brenner's main contributions to the emergence of scalar theory has to do with the processes of reterritorialization: that is, the sociospatial reconfiguration and rescaling of territorial organization through the *form* of cities and states. Central to Brenner's scalar theorizing is Harvey's (1982, 416) argument that a "spatial-fix" comes to be manifested via the production of immobile socioterritorial configurations within which expanded capital accumulation can be generated (see Brenner 1999, 433). Just as these sociospatial configurations are used for capital accumulation, and lead to uneven production at both local and global scales, however, other configurations that are also immobile via a spatial-fix can serve as foundations for resistance: that is, those institutions created to serve local communities. This is not to suggest that ghetto configurations are spatially ideal, in the same way that cities are useful to capitalists. Quite the contrary. The BPP's theorizing about scales does provide, however, useful revolutionary theory about spatial-fixity and resistance, given church, school, and other community resources through which they engaged politically.

Conclusion

As a result of their radical efforts to combat oppression within their own spatial scales of interaction, most often referred to as ghettos, for the sake of the survival of individual children, the BPP's efforts had many historical scalar ramifications. Just as the radicalization of the BPP was largely the result of engaging global revolutionary ideologies, including Marx and Engels, Lenin, Mao, Fanon, Guevara, Castro, and Nkrumah, among others, so too did its own revolutionary praxis flow back out through global currents to inspire other global revolutionary moments. Bobby Seale told me that, as one of the main organizers of the BPP, he talked to very few international organizers about how to set up the free breakfast, free food programs, and other survival programs. Yet, at least in England, Bermuda, Israel, Belize, Australia, and India, groups claiming to have emulated the revolutionary praxis of the BPP, and working in solidarity with the BPP, set up free food programs all over the world (see Clemons and Jones 2001).

Interestingly, at four points in their *Multitude: War and Democracy in the Age of Empire*, Hardt and Negri (2004) criticize the BPP for overly militaristic modes of resistance via its particular forms of "guerrilla formation." In doing so, Hardt and Negri focus on "the gun" as central to the BPP's tactics, and they suggest that the party "misunderstood completely and tragically that the adequate form of resistance changes historically and must be invented for each new situation – specifically, that a gun is no longer an adequate arm for defense" (343). Their argument, however, misses one of the most important points about why the BPP was historically so successful: it focused on "the people" rather than on an abstract notion of "the multitude." The BPP's political strategy was far more complex than Hardt and Negri give the party credit for, despite its political shortcomings. The BPP's struggles were based on a multiscalar revolutionary praxis grounded first and foremost in the fundamentals of social reproduction in an attempt to co-opt biopolitics from below. By putting the reins of population control back in the hands of the people and the vanguard, the BPP was able to frame/orchestrate powerful scale shifts, thus increasing its political power and the spatial terrain over which it had influence. It is precisely the lack of attention to social reproduction in their critique of the BPP, maybe for the reasons that Katz (2001b) and others suggest, that impedes Hardt and Negri. To the contrary, attention to social reproduction and efforts to engage in biopolitics from below are why the BPP's radical anti-hunger/anti-imperial praxis still deserves increased strategic attention.

As Smith (2001, 23) suggests, "scales are the geographical infrastructures that organize social difference, refracting it back as part of the landscape, fixed, naturalized. The production of scale is simultaneously a means of shaping and *containing* social struggle and a means of empowering specific struggles." In this context, the BPP's attempts at marshalling global support via revolutionary intercommunalism provide powerful social theoretical support to the suggestion of Andrew Jonas (1994, 262) that "the language of scale is an anticipation of the future." Huey Newton knew this and began working to mobilize the politics of scale for combatting the brutal inequality within the world's ghettos, but, more fundamentally, to help facilitate social reproduction and survival. The possibility of supplanting biopolitics as usual, and the human misery that it produces, with an emancipatory biopolitics from below offers hope in the face of increased global inequality and disempowerment. Politics of scale offer strategic insights into how, despite its elusive nature, paying special attention to social reproduction through grassroots networks and social movements can respond to empire.

While Foucault did a great deal to push our understanding of power, among other things, he lacked emancipatory political vision.[5] The idea of standing biopolitics on its head for the sake of strategizing the revolutionary importance of social reproduction necessitates utilizing the robust politics of scale literature to spatially juxtapose Foucault's "sovereign" with the BPP's "the people." While the politics of scale literature has provided numerous theoretical contributions, there is still much room for thinking about the political possibilities through reframing and jumping scale in different kinds of organizing. The BPP's efforts should be used as a harbinger of imagining these political possibilities. On the other hand, while scale is important for this story, it is not the most important thing. Some of the blunting of the politics of scale, as discussed by Smith, can be avoided if we use scale to understand the inequalities, suffering, and contradictions within social life as opposed to using these elements of social life to understand the politics of scale.

NOTES

1 The Studies in Political Economy annual conference Towards a Political Economy of Scale, York University, Toronto, 3-5 February 2005.
2 These numbers were provided to me by Bobby Seale (see endnote 3). Since he was the chairman of the party at its peak, he is likely the most reliable source. In his memoir about his experience as BPP chief of staff, David Hilliard put the party's peak membership at "over 4,000 members" (Hilliard and Cole 1993, 3).
3 Verbatim quotations are taken from over thirty interviews with ex-Black Panther Party members from Oakland, Chicago, Boston, Milwaukee, and New Haven between May 2004 and June 2005. In addition, interviews were conducted with people who worked with the BPP.
4 See Tyner (2006) for an alternative, albeit complementary, discussion of Newton's notions of scale.
5 Noticeable throughout his work but most noticeable in his debate with Noam Chomsky (see Foucault and Chomsky 2006).

15
The Empire, the Movement, and the Politics of Scale: Considering the World Social Forum

Janet Conway

In the face of new forms of hegemonic power and changing political terrains at home and abroad, social movements are rescaling. The World Social Forum (WSF) is a key site for the reinvention of the spatial praxis of emancipatory social movements, their interaction and consolidation, and is itself an enactment of a new spatiopolitical praxis. The WSF was initiated in 2000 by a committee of Brazilian organizations as a process to convene groups and movements of civil society opposed to neoliberalism from around the world. Over half a million people have participated in the annual global gatherings since its inception. The WSF's declaration that "another world is possible" is posed against the authoritarian imposition of "neoliberal globalization" on every society in the world and the new relations of colonialism that it enacts. Arturo Escobar calls this process a "new US-based form of imperial globality, an economic-military-ideological order that subordinates regions, peoples, and economies world-wide" (2004, 207). Many participants and commentators understand the WSF as a new and emergent form of counter-hegemonic globalization posed against a new form of empire. There is a complex "politics of scale" (Herod 1997) under way within and among the social movements of the WSF and as constitutive of the WSF itself.[1]

This spatial praxis and the politics of scale constitute a counterhegemonic social practice and alternative to empire. Yet, this politics of scale is neither narrowly an expression of power politics vis-à-vis empire nor a struggle for hegemony among social forces. It is also about a politics of difference, diversity, and recognition in which the specificities of struggles arising from particular places and expressing themselves at a variety of scales are acknowledged and valorized. The emergent scalar practices and discourses and the political debates and struggles over them in the social movements of the WSF and in the WSF itself suggest that scale is a critical axis of "new politics." A new democratic imaginary is coming into view, and a new politics of scale is emerging as a critical element. In this chapter, I situate the World Social Forum in the new imperial context, explore its spatial praxis, and reflect on its significance. Before doing so, however, it is important to take a theoretical detour.

Space, Place, and Scale: Critical Geography and Social Movement Studies

In activist politics, the rescaling of political struggle in the face of imperialist globalization has prompted both intensified processes of transnational networking and renewed attention to "the local," as well as inspiring fierce debates about their relative priority. Scales between "local" and "global," notably "the national," have become relatively decentred although clearly not absent from many expressions of activist politics, including at the WSF.[2] As in much activist practice, such transformations are uneven and contradictory. They seldom unfold with any reference to theoretical debates, nor are they themselves much documented, systematized, or theorized.

Social movement studies in many disciplines are not particularly geographically sensitive. Where spatial aspects are noticed, studies are hampered by the persistence of realist conceptions of space, place, and scale, largely uninformed by two decades of important theoretical developments in critical geography, which are themselves informed by postpositivism, social constructivism, and poststructuralism. Despite a proliferating academic literature in geography (Bosco 2001; Kurtz 2003; Miller and Martin 2000, 2004; Routledge 2000, 2003, 2004), these intellectual breakthroughs have not much penetrated work in the other social sciences, where space and scale continue to be taken for granted. The problems are exacerbated by a widespread and persistent "methodological nationalism" in which the national scale and the (nation-) state remain the unproblematized space and scale of politics. In an era of globalization, the equally unproblematized "global" is partially displacing the national as the given and preeminent geographical signifier. Whatever the limits of social movement scholarship, social movements themselves are inventing new scales of political practice, experimenting with multiscale political practices and reconceiving the relations between scales of movement politics, organization, and mobilization.

Through the 1980s and 1990s, the spatial turn in social theory challenged prevailing assumptions of history/time as dynamic and space as static, dead, or neutral (Foucault 1999; Soja 1999). Space was reconceptualized as socially constructed and social relations, in turn, as sociospatial relations (Harvey 1996). Critical geographers have demonstrated that spatial arrangements are constantly being produced and reproduced through ongoing practices and discourses. In turn, spatial discourses and practices actively condition social reality and the terms of social struggles (Harvey 1989a, 1996; Marston 2000; Massey 1992; Smith 1993; Swyngedouw 1997a). Relatedly, understandings of "place" have also been problematized. Static views of place, in which it was associated with cohesive communities, bounded cultures, and fixed identities, have been replaced with the notion of place as a process (Massey 1994). Places are constantly being produced through social relations and practices that are inherently dynamic and conflictual. This is a new way of seeing place that complicates any inquiry into the relationship between places and their social movements and between place-based movements and transnational movement spaces and practices such as the World Social Forum.

Scholarly work on the "social construction of scale" is situated within these broader theoretical developments in critical geography. In terms of the construction and politics of scale in social movements, a special 1997 issue of the journal *Political Geography* represented an important contribution. Editors Delaney and Leitner assembled work empirically demonstrating the social construction of scale through detailing the concrete practices of specific social actors and the political contexts and ramifications of such scalar practices and narratives. Arguing for a broader understanding of politics, they explicitly selected practices of non-state actors, arguing for a broader understanding of politics than that associated with contestations over state power (Agnew 1997; Delaney and Leitner 1997; Herod 1997; Miller 1997).

Feminists also insist that space and scale are produced through the everyday practices of ordinary people, including, for example, women in households, that scales such as "the body" and "the household" are also socially constructed and need to be understood in a mutually constitutive relationship with other scales of social, political, and economic life (Marston 2000). Nevertheless, much of the scholarship continues to focus on the social construction of scale and on the scale politics of states, capital, and elites, despite regular injunctions that space and scale are also contested from below and are thereby produced or at least co-constituted through the agency of insurgent social forces such as social movements, labour unions, and indigenous peoples. Even work that focuses on agency from below tends to privilege the actions of workers and unions over other kinds of actors and movements and limits the politics of scale in social movements to strategic instrumentalities in frontal struggles with capital, thereby reducing its political significance to macro–political-economic gains vis-à-vis states or capital.

Writing about the spatial praxis of unions and workers, respectively, Herod (1997) and Castree (2000a) make important contributions to our understandings of scale and its social construction in and through the politically laden and conflicted praxis of non-elite agents. Herod is concerned to challenge the capital-centrism of the critical scholarship on scale by demonstrating how scale is actively produced by ordinary people through everyday practices, in this case, of collective bargaining. Furthermore, he counters the widely shared assumption that, in an era of globalization, labour (and by extension, oppositional movements) have to "scale up" to the global level to wage struggles successfully. Herod effectively argues that no single scale (usually the global) is associated with political efficacy and that there is no one scalar logic or direction in successful political mobilization. Movements use different geographical strategies to great effect, which sometimes involves scaling downward as well as upward.

Castree (2000a) comes to similar conclusions, arguing that the successful labour internationalism of the Liverpool dock dispute was accompanied by ongoing struggles at local and national scales. He argues for "a more complex and contingent appreciation of the *multiscalar* dynamics of labor struggles" (272; emphasis added). In my own work on the Metro Network for Social Justice in Toronto and on the Canadian Ecumenical Jubilee Initiative, I call attention to the "politics of multiple scales" in a place-based antiglobalization movement and in a national-scale mobilization anchored in "local" committees and articulated to the international Jubilee 2000 campaign, respectively (Conway 2004, 2006).

Sallie Marston (2000) has suggested that, for those who treat geographical scale as a "relation" rather than a simple descriptor of size or level, scalar narratives are understood as a way of framing reality and have material consequences. Scalar framings are often contested, however, and are not necessarily enduring. In other words, scale is not a "thing"; it is a way of representing sociospatial reality that is politically laden and that shapes social practices (Kelly 1999). It is a way of understanding and ordering the social world (Jones 1998), and deploying scalar narratives functions to order and contain actions and determine their meanings. Hegemonic scalar discourses shape and contain sociospatial practices, restricting them to apparently natural political or geographical arenas and investing them with significance – or not. The manipulation of scale, or the "politics of scale," is a central dimension of power, especially in the current period.[3]

Those interested in the politics of scale seek to discern and analyze scalar processes to expose the workings of power, to challenge it, and to understand the nature of the power inherent in various scalar discourses in order to deploy it. Studying any specific scalar process – that is, any specific set of practices and discourses that constitutes a particular instantiation of "scale" – implies attention to the presence and interplay of diverse forces operating at multiple scales, which constitute the specific process of scale construction under study. Because they are interrelated, interpenetrating, and mutually constituting, no scale can a priori be declared determinative or derivative of other scales. This is a matter of investigation of specific (multi)scalar processes.

In the argument that follows, I draw on these analytical insights on the social construction of space, place, and scale to explore the spatial constitution and the spatial praxis of the World Social Forum. As a worldwide process, the WSF is constituted at a variety of geographical scales. As it is instantiated in specific, geographically grounded events, it assumes a place-specific character, reflecting the local movements and their "place-structured identities" (Miller and Martin 2000) even as the events themselves are products of activist organizing processes operating at multiple scales. This study of the World Social Forum builds on the scholarship reviewed above on the spatial praxis of non-elite social actors. It testifies to continual emergence, increasing relevance, and intensifying experimentation with multiscale praxes in an era of globalization and to the complexities of negotiating new political relations across scales of practice in social movement networks. Before focusing on the spatial constitution and praxis of the WSF, let us first consider the movement that spawned the WSF coupled with the new imperial context against which the World Social Forum is developing.

The Empire and the Movement

In the spring of 1997, midway through the second term of the Clinton presidency, a Washington-based neoconservative think tank launched a project for "the new American century." The group, all men, included Dick Cheney, Donald Rumsfeld, Paul Wolfowitz, and others at the centre of the subsequent Bush administration. The Project for the New American Century (PNAC) argues that in the post-Cold War period, America is the sole superpower. This condition offers extraordinary opportunity and must be actively preserved and guaranteed as far into the future as possible. American global hegemony is central to the globalization of American economic, political, and cultural values and must be secured through undisputed military dominance. The project's authors are straightforward in their views that economic liberalization is both secured through US military might and must proceed in tandem with US strategic interests. Undisputed US domination is the guarantee of global security, democratic freedoms, and individual political rights, grounded in the free market. These are the pillars of the *Pax Americana*.

In a major paper published by PNAC in fall 2000, the authors argue that the *Pax Americana* will only be preserved through the superpower's willingness to regularly wage and win wars, to police strategically important regions, and to renovate the military for undisputed dominance of both outerspace and cyberspace. In an especially chilling passage, the project's architects admit that the implementation of their vision will be long and slow, "absent some catastrophic and catalyzing event – like a new Pearl Harbor" (PNAC 2000). The events of 9/11 provided the new Pearl Harbor.

Coming in the wake of the mass demonstrations in Genoa in which a protester was killed by police and the Italian government shaken by popular demands for justice, 9/11 set the surging anti-globalization movement back on its heels. It also conveniently silenced critics of the Bush administration in the United States, who were growing in number and volume in response to US refusals to ratify the Kyoto Accord, support the International Criminal Court, or renew support for the Anti-Ballistic Missile Treaty. The 9/11 attacks unleashed the hawks in and around the Bush administration and granted them legitimacy overnight as "forces of good" over the axis of evil, then represented by Osama Bin Laden, which quickly expanded to include the Taliban/Afghanistan, Saddam Hussein/Iraq, North Korea, and increasingly Iran. Infinite, open-ended war provides the US ruling establishment with the quasi-legal and moral legitimacy that it needs to periodically demonstrate its capacity for violence, both to suppress dissent at home and to enact regime change whenever and wherever the US administration deems it necessary.

For the anti-globalization movement, the events of 9/11 – preceded by the repression in Genoa, shootings in Gothenburg, riot police and tear gas in Quebec – served to educate a new generation of activists and remind older ones of the centrality of violence to the maintenance of the existing maldistributions of power and wealth, globally and locally. In a movement whose dominant discourses of power so focused on the political and institutional arrangements governing the international economy, some key issues had been obscured: the role of coercive power through police and armies, the ongoing powerful role of nation-states, and the particular global geopolitical role of the United States in configuring neoliberal world order. The growing repression of the movement, coupled with the events of 9/11 and the ensuing war on terrorism at home and abroad, challenged the anti-globalization movement to develop a more complex understanding of power and resistance and to reconfigure its politics in response.

Global opposition to neoliberalism and the emergence of a new movement were fuelled by the war in Iraq. Through the winter of 2003, the anti-globalization movement was transformed by the explosion of a massive, global, anti-war movement opposing an American attack on Iraq. On 15 February 2003, more than 15 million people took to the streets in over 600 towns and cities on five continents in an extraordinary, globally coordinated effort to prevent war. Growing numbers of people and movements readily link US-led military aggression with an imperial civilizational project of global proportion that intersects with, but is not reducible to, the interests of US-dominated, transnational corporations or international financial institutions.

In the wake of 9/11, in the face of rising repression, the criminalization of dissent, and the threat of war, activists reconsidered their strategies and tactics, especially the centrality of highly confrontational mass demonstrations. Many turned to local, community-based, anti-globalization struggles. Many reiterated the irreducible importance of grassroots, place-based, but globally conscious and connected organizing. In the same period, activists in the tens of thousands looked to other places and modes of global convergence. The most significant has been the World Social Forum.

New Forms of Convergence: The World Social Forum

Originally conceived as an alternative to the World Economic Forum held annually in Davos, Switzerland, the WSF was initiated in 2000 by a committee of Brazilian organizations to convene groups and movements of civil society opposed to neoliberalism from around the world. The idea was to create a forum for the free and horizontal exchange of ideas, experiences, and strategies oriented to showcasing and generating alternatives to neoliberalism and building convergence across difference. The gathering would be thoroughly international but anchored geographically and experientially in the global South. The first WSF, held in Porto Alegre, Brazil, in January 2001, attracted 15,000 participants. Its astounding success led organizers to commit to the WSF as a permanent process. Each January since then, the event has taken place, growing exponentially in size, diversity, complexity, and importance.

Although united in opposing neoliberalism, the civil society entities present at the World Social Forum are amazingly diverse in their demographic makeup, organizational forms, cultural expressions, geographical roots and reach, strategies, tactics, and discourses. The WSF is often characterized as a "space of spaces," a "network of networks," and a critical instantiation of the anti-globalization "movement of movements," but it is not itself a social movement (Santos 2004, 6). The WSF is best understood as a "space" in which participants are invited to self-organize, to advance their campaigns, and to mount activities for one another. The WSF is open to any group anywhere in the world that is not a political party and not engaged in armed struggle.[4]

Paul Routledge's concept of the "convergence spaces" of grassroots globalization networks is useful here. Convergence spaces "facilitate the forging of an associational politics that constitute a diverse, contested coalition of place-specific social movements [that] prosecute conflict on a variety of multi-scalar terrains" (2003, 345). They are constituted by both deep diversity and an extraordinary will to find what is common. Face-to-face encounters in events such as the WSF initiate, enable, and reinforce network circuits of communication and coordination across scales, places, and sectors of struggle that extend beyond the space-time of the event.

Central to the functioning of the WSF to date has been the understanding that it is not a deliberative space. The WSF *qua* WSF does not make decisions, issue statements, or embark on common actions. No one can "represent" the WSF. It is not a unitary entity, and its architects repudiate the notion that it should be. This position is becoming increasingly contentious in and beyond the WSF's International Council (IC),[5] but it has been definitive of the WSF thus far.

In 2002, at the second WSF in Porto Alegre, organizers called on participants to organize similar processes in their own places, defined by their own priorities, and at whatever scale made sense to them. Hundreds of social forums are appearing worldwide on every continent and at every scale, inspired by the world event and organized in accordance with the WSF's Charter of Principles. Notably, important and increasingly autonomous regional processes are emerging.[6] In 2006, the World Social Forum was "polycentric," meaning that the global event was dispersed over three sites, Caracas, Venezuela; Bamako, Mali; and Karachi, Pakistan. This innovation in the process is reflective of both the depth and maturity of regional processes and the arguments of some that the WSF has to be more regionally rooted in order to reflect and respond to the specificities of popular struggles under way in different parts of the world.

The development of the World Social Forum, understood as an annual event, is central to my exploration here of the social construction and politics of scale. It is critical, however, to recognize that the WSF is more accurately represented as a worldwide, movement-based, multiscale, and multisited cultural process that is evolving daily. Its ongoing shape-shifting presents multiple problems of representation and analysis.

The world event/process is significantly re-created when it is taken up by groups in different parts of the world, and this changes what follows locally and globally. Likewise, when the World Social Forum is enacted locally and regionally, it assumes specificities that flow from place and scale, the historical-geographical conjuncture in which the process/event occurs, and the discourses, practices, preoccupations, and strategies of its constitutive social movements. Furthermore, particular movements make a claim on particular instantiations of the World Social Forum through the particularities of place or scale and are intervening in the world process, albeit unevenly.

So there is no one World Social Forum even as there are distinguishing features of the Forum as a specific political-cultural form linking otherwise intensely diverse instantiations of the process. The power and potential of the Forum as a new political form and process rest on four features: (1) its character as a non-deliberative yet highly participatory and inclusive space of spaces with multiple centres; (2) its global diffusion as a form and method, through the proliferation of local and regional social forums; (3) the increasing internationalization, interculturalism, and multiculturalism of the global process, signalled by the WSF's move from Brazil to India in 2004 and to Africa in 2007; and (4) a growing recognition of multiplicity, diversity, and pluralism as organizing principles in fostering a new politics for a new world, with the space for many worlds within it. These features have emerged in practice and become definitive even as their significance can as yet be dimly perceived. Their possible meanings depend on how future political practice, experimentation, and debates over the future of the WSF unfold.

The Spatial Praxis of the WSF

In this and any discussion about the WSF, it is critical to maintain a distinction between "the World Social Forum" and "the social movements and activist networks of the WSF." The latter act in and beyond the WSF, understood as event and space, but they also help to constitute the WSF as event and space. The WSF is both more than, and different from, the sum of these movements, and the movements are more than, and different from, the sum of their practices vis-à-vis the WSF. The constituent movements all have their own particular spatialities, spatial praxes, and scalar politics; they also play out in the events and processes that constitute the WSF (Conway 2008a). Is it possible, then, to attribute to the WSF *qua* WSF an identifiable spatial praxis? If so, then what are its attributes? And what are the relations, if any, between the spatial praxis of the WSF and that of its constituent movements? I want to advance four major claims.

The first claim is that, from the beginning, there has been de facto recognition and valorization of the emergence of resistance and alternatives to neoliberalism from the most local to the most global. The creation of conditions for contact, recognition, and interchange among movements and organizations working at a variety of scales, in a range of modes, on a variety of issues and fronts, and with a number of strategic approaches, has been one of the most significant innovations of the World Social Forum. This is a noteworthy departure from the practices of UN-sponsored gatherings, which privilege nationally articulated civil society entities in international forums. The convergence space of the WSF "facilitates an intermingling of scales of political action, where such scales become mutually constitutive" (Routledge 2003, 346).

The regionalization and localization of the World Social Forum to every continent comprise a second key dimension of the WSF's spatial praxis. It must be emphasized that this did not occur as a result of initiatives taken by the WSF architects in Brazil or on the IC but through an extraordinary response to their invitation to participants to organize forums in their own places. The valorization of political activity at multiple scales coupled with that of self-organized activity (*auto-gestion*) helps to account for the global diffusion of the Forum as a particular political form and methodology.

As with the exponential growth of the world event, the proliferation of local and regional processes could not have been foreseen. With the invitation to self-organize, within the terms of the Charter of Principles, the local and regional forums embody the autonomist practices that define the Forum. They are beyond the management and control of any central body, although clearly the regional (i.e., continental or hemispheric) events have a status and investment by the IC in ways that smaller-scale forums do not.[7]

Although there has been a rather traditional scalar vocabulary understood as fixed levels emanating from the IC ("local," "national," "regional") and a de facto hierarchy in terms of the political importance attached to bigness, nationalness, and internationalness in terms of representation at the IC and visibility in the world process, the fact remains that people and groups all over the world have seized the World Social Forum and run with it, at whatever scale makes sense to them, working across the differences that seem most pressing in their own context. This intersection between self-activity/ *auto-gestion* and the proliferation of *scales* of forum processes/events suggests a critical link between the valorization of self-activity of autonomous groupings as a foundational feature of the Forum and the valorization of a variety of scales of sociopolitical activity in producing the global diffusion of the Forum as a particular political form and methodology and in multiplying its power.

Furthermore, the emplacement of World Social Forum processes in so many different contexts roots it in locally specific ways. In turn, those practices and processes take on a dynamic of their own, with their own process innovations, political breakthroughs, multiculturalisms, as well as conflicts and limits (Conway 2008b). At the regional, continental, and hemispheric scales, major processes are developing, accumulating their own histories, knowledges, and sedimented powers. They are becoming somewhat institutionalized through the establishment of regional councils, which are flexing their muscles at the IC in terms of their autonomy, their specificity, their decision-making power over continental-scale WSF processes, and their role in helping to constitute the *World* Social Forum process.

In terms of the politics of place and scale, feminist, indigenous, and queer movements made a significant claim on the WSF through organizing the first Social Forum of the Americas in Quito, Ecuador, in July 2004 (Conway 2007). Although the increased political visibility, substantive political content, process innovations, and important dialogues among these movements that took place in Quito did not neatly transpose themselves to the following world event in 2005 in Porto Alegre, they pointed to the political possibilities in claiming the regional process/space in itself as an intervention in the world process. In the 2006 polycentric WSF in Caracas, the feminist, queer, and indigenous legacies of the first forum in Quito were far more successfully carried over, precisely (although not only) because of the greater weight of the regional councils in the polycentric approach.

In 2005, a France-based initiative sought to identify and document specifically "local" WSF practices, to make them visible to one another, to network them, and to make a claim about their importance in the world process. This initiative is explicitly grounded in an understanding that globalization is produced and contested in specific places, and so is any alternative globalization that is being produced. So the local of the World Social Forum is also making its presence felt at the world-scale process/event. The global diffusion of the Forum and the proliferating place-based and multiscale practices are producing difference within the World Social Forum and are thus transforming the world-scale processes/events, in addition to whatever effects they have on the politics of their specific places and social movement networks.

The option to move the world event geographically and the experimentation with a polycentric approach embody a recognition that place matters in terms of the global event/global process as well as for the place-based processes in the region. This is a third feature of the spatial praxis of the WSF.

In 2002, the WSF's International Council first began to consider the merits of mounting a WSF outside Brazil as a way of further internationalizing the process. Some key leaders recognized the importance of rooting the process and the event in another region of the world – in other words, the significance of the territoriality of the world event in determining who participated in what numbers, the nature of themes, issues, and alternatives under discussion, and the horizon of possible futures.[8] The specific site of the world event invests a place-specific visibility and power to the WSF and is probably the single most important variable in determining the character of its globality. The proposed local and regional forums emerged as an extension of this deliberation and represented an emergent understanding of the WSF as process, not just event, and of the possible value of multiple spaces and processes unfolding at multiple scales and temporalities in multiple regions of the world.

In 2004, the fourth World Social Forum and the first to be held outside Brazil took place in Mumbai, India. It saw over 80,000 people attend from 132 countries, representing 2,660 organizations. Unofficially, as many as 130,000 participated. Unlike the WSF in Brazil, a sizeable majority of participants in Mumbai came as part of mass, poor people's movements – notably movements of *adivasi*, or indigenous peoples, and *dalits*, or "untouchables." The presence of these movements in such numbers foregrounded issues central to the survival of tribal peoples, their subsistence rights to lands, rivers, forests, and water against the destruction wrought by megadevelopment projects, resource extraction, privatization, and corporate control of nature. These movements are rural, communitarian, and oriented to subsistence livelihoods, and they embody the links between bio- and cultural diversity. Their survival struggles forced ecological questions that had heretofore been relatively marginal to the centre of the WSF's agenda. Their presence also posed deep challenges to the modernization, urbanization, and development discourses that continue to underpin the utopias of much of the anti-globalization movement.

In Brazil, the WSF has been peopled predominantly by Brazilians and secondarily by Latin Americans, with about fifteen percent of delegates coming from outside the region in 2003. If anything, by 2005, the Porto Alegre event was even more thoroughly Brazilian, although the participation and visibility of Asians and Africans had also increased. Key mass movement entities in the Brazil events included the Movimiento Sem Terra (MST, the landless movement), the CUT, Via Campesina, and Articulación Feminista Marcosur. Prominent issues and campaigns in 2002 and 2003 included the struggle against the Free Trade Agreement of the Americas, resistance to US intervention in Latin America as in the proposed Plan Puebla Panama and Plan Colombia, and attention to the Argentine economic crisis. Each WSF reflects both the global historical conjuncture and the particular conjuncture and social struggles of the host country and region. For all their impressive diversity, the WSF gatherings in Brazil have been primarily light-skinned affairs of the middle class and non-poor. The massive realities of Afro-Brazil and the indigenous Americas have barely been apparent. Even the Brazilian MST, although a major player in the WSF process, has not been present in its tens of thousands in the space of the WSF.[9]

Place (the region/country but also the specific city) is overwhelmingly significant for the character of the world event and for its contribution to the globality/multiculturalism of the WSF process. It is also significant for its effects on the host movements and indigenous political culture before, during, and after the world event, especially through its politics of diversity and inclusion and the way in which they get embodied in a particular place-based process.[10] Wherever the world event is organized, it enacts its own culturally specific, geographically rooted social movement processes. This place-based dynamic makes for significantly different World Social Forums and is critical to deepening the international, multicultural, and intercivilizational character of the global process and the possibility for genuinely dialogical encounters among movements across difference. Every edition of the World Social Forum is "placed" but transnational. The worldwide process is made up of myriad place-based processes, indisputably localized but both taken as a whole and, in many of its constitutive parts, characterized by an expanding globality.

The fourth aspect of the WSF's spatial praxis has to do with the presence, role, and status of place-based movements in the processes and events constituting the WSF, their own evolving multiscale politics/practices, and the relation of these practices to their "subaltern strategies of localization" (Escobar 2001).[11] For highly localized movements, which are just finding their ways into transnational civil society spaces, or those that have little cross-sectoral coalitional experience, the WSF is a place both to learn of new others and to assert one's own right to be present in and to this worldwide convergence against neoliberalism.

For example, indigenous movements of the Americas have made a claim on the World Social Forum. In making a bid to host the Americas Social Forum (ASF), indigenous groups were among those who brought the forum to Quito, Ecuador, which, with Peru and Bolivia, is home to Aymara and Quechwa peoples and where indigenous peoples make up 40 percent of the population. Ecuador is also home to one of the strongest, most dynamic, and most politically potent indigenous movements in the world. From within the Latin American orbit, the Americas Social Forum in Quito issued a strong challenge to Porto Alegre in the 1,000-strong indigenous people present; in their prominent presence on panels not narrowly about indigenous issues; in the visibility of their art forms, music, and dance throughout the event; in their distinct political discourses, visions, projects, and processes. Key is their twin insistence that they need the World Social Forum and that the worldwide movement against neoliberal globalization needs them, specifically for their defence of diversity as a lived reality and political principle and for their defence of nature – their lands and environments – against the rapacious incursion of resource-extraction corporations and neoliberal, neocolonial states (Chancosa 2004).

Despite the existence of some more nuanced scholarship, notably in geography, many commentators, including on the left, portray such place-based movements as place bound and as the repository of traditional, defensive, parochial, and often reactionary politics.[12] By extension, place-based or localized social movements are assumed to be parochial and defensive or, more kindly, naive and ineffectual in confronting increasingly globalized forms of power. In contrast, anthropologist Arturo Escobar (2001, 163) attributes to place-based movements such as those described here a "novel politics of scale" wherein they enact a place-based localization strategy premised on the defence of local cultures and natures, coupled with active engagement with translocal forces and a multiscale politics linking identity, territory, and culture.

Conclusion: The Empire, the Movement, and the Politics of Scale

As a scholar of social movements and an activist, I have long been concerned to make visible the discourses and practices of emancipatory social movements and inquire into their meanings. I am concerned about scholarship on the left, in geography and elsewhere, contributing to what Escobar (2001, 150) has called "the prose of counter-insurgency" in effectively erasing practices of resistance through too single-minded a focus on the power of capital and states (see also Guha 1988). If we are committed to a constructivist perspective on scale, and we recognize that the manipulation of scale is essential to the exercise of power in the contemporary period, then it seems important to ask whether and how non-elite social actors are also actively remaking scale in response to neoliberal and imperialist globalization, not just in frontal contestation with economic and political elites *but also within and among social movements themselves*.

Far from the centres of world domination, the World Social Forum is helping to give birth to a new kind of worldwide left – democratic, diverse, pluralistic, and broadly convergent in its desire for a world marked by equality, justice, and democracy and its opposition to imperialist globalization. The World Social Forum has been central to the convergence of both anti-globalization and anti-war movements, even as the WSF is not itself a unitary entity and as organizers repudiate the notion that it should be. The Forum is successfully fostering *convergence* among movements worldwide through the promotion of *pluralism*. It is this extraordinary paradox, that embracing diversity is producing unprecedented coordinated action on a global scale, that is key to the generative power of the WSF and suggestive of a new democratic politics on a world scale. Increasingly, the power of the Forum lies also in its global diffusion as a *process* for the creation of *non-deliberative* political spaces through which various movements converge and encounter each other in a variety of ways, in different places, and at different scales.

At the heart of the alternative politics/culture currently emergent in and through the WSF is the recognition and status of difference and multiplicity, including those arising from place and scale.[13] Drawing on insights and approaches in critical geography, I have explored the interrelated character of space, place, and scale, the social construction of scale, and the practice of a politics of multiple scales taking shape in and through the World Social Forum. I have begun to consider the relations between a politics of multiple scales at the WSF and its constitutive place-based movements. In this conclusion, I want to reflect on its relationship to a politics of recognition and difference and, following Escobar, its significance for emancipatory politics in a time of empire.

The recognition and valorization of social struggles and movements at various scales and arising from distinct places enact an expanding politics of diversity and recognition, which acknowledges the multiplicity of alternative visions, values, and worldviews and the presence of existing "other worlds." This praxis implies a break with globocentrism and is signalled by the profound shifts in relations among social movements at different scales that are more horizontal and less hierarchical and characterized by greater reciprocity, dialogue, mutual respect, and recognition. It invokes an alternative sociospatial imaginary of "the movement" as rooted in places/locales that are dispersed, diverse, and increasingly densely networked in a huge variety of ways rather than as a single, unitary, global, counterhegemonic counterforce.

The World Social Forum as an autonomous *space* allows the movements and groups of globalizing civil society to make themselves visible to one another, to encounter and transform one another. This is every bit as important as their effects on hegemonic institutions and regimes and is central to constructing anti-hegemonic power on a global scale, even if it cannot be reduced to this. The recognition of the multiple geographical sites and scales of struggle, the irreducibility of their existence and their significance, and the displacement of a hierarchy of scales of movement practice are central to creating a postcolonial and anti-imperialist politics, to breaking with imperial capitalist modernity and its Eurocentrisms.

Santos (2004) identifies the trans-scalar character of the WSF and the reassertion of the "local" as a key dimension of its newness. Yet, it is not just the putative newness of the WSF but also what it connotes about a new politics in formation that is important. Notwithstanding his problematic grammar of fixed scales, Santos makes an important point:

What is new about contemporary societies is that the scales of social and political life – the local, national and global scales – are increasingly more interconnected ... It is even more true with scales of counter hegemonic struggles. It is obvious that each political practice or social struggle is organized in accordance with a privileged scale, be it local, national or global, but whatever the scale may be, all the others must be involved as conditions of success. The decision on which scales to privilege is a political decision that must be taken in accordance with concrete political conditions. It is therefore not possible to opt in the abstract for any one hierarchy among scales of counter-hegemonic practice or struggle. (2004, 96)

The recognition and valorization of movement politics of multiple scales and the concomitant recognition of contingency and respect for difference arising from place and scale comprise a critical axis of the new politics. The social construction of scale and the politics of scale are not simply operative in terms of power politics, within social movements, or between oppositional movements and elites (although it is also about that). Social movement practices and discourses can also be prefigurative and utopian. The emergent scalar practices and discourses and the political struggles/debates over them are important aspects of a new democratic imaginary, budding in the shadow of empire.

ACKNOWLEDGMENTS

The research for this chapter was supported by the Social Sciences and Humanities Research Council of Canada.

NOTES
1. Leitner and Sheppard (this volume) are surely right in noting that, in much recent scholarship in geography on social movements, scale has become a master concept that can occlude other dimensions of the spatiality of movement politics. Here I write of the "spatial praxis" of the WSF of which the politics of scale is one dimension. Nevertheless, I suspect that my use of the "politics of scale" remains more encompassing than they would prefer.
2. See Santos (2004) for the cleavage at the WSF between national and global strategies and for commentary on how and why the majority do not see themselves

represented by this cleavage. See Sen (2004a) for the reassertion of the "national" meaning *Indian* in the organizing of the Asia Social Forum and the 2004 WSF in Mumbai.

3   The term "politics of scale" is used widely with varying and imprecise meanings. When I use it here, I am referring narrowly to the conscious and purposeful deployment of scalar narratives to shape political outcomes.

4   See the WSF Charter of Principles at http://www.forumsocialmundial.org.br. For commentary, see Sen (2004b). These features remain definitive despite some departures in practice for the WSF in India. For the 2004 WSF in Mumbai, organizers further required that participants declare their opposition to religious communalism and allowed for participation by political parties of the left in organizing the WSF. See Sen (2004a) for commentary.

5   It is critical to maintain a distinction between the WSF and its governing and organizing bodies, the key ones being its International Council and International Secretariat. While IC deliberations are an important pole in shaping the world-scale WSF process, the proliferation, dynamism, geographical dispersion, and multiculturalism of WSF processes continually overwhelm the IC and any occasional attempts to control or represent the WSF.

6   "Regional" social forum "councils" are in formation and have observer status at the International Council. They are increasingly claiming autonomy while often reminding the IC that local and regional processes also constitute the *World* Social Forum. There is often overlap between IC members and leading organizations of various regional processes, but not all IC members are embedded in local or regional processes.

7   The WSF charter is silent on the scale question, and the resulting ambiguity has left space for a variety of practices at a variety of scales. There is a host of interesting research and analysis to be done here exploring why activists organize forums at the scales they do and how they understand the relations between social movements operating at various scales in and beyond their forums.

8   The difference that place makes is also evident at the subglobal level, for example, in the distinctiveness of Florence-, Paris-, and London-based European World Social Forums in 2002, 2003, and 2004, respectively, and in Quito versus Porto Alegre in terms of Latin American-based forums.

9   See Conway (2005) for more extensive discussion of the difference that place makes to the WSF.

10 For further discussion of this point, especially with reference to Indian social movements, see Conway (2005) and Sen (2004a).

11 While all social movements have their own spatialities and territorialities, they are not all place based in the same ways or to the same degrees.

12 They may be, but this is an empirical question.

13 Recognition of the diversities arising from geographic dispersion and place-based movements is not adequate in and of itself. Not all diversity/multiplicity can or should be understood in terms of geographical context alone. Issues of women's equality, the rights of sexual minorities, people with AIDS, people with disabilities, and other "others" highlight the continually contested character of the places/cultures of place-based movements.

Conclusion

Rianne Mahon and Roger Keil

This book has presented work at the intersections of political economy and spatial theory. While it makes reference to all customary spatial concepts on the sociospatial register – territory, place, scale, networks – the book focuses on scale and its articulations (Jessop, Brenner, and Jones 2008). It has brought recent work on scale from a variety of disciplines to bear on some of the classical concerns of political economy. Writing from a Canadian vantage point, this endeavour to some extent reflects the questions arising from Canada's peculiar pathways of societal development. Yet, the book is not centrally about Canada or its traditions of thought and practice. It reaches beyond and self-consciously aims towards a global repositioning of various strands of critical social theory. The contributors cover real and theoretical territory stretching across three continents. Canadian work on the political economies of scale is projected outward onto wider circuits of theory as external perspectives are marshalled to make sense of the world in Canada.

The book creates the space for significant theoretical advances at the interface of political economies and spatiality as well as for empirical explorations guided thereby. In a sense, the chapters of this book treat scales as series of "concrete abstractions," which Mark Gottdiener (1993, xx) – following Marx, Lefebvre, and Harvey – has defined as "both a material product of social relations (the concrete) and a manifestation of relations, a relation itself (the abstract)." Theoretical interventions such as those by Brenner, Jessop, Kipfer, Magnusson, and Miller are easily tied back to (and are themselves part of) the material realities from which they sprang, while the more empirically dense accounts (Ali and Keil, Mahon, Swyngedouw, Wekerle et al., among others) are informed by sophisticated theoretical and conceptual debates. The book's contributors also issue a strong warning against schematic applications of either political economic or scale thinking. Neither works well if applied mechanically to social reality. An inflexible template is not capable of elucidating the complex realities so deftly grasped through Brenner's metaphor of the *mille feuille*.

Scale as Theory, Method, and Practice

Several chapters in this volume operate predominantly on conceptual and methodological levels. To bring out the economic, political, and cultural dimensions of a scalar perspective, Miller focused on three processes and their relationship to scale (borders, territory, and capabilities of different levels). Jessop's chapter began by warning against four fallacies (scalar conflation, reductionism, essentialism, and scalar rejectionism) and then went on to develop four concepts that can improve our understanding of changing sociospatial relations – from place and territory to scale and space. Brenner's chapter used the powerful metaphor of the *mille feuille* to conjugate a complex register of sociospatial relations as they interact with political economies. Finally, Kipfer, relying on Lefebvre's urban theory, mounted a powerful argument against confusing scale with levels of social reality.

Much attention has been paid to one of political economy's classic concerns – the role of state spaces and state scales. Swyngedouw's chapter provided an archeology of the hydraulic spaces created by the scalar politics of the Franco regime in mid-twentieth-century Spain. Leitner and Sheppard's chapter showed how strategies are shaped by state-constructed scalar configurations. Yet, while they accept the existence of scalar strategies and scalar frames, the authors also argued the need for the concept of positionality in order to bring into view connectivity and place. In his comprehensive review, Magnusson posed the question of the relationships of state and politics somewhat differently, asking whether state institutions and processes could be scaled to politics: that is, the "real" politics that govern our lives. We will return to this question at the end.

The book is also not just a methodological discussion of scale but presents, instead, a kaleidoscope of current thinking on societal matters of concern. To frame those matters in political economies of scale is merely one – albeit important – perspective that helps us to understand their complexities. Most chapters show a keen awareness of the global constitution of our world today. Ali and Keil, in particular, simultaneously mobilized thinking on scale and networks/topologies to illuminate the spread of, and the fight against, emerging infectious diseases. They navigated the choppy waters of global health governance as bodies, cities, and their public health systems are restructured and repositioned under the double duress of imminent health threats and shifts in global public health governance (simultaneous downloading and upscaling of responsibilities). The impact of restructuring becomes especially tangible in the emerging relationships of the World Health Organization to local public health agencies, although it is clear that national and provincial levels of government remain in control of most related processes.

Heynen's chapter similarly took the body (naked life, naked survival) and social reproduction as its starting point. The chapter revealed a distinct biopolitics from below – the Black Panther Party provided community breakfasts to poor ghetto children – at an important historical conjuncture in American history. This basic activity signalled a multiscalar critique of the US welfare state and the US Empire that resonated far beyond the confines of the inner city. Through the concept of revolutionary intercommunalism, the Black Panther Party was able to mobilize and build support across various scales of African American communities and beyond.

Mahon's chapter used the notion of scalar hierarchies to explore one of the defining questions – child care provision – of today's collective consumption in advanced industrial societies. The massive entry of women into the world of paid work has raised questions of how to manage daily and intergenerational social reproduction. To be sure, child care advocates have focused their attention on the national and, in Canada, provincial scales, but interscalar hierarchies created by federal-provincial relations leave room for creativity where the need arises (i.e., the local scale).

Howitt came at the significance of the global from a somewhat different angle, but he also noted how scale helped him to think critically about what had been done to Aboriginal peoples (the erasure of their scales and the superimposition of imperial and later federal scalar organization). The historical outcome of these contradictions points towards the negotiation of a new relationship among the chief actors and institutions.

Writing from a neighbouring context down under, Larner, Lewis, and Le Heron embedded their chapter on the New Zealand fashion industry in a discussion of neoliberalism and the scalar world that it has constructed. They asked how best to think about "after neoliberalism" or even neoliberalization. The latter is not understood as a singular, coherent strategy but as a series of events whose direction can only be seen *ex post facto*. The instability of these formations and their internal contradictions are integral to the project's character. A distinct spatial imaginary is woven into this complex story, with a complex understanding of problems, engaging diverse actors operating at different and multiple spatial and temporal scales. Also on the plane of "creative" economic geography, Peck's chapter critiqued the current craze for urban creativity projects, inspired by the work of Richard Florida. For Peck, such economic development strategies clearly form part of a neoliberal scalar politics. Drawing on the examples of Detroit/Michigan, Peck's chapter highlighted the impact of the current extralocal rule regime of neoliberalism, which is designed to exacerbate interlocal competition through "fast policy transfer."

The book points towards scalar politics as the dynamic domain of change. Thus, Conway's chapter looked at the World Social Forum as a multiscalar form. For Conway, the forum should not be understood as a deliberative or hierarchical space – as in state space. In some respects, it represents a "collage," although this term fails to see the impact of the coexistence and action of diverse groups, operating from different scales, on each other. The chapter teased out the constitutive importance of the participative dimension. In this world where empire and movement seem to coexist and co-define each other, place ultimately matters too. This latter point was made forcefully in the chapter by Wekerle, Sandberg, and Gilbert, who argued that place-based knowledge challenges the hierarchy and linearity of scalar analysis. Social movement imagination of place and ecosystem constitutes a powerful narrative of resistance. The chapter reflected on the bioregion as critical to forging multiscalar networked analysis, of which it is the discursive and metabolic centre. As a result of this particular scalar production, nature can be defended – and socialized – on much different terms than the water in Franco's Spain. Yet, their analysis also revealed the possibility that developers, too, can deploy scalar narratives in green language.

Contribution to Ongoing Debates on Scale and in Political Economy

In the introduction, we outlined some important debates that structure the progression of the arguments in the book: the spatial and, more recently, scalar turn in the social sciences; the dramatic restructuring of state spaces and scales as well as the constitutive processes of political discourses and struggles; accumulation and social reproduction; and, finally, the politics of the possible and the scalar strategies deployed by social movements as they seek to reshape the fixed and flowing realities that constitute their everyday lives.

As we have seen throughout the work presented in this volume, in the rescaling of political economies, in an era of "glocalization," the national

Conclusion

still commands a central place, despite the growing insight that, in a post-Westphalian world, other scales of states and societies are claiming a more prominent spot in the considerations of all actors. This is true for both the supra- and the subnational scales with which collective action engages.

The variably grounded metanarrative of neoliberalization has been shown to play a particularly pertinent role in the rescaling of political economies between New Zealand and Australia at one end and North America and Europe at the other. Still, we are also reminded that rescaling is not just a thing of the recent past but has also been a permanent feature of capitalist political economies for a long time. The more historical perspectives of Swyngedouw's chapter on Franco's water policies and Heynen's contribution on the Black Panther Party demonstrate that politics of scale had a major role to play in the middle of the twentieth century, when the nation-state was in its heyday. These two chapters bookend the "political" between the myth-infused policies of the (authoritarian) state and the innovative struggles of a poor people's movement in the literal ghetto. In paraphrasing Warren Magnusson, scaling the state to politics clearly presented a problem for both extremes.

The contributions to this book all implicitly or explicitly recognize the importance of place, which, as we have learned from Bob Jessop, is specific, bounded, characterized by identity and face-to-face communication and everydayness. The debate over whether such places are constituted in a hierarchically layered reality of scales or in topological fashion, cutting across levels of material reality, continues throughout this volume. The editors, however, clearly agree with the thrust of many chapters: the two seemingly contravening positions are not incompatible, as suggested by Marston, Jones, and Woodward (2005). Certainly, there are many factors that make topological and scalar approaches awkward partners in the toolbox of political economists. Nevertheless, several contributors – notably Brenner, Miller, Ali and Keil, Leitner and Sheppard – demonstrate how they can be used in a complementary fashion.

Howitt's chapter, among others, makes it clear that successful contestatory and emancipatory politics may view the scale-network/topology debate in more strategic than theoretical ways. Where and when such politics can intervene powerfully and through which means – scale jumping, scale bending, unscaled, networked, or otherwise – may have more to do with the circumstances of praxis than with the spatiopolitical ontologies that constitute the actors who use those tactics. More broadly, the pervasive political economies (and ecologies) of emancipatory action presented in many chapters highlight the work on the body and biopolitics from below and from above. The chapters dealing with health- and food-related issues (Ali and Keil; Heynen); those on non-human nature, both national and bioregional (Swyngedouw; Wekerle, Sandberg, and Gilbert); the urban (Brenner; Kipfer; Peck; Mahon; Ali and Keil; Larner, Lewis, and Le Heron); and the politics of movements (Miller; Leitner and Sheppard; Conway) allow a framing that oscillates between the constitution of the individual through collective more-than-human practices and the increasing risks associated with our "modern constitution" (Latour 1993).

The question we can now ask more precisely is what implications can we draw from the book for the study of political economy? Here are a few ways in which we believe we can move forward with regard to mobilizing thinking on scale for political economic thought and praxis.

1   What does a multiscalar view contribute to political economy, especially to contemporary debates about glocalization and the place of the national? Clearly, we have a range of options here, from the reluctant abandonment of methodological nationalism in Brenner's and Jessop's chapters to the celebration of the decentred state in Magnusson's chapter. Cities are definitely conceptual hubs in this "rescaling" of thought, although Kipfer's take on the urban question foregrounds the multilevel, rather than the multiscalar, character of the urban. Mahon, Ali and Keil, and Wekerle, Sandberg, and Gilbert privilege the urban, and to some degree the sphere of (collective) consumption, in the thinking about multiscalar political economies, but they locate cities in wider (and tangled) scalar hierarchies. All multi- and trans-scale work associated with this set of questions delivers varying sets of sociospatial imaginaries that drive the interventions of actors both from above and from below.

2   Political economists have traditionally studied processes of human interaction through social divisions (class, race, gender) and institutions. Scale adds a new dimension to the study of processes of human interaction, and our book has turned attention to ways in which scales are articulated with the different processes through which capitalism is sustained and endangered. Interterritorial competition at the basis of the globalized economies is subject to intense scrutiny – with quite diverse results – in Peck's trenchant critique of the "creative city" economies and

in Larner, Lewis, and Le Heron's careful investigation of a localized sector of production in the global economy. Such investigation of scaled processes extends to those of social reproduction and the production of nature. It shows the breadth of work possible in analyzing our social reality today, once the methodological infatuation with the nation-state Leviathan is abandoned.

3   Like other critical political economists, those using the concept of scale are interested not only in understanding the world but also in contributing to the change of it. For example, Kipfer's reflections on Henri Lefebvre's "right to the city" make the case for understanding and acting on the fragmented and homogeneous aspects of urban everyday life. Howitt's chapter illuminates the way that the concept of scale can be strategically deployed to reclaim or reinvent new scales of sociality by those whom colonial history has sought to obliterate. Wekerle, Sandberg, and Gilbert show how scalar concepts can be used to forge multiscalar alliances, a theme that also appears in Conway's analysis of the World Social Forum as a flexible, multiscalar site for the construction of new networks among activists.

4   There is, above all, a need to recognize the limit and potential of scale. To all authors in this volume, it is but one concept that helps us to probe the political economy of space. This insight emerges strongly in the introductory chapters and is powerfully reiterated in Leitner and Sheppard's chapter. It is also borne out by the more empirical chapters, which carefully utilize scale along with a potpourri of other spatial and temporal concepts.

To conclude, political economy has been found wanting when it comes to the theorization of space and scale. When reviewing the contributions to this volume, we may at last find some new openings to address political economy's undertheorization of space and scale. Especially in the chapters that deal with the rescaling of movements and politics, hunger, ecology, and global resistance are contextualized in a powerful analysis of a world of scale politics, which does not automatically lead back to the state as we know it. The fractal edges of this world in motion reflect the opening on which we might pin hopes for a range of possible futures that are ours to make. As Conway demonstrates in the closing contribution to this book, like the turtle to globalization's hare, resistance and contestation constantly challenge the scales and topologies of today's capitalist political economy on a world scale.

References

Abayasekara, Geetha. 1999. Environmental ideology and urban planning: The discourse and practice of "environmental protection" in the urban planning process of Sydney's metropolitan growth. PhD diss., Macquarie University.

Aberley, Doug. 1999. Interpreting bioregionalism: A story from many voices. In *Bioregionalism*, ed. Michael Vincent McGinnis, 13–42. New York: Routledge.

Abraham, Thomas. 2004. *Twenty-first century plague: The story of SARS*. Baltimore: Johns Hopkins University Press.

Abu-Jamal, Mumia. 2004. *We want freedom: A life in the Black Panther Party*. Cambridge, MA: South End Press.

Acosta Bono, Gonzalo, José Luis Gutiérrez Molina, Lola Martínez Macías, and Ángel del Río Sánchez. 2004. *El canal de los presos (1940-1962): Trabajos forzados: De la represión política a la explotación económica*. Barcelona: Crítica.

Adams, Paul. 1996. Protest and the scale of telecommunications. *Political Geography* 15: 419–41.

Affonso, Dyanne D., Gavin J. Andrews, and Lianne Jeffs. 2004. The urban geography of SARS: Paradoxes and dilemmas in Toronto's health care. *Journal of Advanced Nursing* 45, 6: 568–78.

Agamben, Giorgio. 1998. *Homo sacer: Sovereign power and bare life*. Palo Alto: Stanford University Press.

Agius, Parry, Jocelyn Davies, Richard Howitt, and Lesley Johns. 2002. *Negotiating comprehensive settlement of Native title issues: Building a new scale of justice in South Australia*. Canberra: Australian Institute of Aboriginal and Torres Strait Islander Studies.

Agius, Parry, Jocelyn Davies, Richard Howitt, Sandie Jarvis, and Rhiân Williams. 2004. Comprehensive Native title negotiations in South Australia. In *Honour among nations? Treaties and agreements with indigenous people*, ed. Marcia Langton, Maureen Teehan, Lisa Palmer, and Kathryn Shain, 203–19. Melbourne: Melbourne University Press.

Agius, Parry, Tom Jenkin, Richard Howitt, Sandie Jarvis, and Rhiân Williams. 2007. (Re)asserting indigenous rights and jurisdictions within a politics of place: Transformative nature of Native title negotiations in South Australia. *Geographical Research* 45, 2: 194–202.

Agnew, John. 1994. The territorial trap. *Review of International Political Economy* 1, 1: 53–80.
—. 1997. The dramaturgy of horizons: Geographical scale in the "reconstruction of Italy" by the new Italian political parties, 1992-95. *Political Geography* 16: 99–122.
Agnew, John, and Stuart Corbridge. 1994. *Mastering Space*. New York: Routledge.
Aguilar, Louis. 2005. Michigan loses jobs: Rate worst in nation. *Detroit News*, 20 January, 1A.
Alfred, Gerald. 1999. *Peace, power, righteousness: An indigenous manifesto*. Toronto: Oxford University Press.
Ali, S. Harris, and Roger Keil. 2006. Global cities and the spread of infectious disease: The case of severe acute respiratory syndrome (SARS) in Toronto, Canada. *Urban Studies* 43, 3: 1–19.
—. 2008. *Networked disease: Emerging infections in the global city*. Oxford: Wiley-Blackwell.
Allen, John. 2004. The whereabouts of power: Politics, government, and space. *Geografiska Annaler Series B* 86: 119–32.
Altman, Jon, and Melinda Hinkson, eds. 2007. *Coercive reconciliation: Stabilise, normalise, exit Aboriginal Australia*. Melbourne: Arena Publications.
Amin, Ash. 1998. Globalization and regional development: A relational perspective. *Competition and Change* 3: 145–65.
—. 2002. Spatialities of globalization. *Environment and Planning A* 34: 385–99.
Amin, Ash, and Stephen Graham. 1999. Cities of connection and disconnection. In *Unsettling cities*, ed. John Allen, Doreen Massey, and Michael Pryke, 7–37. London: Routledge.
Amin, Ash, and Nigel Thrift. 2002. *Cities*. Oxford: Polity.
Amin, Samir. 1979. *Accumulation on a world scale*. Hassocks, Sussex: Harvester Press.
Anderson, Felicity. 1999. Confidence high in CBD development. *Independent*, 8 December, 7.
Anderson, Kay. 2005. Australia and the "state of nature/Native." *Australian Geographer* 36, 3: 267–82.
—. 2006. *Race and the crisis of humanism*. London: Routledge.
Anthias, Floya. 2002. Where do I belong? Narrating collective identity and translocational positionality. *Ethnicities* 2: 491–514.
Antolín-Fargas, Francesca. 1997. Dotaciones y gestión de los recursos energéticos en el desarollo económico de España. *Papeles de economía española* 73: 193–207.
—. 1999. Iniciativo privada y política pública en el desarollo de la industria eléctrica en España: La hegemonía de la gestión privada, 1875-1950. *Revista de historia económica* 17, 2: 411–45.
Aristotle. 1996. *The politics and the constitution of Athens*. Cambridge, UK: Cambridge University Press.
Asían-Peña, José Luis. 1941. *Elementos de geografía general e historia de España*. 2nd ed. Barcelona: Bosch Casa Editorial.

Balakrishnan, Tattamangalam, and K. Selvanathan. 1990. Ethnic residential segregation in metropolitan Canada. In *Ethnic demography*, ed. Shivalingappa Halli, Frank Torvato, and Leo Driedger, 393–413. Ottawa: Carleton University Press.

Bannerji, Himani. 1995. *Thinking through*. Toronto: Women's Press.

Barciela López, Carlos, and Inmaculada López Ortiz. 2000. La política de colonización del Franquismo: Un complemento de la política de riegos. In *El agua en la historia de España*, ed. Carlos Barcielo López and Joaquin Melgarejo Moreno, 325–68. Alicante: Publicaciones de la Universidad de Alicante.

—. 2003. El fracaso de la política agraria del Primer Franquismo, 1939-1959: Vente años perdidos para la agricultura Española. In *Autarquía y mercado negro: El fracaso económico del Primer Franquismo, 1939-1959*, ed. Carlos Barciela López, 55–93. Barcelona: Crítica.

Bashevkin, Sylvia. 2002. *Welfare hot buttons: Women, work, and social policy reform*. Toronto: University of Toronto Press.

Beatley, Timothy, and Kristy Manning. 1997. *The ecology of place: Planning for environment, economy, and community*. Washington, DC: Island Press.

Bello, Marisol. 2005. Detroit is bracing for a lean new year. *Detroit Free Press*, 30 December, A1.

Berg, Peter, and Raymond Dasmann. 1977. Reinhabiting California. *Ecologist* 7, 10: 399–401.

Berman, Marshall. 1982. *All that is solid melts into air: The experience of modernity*. New York: Simon and Schuster.

Bernal, Antonio Miguel. 1990. Agua para los latifundios anadaluces. In *Agua y modo de producción*, ed. Teresa Pérez Picazo and Guy Lemeunier, 271–310. Barcelona: Crítica.

—. 2004. Los beneficiarios del canal: Latifundios de regadío. In *El canal de los presos (1940-1962): Trabajos forzados – De la represión política a la explotación económica*, ed. Gonzalo Acosta-Bono, José Luis Gutiérrez-Molina, Lola Martínez-Macías, and Ángel del Río Sánchez, 27–36. Barcelona: Crítica.

Berry, Mike. 2005. Melbourne: Is there life after Florida? *Urban Policy and Research* 23: 381–92.

Bill, Amanda. 2003. Creating a label for myself: Fashion design subjectivity and education in the new economy. Paper presented at Making an Appearance: Fashion, Dress, and Consumption, Centre for Critical and Cultural Studies, University of Queensland Creative Industries Faculty, Brisbane, Australia.

The Black Panther. 1973. Chicagoans unite for community control of police. *Black Panther*, 26 May, 2–5.

Black Panther Party (BBP). N.d. *Defend the ghetto*. Pamphlet. Wisconsin Historical Society Archives, Madison, WI.

—. 1966. Black Panther Party platform and program. In *The Black Panthers Speak*, ed. Philip S. Foner. New York: Da Capo Press.

Blaut, James M. 1974. The ghetto as an internal neo-colony. *Antipode* 6, 1: 37–41.

–. 1993. *The colonizer's model of the world: Geographical diffusionism and Eurocentric history.* New York and London: Guilford Press.

Blomfield, Paul. 2002. *The designer fashion industry in New Zealand: A scoping study.* Wellington: Industry New Zealand.

Bluestone, Barry, and Harrison Bennett. 1982. *The deindustrialization of America.* New York: Basic Books.

Bocking, Stephen A. 2005. Protecting the rain barrel: Discourses and the roles of science in a suburban environmental controversy. *Environmental Politics* 14, 5: 611–28.

Boden, Deirdre, and Harvey Molotch. 1994. The compulsion to proximity. In *NowHere: Space, time, and modernity,* ed. Roger Friedland and Deirdre Boden, 257–86. Berkeley: University of California Press.

Boltanski, Luc, and Eve Chiapello. 2006. *The new spirit of capitalism.* London: Verso.

Bosco, Fernando J. 2001. Place, space, networks, and the sustainability of collective action: The Madres de Plaza de Mayo. *Global Networks* 1, 4: 307–29.

Boudreau, Julie-Anne, and Roger Keil. 2001. Seceding from responsibility? Secession movements in Los Angeles. *Urban Studies* 38: 1701–31.

Bourne, Larry S. 2000. Urban Canada in transition to the twenty-first century: Trends, issues, and visions. In *Canadian cities in transition,* ed. Trudi Bunting and Pierre Filion, 26–52. Toronto: Oxford University Press.

Boychuk, Gerard. 1998. *Patchworks of purpose: The development of social assistance in Canada.* Montreal: McGill-Queen's University Press.

Bradford, Neil. 2002. Why cities matter: Policy research perspectives for Canada. CPRN Policy Research Paper F/23. http://www.cprn.ca.

Braudel, Fernand. 1984. *The perspective of the world.* Berkeley: University of California Press.

Braun, Bruce, and Noel Castree, eds. 1998. *Remaking reality.* London: Routledge.

Brenner, Neil. 1997. Global, fragmented, hierarchical: Henri Lefebvre's geographies of globalization. *Public Culture* 10, 1: 137–69.

–. 1998a. Between fixity and motion: Accumulation, territorial organization, and the historical geography of spatial scales. *Environment and Planning D: Society and Space* 16: 459–81.

–. 1998b. Global cities, "glocal states": Global-city formation and state territorial restructuring in contemporary Europe. *Review of International Political Economy* 5, 1: 1–37.

–. 1999. Globalization as reterritorialization: The re-scaling of urban governance in the European Union. *Urban Studies* 36, 3: 431–51.

–. 2000. The urban question as a scale question: Reflections on Henri Lefebvre, urban theory, and the politics of scale. *International Journal of Urban and Regional Research* 24, 2: 361–78.

–. 2001a. The limits to scale? Methodological reflections on scalar structuration. *Progress in Human Geography* 25, 4: 591–614.

–. 2001b. State theory in the political conjuncture: Henri Lefebvre's comments on a new state form. *Antipode* 33, 5: 784–807.

–. 2004. *New state spaces: Urban governance and the rescaling of statehood.* Oxford: Oxford University Press.

Brenner, Neil, Bob Jessop, Martin Jones, and Gordon MacLeod. 2003. State space in question. In *State/space: A reader*, ed. Neil Brenner, Bob Jessop, Martin Jones, and Gordon MacLeod, 1–26. Oxford: Blackwell.

–. 2006a. State/space and the political economy of capitalism, part one: Rethinking sociospatiality. Lecture at the National Institute for Regional and Spatial Analysis, National University of Ireland, Maynooth, 15 May.

–. 2006b. State/space and the political economy of capitalism, part two: Geographies of state spatial restructuring after Atlantic Fordism. Lecture at the National Institute for Regional and Spatial Analysis, National University of Ireland, Maynooth, 15 May.

Brenner, Neil, and Roger Keil, eds. 2006. *The global cities reader.* New York: Routledge.

Brenner, Neil, Jamie Peck, and Nik Theodore. 2005. Neoliberal urbanism: Cities and the rule of markets. DEMOLOGOS Working Paper, Department of Geography, University of Wisconsin, Madison.

Brodie, Janine. 1989. The political economy of regionalism. In *The new Canadian political economy*, ed. Wallace Clement and Glen Williams, 240–61. Montreal: McGill-Queen's University Press.

–. 1990. *The political economy of Canadian regionalism.* Toronto: Harcourt, Brace, Jovanovich.

Brown, Elaine. 1992. *A taste of power: A black woman's story.* New York: Pantheon Books.

Brown, Michael. 1995. Sex, scale, and the "new urban politics": HIV-prevention strategies from Yaletown, Vancouver. In *Mapping desire: Geographies of sexualities*, ed. David Bell and Gill Valentine, 245–63. London: Routledge.

–. 1997. *Replacing citizenship: AIDS activism and radical democracy.* New York: Guilford.

Buell, Frederick. 2004. *From apocalypse to way of life: Environmental crisis in the American century.* New York: Routledge.

Buesa, Mikel. 1986. Política industrial y desarollo del sector eléctrico en España (1940-1963). *Información comercial española*, 121–35.

Bulkeley, Harriet. 2005. Reconfiguring environmental governance: Towards a politics of scales and networks. *Political Geography* 24: 875–902.

Bullón, Eloy. 1941. Reformas urgentes en la enseñanza de la geografía. *Estudios geográficos* 5: 661–78.

Bunnell, Tim, and Neil Coe. 2005. Re-fragmenting the "political": Globalization, governmentality, and Malaysia's multimedia super-corridor. *Political Geography* 35: 831–49.

Burleigh Evatt and New Zealand Institute of Economic Research. 2001. *Textile and clothing industry preliminary report Part A: Breaking with past – Patterns of uncompetitive behaviour.* Wellington: Industry New Zealand.

Butler, Judith. 1990. *Gender trouble: Feminism and the subversion of identity.* London: Routledge.
Calvo, Oscar. 2001. Bienvenido, Mister Marshall! La ayuda económica americana y la economía española en la década de 1950. *Revista de historia económica* 19 (special issue): 253-75.
Campbell, David, and Michael Dillon, eds. 1993. *The political subject of violence.* Manchester: Manchester University Press.
Capel, Horacio. 1976. La geografía española tras la Guerra Civil. *Geo crítica* 1: 5-35.
Carr, Raymond. 1995. *España: De la restauración a la democracia, 1875-1980.* Barcelona: Editorial Ariel.
—. 2001. *Modern Spain, 1875-1980.* Oxford: Oxford University Press.
Castells, Manuel. 1977. *The urban question.* London: Edward Arnold.
—.1996. *The rise of the network society.* Oxford: Blackwell.
—. 2000. *The rise of the network society.* Vol. 1. *The information age: Economy, society, and Culture.* 2nd ed. Oxford: Blackwell.
Castree, Noel. 1995. On theory's subject and subject's theory: Harvey, capital, and the limits to classical Marxism. *Environment and Planning A: Society and Space* 27: 269-97.
—. 2000a. Geographic scale and grass-roots internationalism: The Liverpool dock dispute, 1995-1998. *Economic Geography* 76: 272-92.
—. 2000b. Marxism and the production of nature. *Capital and Class* 72: 5-36.
—. 2002. False antitheses? Marxism, nature, and actor-networks. *Antipode* 34, 2: 111-46.
Castree, Noel, and Bruce Braun, eds. 2001. *Social nature: Theory, practice, and politics.* Oxford: Blackwell.
Central Intelligence Agency (CIA). 2003. SARS: Lessons from the first epidemic of the 21st century – A collaborative analysis with outside experts (unclassified). Office of Transnational Issues, 29 September.
Cerny, Philip. 1995. Globalization and the changing logic of collective action. *International Organization* 49, 4: 595-625.
—. 2004. Mapping varieties of neoliberalism. Paper presented at the International Studies Association, Montreal.
Chambers, Colin, and L. Anders Sandberg. 2007. Pits, peripheralization, and the politics of scale: Struggles over locating extractive industries in the Town of Caledon, Ontario, Canada. *Regional Studies* 41, 3: 327-38.
Chancosa, Blanca. 2004. Interview with the author. Translated by Carlos Torres. Quito, Ecuador.
Chomsky, Noam. 1993. *Year 501: The conquest continues.* London: Verso.
Churchill, Ward, and Jim Vander Wall. 2002. *The COINTELPRO papers: Documents from the FBI's secret wars against dissent in the United States.* Cambridge, MA: South End Press.

References

City of Vancouver. 2002. *Moving forward: Child care: A cornerstone of child development services*. Vancouver: City of Vancouver.

Clark, Helen. 2002. Implementing a progressive agenda after fifteen years of neoliberalism: The New Zealand experience. Presentation to London School of Economics, 21 February.

Cleaver, Kathleen, and George Katsiaficas, eds. 2001. *Liberation, imagination, and the Black Panther Party: A new look at the Panthers and their legacy*. New York: Routledge.

Clemons, Michael, and Charles E. Jones. 2001. Global solidarity: The Black Panther Party in the international arena. In *Liberation, imagination, and the Black Panther Party: A new look at the Panthers and their legacy*, ed. Kathleen Cleaver and George Katsiaficas, 20–39. New York: Routledge.

Collinge, Chris. 1999. Self-organization of society by scale: A spatial reworking of regulation theory. *Environment and Planning D: Society and Space* 17, 5: 557–74.

–. 2005. The différance between society and space: Nested scales and the returns of spatial fetishism. *Environment and Planning D: Society and Space* 23, 2: 189–206.

–. 2006. Flat ontology and the deconstruction of scale: A response to Marston, Jones, and Woodward. *Transactions of the Institute of British Geographers* 30, 2: 244–51.

Conway, Janet. 2004. *Identity, place, knowledge: Social movements contesting globalization*. Halifax: Fernwood.

–. 2005. The empire, the movement, and the politics of scale: Considering the World Social Forum – Towards a political economy of scale. York University, Toronto. http://www.carleton.ca/polecon/scale/conway.rtf.

–. 2006. Toward a movement of multiple scales: The Canadian Jubilee 2000 Initiative. In *Nature's revenge: Re-claiming sustainability in an age of corporate globalization*, ed. Mike Gismondi, James Goodman, and Josée Johnston, 203–24. Toronto: Broadview Press.

–. 2007. Transnational feminisms and the World Social Forum: Encounters and transformations in anti-globalization spaces. *Journal of International Women's Studies* 8, 3: 49–70.

–. 2008a. Geographies of transnational feminism: Place and scale in the spatial praxis of the World march of Women. *Social Politics: International Studies in Gender, State and Society* 15, 2: 1–25.

–. 2008b. Reading Nairobi: Place, space and difference at the 2007 World Social Forum. *Societies without Borders* 3, 1: 48–70.

Cool Cities Initiative. 2004. *Michigan's Cool Cities Initiative: A reinvestment strategy*. Lansing: State of Michigan.

Cortner, Hanna J., and Margaret A. Moote. 1999. *The politics of ecosystem management*. Washington, DC: Island Press.

Cox, Kevin. 1990. Territorial structures of the state: Some conceptual issues. *Tijdschrift voor economische en sociale geografie* 81, 4: 251–66.

–, ed. 1997. *Spaces of globalization*. New York: Guilford.
–. 2002. *Political geography: Territory, state, and society*. Cambridge, MA: Blackwell.
Craig, David, and Doug Porter. 2004. The third way and the Third World: Poverty reduction and social inclusion strategies in the rise of "inclusive" liberalism. *Review of International Political Economy* 12, 2: 226–63.
Crain, Keith. 2007. We really are in a single-state recession. *Crain's Detroit Business*, 6 November, 14.
Crain's Detroit Business. 2006. Young people can be Detroit's catalyst. *Crain's Detroit Business*, 17 April, 8.
Cresswell, Tim. 2002. Theorizing place. In *Theorizing place, placing mobility: The politics of representation in a globalized world*, ed. Ginette Verstraete and Tim Cresswell, 11–32. Amsterdam: Rodopi.
Crewe, Louise, and Jonathan Beaverstock. 1998. Fashioning the city: Cultures of consumption in contemporary urban spaces. *Geoforum* 29, 3: 287–308.
Cross, Sherrie. Forthcoming. The scale politics of reconciliation. PhD diss., Macquarie University, Sydney.
Cunningham, David. 2005. The concept of metropolis: Philosophy and urban form. *Radical Philosophy* 133: 13–25.
Dahl, Robert A. 1990. *After the revolution?* New Haven: Yale University Press.
Davis, Mike. 2005. *The monster at our door: The global threat of avian flu*. New York: New Press.
Debanné, Anne-Marie, and Roger Keil. 2004. Multiple disconnections: Environmental justice and urban water in Canada and South Africa. *Space and Polity* 8, 2: 209–25.
Del Moral Ituarte, Leandro. 1999. La política hidráulica en España de 1936 a 1996. In *El agua en los sistemas agrarios: Una perspectiva histórica*, ed. Ramon Garrabou and José Manuel Naredo, 181–95. Madrid: Fundación Argentaria.
Delaney, David, and Helga Leitner. 1997. The political construction of scale. *Political Geography* 16: 93–97.
Deleuze, Gilles, and Felix Guattari. 1988. *A thousand plateaus: Capitalism and schizophrenia*. Minneapolis: University of Minnesota Press.
Demeritt, David. 2002. What is "the social construction of nature"? A typology and sympathetic critique. *Progress in Human Geography* 26, 2: 255–79.
Demirovic, Alex. 1992. Regulation und Hegemonie: Intellektuelle, Wissenspraktiker, und Akkumulation. In *Hegemonie und Staat*, ed. Alex Demirovic, Hans-Peter Krebs, and Thomas Sablowski, 128–57. Muenster: Westfaelisches Dampfboot.
Desfor, Gene, and Roger Keil. 2004. *Nature and the city*. Tucson: University of Arizona Press.
Desfor, Gene, Roger Keil, Stefan Kipfer, and Gerda Wekerle. 2005. From surf to turf: No limits to growth in Toronto? *Studies in Political Economy* 77: 131–56.
Desjardins, Ghislaine. 1992. An historical overview of child care in Quebec. In *Canadian child care in context: Perspectives from the provinces and territories*, vol. 2, ed. Alan Pence, 31–46. Ottawa: Statistics Canada.

Detroit Renaissance. 2006. *Road to renaissance.* Detroit: Detroit Renaissance.
Díaz-Marta Pinilla, Manuel. 1997 [1969]. *Las obras hidráulicas en España.* Aranjuez: Ediciones Doce Calles.
Dicken, Peter, Philip F. Kelly, Kris Olds, and Henry Yeung. 2001. Chains and networks, territories and scales. *Global Networks* 1, 2: 89–112.
Dirección General de Obras-Hidráulicas. 1990. *Plan hidrológico: Síntesis de la documentación básica.* Madrid: Ministerio de Obras Públicas y Urbanismo.
Dreher, Christopher. 2002. Be creative – or die. *Salon,* 6 June. http://dir.salon.com/story/books/int/2002/06/06/florida/index.html.
Driedger, Leo. 2003. Changing boundaries: Sorting space, class, ethnicity, and race in Ontario. *Canadian Review of Sociology and Anthropology* 40, 5: 593–621.
Duncan, Simon, and Mark Goodwin. 1988. *The local state and uneven development.* Cambridge, UK: Polity.
Elden, Stuart. 2004. *Understanding Henri Lefebvre: Theory and the possible.* London: Continuum.
Engels, Friedrich. 1881. A fair day's wages for a fair day's work. *Labour Standard,* 7 May. http://www.marxists.org/archive/marx/works/1881/05/07.htm.
–. 1958 [1844]. *The condition of the working class in England.* Stanford: Stanford University Press.
Entrikin, J. Nicolas. 1991. *The betweenness of place: Towards a geography of modernity.* Basingstoke: Macmillan.
Erickson, H. 2003. Create Detroit: Who needs it? We do! *Detroiter,* November. http://www.thedetroiter.com.
Escobar, Arturo. 2001. Culture sits in places: Reflections on globalism and subaltern strategies of localization. *Political Geography* 20: 139–74.
–. 2004. Beyond the Third World: Imperial globality, global coloniality, and anti-globalization social movements. *Third World Quarterly* 25, 1: 207–30.
Esping-Andersen, Gøsta. 1990. *Three worlds of welfare capitalism.* Princeton: Princeton University Press.
Faludi, Andreas, and Bas Waterhout. 2002. *The making of the European spatial development perspective.* London: Routledge.
Ferguson, James, and Akhil Gupta. 2002. Spatializing states: Toward an ethnography of neoliberal governmentality. *American Ethnologist* 29: 981–1002.
Ferguson, Rob. 2003. SARS tab may top $2 billion: Bank. *Toronto Star,* 26 April, D1.
Fernández de Valderrama, Gabriel. 1964. España-USA, 1953-1964. *Economía financiero* 6: 14–51.
Fidler, David P. 2004a. Germs, governance, and global public health in the wake of SARS. *Journal of Clinical Investigation* 113, 6: 799–804.
–. 2004b. *SARS, governance, and the globalization of disease.* New York: Palgrave Macmillan.
Florida, Richard. 2002a. *The rise of the creative class: And how it's transforming work, leisure, community, and everyday life.* New York: Basic Books.
–. 2002b. The rise of the creative class. *Washington Monthly,* May, 15–25.

—. 2004. Revenge of the squelchers. *Next American City* 5: i–viii.
—. 2005a. *Cities and the creative class*. New York: Routledge.
—. 2005b. *The flight of the creative class: The new global competition for talent*. New York: HarperBusiness.
Flusty, Steven. 2004. *De-Cocacolonization: Making the globe from inside out*. New York: Routledge.
Forsey, Helen. 2005. Betting the farm. *Canadian Dimension*, July-August, 21–27.
Foucault, Michel. 1990. *The history of sexuality: An introduction*. New York: Vintage.
—. 1994. The birth of biopolitics. In *Michel Foucault: Ethics, subjectivity, and truth*, ed. Paul Rabinow, 73–79. New York: New Press.
—. 1997. What is enlightenment? In *Michel Foucault: Ethics, subjectivity, and truth*, ed. Paul Rabinow, 303–19. New York: New Press.
—. 1999. Space, power, and knowledge. In *The cultural studies reader*, ed. Simon During, 134–41. London: Routledge.
—. 2004. *Naissance de la biopolitique: Cours au Collège de France, 1978-1979*. Paris: Seuil-Gallimard.
Foucault, Michel, and Noam Chomsky. 2006 [1971]. *The Chomsky-Foucault Debate: On Human Nature*. New York: New Press.
Fowke, Vernon. 1957. *The national policy and the wheat economy*. Toronto: University of Toronto Press.
Frank, Thomas. 2000. *One market under God*. New York: Doubleday.
Fraser, Malcolm. 2000. The past we need to understand: Vincent Lingiari Memorial Lecture, August 1992. Darwin, Australia. http://www.austlii.edu.au/au/other/IndigLRes/car/2000/2408.html.
Freeman, Carla. 2001. Is local:global as feminine:masculine? Rethinking the gender of globalization. *Signs: Journal of Women in Culture and Society* 26: 1007–36.
Friendly, Martha, and Jane Beach. 2005. *Early childhood education and care in Canada 2004*. Toronto: University of Toronto Childcare Resource and Research Unit. http://www.crru.ca.
Froehling, Oliver. 1999. Internauts and guerrilleros: The Zapatista rebellion in Chiapas, Mexico, and its extension into cyberspace. In *Virtual geographies: Bodies, space, and relations*, ed. Mike Crang, Phil Crang, and Jon May, 178–201. London: Routledge.
Fusi, J.P., and J. Palafox. 1989. *España 1808-1996: El desafío de la modernidad*. Madrid: Editorial Espasa.
Gale, Anne-Maree. 2001. Fashioned with thought. *Venture* June: 14–16.
Gallo, Max. 1974. *Spain under Franco: A history*. New York: E.P. Dutton and Company.
Galtung, Johan. 1971. A structural theory of imperialism. *Journal of Peace Research* 2: 81–116.
Gandy, Matthew. 2002. *Concrete and clay: Reworking nature in New York City*. Cambridge, MA: MIT Press.

References

Gandy, Matthew, and Almuddin Zumla, eds. 2002. *The return of the white plague: Global poverty and the "new" tuberculosis.* London: Verso.

García-Alvarez, Jácobo. 2002. *Provincias, regiones, y comunidades autónomas: La formación del mapa político de España.* Temas del Senado 8. Madrid: Secretaría General del Senado, Dirección de Estudios y Documentación, Departamento de Publicaciones.

Gardiner, Michael E. 2000. *Critiques of everyday life.* London: Routledge.

Garrett, Laurie. 1996. The return of infectious disease. *Foreign Affairs* 75, 1: 66–79.

—. 2005. The next pandemic? *Foreign Affairs* 84, 4: 3–23.

Garrido Morrión, Joaquin. 1957. Desarrollo hidroelectrico Español en la producción de energia desde 1939 a 1955 en relación con los recursos hidroelectricos totales de España. *Revista de obras publicas,* December, 661–67.

Geisler, Charles C., and Barbara L. Benford. 1998. Ecosystem management: Who's entitled? In *Who owns America? Social conflict over property rights,* ed. Harvey M. Jacobs, 131–56. Madison: University of Wisconsin Press.

Gellner, Ernst. 1983. *Nations and nationalism.* Oxford: Blackwell.

Gibbs, David, Andrew Jonas, and Aidan While. 2002. Changing governance structures and the environment: Theorising the links between economy and environment at the local and regional scale. *Journal of Environmental Policy and Planning* 5, 3: 235–54.

Gibson, Chris, and Natascha Klocker. 2005. The "cultural turn" in Australian regional economic development discourse: Neoliberalising creativity? *Geographical Research* 43: 93–102.

Gibson-Graham, Julie-Katherine. 1994. "Stuffed if I know": Reflections on post-modern feminist research. *Gender, Place, and Culture* 1, 2: 205–24.

Giddens, Anthony. 1984. *The nation state and violence.* Berkeley: University of California Press.

Gilbert, Liette, L. Anders Sandberg, and Gerda R. Wekerle. Forthcoming. Building bioregional citizenship: The case of the Oak Ridges Moraine, Ontario, Canada. *Local Environment: The International Journal of Justice and Sustainability.*

—. 2008. Una mirada al prisma biorregional: Construcción de vivienda y conservación de la naturaleza en la Gran Región de Toronto. In *Norte América: Construccíon de espacios regionales,* ed. Alejandro Mercado Celis, Graciela Martinez-Zalce, and Miriam Alfie Cohen, 125–55. México: Metropolitana-Cuajimatpa.

Gilbert, Liette, Gerda R. Wekerle, and L. Anders Sandberg. 2005. Local responses to development pressures: Conflictual politics of sprawl and environmental conservation. *Cahiers de Géographie du Québec* 49: 377–92.

Gillmor, Don. 2004. Coming soon. *Toronto Life,* February, 60–65.

Gil-Olcina, Antonio. 2003. Perduración de los planes hidráulicos en España. In *La directiva marco del agua: Realidades y futuros,* ed. Pedro Arrojo-Agudo and Leandro del Moral Ituarte, 29–61. Zaragoza: Fundación Nueva Cultura del Agua, Institución Fernando el Católico, Universidad de Zaragoza.

Glassman, Jim. 1999. State power beyond the "territorial trap": The internationalization of the state. *Political Geography* 18: 669–96.

—. 2001. From Seattle (and Ubon) to Bangkok: The scales of resistance to corporate globalization. *Environment and Planning D: Society and Space* 19: 513–33.

Gómez De Pablos González, Manuel. 1973a. El Centro de Estudios Hidrográficos y la planificación hidráulica española. *Revista de obras publicas* 120: 241–48.

—. 1973b. El desarollo de los recursos hidráulicos en España. *Revista de obras publicas* 120: 337–44.

Gómez Mendoza, Josefina. 1992. Regeneracionismo y regadíos. In *Hitos históricos de los regadíos españoles*, ed. Antonio Gil Olcina and Antonio Morales Gil, 231–62. Madrid: Ministerio de Agricultura, Pesca, y Alimentación.

—. 1997. La formación de la escuela española de geografía (1940-1952). *Ería* 42: 107–46.

Goodwin, Mark, Simon Duncan, and Stephen Halford. 1993. Regulation theory, the local state, and the transition of urban politics. *Environment and Planning D: Society and Space* 11, 1: 67–88.

Goonewardena, Kanishka. 2005. The urban sensorium: Space, ideology, and the aestheticization of space. *Antipode* 37: 58–72.

Goonewardena, Kanishka, and Stefan Kipfer. 2005. Spaces of difference. *International Journal of Urban and Regional Research* 29, 3: 69–87.

Gordon, David. 1978. Capitalist development and the history of American cities. In *Marxism and the metropolis*, ed. William Tabb and Lewis Sawers, 25–63. New York: Oxford University Press.

Gostin, Lawrence, Ronald Bayer, and Amy L. Fairchild. 2003. Ethical and legal challenges posed by severe acute respiratory syndrome: Implications for the control of severe infectious disease threats. *Journal of the American Medical Association* 290: 3229–37.

Gottdiener, Mark. 1993. A Marx for our time: Henri Lefebvre and the production of space. *Sociological Theory* 11, 1: 129–34.

Graham, Stephen, and Simon Marvin. 2001. *Splintering urbanism*. New York: Routledge.

Gramsci, Antonio. 1971. *Selections from the prison notebooks*. Trans. and ed. Quintin Hoare and Geoffrey Nowell Smith. London: Lawrence and Wishart.

Griffen, Sandra. 1992. Addendum: Child care in British Columbia, 1988-1990. In *Child care in context: Perspectives from the provinces and territories*, vol. 1, ed. Alan Pence, 87–101. Ottawa: Statistics Canada.

Grumbine, R. Edward. 1994. What is ecosystem management? *Conservation Biology* 8, 1: 37–38.

Guha, R. 1988. The prose of counterinsurgency. In *Selected subaltern studies*, ed. R. Guha and G. Spivak, 37–44. Delhi: Oxford University Press.

Häkli, Jouni. 2001. In the territory of knowledge: State-centered discourses and the construction of society. *Progress in Human Geography* 25, 3: 403–22.

Hall, Peter. 2000. Creative cities and economic development. *Urban Studies* 37, 4: 639–49.

Hamel, Pierre, Julie-Anne Boudreau, and Roger Keil. 2005. Comparing metro governance: The cases of Montreal and Toronto. Typescript.
Haraway, Donna. 1988. Situated knowledges: The science question and the privilege of partial perspective. *Feminist Studies* 14: 575-99.
Harcourt, Wendy, and Arturo Escobar. 2002. Women and the politics of place. *Development* 45, 1: 7-14.
Hardt, Michael, and Antonio Negri. 2000. *Empire.* Cambridge, MA: Harvard University Press.
—. 2004. *Multitude: War and democracy in the age of empire.* New York: Penguin Press.
Harvey, David. 1982. *The limits to capital.* Chicago: University of Chicago Press.
—. 1985. The geopolitics of capitalism. In *Social relations and spatial structures,* ed. Derek Gregory and John Urry, 128-63. London: Macmillan.
—. 1988 [1973]. *Social justice and the city.* Oxford: Blackwell.
—. 1989a. *The condition of postmodernity.* Oxford: Blackwell.
—. 1989b. From managerialism to entrepreneurialism: The transformation in urban governance in late capitalism. *Geografiska annaler B* 71: 3-17.
—. 1989c. *The urban experience.* Oxford: Blackwell.
—. 1995. Cities or urbanization? *City* 1, 2: 38-61.
—. 1996. *Justice, nature, and the geography of difference.* Oxford: Basil Blackwell.
—. 2000a. Reinventing geography. *New Left Review* 4: 75-97.
—. 2000b. *Spaces of hope.* Berkeley: University of California Press.
—. 2001. *Spaces of capital: Towards a critical geography.* New York: Routledge.
—. 2003. *The new imperialism.* Oxford: Oxford University Press.
—. 2006a. Space as a keyword. In *David Harvey: A critical reader,* ed. Noel Castree and Derek Gregory, 270-93. New York: Routledge.
—. 2006b. *Spaces of global capitalism.* London: Verso.
Haug, Frigga. 1994. Alltagsforschung als zivilgesellschaftliches Projekt. *Das Argument* 206: 6-13.
—. 2003. Alltagsforschung. In *Historisch-Kritisches Wörterbuch des Feminismus,* vol. 1, ed. Frigga Haug, 639-58. Hamburg: Argument Verlag.
Haughton, Graham, and Dave Counsell. 2004. *Regions, spatial strategies, and sustainable development.* London: Routledge.
Held, David. 1996. *Models of democracy.* Cambridge, UK: Polity Press.
Henderson, Jeffrey, Peter Dicken, Martin Hess, Neil Coe, and Henry W.-C. Yeung. 2002. Global production networks and the analysis of economic development. *Review of International Political Economy* 9: 436-64.
Hernández, José Miguel. 1994. La planificación hidrológica en España. *Revista de estudios agro-sociales* 167: 13-25.
Herod, Andrew. 1991. The production of scale in United States labor relations. *Area* 23, 1: 82-88.
—. 1997. Labor's spatial praxis and the geography of contract bargaining in the US east coast longshore industry, 1953-1989. *Political Geography* 16, 2: 145-69.

—. 2001. *Labor geographies: Workers and the landscapes of capitalism*. New York: Guilford.

Herod, Andrew, and Melissa Wright. 2002. Introduction: Theorizing scale. In *Geographies of power: Placing scale*, ed. Herod Andrew and Melissa Wright, 1–14. Malden, MA: Blackwell.

Hertzman, Clyde. 2004. *Making early childhood development a priority: Lessons from Vancouver*. Vancouver: Canadian Centre for Policy Alternatives British Columbia.

Hess, Rémi. 1988. *Henri Lefebvre et l'aventure du siècle*. Paris: Metailie.

Hettne, Bjørn. 1997. Europe in a world of regions. In *A new Europe in the changing global system*, ed. Richard Falk and Tamás Szentes, 16–40. Tokyo: United Nations University Press.

Heyman, David. 2005. Interview. World Health Organization, Geneva, 28 September.

Heynen, Nik, Maria Kaika, and Erik Swyngedouw, eds. 2005. *In the nature of cities: Urban political ecology and the politics of urban metabolism*. London: Routledge.

Hilliard, David, and Lewis Cole. 1993. *This side of glory: The autobiography of David Hilliard and the story of the Black Panther Party*. Boston: Little, Brown.

Hilliard, David, and Donald Weise. 2002. *The Huey P. Newton reader*. New York: Seven Stories Press.

Hirsch, Joachim. 1997. Globalization of capital, nation-states, and democracy. *Studies in Political Economy* 54: 39–58.

Hirsch, Joachim, and Roland Roth. 1986. *Das neue Gesicht des Kapitalismus*. Hamburg: VSA.

Hirst, Paul, and Graham Thompson. 1995. Globalization and the future of the nation state. *Economy and Society* 24: 409–42.

Hobbes, Thomas. 1996 [1651]. *Leviathan*. Cambridge, UK: Cambridge University Press.

Hobsbawm, Eric. 1962. *The age of revolution: Europe 1789-1848*. London: Weidenfeld and Nicolson.

—. 1994. *The age of extremes: The short twentieth century, 1914-1991*. London: Michael Joseph.

Hodgson, Peter. 2001. New support for NZ's business incubators. Media release, New Zealand Government, 27 April.

Hoefle, Scott W. 2006. Eliminating scale and killing the goose that laid the golden egg? *Transactions of the Institute of British Geographers* 30, 2: 238–43.

Howitt, Richard. 1993a. People without geography? Marginalisation and indigenous peoples. In *Marginalisation in theory and practice*, ed. Richard Howitt, 37–52. Sydney: Economic and Regional Restructuring Research Unit, Departments of Economics and Geography, University of Sydney.

—. 1993b. "A world in a grain of sand": Towards a reconceptualisation of geographical scale. *Australian Geographer* 24, 1: 33–44.

—. 1997. Getting the scale right: The geopolitics of regional agreements. *Northern Analyst* 2: 15–17.

—. 1998. Scale as relation: Musical metaphors of geographical scale. *Area* 30, 1: 49–58.

—. 2001. *Rethinking resource management: Justice, sustainability, and indigenous peoples*. London: Routledge.

–. 2002a. A nation in dialogue: Recognition, reconciliation, and indigenous rights in Australia. *Hagar* 2, 2: 261–75.
–. 2002b. Scale and the other: Levinas and geography. *Geoforum* 33: 299–313.
–. 2003. Scale. In *A companion to political geography*, ed. John Agnew, Katharyne Mitchell, and Gerald Toal, 138–57. Oxford: Blackwell.
–. 2006. Scales of coexistence: Tackling the tension between legal and cultural landscapes in post-*Mabo* Australia. *Macquarie Law Journal* 6: 49–64.
Howitt, Richard, and Susan Jackson. 1998. Some things do change: Indigenous rights, geographers, and geography in Australia. *Australian Geographer* 29, 2: 155–73.
Hudson, Raymond. 2001. *Producing places*. New York: Guilford.
Human Rights and Equal Opportunity Commission (HREOC). 1997. *Bringing them home: National inquiry into the separation of Aboriginal and Torres Strait islander children from their families*. Sydney: HREOC.
Hutton, Thomas. 2004. Postindustrialism, postmodernism, and the reproduction of Vancouver's central area: Retheorizing the 21st century city. *Urban Studies* 41, 10: 1953–82.
Institute on Governance, Health Governance. http://www.iog.ca/knowledge_areas.asp?pageID=23.
Japel, Christa, Richard E. Tremblay, and Sylvana Coté. 2005. La qualité, ca compte! *Choix* 11, 4: 1–42.
Jay, Martin. 1984. *Marxism and totality*. Berkeley: University of California Press.
Jensen, Ole B., and Tim Richardson. 2004. *Making European space*. London: Routledge.
Jenson, Jane. 1989. Different but not exceptional: Canada's permeable Fordism. *Canadian Review of Sociology and Anthropology* 26, 1: 69–94.
–. 2002. Against the current: Child care and family policy in Quebec. In *Child care at the crossroads: Gender and welfare state restructuring*, ed. Sonya Michel and Rianne Mahon, 309–32. New York: Routledge.
–. 2006. Rolling out or backtracking on Quebec's child care system? Ideology matters. Paper presented at the Annual Meeting of the Canadian Political Science Association, York University, Toronto, June.
Jenson, Jane, and Rianne Mahon. 2002. Bringing cities to the table: Child care and intergovernmental relations. Canadian Policy Research Networks Discussion Paper F26, Ottawa, October.
Jenson, Jane, Rianne Mahon, and Manfred Bienefeld, eds. 1993. *Production, space, identity: Political economy faces the 21st century*. Toronto: Canadian Scholars' Press.
Jessop, Bob. 1982. *The capitalist state*. Oxford: Martin Robertson.
–. 1993. Towards a Schumpeterian workfare state. *Studies in Political Economy* 40: 7–39.
–. 2000. The crisis of the national spatio-temporal fix and the tendential ecological dominance of globalizing capital. *International Journal of Urban and Regional Research* 24, 2: 323–60.
–. 2001. Institutional (re)turns and the strategic-relational approach. *Environment and Planning A* 33, 1: 1213–37.

—. 2002a. *The future of the capitalist state.* Cambridge, UK: Polity.
—. 2002b. Liberalism, neoliberalism, and urban governance: A state-theoretical perspective. In *Spaces of neoliberalism: Urban restructuring in North America and Western Europe*, ed. Neil Brenner and Nik Theodore, 105–25. Oxford: Blackwell.
—. 2004a. Critical semiotic analysis and cultural political economy. *Critical Discourse Studies* 1, 2: 159–74.
—. 2004b. The European Union and recent transformations in statehood. In *The state of Europe: Transformations of statehood from a European perspective*, ed. S. Puntscher Riekmann, M. Mokre, and M. Latzer, 75–94. Frankfurt: Campus Verlag.
—. 2006. Spatial fixes, temporal fixes, and spatio-temporal fixes. In *David Harvey: A critical reader*, ed. Noel Castree and Derek Gregory, 142–66. Oxford: Blackwell.
Jessop, Bob, Neil Brenner, and Martin Jones. 2008. Theorizing socio-spatial relations. *Environment and Planning D: Society and Space* 26, 3: 389–401.
Jonas, Andrew. 1994. The scale politics of spatiality. *Environment and Planning D: Society and Space* 12: 257–64.
Jones, Charles E. 1998. *The Black Panther Party (reconsidered).* Baltimore: Black Classic Press.
Jones, Katherine. 1998. Scale as epistemology. *Political Geography* 17: 25–28.
Jones, Martin R. 2005. Travels in "phase space": Regions and the limits to thinking space relationally. Paper presented at the Regional Studies Association Meeting, Aalborg, Denmark, May.
Jones, Martin, and Gordon MacLeod. 2004. Regional spaces, spaces of regionalism: Territory, insurgent politics, and the English question. *Transactions of the Institute of British Geographers* 29: 433–52.
Judd, Denis R. 1998. The case of the missing scales: A commentary on Cox. *Political Geography* 17, 1: 29–34.
Jung, Hyunjoo. 2004. Place, space, and scale in contentious politics: The case of greenbelt movements in South Korea between 1998 and 1999. PhD diss., University of Minnesota, Minneapolis.
Kaffer, Nancy. 2005. Crimson haze. *Metro Times*, 9 March. http://www.metrotimes.com/editorial/story.asp?id=7419.
Kaika, Maria. 2005. *Cities of flows: Modernity, nature, and the city.* London: Routledge.
—. 2006. Dams as symbols of modernization: The urbanization of nature between geographical imagination and materiality. *Annals, Association of American Geographers* 96, 2: 276–301.
Kant, Immanuel. 1991. An answer to the question: "What is enlightenment?" In *Kant: Political writings*, ed. H.S. Reiss, 54–60. Cambridge, UK: Cambridge University Press.
Katz, Cindi. 2001a. On the grounds of globalization: A topography for feminist political engagement. *Signs: Journal of Women in Culture and Society* 26, 4: 1213–34.
—. 2001b. Vagabond capitalism and the necessity of social reproduction. *Antipode* 34: 709–28.

–. 2004. *Growing up global: Economic restructuring and children's everyday lives.* Minneapolis: University of Minnesota Press.

Katznelson, Ira. 1993. *Marxism and the city.* Oxford: Clarendon.

Keck, Margaret, and Kathryn Sikkink. 1998. *Activists beyond borders: Advocacy networks in international politics.* Ithaca: Cornell University Press.

Keeling, David J. 1995. Transport and the world city paradigm. In *World cities in a world-system,* ed. Paul Knox and Peter J. Taylor, 115–31. Cambridge, UK: Cambridge University Press.

Keil, Roger. 1987. David Harvey und das Projekt einer materialistischen Stadttheorie. *Prokla* 69, 4: 132–47.

–. 1998. Globalization makes states: Perspectives of local governance in the age of the world city. *Review of International Political Economy* 5, 4: 616–46.

–. 2002. From Los Angeles to Seattle: World city politics and the new global resistance. In *From ACT UP to the WTO: Urban protest and community building in the era of globalization,* ed. Ronald Hayduk and Benjamin Shepard, 326–32. London: Verso.

–. 2005. Urban political ecology, progress report 2. *Urban Geography* 26, 7: 640–51.

Keil, Roger, and S. Harris Ali. 2008. SARS and the restructuring of health governance in Toronto. In *Networked disease: Emerging infections in the global city,* ed. S. Harris Ali and Roger Keil, 55–69. Oxford: Wiley-Blackwell.

Keil, Roger, and Julie-Anne Boudreau. 2005. Metropolitics and metabolics: Rolling out environmentalism in Toronto. In *In the nature of cities: Urban political ecology and the politics of urban metabolism,* ed. Nikolas Heynen, Maria Kaika, and Erik Swyngedouw, 41–60. New York: Routledge.

Keil, Roger, and Neil Brenner. 2003. Globalisierung, global cities, und die neuen Räume der Politik. In *Globalisierung und der Strukturwandel des Politischen,* ed. Albert Scharenberg and Oliver Schmidtke, 254–76. Münster: Westfälisches Dampfboot.

Keil, Roger, and Anne-Marie Debbané. 2005. Scaling discourse analysis: Experiences from Hermanus, South Africa, and Walvis Bay, Namibia. *Journal of Environmental Policy and Planning* 7, 3: 257–76.

Kelly, Philip F. 1999. The geographies and politics of globalization. *Progress in Human Geography* 23, 3: 379–400.

King, Nicholas B. 2004. The scale politics of emerging diseases. *Osiris* 19: 62–76.

Kipfer, Stefan. 2007. Fanon and space: Colonization, urbanization, and liberation from the colonial to the global city. *Environment and Planning D: Society and Space* 25, 4: 701–26.

Kipfer, Stefan, and Roger Keil. 2002. Toronto Inc? Planning the competitive city in the new Toronto. *Antipode* 34, 2: 227–64.

Kirsch, Scott, and Don Mitchell. 2004. The nature of things: Dead labour, nonhuman actors, and the persistence of Marxism. *Antipode* 36, 4: 786–806.

Klein, Sarah. 2004a. Creation station. *Metro Times,* 10 March. http://www.metrotimes.com/editorial/story.asp?id=6019.

—. 2004b. Hipster economics. *Metro Times*, 25 February. http://www.metrotimes.com/editorial/story.asp?id=5965.

Kline, Daniel T. 2006. Theorizing the child in late medieval English culture. Paper presented at the Conference on Medieval Children 1200-1500, University of Kent, UK, June 14-16.

Knopp, Larry. 1997. Sexuality and urban space: Gay male identities, communities, and cultures in the U.S., U.K., and Australia. In *Geographies of resistance*, ed. Steven Pile and Michael Keith, 149-76. London: Routledge.

Kofman, Eleonore. 1998. Whose city? Gender, class, and immigrants in globalizing European cities. In *Cities of difference*, ed. Ruth Fincher and Jane M. Jacobs, 279-300. New York: Guilford.

Krätke, Stefan. 2004. City of talents? Berlin's regional economy, socio-spatial fabric, and "worst practice" urban governance. *International Journal of Urban and Regional Research* 28: 511-29.

Kropotkin, Peter. 1995. *Kropotkin: "The conquest of bread" and other writings*, ed. Marshall S. Shatz. Cambridge, UK: Cambridge University Press.

Kurtz, Hilda. 2003. Scale frames and counter-frames: Constructing the problem of environmental injustice. *Political Geography* 22: 887-916.

—. 2004. The politics of environmental justice as the politics of scale: St. James Parish, Louisiana, and the Shintech siting controversy. In *Geographies of power: Placing scale*, ed. Andrew Herod and Melissa Wright, 249-73. Oxford: Blackwell.

Lacoste, Yves. 1990. *Geographie und politisches Handeln*. Berlin: Kleine Kulturwissenschaftliche Bibliothek.

Landry, Charles. 2000. *The creative city: A toolkit for urban innovators*. London: Earthscan Publications.

Lane, Amy. 2007. Granholm to propose new revenue-sharing plan. *Crain's Detroit Business*, 29 January, 32.

Langford, Thomas. 2003. From social movement to marginalized interest group: Advocating for quality child care in Alberta, 1965-86. In *Changing child care: Five decades of child care advocacy and policy in Canada*, ed. Susan Prentice, 63-80. Halifax: Fernwood.

—. 2006. Alberta's day care controversy. Typescript, Department of Political Science, University of Calgary.

Läpple, Dieter. 1978. Gesellschaftlicher Reproduktionsprozess und Stadtstrukturen. In *Stadtkrise und soziale Bewegungen*, ed. Margit Mayer, Roland Roth, and Volkhard Brandes, 23-54. Frankfurt am Main: Europäische Verlagsanstalt.

Larner, Wendy. 1998. Hitching a ride on the tiger's back: Globalisation and spatial imaginaries in New Zealand. *Environment and Planning D: Society and Space* 16: 599-614.

—. 2001. Governing globalisation: The New Zealand call centre attraction initiative. *Environment and Planning A* 33, 2: 297-313.

Larner, Wendy, and David Craig. 2005. "After neoliberalism"? Community activism and local partnerships in Aotearoa New Zealand. *Antipode* 37, 3: 402–24.

Larner, Wendy, and Richard Le Heron. 2002. The spaces and subjects of a globalizing economy: A situated exploration of method. *Environment and Planning D: Society and Space* 20: 753–74.

—. 2004. Global benchmarking: Participating at a distance in the global economy. In *Global governmentality: New perspectives on international rule*, ed. Wendy Larner and William Walters, 212–32. London: Routledge.

—. 2005. Neoliberalising spaces and subjectivities: Reinventing New Zealand universities. *Organization* 12, 6: 843–62.

Larner, Wendy, Richard Le Heron, and Nick Lewis. 2007. Co-constituting "after neoliberalism"? Political projects and globalising governmentalities in Aotearoa New Zealand. In *Neo-liberalization: States, networks, people*, ed. Kim England and Kevin Ward, 223–47. Oxford: Blackwell.

Larner, Wendy, and Maureen Molloy, with Alison Goodrum. 2007. Globalisation, cultural economy, and not-so-global cities. *Environment and Planning D: Society and Space* 25, 3: 381–400.

Larner, Wendy, and William Walters. 2004. Globalisation as governmentality. *Alternatives* 29, 5: 495–514.

Latham, Alan. 2002. Retheorizing the scale of globalization: Topologies, actor networks, and cosmopolitanism. In *Geographies of power: Placing scale*, ed. Andrew Herod and Melissa Wright, 115–44. Oxford: Blackwell.

Latour, Bruno. 1993. *We have never been modern*. Cambridge, MA: Harvard University Press.

—. 2005. *Reassembling the social: An introduction to actor-network theory*. Oxford: Oxford University Press.

Law, John, and John Urry. 2004. Enacting the social. *Economy and Society* 33, 3: 390–410.

Lawless, Paul. 2002. Power and conflict in pro-growth regimes: Tensions in economic development in Jersey City and Detroit. *Urban Studies* 39: 1329–46.

Laws, Serena. 2004. Legal aid in the neoliberalized state. Seminar paper, Department of Geography, University of Minnesota, Minneapolis.

Le Heron, Richard. 2003. Creating food futures: Reflections of food governance issues in New Zealand's agri-food sector. *Journal of Rural Studies* 19, 1: 111–25.

Lee, Kelley, Suzanne Fustukian, and Kent Buse. 2002. An introduction to global health policy. In *Health policy in a globalizing world*, ed. Kelley Lee, Suzanne Fustukian, and Kent Buse, 3–17. Cambridge, UK: Cambridge University Press.

Lee, Roger, and Jane Wills, eds. 1997. *Geographies of economies*. London: Arnold.

Lefebvre, Henri. 1968. *L'irruption : De Nanterre au sommet*. Paris: Anthropos.

—. 1970a. *Du rural à l'urbain*. Paris: Anthropos.

—. 1970b. *Le manifeste différentialiste*. Paris: Gallimard.

—. 1972. *La pensée marxiste et la ville*. Paris: Casterman.

–. 1976. *De l'état I: L'état dans le monde moderne*. Paris: Union Générale d'Éditions.
–. 1977. *De l'état III: Le mode de production étatique*. Paris: Union Générale d'Éditions.
–. 1978. *De l'état IV: Les contradictions de l'état moderne: La dialectique et/de l'état*. Paris: Union Générale d'Éditions.
–. 1979. Space: Social product and use value. In *Critical sociology: European perspective*, ed. J.W. Freiburg, 285–95. New York: Irvington Publishers.
–. 1981. *Critique de la vie quotidienne III: De la modernité au modernisme (Pour une métaphilosophie du quotidien)*. Paris: L'Arche.
–. 1991 [1974]. *The production of space*. Trans. Donald Nicholson-Smith. Oxford: Blackwell.
–. 1996. *Writings on Cities*. Trans. Eleonore Kofman and Elizabeth Lebas. Oxford: Blackwell.
–. 1997 [1964]. *Métaphilosophie*. Préface by Georges Labica. Paris: Syllepse.
–. 2002. *Critique of everyday life volume II: Foundations for a sociology of the everyday*. Trans. John Moore. London: Verso.
–. 2003a. Myths in everyday life. In *Henri Lefebvre: Key Writings*, ed. Stuart Elden, Elizabeth Lebas, and Eleonore Kofman, 100–8. New York: Continuum.
–. 2003b. State (from *Le retour de la dialectique*). In *Henri Lefebvre: Key Writings*, ed. Stuart Elden, Elizabeth Lebas, and Eleonore Kofman, 61–64. New York: Continuum.
–. 2003c [1970]. *The urban revolution*. Trans. Robert Bononno. Minneapolis: University of Minnesota Press.
–. 2009 [1974]. Reflections on the politics of space. In *State, Space, World: Selected Essays*, ed. N. Brenner and S. Elden, 167–84. Minneapolis, MN: University of Minnesota Press.
Leibovitz, Joseph. 1999. New spaces of governance: Re-reading the local state in Ontario. *Space and Polity* 3, 2: 199–216.
Leitner, Helga. 1997. Reconfiguring the spatiality of power: The construction of a supranational migration framework for the European Union. *Political Geography* 15: 123–43.
–. 2004. The politics of scale and networks of spatial connectivity: Transnational interurban networks and the rescaling of political governance in Europe. In *Scale and geographic inquiry: Nature, society, and method*, ed. Eric Sheppard and Robert McMaster, 236–55. Oxford: Blackwell.
Leitner, Helga, and Byron Miller. 2007. Scale and the limitations of ontological debate: A commentary on Marston, Jones, and Woodward. *Transactions of the Institute of British Geographers* 32, 1: 116–25.
Leitner, Helga, Claire Pavlik, and Eric Sheppard. 2002. Networks, governance, and the politics of scale: Inter-urban networks and the European Union. In *Geographies of Power, Placing Scale*, ed. Andrew Herod and Melissa Wright, 274–303. Oxford: Blackwell.
Leitner, Helga, Jamie Peck, and Eric Sheppard, eds. 2007. *Contesting neoliberalism: Urban frontiers*. New York: Guilford.

Leitner, Helga, and Eric Sheppard. 2002. "The city is dead, long live the net": Harnessing European interurban networks for a neoliberal agenda. In *Spaces of neoliberalism*, ed. Neil Brenner and Nik Theodore, 148–71. Oxford: Blackwell.

Leslie, Carolyn. 2003. Charge it darling. *Venture*, February, 20–22.

Lewis, Nick. 2004. Embedding the reforms in New Zealand schooling: After neoliberalism? *Geojournal Special Issue: Reinventing Government: The Changing Geography of New Zealand after Restructuring* 59, 2: 149–60.

Li, Peter. 1998. *Chinese in Canada*. London: Oxford University Press.

Liedtke, Boris N. 1998. *Embracing a dictatorship: US relations with Spain, 1945-1953*. Oxford/London: St. Martin's Press/Macmillan.

Lim, Sue, Tom Closson, Gillian Howard, and Michael Gardam. 2004. Collateral damage: The unforeseen effects of emergency outbreak policies. *The Lancet Infectious Diseases* 4: 697–703.

Lipietz, Alain. 1987. *Mirages and miracles: The crisis in global Fordism*. London: Verso.

–. 1992. *Towards a new economic order: Post-Fordism, ecology, and democracy*. New York: Oxford University Press.

Lister, Ruth, Fiona Williams, Anneli Anttonen, Jet Bussemaker, Ute Gerhard, Jacqueline Heinen, Stina Johansson, Arnlaug Leira, Birte Siim, Constanza Tobio, and Anna Gavanas. 2007. *Gendering citizenship in Western Europe: New challenges for citizenship research in a cross-national context*. Bristol: Policy Press.

Lloyd-Jenkins, Douglas. 2003. The geography of High Street. Paper presented at the 22nd Conference of the New Zealand Geographical Society, 6–11 July.

Logan, John, and Harvey Molotch. 1987. *Urban fortunes*. Berkeley: University of California Press.

Logan, Shannon, and Gerda R. Wekerle. 2008. Neoliberalizing an environmental governance? Land trusts, private conservation and nature on the Oak Ridges Moraine. *Geoforum* 39, 6: 2097–2108.

Low, Donald E. 2003. SARS: Lessons from Toronto. In *Learning from SARS: Preparing for the next disease outbreak*, ed. Stacey Knobler, Adel Mahmoud, Stanley Lemon, Alison Mack, Laura Sivitz, and Katherine Oberholtzer, 63–70. Washington: National Academies Press.

Löwy, Ilana. 1994. On hybridizations, networks, and new disciplines: The Pasteur Institute and the development of microbiology in France. *Studies in History and Philosophy of Science* 25, 5: 655–88.

MacLeod, Gordon, and Mark Goodwin. 1999. Space, scale, and state strategy: Rethinking urban and regional governance. *Progress in Human Geography* 23, 4: 503–27.

Macpherson, Crawford Brough. 1953. *Democracy in Alberta: Social Credit and the party system*. Toronto: University of Toronto Press.

Magnusson, Warren. 1996. *The search for political space: Globalization, social movements, and the urban political experience*. Toronto: University of Toronto Press.

—. 2000. Politicizing the global city. In *Democracy, citizenship, and the global city*, ed. Engin Isin, 289–307. London: Routledge.
Mahon, Rianne. 1999. "Yesterday's modern times are no longer modern": Swedish unions confront the double shift. In *The brave new world of European labor*, ed. George Ross and Andrew Martin, 125–66. New York: Bergahn Press.
—. 2000. The never-ending story: The struggle for universal child care in the 1970s. *Canadian Historical Review* 81, 4: 583–615.
—. 2002. Gender and welfare state restructuring: Through the lens of child care. In *Child care policy at the crossroads*, ed. Sonya Michel and Rianne Mahon, 1–30. New York: Routledge.
—. 2005a. Child care as citizenship right: Toronto in the 1970s and 1980s. *Canadian Historical Review* 86, 2: 285–316.
—. 2005b. Rescaling social reproduction: Childcare in Toronto/Canada and Stockholm/Sweden. *International Journal of Urban and Regional Research* 29, 2: 341–57.
—. 2006a. *Learning from each other: Early learning and child care experience in Canadian cities.* Produced for the Cities of Toronto and Vancouver with the assistance of Jane Jenson and Katherine Mortimer. Toronto: City of Toronto.
—. 2006b. The OECD and the reconciliation agenda: Competing blueprints. In *Children, changing families, and welfare states*, ed. Jane Lewis, 172–97. Cheltenham: Edward Elgar.
—. 2006c. Of scalar hierarchies and welfare redesign: Childcare in three Canadian cities. *Transactions of the Institute of British Geographers* 31, 4: 452–66.
Mahon, Rianne, and Laura Macdonald. 2006. Poverty policy and politics in Canada and Mexico: Inclusive liberalism. Paper presented at the 16th Conference of the International Sociological Association, Durban, South Africa, August, 2006.
Maier, Charles. 2000. Consigning the twentieth century to history: Alternative narratives for the modern era. *American Historical Review* 105, 3: 807–31.
Malanga, Steven. 2004. The curse of the creative class. *City Journal* 14, 1: 36–45.
—. 2005. Florida daze. *City Journal* 15, 2: 7–9.
Maluquer de Motes, Jordi. 1983. La despatrimonialización del agua: Movilización de un recurso natural fundamental. *Revista de historia económica* 1, 2: 76–96.
Mann, Michael. 1988. The autonomous power of the state: Its origins, mechanisms, and results. In *States, war, and capitalism*, ed. Michael Mann, 1–32. Cambridge, MA: Blackwell.
Manne, Robert. 2001. In denial: The stolen generations and the right. *Australian Quarterly Essay* 1: 1–113.
MAPA. 1990. *Historia y evolución de la colonización agraria en España.* Vol. II: *Política administrativa y economica de la colonización agraria: Analysis institucional y financiero (1936-1977).* Madrid: Ministerio para las Administraciones Publicas.
Marston, Sallie. 2000. The social construction of scale. *Progress in Human Geography* 24, 2: 219–42.

—. 2004. A long way from home: Domesticating the social production of scale. In *Scale and geographic inquiry*, ed. Eric Sheppard and Robert B. McMaster, 170–91. Oxford: Blackwell.
Marston, Sallie A., John Paul Jones III, and Keith Woodward. 2005. Human geography without scale. *Transactions of the Institute of British Geographers* 30: 416–32.
Marston, Sallie, and Neil Smith. 2001. States, scales, and households: Limits to scale thinking? *Progress in Human Geography* 25, 4: 615–19.
Martin, Deborah G. 1999. Transcending the fixity of jurisdictional scale. *Political Geography* 18: 33–38.
—. 2003. "Place framing" as place-making: Constituting a neighborhood for organizing and activism. *Annals of the Association of American Geographers* 93: 730–50.
Martin, Deborah G., and Byron Miller. 2003. Spaces and contentious politics. *Mobilization: An International Journal* 8: 143–56.
Martin, Francis. 2002. Threading a path ahead. *Venture*, July-August, 15–19.
Martín-Mendiluce, José María. 1996. Los embalses en España: Su necesidad y transcendencia económica. *Revista de obras publicas* (3354): 7–24.
Marx, Karl. 1964. *Economic and philosophic manuscripts of 1844*. New York: International Publishers.
—. 1976 [1867]. *Capital*. Trans. Ben Fowkes. New York: Penguin.
—. 1977. *Selected Writings*. Ed. David McLellan. Oxford: Oxford University Press.
Marx, Karl, and Friedrich Engels. 1998. *The German ideology*. New York: Prometheus Books.
Massey, Doreen. 1984. Introduction: Geography matters. In *Geography Matters! A reader*, ed. Doreen Massey and John Allen, 1–11. Cambridge, UK: Cambridge University Press.
—. 1985. *Spatial divisions of labour*. London: Macmillan.
—. 1991. A global sense of place. *Marxism Today*, June, 24–29.
—. 1992. Politics and space/time. *New Left Review* 196: 65–84.
—. 1994. *Space, place, and gender*. Minneapolis: University of Minnesota Press.
—. 1995. Places and their pasts. *History Workshop Journal* 39: 182–92.
—. 2005. *For space*. London: Sage.
Masson, Jack, and Edward LeSage Jr. 1994. *Alberta's local governments: Politics and democracy*. Edmonton: University of Alberta Press.
Mayer, Jonathan D. 2000. Geography, ecology, and emerging infectious diseases. *Social Science and Medicine* 50: 937–52.
McAdam, Douglas, Sidney Tarrow, and Charles Tilly. 2001. *Dynamics of contention*. Cambridge, UK: Cambridge University Press.
McCann, Eugene J. 2003. Framing space and time in the city: Urban policy and the politics of spatial and temporal scale. *Journal of Urban Affairs* 25, 2: 159–78.
—. 2007. Inequality and politics in the creative city-region: Questions of livability and state strategy. *International Journal of Urban and Regional Research* 31, 1: 188–96.
McCarthy, Jan. 2003. Fashioning a business. *Press*, 24 March, 6.

McCarthy, John. 2002. Entertainment-led regeneration: The case of Detroit. *Cities* 19: 105–11.

McDonell, Linda. 1992. An historical overview of child care in British Columbia. In *Childcare in context: Perspectives from the provinces and territories*, vol. 1, ed. Alan Pence, 19–42. Ottawa: Statistics Canada.

McDowell, Linda. 1999. *Gender, identity, and place: Understanding feminist geographies.* Minneapolis: University of Minnesota Press.

—. 2001. Linking scales: Or how scales about gender and organizations raise new issues for economic geography. *Economic Geography* 1, 4: 227–50.

McHugh, Paul G. 1996. The legal and constitutional position of the crown in resource management. In *Resources, nations, and indigenous peoples: Case studies from Australasia, Melanesia, and Southeast Asia*, ed. Richard Howitt, John Connell, and Philip Hirsch, 300–16. Melbourne: Oxford University Press.

McLeod, Mary. 1997. Henri Lefebvre's critique of everyday life. In *Architecture of the everyday*, ed. Stephen Harris and Deborah Berke, 9–29. New York: Princeton Architectural Press.

McMaster, Robert, and Eric Sheppard. 2004. Introduction: Scale and geographic inquiry. In *Scale and geographic inquiry: Nature, society, and method*, ed. Robert McMaster and Eric Sheppard, 1–22. Oxford: Blackwell.

McMichael, Philip. 2006. Peasant prospects in the neoliberal age. *New Political Economy* 11, 3: 407–18.

McQuirk, Pauline. 2003. Producing the capacity to govern in global Sydney: A multi-scaled account. *Journal of Urban Affairs* 25, 2: 201–25.

Melgarejo Moreno, Joaquín. 1995. *La intervención del estado en la cuenca del segura, 1926-1986.* Valencia: Institut de Cultura "Juan Gil-Albert."

—. 2000. De la política hidráulica a la planificación hidrológica: Un siglo de intervención del estado. In *El agua en la historia de España*, ed. Carlos Barcielo López and Joaquín Melgarejo Moreno, 273–321. Alicante: Publicaciones de la Universidad de Alicante.

Mercer, David. 1997. Aboriginal self-determination and indigenous land title in post-*Mabo* Australia. *Political Geography* 16, 3: 189–212.

Merrifield, Andy. 2002. *Dialectical Marxism: Social struggles in the contemporary city.* New York: Monthly Review Press.

—. 2006. *Henri Lefebvre: A critical introduction.* New York: Routledge.

Mettler, Suzanne. 1998. *Dividing citizens: Gender and federalism in New Deal public policy.* Ithaca: Cornell University Press.

Michel, Sonya, and Rianne Mahon, eds. 2002. *Child care policy at the crossroads: Gender and welfare state restructuring.* New York: Routledge.

Michigan. Office of the Governor. 2003. *Michigan cool cities initial report.* Lansing: State of Michigan.

Miller, Byron. 1994. Political empowerment, local-central state relations, and geographically shifting political opportunity structures: Strategies of the Cambridge, Massachusetts, Peace Movement. *Political Geography* 13, 5: 393–406.

—. 1997. Political action and the geography of defense investment: Geographical scale and the representation of the Massachusetts miracle. *Political Geography* 16: 171–85.
—. 2000. *Geography and social movements: Comparing antinuclear activism in the Boston area.* Minneapolis: University of Minnesota Press.
Miller, Byron, and Deborah Martin. 2000. Missing geography: Social movements on the head of a pin. In *Geography and social movements: Comparing anti-nuclear activism in the Boston area*, ed. Byron Miller, 1–38. Minneapolis: University of Minnesota Press.
—. 2004. Spaces of mobilization: Transnational social movements. In *Spaces of democracy: Geographical perspectives on citizenship, participation, and representation*, ed. Clive Barnett and Murray Low, 223–46. London: Sage.
—. 2005. Modes of governance, modes of resistance: Contesting new liberalism in Calgary. Typescript, University of Calgary.
—. 2007. Modes of governance, modes of resistance: Contesting neoliberalism in Calgary. In *Contesting neoliberalism: Urban frontiers*, ed. Helga Leitner, Jamie Peck, and Eric Sheppard, 223–49. New York: Guilford.
Ministerio de Medio Ambiente. 2000. *Plan hidrólogico nacional: Análisis de antecedentes y transferencias planteadas*. Madrid: Ministerio de Medio Ambiente.
Ministry of Municipal Affairs and Housing. Province of Ontario. 2001. *Oak Ridges Moraine Conservation Act 2001*. Toronto: Queen's Printer.
—. 2002. *Oak Ridges Moraine Conservation Plan 2002*. Toronto: Queen's Printer.
—. 2005. *Greenbelt Protection Plan 2005*. Toronto: Queen's Printer.
Mitchell, Katharyne, Sallie Marston, and Cindi Katz. 2004. *Life's work: Geographies of social reproduction*. Oxford: Blackwell.
Mohanty, Chandra T. 2003. *Feminism without borders*. Durham: Duke University Press.
Moore, Donald S. 1997. Remapping resistance: "Ground for struggle" and the politics of place. In *Geographies of resistance*, ed. Steven Pile and Michael Keith, 87–106. London: Routledge.
Morrison, Judith. 2000. *Uniting the voices: Decision making to negotiate for Native title in South Australia*. Adelaide: Aboriginal Legal Rights Movement. http://www.iluasa.com/documents/.
Morse, Stephen. 1993. *Emerging viruses*. London: Oxford University Press.
Murdoch, Jonathan. 1998. The spaces of actor-network theory. *Geoforum* 29, 4: 357–74.
Murdoch, Jonathan, and Graham Day. 1998. Middle class mobility, rural communities, and the politics of exclusion. In *Migration into rural areas: Theories and issues*, ed. Paul Boyle and Keith Halfacree, 186–99. New York: John Wiley and Sons.
Murphy, Ryan. 2004. Boycott United Airlines! Defending the queer workplace, contesting neoliberalism. Seminar paper, Department of Geography, University of Minnesota, Minneapolis.
Myers, Fred. 1986. *Pintupi country, Pintupi self: Sentiment, place, and politics among Western Desert Aborigines*. Washington/Canberra: Smithsonian Institution/Australian Institute of Aboriginal and Torres Strait Islander Studies.
Myrdal, Gunnar. 1957. *Rich lands and poor*. New York: Harper and Brothers.

Nagar, Richa, and Susan Geiger. 2007. Reflexivity, positionality, and identity in feminist fieldwork: Beyond the impasse. In *Politics and practice in economic geography*, ed. Adam Tickell, Trevor Barnes, Jamie Peck, and Eric Sheppard, 267–88. Beverly Hills: Sage.

Natter, Wolfgang, and Wolfgang Zierhofer. 2002. Political ecology, territoriality, and scale. *GeoJournal* 58, 4: 225–32.

Naylor, David. 2003. *Learning from SARS: Renewal of public health in Canada: A report of the National Advisory Committee on SARS and Public Health*. Ottawa: Health Canada.

New Zealand Institute of Economic Research (NZIER). 2002. *Creative industries in New Zealand: Economic contribution*. Wellington: New Zealand Trade and Enterprise.

Newton, Huey P. 1972. *To die for the people*. New York: Random House.

—. 1973. *Revolutionary suicide*. New York: Harcourt, Brace, Jovanovich.

—. 2002a. Speech delivered at Boston College: November 18, 1970. In *The Huey P. Newton reader*, ed. David Hilliard and Donald Weise, 160–75. New York: Seven Stories Press.

—. 2002b. Uniting against a common enemy: October 23, 1971. In *The Huey P. Newton reader*, ed. David Hilliard and Donald Weise, 234–40. New York: Seven Stories Press.

Next American City. 2004a. The great creative class debate continues: The Peabody Institute Forum. *Next American City* 6: 19–22.

—. 2004b. How four cities are responding to the great creative class debate. *Next American City* 7: 16–24.

Ng, Mee Kam, and Peter Hills. 2003. World cities or great cities? A comparative study of five Asian metropolises. *Cities* 20, 3: 151–65.

Niño, Antonio. 2003. 50 años de relaciones entre España y Estados Unidos. *Cuadernos de historia contemporánea* 25: 9–33.

Noss, Reed. 2001. Presentation at Richmond Hill Council, Richmond Hill, ON, 18 January. Fieldnotes from participant observation.

Núñez, Gregorio. 2003. Las empresas eléctricas: Crisis de crecimiento en un contexto de crisis política. In *Los empresarios de Franco: Política y economía en España, 1936-1957*, ed. Glicerio Sánchez Recio and Julio Tascón Fernández, 121–44. Barcelona: Crítica.

O'Brien, Richard. 1990. *Global financial integration: The end of geography*. London: Pinter.

Office of the Prime Minister. 2002. *Growing an innovative New Zealand*. Wellington: Government of New Zealand.

Olds, Kristopher, and Henry Yeung. 2005. Pathways to global city formation: A view from the developmental city-state of Singapore. *Review of International Political Economy* 11, 3: 489–521.

Ollman, Bertell. 1993. *Dialectical investigations*. New York: Routledge.

Ong, Aihwa. 1999. *Flexible citizenship: The cultural logics of transnationality*. Durham: Duke University Press.

Orloff, Ann. 2004. Farewell to maternalism? State policies and mothers' employment. Paper presented at the 2004 meetings of Research Committee 19 of the International Sociology Association, Paris, 2–5 September.

Ortí, Alfonso. 1984. Política hidráulica y cuestión social: Orígenes, étapas, y significados del regeneracionismo hidráulico de Joaquín Costa. *Revista agricultura y sociedad* 32: 11–107.
Oslender, Ulrich. 2004. Fleshing out the geographies of social movements: Black communities on the Colombian Pacific Coast and the "aquatic space." *Political Geography* 23: 957–85.
Paasi, Anssi. 2002. Bounded spaces in the mobile world: Deconstructing "regional identity." *Tijdschrift voor economische en sociale geografie* 93, 2: 137–48.
–. 2004. Place and region: Looking through the prism of scale. *Progress in Human Geography* 28, 4: 536–46.
Panitch, Leo, and Sam Gindin. 2003. Global capitalism and American Empire. In *The imperial challenge: Socialist register 2004*, ed. Leo Panitch and Colin Leys, 1–42. New York: Monthly Review Press.
Patano, Sandra, and L. Anders Sandberg. 2005. Winning back more than words? Power, discourse, and quarrying on the Niagara Escarpment. *Canadian Geographer* 49: 25–41.
Paul, Ari. 2005. 32 flavors of cool: Making over Michigan. *Next American City* 7: 18–19.
Paul, Darel E. 2005. *Rescaling international political economy: Subnational states and the regulation of the global political economy*. New York: Routledge.
Pearson, Noel. 1997. The concept of Native title at common law. In *Our land is our life: Land rights – past, present, and future*, ed. Galarrwuy Yunupingu, 150–61. St. Lucia: University of Queensland Press.
Peck, Jamie. 2001a. American recession. *Transactions of the Institute of British Geographers* 27: 131–35.
–. 2001b. *Workfare states*. New York: Guilford.
–. 2002a. Labor, zapped/growth, restored? Three moments of neoliberal restructuring in the American labor market. *Journal of Economic Geography* 21: 179–220.
–. 2002b. Political economies of scale: Fast policy, interscalar relations, and neoliberal workfare. *Economic Geography* 78: 331–60.
–. 2003. The rise of the workfare state. *Kurswechsel* 3: 75–87.
–. 2005. Struggling with the creative class. *International Journal of Urban and Regional Research* 24: 740–70.
Peck, Jamie, and Adam Tickell. 1994. Searching for a new institutional fix: The after Fordist crisis and global-local disorder. In *Post-Fordism: A reader*, ed. Ash Amin, 280–316. Malden, MA: Blackwell.
–. 2002. Neoliberalising space. *Antipode* 34: 381–404.
Peiris, J.S.M., et al. 2003. Coronavirus as a possible cause of severe acute respiratory syndrome. *Lancet* 361: 1319–25.
Pérez, Joseph. 1999. *Historia de España*. Barcelona: Crítica.
Pile, Steven, and Michael Keith, eds. 1997. *Geographies of resistance*. London: Routledge.
Pred, Allan. 1981. "Social Reproduction and the Time-Geography of Everyday Life." *Geografiska annaler: Series B, Human Geography* 63, 1: 5–22.

Prentice, Susan. 1988. Kids are not for profit: The politics of child care. In *Social movements/social change*, ed. F. Cunningham, S. Findlay, M. Kadar, A. Lennon, and E. Silva, 98–128. Toronto: Between the Lines.

—. 1993. Militant mothers in domestic times: Toronto's postwar child care struggle. PhD diss., York University, Toronto.

Preston, Paul. 1990. *The politics of revenge: Fascism and the military in twentieth century Spain*. London: Unwin Hyman.

—. 1995. *Franco: A biography*. London: Fontana Press.

Preston, Paul, and Frances Lannon, eds. 1990. *Elites and power in twentieth-century Spain*. Oxford: Clarendon Press.

Preston, Richard. 1989. *The hot zone*. New York: Bantam Doubleday Dell Publishing.

Price-Smith, Andrew T. 2002. *The health of nations: Infectious disease, environmental change, and their effects on national security and development*. Cambridge, MA: MIT Press.

Prigge, Walter. 1995. Urbi et Orbi: Zur Epistemologie des Städtischen. In *Capitales Fatales: Urbanisierung und Politik in den Finanzmetropolen Frankfurt und Zürich*, ed. Hansruedi Hitz, Roger Keil, Ute Lehrer, Walter Ronneberger, Christian Schmid, and Richard Wolff, 176–87. Zurich: Rotpunktverlag.

Project for the New American Century. 1997. Statement of principles. http://www.newamericancentury.org/.

—. 2000. Rebuilding America's defenses: Strategy, forces, and resources for a new century. http://www.newamericancentury.org/.

Puente Diaz, Gregorio. 1949. La energia electrica en España. *Información comercial española* (numero extraordinario dedicada a la electridad española): 55–59.

Puig, Núria. 2003. La ayuda económica Norteamericana y los empresarios españoles. *Cuadernos de historia contemporánea* 25: 109–29.

Puig, Núria, and Adoración Álvaro. 2002. Estados Unidos y la modernación de los empresas españoles, 1950-1975: Un estudio preliminar. *Historia del presente* 1: 9–29.

Punter, John. 2003. *The Vancouver achievement: Urban planning and design*. Vancouver: UBC Press.

Reguera-Rodríguez, Antonio Theodore. 1991. Fascismo y geopolítica en España. *GeoCrítica* 94: 11–63.

Reher, David S. 2003. Perfiles demográficos de España, 1940-1960. In *Autarquía y mercado negro: El fracaso económico del primer Franquismo, 1939-1959*, ed. L.C. Barciela, 1–26. Barcelona: Crítica.

Reinicke, Wolfgang H., and Jan Martin Witte. 2000. Interdependence, globalisation, and sovereignty: The role of non-binding international legal accords. In *Commitment and compliance: The role of non-binding norms in the international legal system*, ed. Dinah H. Shelton, 75–99. Oxford: Oxford University Press.

Revista de Obras Públicas (ROP). 1940a. Número extraordinario, dedicado a la cruzada española, 1936-1939. *Revista de obras publicas* (special issue).

—. 1940b. *Revista de obras publicas* 88 (1 March).
Reynolds, Gretchen. 2004. The flu hunters. *New York Times Magazine*, 7 November, 36–43, 52, 68, 92–93.
Reynolds, Henry. 1998. *This whispering in our hearts*. Sydney: Allen and Unwin.
Richmond Hill Council Public Hearing. 2000. Submissions by public, Archives of Richmond Hill Library, 23 February.
Robbins, Paul. 2004. *Political ecology*. Oxford: Blackwell.
Rodríguez Ferrero, Noelina. 2001. *Los regadíos de iniciativa pública en la Cuenca del Guadalquivir: Un análisis económico*. Granada: Editorial Universidad de Granada.
Rodríguez, Saturnino. 1999. *El NO-DO: Catecismo social de una epoca*. Madrid: Editorial Complutense.
Rodwin, Victor. 2008. Health and disease in global cities: A neglected dimension of national health policy. In *Networked disease: Emerging infections in the global city*, ed. Harris Ali and Roger Keil, 27–48. Oxford: Blackwell.
Rodwin, Victor G., and Michael G. Gusmano. 2002. The World Cities Project: Rationale, organization, and design for comparison of megacity health systems. *Journal of Urban Health: Bulletin of the New York Academy of Medicine* 79, 4: 445–63.
Rose, Damaris, and Nathalie Chicoine. 1991. Access to school daycare services: Class, family, ethnicity, and space in Montreal's old and new inner city. *GeoForum* 22, 2: 185–201.
Rose, Deborah Bird. 1992. *Dingo makes us human: Life and land in an Aboriginal Australian culture*. Cambridge, UK: Cambridge University Press.
Rose, Gillian. 1997a. Performing inoperative community: The space and the resistance of some community arts projects. In *Geographies of resistance*, ed. Steven Pile and Michael Keith, 184–202. London: Routledge.
—. 1997b. Situating knowledges: Positionality, reflexivities, and other tactics. *Progress in Human Geography* 21: 305–20.
Rose, Nik. 1999. *Powers of freedom: Reframing political thought*. Cambridge, UK: Cambridge University Press.
—. 2002. The seductions of resistance: Power, politics, and a performative style of systems. *Environment and Planning D: Society and Space* 20: 383–400.
Rosenau, James, and Ernst-Otto Czempiel, eds. 1992. *Governance without government: Order and change in world politics*. Cambridge, UK: Cambridge University Press.
Ross, Kristin. 1995. *Fast cars, clean bodies: Decolonization and the reordering of French culture*. Cambridge, MA: MIT Press.
Rössler, Mechtild. 1989. Applied geography and area research in Nazi society: Central place theory and planning, 1933 to 1945. *Environment and Planning D: Society and Space* 7: 419–31.
Rousseau, Jean. 2000. The new political scales of citizenship in a global era: The politics of hydroelectric development in the James Bay region. PhD diss., Carleton University, Ottawa.

Routledge, Paul. 2000. "Our resistance will be as transnational as capital": Convergence space and strategy in globalizing resistance. *GeoJournal* 52: 25–33.
—. 2003. Convergence space: Process geographies of grassroots globalisation networks. *Transactions of the Institute of British Geographers* 28: 333–49.
—. 2004. Convergence of commons: Process geographies of people's global action. *The Commoners* 8: 1–20.
Rowse, Tim. 1988. From houses to households? The Aboriginal Development Commission and economic adaptation by Alice Springs Town Campers. *Social Analysis* 24: 50–65.
Royal Commission on the Future of the Toronto Waterfront. 1992. *Regeneration: Toronto's waterfront and sustainable city.* Toronto: Queen's Printer.
Ruggie, John. 1993. Territoriality and beyond: Problematizing modernity in international relations. *International Organization* 47, 1: 139–74.
Ryan, Christopher. 2001. Cutting an identity. *Venture*, 6 June, 11.
Sack, Robert. 1986. *Human territoriality: Its theory and history.* New York: Cambridge University Press.
Samers, Michael. 2002. Immigration and the global city hypothesis: Towards an alternative research agenda. *International Journal of Urban and Regional Research* 26, 2: 389–402.
Sánchez-Albornoz, Nicolás. 2004. Saña y negocio en le trabajo forzado. In *El canal de los presos (1940-1962): Trabajos forzados: De la represión política a la explotación económica*, ed. Gonzalo Acosta Bono, José Luis Gutiérrez Molina, José Luis Martínez, Lola Macías, and Angel del Río Sánchez, xxi-xxv. Barcelona: Crítica.
Sánchez de Toca, Joaquín. 1911. *Reconstitución de España en vida de economía política actual.* Madrid: Jaime Ratés Martín Impresor.
Sánchez-Pérez, Francisca. 1981. Acceso al profesorado en la geografía española (1940-1979). *GeoCrítica* 32: 5–51.
Sánchez-Recio, Glicerio. 2003. El Franquismo como red de intereses. In *Los empresarios de Franco: Política y economía en España, 1936-1957*, ed. Glicerio Sánchez Recio and Julio Tascón Fernández, 13–22. Barcelona: Crítica.
Sánchez-Rey, Agustín. 2003. El papel de la Revista de obras públicas en la prensa española: Un medio de información testigo de tres siglos. *Revista de obras públicas* (3434): 17–38.
Santos, Boaventura de Sousa. 2004. *The World Social Forum: A user's manual.* http://www.ces.uc.pt/bss/documentos/fsm_eng.pdf.
Sassen, Saskia. 1991. *The global city: New York, London, Tokyo.* Princeton: Princeton University Press.
—. 2000. *Cities in a world economy.* 2nd ed. Thousand Oaks, CA: Pine Forge Press.
—. 2003. Globalization or denationalization? *Review of International Political Economy* 10, 1: 1–22.
Sax, Joseph L. 1993. Property rights and the economy of nature: Understanding *Lucas v. South Carolina Coastal Council. Stanford Law Review* 45: 1433–55.

Sayer, Andrew. 1992. *Method in social science.* New York: Routledge.
—. 2000. *Realism and social science.* London: Sage.
Sayre, Nathan F. 2005. Ecological and geographical scale: Parallels and potential for integration. *Progress in Human Geography* 29, 3: 276–90.
Schmid, Christian. 2003. Raum und Regulation: Henri Lefebvre und der Regulationsansatz. In *Fit für den Postfordismus? Theoretisch-politische Perspektiven des Regulationsansatzes,* ed. Ulrich Brand and Werner Raza, 217–42. Munster: Westfälisches Dampfboot.
—. 2005. *Stadt, Raum, und Gesellschaft: Henri Lefebvre und die Produktion des Raumes.* PhD diss., University of Zurich.
Schmitter, Philippe C. 1992. Representation and the future Euro-polity. *Staatswissenschaft und Staatspraxis* 3, 3: 379–405.
Scott, Allen J. 1988. *New industrial spaces.* Berkeley: University of California Press.
—. 2000. *The cultural economy of cities: Essays on the geography of image-producing industries.* London: Sage.
Scott, Joan, and David Trubek. 2002. Mind the gap: Law and new approaches to governance in the European Union. *European Law Journal* 8, 1: 1–18.
Seale, Bobby. 1978. *A lonely rage: The autobiography of Bobby Seale.* New York: Times Books.
—. 1991. *Seize the time: The story of the Black Panther Party and Huey P. Newton.* Baltimore: Black Classic Press.
Sen, Jai. 2004a. The long march to another world: Reflections of a member of the WSF India Committee in 2002 on the first year of the World Social Forum process in India. In *World Social Forum: Challenging empires,* ed. Jai Sen, Anita Anand, Arturo Escobar, and Peter Waterman, 293–311. New Delhi: Viveka Foundation.
—. 2004b. A tale of two charters. In *World Social Forum: Challenging empires,* ed. Jai Sen, Anita Anand, Arturo Escobar, and Peter Waterman, 72–75. New Delhi: Viveka Foundation.
Sewell, William H. Jr. 2001. Space in contentious politics. In *Silence and voice in contentious politics,* ed. Ronald R. Aminzade, Jack A. Goldstone, Doug McAdam, Elizabeth J. Perry, Sidney Tarrow, and Charles Tilly, 51–88. Cambridge, UK: Cambridge University Press.
Shakur, Assata. 1987. *Assata, an autobiography.* Westport, CT: Lawrence Hill.
Sharp, Nonie. 1993. *Stars of Tagai: The Torres Strait Islanders.* Canberra: Aboriginal Studies Press.
Shaw, Martin. 2000. *Theory of the global state.* Cambridge, UK: Cambridge University Press.
Shen, Jianfa. 2004. Cross-border urban governance in Hong Kong: The role of state in a globalizing city-region. *Professional Geographer: Forum and Journal of the Association of American Geographers* 56, 4: 530–43.
Sheppard, Eric. 2002. The spaces and times of globalization: Place, scale, networks, and positionality. *Economic Geography* 78: 307–30.

—. 2006. Positionality and globalization in economic geography. In *The changing economic geography of globalization*, ed. Giovanna Vertova, 45–72. London: Routledge.

Sheppard, Eric, and Robert B. McMaster. 2004a. Introduction: Scale and geographical inquiry: Contrasts, intersections, and boundaries. In *Scale and geographic inquiry: Nature, society, and method*, ed. Eric Sheppard and Robert B. McMaster, 1–22. Oxford: Blackwell.

—. 2004b. Scale and geographic inquiry: Contrasts, intersections, and boundaries. In *Scale and geographic inquiry*, ed. Eric Sheppard and Robert M. McMaster, 256–67. Oxford: Blackwell.

Sibley, David. 1995. *Geographies of exclusion*. London: Routledge.

Silvern, Steven E. 1999. Scales of justice: Law, American Indian treaty rights, and the political construction of scale. *Political Geography* 18, 6: 639–68.

Simpson, James. 1995. *Spanish agriculture: The long siesta, 1765-1965*. Cambridge, UK: Cambridge University Press.

Slater, David. 1997. Spatial politics/social movements: Questions of (b)orders and resistance in global times. In *Geographies of resistance*, ed. Steven Pile and Michael Keith, 258–76. London: Routledge.

Smith, David, and Michael Timberlake. 2001. World city networks and hierarchies, 1977-1997: An empirical analysis of global air travel links. *American Behavioral Scientist* 44, 10: 1656–78.

Smith, Dorothy. 1987. *The everyday world as problematic: A feminist sociology*. Toronto: University of Toronto Press.

Smith, Jonathan M., Andrew Light, and D. Roberts. 1998. Introduction: Philosophies and geographies of place. In *Philosopnies of place*, ed. Andrew Light and Jonathan M. Smith, 1–19. Lanham, MD: Rowan and Littlefield.

Smith, Neil. 1984. *Uneven development: Nature, capital, and the production of space*. Oxford: Blackwell.

—. 1991. *Uneven development: Nature, capital, and the production of space*. 2nd ed. Oxford: Blackwell.

—. 1992a. Contours of a spatialized politics: Homeless vehicles and the production of geographical space. *Social Text* 33: 54–81.

—. 1992b. Geography, difference, and the politics of scale. In *Postmodernism and the social sciences*, ed. Joe Doherty, Elspeth Graham, and Mo Malek, 57–79. London: Macmillan.

—. 1993. Homeless/global: Scaling places. In *Mapping the futures*, ed. Jon Bird, Barry Curtis, Tim Putnam, George Robertson, and Lisa Tickner, 87–119. London: Routledge.

—. 1995. Remaking scale: Competition and cooperation in prenational and postnational Europe. In *Competitive European peripheries*, ed. Heikki Eskelinen and Folke Snickars, 59–74. Berlin: Springer Verlag.

—. 1997. The Satanic geographies of globalization: Uneven development in the 1990s. *Public Culture* 10, 1: 169–92.

—. 2001. New geographies and old ontologies: Optimism of the intellect. *Radical Philosophy* 106: 21–30.
—. 2002. New globalism, new urbanism: Gentrification as global strategy. In *Spaces of neoliberalism: Urban restructuring in North America and Western Europe,* ed. Neil Brenner and Nik Theodore, 80–103. Oxford: Blackwell.
—. 2003. Foreword. In *The urban revolution,* by Henri Lefebvre, trans. Robert Bononno, vii–xxiii. Minneapolis: University of Minnesota Press.
—. 2004. Scale bending and the fate of the national. In *Scale and geographic inquiry: Nature, society, and method,* ed. Robert McMaster and Eric Sheppard, 192–212. Oxford: Blackwell.
—. 2005. Neo-critical geography: Or, the flat pluralist world of business class. *Antipode* 37: 887–99.
Smith, Neil, and Ward Dennis. 1987. The restructuring of geographical scale: Coalescence and fragmentation of the northern core region. *Economic Geography* 63, 2: 160–82.
Smith, Richard. 2006. World city topologies. In *The global cities reader,* ed. Neil Brenner and Roger Keil, 400–6. London: Routledge.
Sneddon, Chris. 2003. Reconfiguring scale and power: The Khong-Chi-Mun Project in northeast Thailand. *Environment and Planning A* 35, 12: 2229–50.
Soja, Edward. 1980. The socio-spatial dialectic. *Annals of the Association of American Geographers* 70: 207–25.
—. 1985. Regions in context: Spatiality, periodicity, and the historical geography of the regional question. *Environment and Planning D: Society and Space* 3: 175–90.
—. 1989. *Postmodern geographies: The reassertion of space in critical social theory.* London: Verso.
—. 1999. History: Geography: Modernity. In *The cultural studies reader,* ed. Simon During, 113–25. London: Routledge.
Songel González, Juan María. 2003. La Revista de obras públicas entre 1939 y 1959: Desde la autarquía al plan de etabilización. *Revista de obras publicas* (3434): 83–98.
Sørensen, Georg. 2001. *The transformation of the state.* Basingstoke: Palgrave.
Sousanis, Nick. 2004. Rise and shine Detroit! *Detroiter,* March. http://www.thedetroiter.com/MAR04/createdetroit.html.
Specter, Michael. 2005. Nature's bioterrorist: Is there any way to prevent a deadly avian-flu pandemic? *New Yorker,* 28 February, 50–61.
Spruyt, Hendrik. 1994. *The sovereign state and its competitors.* Princeton: Princeton University Press.
St. John, Ron. 2003. The Canadian hospital: The infectious disease border. Paper presented at Medical Emergencies and the Law: Conference on SARS, Global Epidemics, and Other Disasters, Joint Program of Osgoode Hall Law School of York University and the Faculty of Medicine, University of Toronto, 16 September.
Staeheli, Lynn A. 1994. Empowering political struggle: Spaces and scales of resistance. *Political Geography* 13, 5: 387–91.

Stanner, William E.H. 1979. *White man got no dreaming: Essays 1938-1973*. Canberra: ANU Press.

Steigerwald, B. 2004. Q&A: Florida sees a "different role" for government. *Pittsburgh Tribune-Review*, 11 April.

Storper, Michael. 1996. *The regional world*. New York: Guilford.

Storper, Michael, and Richard Walker. 1989. *The capitalist imperative*. Cambridge, MA: Blackwell.

Suárez-Fernandez, Luis. 1984. *Francisco Franco y su tiempo*. Vol. 5. Madrid: Fundación Nacional Francisco Franco.

Sugrue, Thomas J. 2005. *The origins of the urban crisis*. 2nd ed. Princeton: Princeton University Press.

Sum, Ngai Ling. 1997. Time-space embeddedness and geo-governance of cross-border regional modes of growth: Their nature and dynamics in East Asian cases. In *Beyond market and hierarchy*, ed. Ash Amin and Jerzy Hausner, 159–95. Cheltenham: Edward Elgar.

Sutton, Peter. 1995. *Country: Aboriginal boundaries and land ownership in Australia*. Canberra: Aboriginal History.

Swainson, Gail. 2000. Expert explains new view on the moraine. *Toronto Star*, 13 July, D3.

Swyngedouw, Erik. 1992. The mammon quest: "Glocalisation," interspatial competition, and the monetary order – The construction of new scales. In *Cities and regions in the new Europe*, ed. Mick Dunford and Grigoris Kafkalas, 139–68. London: Belhaven Press.

–. 1996. The city as a hybrid: On nature, society, and cyborg urbanisation. *Capitalism, Nature, Socialism* 7, 1: 65–80.

–. 1997a. Excluding the other: The production of scale and scaled politics. In *Geographies of economies*, ed. Roger Lee and Jane Wills, 167–76. London: Arnold.

–. 1997b. Neither global nor local: "Glocalization" and the politics of scale. In *Spaces of globalization: Reasserting the power of the local*, ed. Kevin Cox, 137–66. New York: Guilford.

–. 1997c. Power, nature, and the city: The conquest of water and the political ecology of urbanization in Guayaquil, Ecuador, 1880-1980. *Environment and Planning A* 29, 2: 311–32.

–. 2000. Authoritarian governance, power, and the politics of rescaling. *Environment and Planning D: Society and Space* 18 :63–76.

–. 2004a. Globalisation or "glocalisation"? Networks, territories, and rescaling. *Cambridge Review of International Affairs* 17, 1: 25–48.

–. 2004b. Scaled geographies: Nature, place, and the politics of scale. In *Scale and geographic inquiry: Nature, society, and method*, ed. Eric Sheppard and Robert McMaster, 129–53. Oxford: Blackwell.

–. 2004c. *Social power and the urbanisation of water: Flows of power*. Oxford: Oxford University Press.

—. 2006. Circulations and metabolisms: (Hybrid) natures AND (cyborg) cities. *Science as Culture* 15, 2: 105-22.

Swyngedouw, Erik, and Guy Baeten. 2001. Scaling the city: The political economy of "glocal" development – Brussels' "conundrum." *European Planning Studies* 9, 7: 827-49.

Swyngedouw, Erik, and Nik Heynen. 2003. Urban political ecology, justice, and the politics of scale. *Antipode* 35, 5: 898-918.

Swyngedouw, Erik, and Maria Kaika. 2003. The making of "glocal" urban modernities. *City* 7, 1: 5-21.

Swyngedouw, Erik, Frank Moulaert, and Arantxa Rodriguez. 2002. Neoliberal urbanization in Europe: Large-scale urban development projects and the new urban policy. In *Spaces of neoliberalism: Urban restructuring in North America and Western Europe*, ed. Neil Brenner and Nik Theodore, 195-229. Oxford: Blackwell.

Sziarto, Kristin. 2003. Faith vs. neoliberalism? Religion-labor networks, neoliberalized spaces, and workers' practices. Paper presented at the Conference on Contested Urban Futures, University of Minnesota, November.

Sziarto, Kristin, and Helga Leitner. 2006. Migrant labor and spaces of social justice activism. Paper presented at the annual meeting of the Association of American Geographers, Chicago, March.

Tarrow, Sidney. 2001. Silence and voice in the study of contentious politics: Introduction. In *Silence and voice in contentious politics*, ed. Ronald R. Aminzade, Jack A. Goldstone, Doug McAdam, Elizabeth J. Perry, Sidney Tarrow, and Charles Tilly, 1-13. Cambridge, UK: Cambridge University Press.

Taylor, Bron. 2000. Bioregionalism: An ethics of loyalty to place. *Landscape Journal* 19, 1-2: 50-72.

Taylor, Peter J. 1993. *Political geography: World-economy, nation-state, and locality.* 3rd ed. New York: Longman.

—. 1994. The state as container: Territoriality in the modern world-system. *Progress in Human Geography* 18, 2: 151-62.

—. 2000. World cities and territorial states under conditions of contemporary globalization. *Political Geography* 19: 5-32.

—. 2004. Is there a Europe of cities? World cities and the limitations of geographical scale analyses. In *Scale and geographic inquiry*, ed. Eric Sheppard and Robert B. McMaster, 213-35. Oxford: Blackwell.

Telò, Mario. 2002. Governance and government in the European Union: The open method of coordination. In *The new knowledge economy in Europe*, ed. Maria João Rodrigues, 242-72. Cheltenham: Edward Elgar.

Termis-Soto, Fernando. 2005. *Renunciando a todo: El régimen franquista y los Estados Unidos desde 1945 hasta 1963.* Madrid: Biblioteca Nueva.

Thayer, Robert. 2004. *LifePlace: Bioregional thoughts and practice.* Berkeley: University of California Press.

Thrift, Nigel. 1995. A hyperactive world. In *Geographies of global change*, ed. Ronald Johnston, Peter Taylor, and Michael Watts, 18–35. Malden, MA: Blackwell.

Torán, José. 1971. Visita al Jefe del Estado del Comite Español de Grandes Presas. *Revista de obras públicas*, April, 314–15.

Torán, José, and J. Alberto Herreras. 1977. Las grandes presas en el desarollo de los recursos hidráulicos: La experiencia española. *Revista de obras públicas*, April, 259–66.

Tranche, Rafael, and Vicente Sánchez-Biosca. 2002. *NO-DO: El tiempo y la memoria*. Madrid: Cátedra/Filmoteca Española.

Tyner, James. 2006. Defend the ghetto: Space and the urban politics of the Black Panther Party. *Annals of the Association of American Geographers* 96: 105–18.

Urry, John. 2004. Connections. *Environment and Planning D: Society and Space* 22: 22–37.

Valcourt, Josee, and Louis Aguilar. 2006. A third of plant jobs evaporate in Michigan. *Detroit News*, 20 April, 1A.

Valentine, Gill. 2002. People like us: Negotiating sameness and difference in the research process. In *Feminist geography in practice*, ed. Pamela Moss, 116–26. Oxford: Blackwell.

Vallarino, Eugenio. 1992. Política hidráulica. *Revista de obras públicas*, March-April, 67–72.

Van Houtum, Henk, Oliver Kramsch, and Wolfgang Zierhofer, eds. 2005. *B/ordering Space*. Hants, UK: Ashgate.

Van Rijn, Nicolaas. 2003. Tourist business in meltdown. *Toronto Star*, 26 April, B1.

Veltz, Pierre. 1996. *Mondialisation, villes, et territoires: L'économie archipel*. Paris: Presses Universitaires de France.

Vera-Rebollo, J. Fernando 1995. Competencia de usos y planificación fluvial. In *Planificación hidráulica en España*, ed. A. Gil-Olcina and A. Morales-Gil, 307–78. Murcia: Fundación Caja del Mediterráneo.

Verstraete, Ginette, and Tim Cresswell, eds. 2002. *Theorizing place, placing mobility: The politics of representation in a globalized world*. Amsterdam: Rodopi.

Vicens Gómez-Tortosa, José A. 1961. Resultados obtenidos hasta la fecha con la regulación hidráulica en España. *Revista de obras publicas*, June, 436–41.

Vicens Vives, Jaime. 1940. *España: Geopolítica del estado y del imperio*. Barcelona: Editorial Yunque.

—. 1941a. Algunos caracteres geopolíticos de la expansión mediterránea de España. *Geopolítica* 19, 1: 5–11.

—. 1941b. Spanien und die Geopolitische Neuordnung der Welt. *Zeitschrift für Geopolitik* 18, 5: 256–63.

Viñas, Angel. 1981. *Los pactos secretos de Franco con Estados Unidos: Bases, ayuda económica, recortes de soberanía*. Barcelona: Ediciones Grijalbo.

Vincent, Andrew. 1987. *Theories of the state*. 1987. Oxford: Blackwell.

Wainwright, Joel. 2007. Spaces of resistance in Seattle and Cancun. In *Contesting neoliberalism: Urban frontiers*, ed. Helga Leitner, Jamie Peck, and Eric Sheppard, 179–203. New York: Guilford.

Wainwright, Joel, Scott Prudham, and Jim Glassman. 2000. The battles in Seattle: Microgeographies of resistance and the challenge of building alternative futures. *Environment and Planning D: Society and Space* 18: 5–13.

Walker, Neil. 2000. Flexibility within a metaconstitutional frame: Reflections on the future of legal authority. In *Constitutional change in the EU: From uniformity to flexibility?* ed. Gráinne de Búrca and Joanne Scott, 9–30. Oxford: Hart Publishing.

Walker, Peter. 2003. Reconsidering "regional" political ecologies: Toward a political ecology of the rural American west. *Progress in Human Geography* 27: 7–24.

Walker, Richard. 1986. A theory of suburbanization: Capitalism and the construction of urban space in the United States. In *Production, work, and territory*, ed. Allen Scott and Michael Storper, 384–429. New York: Methuen.

Walker, Rob. 1993. *Inside/outside: International relations as political theory*. New York: Cambridge University Press.

Walters, Vernon. 1993. El acuerdo sobre los bases entre España y Estado Unidos cuarenta años déspues. *Política exterior* 36, 7: 160–75.

Wallace, Carey. 2004. Does civic creativity pay? *Metro Times*, 25 February. http://www.metrotimes.com/editorial/story.asp?id=5959.

Wallerstein, Immanuel. 1974. *The modern world-system I*. New York: Academic Publishers.

Walling, Dayne. 2004. Contesting neoliberalism at the metropolitan scale: A case study of the alliance for metropolitan stability in Minneapolis/St. Paul. Seminar paper, Department of Geography, University of Minnesota, Minneapolis.

War. 1972. The world is a ghetto. Los Angeles, CA: Avenue Records.

Waters, William F. 2001. Globalization, socioeconomic restructuring, and community health. *Journal of Community Health* 26, 2: 79–92.

Weber, Max. 2002. *The Protestant ethic and the spirit of capitalism*. Oxford: Blackwell.

Wekerle, Gerda R. 2000. Civil society: A challenge to planners. *Planners Network* 142, 3: 16–17.

–. 2001. Resisting sprawl: Environmental challenges and sustainable regional planning. In *Proceedings of Leading Edge Conference*, Niagara Escarpment Commission. http://www.escarpment.org/leading-edge/LE01/papers/Wekerle.pdf.

–. 2008. The chill factor: Land use conflicts and resistance to growth in the Toronto region. *Plan Canada* 48, 3: 14–17.

Wekerle, Gerda R., and Teresa V. Abbruzzese. 2009. Producing regionalism: Regional movements, ecosystems and equity in a fast and slow growth region. *Geojournal*.

Wekerle, Gerda R., L. Anders Sandberg, and Liette Gilbert. 2009. Taking a stand in exurbia: Environmental movements to preserve nature and resist sprawl. In *Environmental conflicts and democracy in Canada*, ed. Laurie Adkin, 279–97. Vancouver: UBC Press.

–. Forthcoming. *Resisting sprawl: The politics of a bioregion*. Toronto: University of Toronto Press.

Wekerle, Gerda R., L. Anders Sandberg, Liette Gilbert, and Matthew Binstock. 2007. Nature as a cornerstone of growth: Regional and ecosystems planning in the Greater Golden Horseshoe. *Canadian Journal of Urban Research* 16, 1: 20–38.

Whatmore, Sarah, and Lorraine Thorne. 1997. Nourishing networks: Alternative geographies of good. In *Globalising food: Agrarian questions and global restructuring*, ed. David Goodman and Michael Watts, 287–304. London: Routledge.

Wilgoren, Jodi. 2005. Shrinking, Detroit faces fiscal nightmare. *New York Times*, 2 February, A12.

Williams, Fiona. 1995. Race/ethnicity, gender, and class in welfare states: A framework for comparative analysis. *Social Politics* 2, 2: 127–59.

Williams, Landon. 1969. Black capitalism and what it means. *The Black Panther*, 23 March, 2–3.

Williams, Nancy M. 1983. Yolngu concepts of land ownership. In *Aborigines, land, and land rights*, ed. N. Peterson and M. Langton, 94–109. Canberra: Australian Institute of Aboriginal Studies.

–. 1986. *The Yolngu and their land: A system of land tenure and the fight for its recognition*. Canberra: Australian Institute of Aboriginal Studies.

Williams, Raymond. 1973. *The country and the city*. New York: Oxford University Press.

Wolf, Eric. 1982. *Europe and the people without history*. Berkeley: University of California Press.

Wood, Andrew M. 2005. Comparative urban politics and the question of scale. *Space and Polity* 9, 3: 201–15.

World Health Organization (WHO). 2004. Update 95: SARS – Chronology of a serial killer. http://www.who.int/csr.

–. 2003. Severe acute respiratory syndrome: Singapore. *Weekly Epidemiological Record* 78: 161.

Wright, Melissa. 2006. Differences that matter. In *David Harvey: A critical reader*, ed. Noel Castree and Derek Gregory, 80–101. Oxford: Blackwell.

Wu, Jianguo. 1999. Hierarchy and scaling: Extrapolating information along a scaling ladder. *Canadian Journal of Remote Sensing* 25: 367–80.

York, Geoffrey. 2005. Virus hunter. *Globe and Mail*, 10 December, F3.

Yulong, Shi, and Chris Hamnett. 2001. The potential and prospect for global cities in China: In the context of the world system. *Geoforum* 33: 121–35.

Zimmerer, Karl. 2000. Re-scaling irrigation in Latin America: The cultural images and political ecology of water resources. *Ecumene* 7, 1: 1–35.

Contributors

S. HARRIS ALI is an Associate Professor at the Faculty of Environmental Studies at York University, Toronto. His research interests involve the study of environmental health issues and the sociology of disasters and risk from an interdisciplinary perspective. He has published on toxic contamination events and disease outbreaks in such journals as: *Social Problems, Social Science and Medicine,* and *Antipode.* He has recently co-edited a volume (with Roger Keil) on SARS and other infectious diseases, entitled *Networked Disease: Emerging Infections in the Global City* (2008).

NEIL BRENNER is Professor of Sociology and Metropolitan Studies at New York University and the author of *New State Spaces: Urban Governance and the Rescaling of Statehood* (2004). He has also co-edited several volumes, including *Henri Lefebvre, State, Space, World: Selected Essays* (with Stuart Elden, 2009); *The Global Cities Reader* (with Roger Keil, 2006); *Spaces of Neoliberalism* (with Nik Theodore, 2002); and *State/Space: A Reader* (with Bob Jessop, Martin Jones, and Gordon MacLeod, 2003). His research focuses on various issues in critical urban and regional studies, urban theory, state theory, and comparative geopolitical economy.

JANET CONWAY is Canada Research Chair in Social Justice and Associate Professor in the Department of Sociology at Brock University. She writes on contemporary social movements and is presently working on a book on the World Social Forum. She is author of two books: *Identity, Place, Knowledge: Social Movements Contesting Globalization* (2004) and *Praxis and Politics: Knowledge Production in Social Movements* (2006). Her work has been published in journals of politics, law, geography, women's studies, and sociology.

LIETTE GILBERT is an Associate Professor and Associate Dean in the Faculty of Environmental Studies at York University in Toronto. Her research focuses on the politics of immigration, multiculturalism, and citizenship, as well as on urban and environmental politics. She is currently co-authoring a book on the politics of environmental conservation of the Oak Ridges Moraine with Gerda Wekerle and Anders Sandberg. Recent articles have been published in *International Journal of Urban and Regional Research, Space and Polity, City, Citizenship Studies, Local Environments,* and *Cahier de Géographie du Québec.*

NIK HEYNEN is an Associate Professor of Geography at the University of Georgia in Athens. His research focuses on the intersection of urban political economy, urban political ecology, and radical social theory. He is working on a book about the Black Panther Party's radical anti-hunger programs and co-edited *In the Nature of Cities: Urban Political Ecology and the Politics of Urban Metabolism* (with Maria Kaika and Erik Swyngedouw, 2006) and *Neoliberal Environments: False Promises and Unnatural Consequences* (with James McCarthy, Scott Prudham, and Paul Robbins, 2007).

RICHARD HOWITT is Head of Department, Environment and Geography, and Director of Environmental Management at Macquarie University, Sydney, Australia. His research has considered the practical and theoretical implications of a relational conception of geographical scale in a series of papers from the early 1990s when he first considered the idea of scale as comprising three interrelated elements – size, level, and relation. His theorizations of geographical scale draw on applied research in the fields of indigenous rights, regional development, self-determination, and the strategies of transnational resource corporations.

BOB JESSOP is Distinguished Professor of Sociology, Founding Director of the Institute for Advanced Studies, and Co-Director of the Cultural Political Economy Research Centre at Lancaster University, England. He is best known for his contributions to state theory, the regulation approach, postwar political economy, strategic-relational theory, and the nature of governance and governance failure. Recently, he has been working on the knowledge-based economy, issues of scale, and the implications of the concept of compossibility for social theory. His most recent publications include: *The Future of the Capitalist State* (2002), *Beyond the Regulation Approach* (with Ngai-Ling Sum, 2006), and *State Power: A Strategic-Relational Approach* (2007).

ROGER KEIL is the Director of the City Institute at York University and Professor in the Faculty of Environmental Studies at York University, Toronto. Among his publications are: *The Global Cities Reader* (co-edited with Neil Brenner, 2006), *Networked Disease: Emerging Infections and the Global City* (co-edited with S. Harris Ali, 2008), and *Changing Toronto: Governing the Neoliberal City* (co-edited with J.A. Boudreau and D. Young, 2009). Keil's current research is on suburban infrastructure, cities and infectious disease, and regional governance. Keil is the co-editor of the

International Journal of Urban and Regional Research and a co-founder of the International Network for Urban Research and Action.

STEFAN KIPFER teaches urban environments, urban politics, and urban-regional planning at the Faculty of Environmental Studies at York University, Toronto. He has published numerous contributions to urban theory and urban politics and is co-editor (with Kanishka Goonewardena, Richard Milgrom, and Christian Schmid) of *Space, Difference, Everyday Life: Reading Henri Lefebvre* (2008). His current work centres on transnational comparisons of urban-regional politics and the intellectual meeting points of metropolitan marxism and anti-colonial traditions.

WENDY LARNER is Professor of Human Geography and Sociology at the University of Bristol. Her research interests include globalization, governance, and gender, and her publications span the fields of political economy, governmentality, economic geography, and social policy.

RICHARD LE HERON is Professor of Geography, School of Geography, Geology and Environmental Science, University of Auckland, New Zealand. His research interests include agri-food developments in the globalizing economy, nature-society relations, geographies of accumulation, new economic spaces under neoliberalism, trans-disciplinarity, and knowledge production and conditions for co-learning. He has recently co-edited *Agri-food Commodity Chains and Globalising Networks* (2008).

HELGA LEITNER is Professor of Geography and a faculty member in the Institute for Global Studies and the Interdisciplinary Center for the Study of Global Change at the University of Minnesota, Minneapolis. She has published three books and has written numerous articles and book chapters on the political economy of urban development, urban neoliberalism, the politics of citizenship and immigrant incorporation, the politics of scale, and the spatialities of contentious politics. Her current research interests include geographies of governance and citizenship, and the remaking of global urbanism.

NICK LEWIS is a political and economic geographer at the University of Auckland, New Zealand. His research interests are diverse, stretching from the spatial imaginaries embedded in Brand New Zealand, through the value chains of Auckland firms, biological economies, the wine industry, international education, and the politics of representation in community development. His doctoral research was on the audit culture and technologies of the Education Review Office in New Zealand. Nick sits on the Management Group of the Building Research Capability in the Social Sciences Network and is a member of He Waka Tangata.

WARREN MAGNUSSON is Professor of Political Science at the University of Victoria. His books include *A Political Space: Reading the Global through Clayoquot Sound* (co-edited with Karena Shaw, 2003) and *The Search for Political Space: Globalization, Social Movements, and the Urban Political Experience* (1996).

RIANNE MAHON is Director of the Institute of Political Economy at Carleton University. While her earlier work focused on unions and labour market restructuring in Canada and Sweden, over the past decade, she has produced numerous articles and book chapters on the politics of childcare. Recent publications include "Varieties of Liberalism: Canadian Social Policy from the 'Golden Age' to the Present," *Social Policy and Administration* (2008), and *The OECD and Transnational Governance*, co-edited with Stephen McBride (2008). Her current research project looks at the OECD and "policy learning" in Canada, Sweden, and Korea as this pertains to reconciliation of work and life policies. She is a co-editor of the journal *Social Politics*.

BYRON MILLER is Associate Professor of Geography and Director of the Urban Studies Program at the University of Calgary. His recent work has focused on the geographic structuring of social movements, technologies of governance, contestation of multi-level governance, and the politics of urban sustainability. The author of *Geography and Social Movements: Comparing Antinuclear: Spatialities and Social Movements* (with Walter Nicholls and Justin Beaumont) *Activism in the Boston Area* (2000), he is currently co-editing *Spaces of Contention: Spatialities and Social Movements* (with Walter Nicholls and Justin Beaumont) and *Alberta Plundered: a First World Political Ecology* (with Laurie Adkin, Randolph Haluza-DeLay, and Naomi Krogman).

JAMIE PECK is Canada Research Chair in Urban and Regional Political Economy and Professor of Geography at the University of British Columbia. His recent publications include *Contesting Neoliberalism: Urban Frontiers* (co-edited with Helga Leitner and Eric Sheppard, 2007) and *Politics and Practice in Economic Geography* (co-edited with Adam Tickell, Eric Sheppard, and Trevor Barnes, 2007).

ANDERS SANDBERG is a Professor and Associate Dean in the Faculty of Environmental Studies at York University, Toronto. He is co-author (with Peter Clancy) of *Against the Grain: Foresters and Politics in Nova Scotia* (2000), and he is currently co-authoring a book on the Oak Ridges Moraine with Gerda Wekerle and Liette Gilbert. Recent articles have appeared in *Environmental Politics, Regional Studies, Journal of Historical Geography, The Canadian Geographer,* and *Society and Natural Resources.*

Contributors

Eric Sheppard is Regents Professor of Geography, and Associate Director of the Interdisciplinary Center for Global Change at the University of Minnesota. He has co-authored and co-edited numerous books, most recently, *Politics and Practice in Economic Geography* (co-edited with Adam Tickell, Jamie Peck, and Trevor Barnes, 2007), and *Contesting Neoliberalism: Urban Frontiers* (co-edited with Helga Leitner and Jamie Peck, 2007). He has published over one hundred refereed articles and book chapters. Current research interests include the spatiality of capitalism and globalization, contestations of neoliberalism, urban politics, environmental justice, the free trade doctrine, and critical GIS.

Erik Swyngedouw is Professor of Geography at Manchester University, in the School of Environment and Development. He has a background in engineering, planning, and geography. Over the past twenty years, he has worked on a range of related issues: geographical political economy, with special attention to transformations in the capitalist space economy; urban and regional development and governance; and political-ecology, with particular emphasis on the governance, politics, and economics of water resources. Recent books include *In the Nature of Cities: Urban Political Ecology and the Politics of Urban Metabolism* (co-edited with Nik Heynen and Maria Kaika, 2006) and *Social Power and the Urbanization of Water: Flows of Power* (2004).

Gerda R. Wekerle is a Professor in the Faculty of Environmental Studies, York University, and Coordinator of the Graduate Program in Planning. She is co-authoring a book on the politics of environmental conservation, environmental politics, and planning on the Oak Ridges Moraine with L. Anders Sandberg and Liette Gilbert. She has published four books and numerous articles and book chapters on housing, urban and regional development, urban security, urban movements, urban politics, planning and growth, urban agriculture, gender and cities, environmental politics, and environmental governance. Current research interests include the policy stories of state actors involved in developing urban growth management policies, gender and the neoliberal city, and the politics of urban gardens.

Index

Note: "(f)" after a page number indicates a figure. "(m)" after a page number indicates a map. "(t)" after a page number indicates a table.

Aberley, Doug, 250–51, 263
Aboriginal absence/presence, 143, 144, 146
Aboriginal Legal Rights Movement (ALRM), 154n10
Aboriginal rights. *See* rights, indigenous
Aboriginal and Torres Strait Islander Commission (ATSIC), 143
activists/activism: civil rights, 239, 241; environmental, 257, 260–61; GLBT, 237–38; immigrant rights, 239, 240–42; religion/labour, 237; urban, 237–39; women's liberation, 223
actor-network theory (ANT), 15, 51
African Americans, 266, 269, 271–75. *See also* Black Panther Party (BPP)
"after neoliberalism": community-based development, 179–82, 186–88, 189; defined, 179–80; economic/social configurations, 191–92; national strategies, 184–86, 192; and the state, 178. *See also* roll-out neoliberalism
Agamben, Giorgio, 266
agency, 15–16, 63–64, 283
Agnew, John, 8
Alfred, Gerald, 154n6

American Center for Law and Justice, 238
Americas Social Forum (ASF), 294
Amin, Ash, 14, 16–17, 48
anti-globalization movement, 64, 286–87. *See also* World Social Forum (WSF)
Aristotle, 105, 106, 109
Artajo, Alberto Martín, 136–37, 139n2
Asia Social Forum, 297n2
Atlantic Fordist economies, 99–100
attribution of similarity, 277–78
Auckland, 187, 189–90
Auckland University of Technology (AUT), 190
Austinization, 161–62
auto-gestion, 290, 291
Aznar, José María, 121

Baeten, Guy, 69
Baker, Gilbert, 238
Bamako, 288
Bashevkin, Sylvia, 212
Beatley, Timothy, 258
Bienvenido Mr. Marshall!, 134, 135(f)
biopolitics from below, 266, 267–71, 271–75

biopower, 267
bioregionalism, 250–51, 263–64
Black Panther Party (BPP), 271, 275–78; and black community, 266, 271, 273–75; black nationalism, 273–75; and Chicago police, 274–75; community control, 274–75; emancipatory politics, 265–67, 267–71, 271–75, 275–77; FBI and, 272, 274; global social movement, 271–72, 274, 275; membership, 271–72, 280n2; politics of survival, 266, 267–68, 277; revolutionary intercommunalism, 271, 275–78; revolutionary praxis, 275–77, 279; revolutionary work, 272–73; scale shifting, 276–78; survival programs, 265–66, 271–72, 274, 275; Ten Point Political Platform, 271. *See also* African Americans
Blaut, James, 273
Boudreau, Julie-Anne, 215, 222
boundaries: characteristics, 58; construction, 56–57; elimination, 276; functions, 94; greenbelt, 261–62; infectious diseases, 206; and political action, 117, 118; porousness, 62, 207–8; regional, 61–62; scale as, 53–54; vs sovereignty, 207–8
Brand New Zealand, 183, 190, 192
Brazil, 293
Brenner, Neil, 8, 13, 17–19, 67–69, 75–76, 82n1, 195, 212, 231, 278
Bridges, Styles, 133
British Columbia Action Coalition, 217
Brodie, Janine, 6, 7
Burleigh Evatt Report, 185
Buse, Kent, 207
Bush administration, 285, 286
Butler, Judith, 243

Calgary Children's Initiative, 225
Calgary Local Council of Women, 223
Canada Assistance Plan (CAP), 211–12
Canada Health and Social Transfer Fund, 212
Canterbury Development Corporation (CDC), 188
capital, 166; accumulation, 46, 278; circulation, 38–41, 39–41; flight, 160, 163, 176, 184 (*See also* creative flight); flows, 13, 100, 161, 166, 261; human, 160; industrialization of, 35–36, 43–44; state, 128–29; talent as, 163–64
capitalism: deep structures, 42–43; geographies of, 34–36, 34(f); globalizing, 44–45; imperialistic, 5–6; neocapitalism, 71; phases, 27, 35–36, 37–38, 43, 76; scalar dynamics, 57–59; and social reproduction, 267
capitalists, 39, 40–41; fairness, 270
Caracas, 288, 291
Carr, Raymond, 134
Castells, Manuel, 48, 67, 69, 75, 250
Castree, Noel, 19, 284
Centres locales des services communautaire (CLSCs), 220–21, 222
Centres de la petite enfance (CEPs), 221–22
centrism: capital-, 284; globo-, 296; national, 10; network-, 48, 92; place-, 31, 92; scale-, 31–32, 89, 232, 234–36
chaotic concept, 52, 63, 65n2
Cheney, Dick, 285
Chicago, 274–75
Chicago School, 73
Chicoine, Nathalie, 221
child care: centralization, 212, 213; as citizen right, 214; federal level,

209–10, 211–13; and interscalar rule regimes, 18, 211–12, 213–16, 217, 219, 223, 225–26; neoliberal government and, 213, 214, 215; political opportunity structure, 214, 216–18, 219, 224; provincial control, 213; regulation, 210, 212, 223; rescaling, 210–11; social democratic model, 210–11, 214, 215–16; uneven access, 210–11, 216, 219, 221; as welfare service, 212; welfare state redesign and, 210–11
child care provision (Calgary): commercial sector, 223–24, 225, 228n9; daycare counsellor, 223; feminists and, 223; neoliberal government and, 224–25; non-profit spaces, 228n10; provincial role, 222–23, 224
child care provision (Montreal): federal funding, 220; municipal role, 221–22; neighbourhood scale, 220–21; non-profit spaces, 220, 221; provincial control, 219–21; Quebec model, 220; spaces, 210–11, 221
child care provision (Toronto): non-profit spaces, 215–16; provincial policy, 214–15; spaces, 211; system, 214, 215–16
child care provision (Vancouver): advocates network, 216–17, 219; child care coordinator, 218; children's advocate, 218; funding, 216, 218–19; non-profit spaces, 219; political opportunity structure, 217, 226, 227n6; provincial policy, 217; social democratic government, 217; spaces, 211
Child and Family Services Authority (CFSA), 224–25
Christaller, Walter, 5

Christchurch, 187, 188
citizen police boards, 274–75
citizenship rights, 145, 148, 154, 239, 241, 299n13
city, 70, 71–72. *See also* creative cities; *specific cities*
civil disobedience, 241, 245n5
Clark, Mark, 274
Cleaver, Eldridge, 265
Closson, Tom, 197
Coalition for Improved Day Care Services, 217
co-implication of spatialities, 232, 239–40, 240–42, 245
Cold War, 3–4, 6
collaborative partnering governmentality, 189
Collinge, Chris, 19, 65n3, 97, 235
colonization, 5, 80, 141, 273
community capacity, 189–90, 191
Community Employment Group, 189
competitiveness: importance, 100; interurban, 159–61, 163–64, 166; social investment and, 215
Confederation of Progressive Electors (COPE), 217, 227n6
Conseil régional de développement (CRD), 221, 222
contentious politics: and politics of place, 22–23, 237; and politics of scale, 232–34; and scale shifting, 54, 277; and sociospatial positionality, 243–45; spatiality of, 231–32, 236–39; and the state, 245n2; states and, 244n2
convergence spaces, 288, 295
Conway, Janet, 19
Cool Cities program, 169–71, 174–75
Corps of Engineers, 129–30
Coté, Sylvana, 221
Cox, Kevin, 40

Craig-Kennedy farmworkers' bill, 242
CreateDetroit, 171–73, 174
creative cities: advocates, 169–70, 173; concept, 160; and international talent market, 161; and neoliberal urbanism, 159–61, 166, 167(t), 169, 175–76; policies, 169, 174–75; strategies, 169–71, 175–76, 187–89, 190; thesis, 167(t), 168–69; urban cargo cult, 166; urban governance and, 186–89. *See also* Cool Cities program; CreateDetroit; designer fashion industry (NZ); *specific creative cities*
creative class, 160–61, 165–66, 170–71; class consciousness, 163; thesis, 159, 161–68; and urban economic development, 161–68
Creative Communities Scheme, 190, 192
creative economy, 159–61, 163, 166–68, 175–76; logic of, 163–64; strategies, 169–73, 173–75
creative flight, 163–64, 170–71, 176
creative incubators, 165–66, 168, 187–88, 189–90
creative industries, 185–86, 188
Creative New Zealand, 190–91, 192
creativity credo, 160, 166, 167(t), 168
crisis: of capitalism, 44; of cities, 7, 74; economic, 171, 173, 293; of Fordism, 6, 11, 59, 100–1; Keynesian welfare state, 12, 100, 101; nation-state, 88, 100
critical geography, 282–85, 296
critical political economy, 3, 6, 106, 119
Cross, Sherrie, 154n9
cultural economy, 182, 184
culture of forgetting, 147
customary law, 144, 148–49, 150, 151, 155n15

Day Nursery Act (DNA), 214
Debanné, Anne-Marie, 20
decentralization, 171, 197, 198–99, 224–25
Delaney, David, 283
Deleuze, Gilles, 14–15
Delgamuukw v. British Columbia, 119n1
Demirovic, Alex, 83n6
designer fashion industry (NZ): Blomfield scoping report, 181, 185; and clothing industry, 182, 185, 186; creative incubators, 187–88, 189–90; fashion cluster initiative, 188; global focus, 182–84, 190, 191; government engagement, 182; and inclusion / diversity, 191; institutionalized, 185; and knowledge economy, 178, 181, 184–86, 188; local focus, 186–89, 189–91; and Maori community, 189–90, 191; and national economy, 182, 183, 185–86; national focus, 184–86; profile, 180–81; roles, 182–84, 185–86, 189–91; social development project, 178, 181, 189–91, 194n1; sponsorship, 182, 183; and urban regeneration, 178, 181, 186–89. *See also* "after neoliberalism"; New Zealand; *specific participating cities*
Desjardins, Ghislaine, 220–21
Detroit: creative cities strategies, 161, 171–73, 173–74; economic decline, 173–75. *See also* Michigan
Detroit Renaissance, 174
devolution of responsibilities, 232, 269
diffusion: global, 289, 290, 291, 292, 295; rapid, 22, 168; spatial, 201–2
diffusion/brokerage, 277–78
discourse: bioregionalism, 256–58; bioregionalism/ecosystems, 249,

259; conservation, 256–57; ecosystem management, 256–57; hegemonic scalar, 284
divisions of labour: capitalist, 7, 29, 41; creative, 162–63, 165, 166; scalar, 45, 88, 96–98, 97, 98, 99–100; spatial, 34(f), 35–36, 39, 41, 43, 47, 58, 166
dominant scales, 97–98, 98–99; international, 136–37
Dunedin, 187
Dunedin Incubator, 188
Durazo, Maria Elena, 240

economic geography, 15, 58–59
ecosystem management, 256–58, 260; multiple scales, 252–53
emancipatory politics, 265–67, 275–77, 287–89
emerging infectious disease (EID), 196, 200–1, 204
empire, 266, 267, 275–77; new form, 281
Engels, Friedrich, 19, 270, 272
ENGOs: national, 253, 254(t), 255, 257; provincial, 253; regional, 253, 254, 254(t), 257; transnational, 253, 254(t), 256. *See also specific ENGOs*
environmental conflict. *See* greenbelt conflict (ON); Oak Ridges Moraine conflict
Environmental Defence Canada, 255, 257
environmental movements, 254–56, 259, 260–61. *See also* ENGOs; *specific environmental conflicts*
erasure: consequences, 151; customary law, 148; indigenous governance, 145–48, 154n9; indigenous rights, 142, 145; practices of resistance, 295
Escobar, Arturo, 233, 256, 281, 295, 296

Esping-Andersen, Gøsta, 227n1
European Spatial Development Planning Process, 98
European Union, 13, 61–62, 100–2, 138, 233

Family and Community Support Services (FCSS), 223, 228n10
Fashion Incubator of New Zealand (FASHINZ), 189–90
Federation of Ontario Naturalists, 253, 257
feminists, 9, 80, 283
Fidler, David P., 199
Finland, 61–62
First Nations: everyday life, 72, 75, 83n6, 111; judged, 109–10, 112, 113; land claim decisions, 119n1; political organization, 108–9; political possibilities, 115–18, 118–19; as role model, 118–19; self-government, 106–7, 109, 117; treaty negotiations, 108; way of life, 109–10, 112; zones of impermissibility, 111–12, 114, 115–16. *See also* Aboriginal absence/presence; indigenous nations; indigenous rights
Florida, Richard, 159, 161–68, 171, 172–73, 175–76
Fordism, 6–7, 9, 11, 59–60, 99–100, 100–1
Foucault, Michel, 17, 94, 268, 280, 280n5
Franco Behamonde, Francisco, 121–22, 123–27, 132; political economic vision, 123–24, 127–33
Frank, Gunder, 10
Free Breakfast for Children Program, 265–66, 271–72, 274. *See also* Black Panther Party (BPP)
Fustukian, Suzanne, 207

García Berlanga, Luis, 134
Gardam, Michael, 197
Garrett, Laurie, 200
generic scalar continuum, 275–78
geographical differences, 29–30, 34–36, 73–74, 82n2
geographical scale, 28, 141, 151–52, 234
geographies: Aboriginal, 150–52; of economic growth, 159; network, 46–48; of resistance, 238–39; of social processes, 31–32; of USD, 27, 28–29, 34–36, 34(f)
geography/geographers, 4–5, 130–31
ghetto, 266, 269, 273, 278
Glassman, Jim, 239
GLBT community, 165
global capitalism, 30, 259–62
global cities network, 14–15, 202–4, 205–6
global convergence, 287–89, 295
global diffusion, 288–89, 290–92
global governmentality: and nation-state, 117–18
global health governance, 196–97, 198–99, 206–7. See also public health governance
global networks, 183, 277–78
global North, 36
global South, 287
globalization: capital circulation, 42; counterhegemonic, 281; designer fashion industry, 178, 181, 182–84; and geographical differences, 27; governmental rationality, 193; vs internationalization, 75–76; interpretations, 48; neoliberal, 88; politics, 16–17; privileged network, 188; as reterritorialization, 278; technological connectivity, 203; and workers, 19
glocal enclaves, 92, 104n7

glocalization, 92, 104n6; neoliberal, 12
glurbanization, 92, 104n6
Gómez De Pablos Gonzáles, Manuel, 121–22
Goonewardena, Kanishka, 79
Gottdiener, Mark, 301
governance: of child care, 209–10; colonial vs indigenous, 142–43, 144; and creative elite, 176; metropolitan, 205–6; and multiple spatial imaginaries, 177–78; scaled construction of, 145; scales of, 145–48, 195–96; space and, 94
governmentality, 17, 117–18
Graham, Stephen, 104n7
Gramsci, Antonio, 18, 83n6
greenbelt conflict (ON), 251, 254–55, 257, 260
Greenbelt Foundation, 255, 257
Greenbelt Plan, 248(m), 252
Greenbelt Protection Act, 257, 260
Growth and Innovation Framework, 185

Hamel, Pierre, 215, 222
Hamnett, Chris, 203
Hampton, Fred, 274
Harcourt, Wendy, 256
Hardt, Michael, 267, 276, 279
Harvey, David, 8, 10, 18, 67, 69, 70, 71, 75, 82n1, 83n6, 233, 278; critique of, 103n3
Haug, Frigga, 80
health governance. See public health governance
hegemony, 6, 285–86; scalar compression and, 276–77
Herod, Andrew, 19, 58–59, 284
Hertzman, Clyde, 219
Hess, Rémi, 77
hierarchies: and agency, 18; concepts of, 17–18; nested structures, 40–41,

196–99, 200–1, 208; of networks, 47, 96; scalar, 55, 209–10, 225, 226; vertical, 16–17, 41, 235–36
hierarchy theory, 17–18, 235–36
High Court (Australia), 144–45, 152n1
Hilliard, David, 276, 280n2
history, 4–5, 111, 112–13, 114
Hobbes, Thomas, 114
homo creativus, 160, 165–66
Hoover, J. Edgar, 272, 274
Hotel Employees and Restaurant Employees International Union (HERE), 240
hotspots, 252, 253, 254
Howard, Gillian, 197
Howitt, Richard, 19, 51
Hutton, Thomas, 217, 219

identity: bioregional, 263–64; and consciousness, 60–61; national, 233, 250, 275; place and, 7–8, 23, 95, 250, 254(f), 305; politics of, 87, 105–6, 114–15; scale and, 152–53; territorial, 236
ideology, 127, 133–34, 261, 274; revolutionary, 271, 275–78
imaginaries: agricultural, 261; alternative, 293, 296; bioregional, 249, 257–58, 260–61; BPP, 271; democratic, new, 281, 297; developmental, 259–60; economic, 159; futuristic, 111–12, 275; multiple spatial, 178; social movements, 249
imaginaries, spatial, 96–97; global, 182, 184, 190; multiple, 178, 193–94; national, 184; urban, 188
immigrant rights, 233–34, 237–38, 239, 240–42
Immigrant Workers Freedom Ride (IWFR), 239–42
immigration policy, 233, 240–42

imperialism, 5, 266–67, 273–74, 275–77, 281
indigenous nations: coerced reconciliation, 143; customary law, 144, 148–49, 150, 151, 155n15; governance, 148–50, 151, 153n4, 155n14; land claims, 153n5; marginalization, 112, 152n1; new order vs, 146; politics, 149, 150–51; rescaling geographies, 150–52; self-determination, 143; self-government, 146–47. *See also* Aboriginal absence/presence; First Nations; Native title
indigenous rights, 141–43, 144–45, 147, 148–49, 154n6, 154n10
Industry New Zealand, 184–85, 186, 190, 192, 194n2
Information and Communications Technologies (ICTs), 185
inner cities. *See* ghetto
Innis, Harold, 6
institutions: capacity, 66n5; global regulatory, 55–56; state, 40–41; territorial, 38–39, 54–55, 56
International Health Regulations (IHR), 199
international political economy (IPE), 11
internationalism, 284
intersections: political economy/spatial theory, 301; politics of place/scale, 251–52, 259–60; scale/identity/place making, 263–64

Japel, Christa, 221
Jay, Martin, 82n5
Jessop, Bob, 8, 11, 12, 13, 19, 193, 195, 196
Jonas, Andrew, 279
Jones, John Paul, III, 16–18, 23n3, 51, 53, 92, 195

Kaika, Maria, 70
Karachi, 288
Katz, Cindi, 267–69, 279
Keck, Margaret, 238
Keil, Roger, 20, 215, 222
Keynesian welfare state: crisis, 100; national scale, 12; pan-Canadian, 225–26, 227n4; turn to workfare, 9–10, 101, 209, 210–11, 212–13, 226–27, 269; US, 273
King, Nicholas B., 200
Klein government, 224–25
knowledge economy. *See* creative cities; designer fashion industry (NZ)
Kropotkin, Peter, 272
Kurtz, Hilda, 19

Labor in the Pulpits, 237–38
Langford, Thomas, 223
Lassiter, Mark, 175
Latour, Bruno, 15–16, 51, 64
Lee, Kelley, 207
Lefebvre, Henri, 28, 30, 32–33, 82n1, 83n6; levels of analysis, 72, 76, 79; in scale debates, 68–71; theory of space production, 74; urban question, 67, 71–74
Leibovitz, Joseph, 211, 216
Leitner, Helga, 15, 16, 46, 65, 236, 238, 244n4, 283
liberal bias: in federal policy, 210, 211, 213; Ontario, 214; welfare regime, 211, 213
liberal democrats, 106
Liberal government (BC), 228n9
Liberal government (ON), 261
Light, Andrew, 250, 262
Lim, Sue, 197
Local Initiative Projects, 220
local political culture, 214–15, 222
local scale, 175–76, 198, 211

London Fashion Week, 183

Mabo decision, 144, 152n1
Mahon, Rianne, 209–28, 269, 301–7
Malevich, Casimir, 11
Manning, Kristy, 258
Maori community, 189–90, 191
Marston, Sallie, 9, 16–18, 23n3, 51, 53, 67, 82n1, 153n2, 210, 284
Martin, Deborah, 225
Marvin, Simon, 104n7
Marx, Karl, 5, 27–28, 105, 106, 114, 270; conception of the future, 111–12
marxism, 69, 71, 79–80, 81
Massey, Doreen, 7–8
Mayer, Jonathan D., 201
McAdam, Douglas, 277
McCain-Kennedy immigration bill, 242
McDowell, Linda, 9, 92
McMaster, Robert, 8, 17
McQuirk, Pauline, 216
Merrifield, Andy, 81
meshworks, 249, 256
metagovernance, 13, 100–2, 104n10
metaphilosophy, 78
methodological nationalism, 10, 282
methodological territorialism, 31
Metro Task Force on Services to Young Children and Families, 215
Mettler, Suzanne, 269
Michigan, 169–71, 171–73, 173–74, 174–75. *See also* Detroit
microbial traffic, 199–200, 201–2, 202–4
micropublic, 242
mille-feuille metaphor, 32, 33
Miller, Byron, 19, 225
Ministry of Natural Resources (ON), 257
Minneapolis-St. Paul, 234, 237–38
Minnesota, 232
modernity, 108–10, 113
Mohanty, Chandra, 243

moment of 1968, 74, 78
Montreal Citizen's Movement (MCM), 222
moral time frame, 258
Morse, Stephen, 201
Moulaert, Frank, 69
Movimiento Sem Terra (MST), 293
Multilateral Framework Agreement on Early Childhood Learning and Care, 213
Mumbai, 292–93, 297n2, 298n4
municipal level: child care provision, 215; political parties, 217, 227n6; public health system, 197–98
Murphy, Ryan, 237

narratives: conflicting, 262; creative city, 176; of dispossession, 141, 152n1; governance, 143; of scale, 262, 284, 298n3; of scale and place, 249–51
National Child Benefit, 212–13
national scale, 42, 43–44, 44–45, 57; coalition, 242; dominant, 97–98, 98–99, 100, 123–33; governance, 143–44, 145–46; government, 166, 168; integration, 128–29; nodal, 97–98, 133–37
nation-state: absolute power, 125; vs capital, 276; extensiveness, 58; ideal, 106; as imagined universal, 111; mode of production vs, 114; nodal level, 189; question of size, 106–8; role in health governance, 205–6; scalar nature, 87–88; as scale manager, 18; sovereignty, 198, 207–8; territorial structures, 38–41; viability, 106
Native title: extinguishment, 144–45, 148, 153n5; negotiations, 149, 151, 154n10, 154nn12–13; recognition, 142, 152n1

Native Title Act, 152n1
Native Title Management Committees (NTMCs), 149
Native title rulings, 144–45, 152n1
nature: constructions of, 254(t); social production, 122–23, 124–25
Nature Conservancy of Canada, 253
Negri, Antonio, 267, 276, 279
neocolonialism, 40, 273, 294
neoliberalism: global opposition (See World Social Forum (WSF)); and global-urban terrain, 168–69; policies, 168–69, 224–25, 228n9, 251; and urban policy making, 159–61, 166; and welfare state restructuring, 210–11, 213, 214, 215
nested hierarchical structures, 17, 40–41, 56–57, 91, 96, 153, 196–99, 200–1
nested scales, 208, 232, 234, 235, 236, 270
nested territorial structures, 54–55, 56–58, 62–63, 65n3, 104n5, 235
network analysis: vs scalar analysis, 51–52, 64
networking: defined, 95–96; interlocal, 244; politics of, 238–39, 240–41, 242, 252–56, 277–78, 287–89; principle, 32; role, 45–46; Spain, 125, 133, 136, 137; strategies, 47; transnational, 282; vertically/horizontally, 253–25
networks: attributes, 16; capital accumulation, 46; community organizing, 240; cyber-, 235; hierarchical relations, 96; rescaling, 122, 133–34, 136–37; scalar constitution, 64–65; of spatial connectivity, 17; topography, 96, 199, 201–2, 206–7, 208; and USD, 45–48; vs scale, 15–16, 235; of the WSF, 288–89, 289–90

networks of interest (Spain): civil engineers, 129–30; electricity companies, 128–29; film industry, 131–32; geographers, 130–31; landowners *(latifundistas)*, 127–28; the press, 132–33; scalar production of, 127; United States, 136–37; Western Atlantic alliances, 137
New American Opportunity Campaign (NAOC), 242
New York City, 242
New Zealand: creative cities strategies, 185, 187–89, 190–91, 192; government, 179, 184; government agencies, 185–86, 189, 190, 192, 194n2; neoliberalization, 177–78; rebranding, 182, 183, 184. See also designer fashion industry (NZ)
New Zealand Fashion Week, 183
New Zealand Four designers, 182
Newton, Huey P., 265, 273, 275–78, 279–80. See also Black Panther Party (BPP)
Niagara Escarpment-Oak Ridges-Algonquin to Adirondacks Heritage (NOAH) project, 257
nodal scales, 97–98, 133–37
Noss, Reed, 257
Noticiario Español Cinematográfico (NO-DO), 131–32

Oak Ridges Moraine Committee, 255
Oak Ridges Moraine conflict, 247–48, 248(m); actors, 252–56, 254(t); construction of, 259–60; and government, 255–56, 261; government agencies, 253, 255, 257; regional citizens' movement, 250–51; rescaling, 257–58; scales, 252–56, 254(t); suburban development, 251–52, 262

Oak Ridges Moraine Conservation Act, 252, 257
Oak Ridges Moraine Conservation Plan, 252, 260
Oak Ridges Moraine Foundation and Trust, 255, 257
Oakland, 271, 272
Office de services de garde à l'enfance (OSGE), 220–21
Ollman, Bertell, 152
Ontario Greenbelt Alliance, 254
Ontario Municipal Board, 253, 255, 257
ontology of networks, 48
ontology of social sites, 16, 18
Opportunities for Youth, 220
Orfield, Myron, 234
organized labour, 237, 240–42
Oslender, Ulrich, 239

Paasi, Anssi, 60–61, 62, 92
Pacific Island communities, 189–90
Pact of Madrid, 136–37, 139n2
Parti Québécois government, 221
Paul, Darel E., 10–11
Pavlik, Claire, 15, 16, 65
Pax Americana, 286–87
Peck, Jamie, 12, 18, 59, 60, 210, 212, 225, 269
Peiris, Malik, 200
Pembina Institute, 255
phase space, 92–93
place: constructions of, 250, 261; defined, 7–8, 95; and identity, 7–8, 23, 95, 250, 254(f), 305; principle, 31; as process, 283; resignification, 237–38; of social space, 33, 145; and USD, 34–37; and the WSF, 293
plug-and-play communities, 160, 165–66
policy networks, 15

polis, 109–11, 117
political ecology, 10, 270
political economy: of agriculture, 261; and Canadian history, 6; capitalist, 266, 267, 270; critique, 68; geographical, 67; of hunger, 270; limits, 76; Marxian, 105–6; metaphorics, 14; multiscalar approach, 13–14; and nature, 10; and political possibility, 115–18; and politics, 114–15; of scale, 17–18; scaled, 49; science of the state, 119; urban, structure of, 273; US, 266
political economy of scale, 48–49, 79–80, 115, 209–10
political science: Aristotelian, 105; and geography, 4
political space, 106, 289, 295
politics: activist, 282; anti-imperialist, 296; constitutive effects, 178; of difference/recognition, 281, 296; of hunger, 272; of identity, 87, 105–6, 114–15; of inclusion/exclusion, 9; indigenous-scale, 141–42, 152n1; of intercultural relations, 152n1; of mobility, 239, 240–42; and the modern state, 106–12; of multiple scales, 284, 296; multiscalar, 11, 249–50; of networking, 238–39, 240–41, 242, 252–56, 277–78, 287–89; of recognition, 142; of regulation/governance, 16–17; of scale, 19, 295; of security, 114–15; of self-determination, 153n4; socialist, 111; of space, 241–42; uncertainty of, 116–17
politics of place: in contentious politics, 22–23, 236–38, 248–49, 252–53; and global capitalism, 259–62; scaled, 249, 251–52, 262, 291–92; transformed, 252–53

politics of scale, 45; BPP, 266; in contentious politics, 196, 231–32; defined, 298n3; and EIDs, 200–1; and political economy, 105; and power, 283–84, 284–85; and social reproduction, 267–69; spatial framework, 275–78, 276–77; tasks, 249–50; theoretical power of, 267
Porto Alegre, 287, 288, 291, 293, 294
positionality. *See* sociospatial positionality
postnational state, 12, 100–1
postwar order, 74, 77, 98–99, 136–37, 226
post-Westphalian world, 101, 197, 199, 200, 305
power: anti-hegemonic, 296; dimensions, 283–84, 284–85; institutional, 55–57, 65n3; international capital flows, 100; relations, 47, 235–36, 243–44, 270, 272
Preston, Richard, 200
production: of consent, 131–33; of political space, 106; of regional identity, 60–62; of scale, 8–9, 56–58, 63, 68, 70–71, 79, 89, 90–91, 122, 279 (*See also* scale, social construction of); of socionature, 122–23
Project for the New American Century (PNAC), 285–86
prose of counter-insurgency, 295
public health governance: global, 196–97, 198–99, 206–7; hierarchical system, 197–98; metropolitan scale, 200; multiscalar conflict, 205–6; neighbourhood scale, 198; neoliberal, 197–99; nested scales, 196–99, 200–1, 208; networks, 199, 201–2, 206–7, 208; post-SARS, 199–201; post-Westphalian, 197–201; topological networks, 199, 201–2,

206–7, 208; in Westphalian world, 196–97. *See also* Severe Acute Respiratory Syndrome (SARS)
Punter, John, 218, 227n6

Quito, 291

radical anti-hunger politics, 266, 267–68, 277
Raglan, 190
Reference re Secession of Quebec, 119n1
reflexivity, 108–10
reframing: discourse, 242, 244; issues, 63, 199, 249, 254, 287–89; place, 283; scalar, 63, 249, 263, 280
regimes of accumulation: Fordist, 59–60; primitive, 142–45, 143, 144, 146
regional scale, 247, 249, 250–51, 252, 260, 288–89, 298n6
regionalism, 263–64
regulation: of child care, 210, 212, 223; of inclusivity/exclusivity, 64; of migration, 202; modes of, 100; multilevel, 100–1, 114; multiscalar, 196, 198, 199–200, 202, 204–5; politics of, 16–17; of public health, 198, 199–200, 202; self-, 100–1, 114; social reproduction, 83n6, 270, 272; territorialization and, 37, 60, 70; theory, 59–60, 83n6
Reinicke, Wolfgang H., 207
relativization of scale, 98–99, 100
rescaling: Aboriginal geographies, 150–52; Aboriginal governance, 148–50, 151, 155n14; after-Fordist, 59–60; ecosystem management, 256–57; global health governance, 198–99; vs globalization, 11; indigenous rights, 149; local organizations, 232; periodic, 235–36; political struggle, 282; processes, 4, 45; regional politics, 252–53; responsibilities/capacities, 54–55, 56, 60, 62; revolutionary praxis, 278–79; social movements, 63, 281; social services, 227n5; waves, 43, 44–45; welfare, 269. *See also* scalar shifting
resistance. *See specific resistance movements*
restructuring, neoliberal: child care, 224–25; economic/social space, 9–10; formal politics, 16–17; global order, 7; and interplace relations, 36–37; post-1970s, 44–45; social services, 212
reticulation. *See* networking
Revista de obras públicas, 129–30
revolution: of geohistorical relationships, 6; mediation of, 78–79; metaphorics, 4–5; social reproduction and, 268–69; urban, 72, 75
Reynolds, Henry, 154n6
rhetoric: creative city, 169; development, 125, 128, 133–34; environmental, 257–58; national autarchy, 136; universalist, 167(t)
Richmond Hill, 255
rights: citizenship, 145, 148, 154, 239, 241, 299n13; to the city, 73–74; cultural, 138; to difference, 73–74; of ecosystems, 261; GLBT, 237–38, 298n11; immigrant, 233–34, 237–38, 239, 240–42; indigenous, 141–43, 144–45, 147, 148–49, 154n6, 154n10; political, 286; property, 260, 261–62; to subsistence, 292–93; title, 148, 153; women, 223, 298n11; workers, 237, 241–42
Robbins, Paul, 249
Roberts, D., 250, 262
Robertson, Pat, 238
Rodriguez, Arantxa, 69
Rodríguez, Saturnino, 132

Index

Rodríguez Zapatero, José Luis, 121
Rodwin, Victor, 198
roll-out neoliberalism, 189, 210, 226–27. *See also* "after neoliberalism"
Rose, Damaris, 221
Rousseau, Jean, 19
Routledge, Paul, 288
Rowell-Sirois Commission, 212, 227n4
Rowse, Tim, 153n2
Royal Commission on the Future of the Toronto Waterfront, 256
Rumsfeld, Donald, 285

San Francisco, 237–38, 274
Sánchez-Albornoz, Nicolás, 128
Santos, Boaventura de Sousa, 296–97, 297n2
SARS. *See* Severe Acute Respiratory Syndrome (SARS)
Save the Rouge Valley System, 255, 257, 258
Sayer, Andrew, 65n2
Sayre, Nathan F., 236, 251
scalar analysis: alternatives, 63–64, 65n2, 304; critics, 51–52; defined, 96; limits, 87–88, 231–32, 252; polyvalence, 96; process, 90–93, 104n4; value, 148–49. *See also* scalar fallacies
scalar concepts, 51, 96–97, 307
scalar fallacies, 302; conflationism, 89; essentialism, 80, 89–91, 103n3; reductionism, 89; rejectionism, 90, 91
scalar fix, 45; after-Fordist, 59; creativity, 159–60, 168, 174–75; Fordist, 9, 99–100; neoliberal, 11–12, 44, 168–69, 174–75, 225. *See also* spatial fix
scalar framing, 233–34, 243–44, 257, 258–59, 275, 284; reframing, 63, 199, 249, 254, 263, 280

scalar production. *See* production, of scale
scalar remaking, 125, 127, 138, 176
scalar shifting. *See* scale shifting
scalar theory: limits, 70–71, 90
scalar transformation, 122–27, 133–37
scalar traps, 103n1. *See also* scalar fallacies
scalar turns, 8–10, 11–12, 20–21, 87–90, 99, 103, 304; forms, 88
scale: and agency, 15–16; as bordering practice, 53; conceptions, 52; constructions of, 253–54, 263; and contentious politics, 232–34; critical scholarship on, 284; defined, 62, 96, 152; as discursive frame, 250; global, 57, 58; household as, 80, 153n2; and identity, 152–53; as level, 55–56, 65n3; as master concept, 297n1; metaphorics, 17; mobilization of, 123; narratives of, 262, 284, 298n3; of a network, 16–17; vs networks, 235; for political organization, 108–9; as *relatum*, 90–91, 92; as size, 53–54, 56–57; social construction of, 8, 51, 53, 70–71, 103, 153n2, 283–85, 289, 296–97. *See also* geographical scale
scale debate, 8, 51, 67, 68–71, 80, 81
scale dominance. *See* dominant scales
scale jumping: defined, 19, 98; disease diffusion, 195–96; SARS coronavirus, 201, 202–4, 206–7; social movements, 54–55, 233, 275
scale politics: and accountability, 150; of indigenous rights, 147; neoliberal, 160–61, 164, 175–76
scale production processes, 52–57, 62–63
scale question. *See* scale debate
scale shifting, 54–55, 57, 59, 65n3, 277–78, 279. *See also* scale jumping

scale theory, 14, 17, 18–19; antiscalar backlash, 16, 90; vs place theory, 225–27, 236; and the urban, 70; and USD, 267
scaled politics. *See* politics of place, scaled
scales: construction of, 254(t); differentiation of, 45; of everyday life, 283; extrabodily, 270; geographically extensive, 55–56; of indigenous governance, 147, 154n9; interconnected, 297; marginal, 98; multiple, 205–6, 252–53; proliferation, 291; of social/political life, 297; socially produced, 266; urban, 57, 58; urban/regional, 42
scaling: health policies, 198; of levels, 76; multiple processes, 91; the *polis*, 109–11, 117; politics, 106, 111; principle, 31–32; of time, 259; the urban, 71
scaling processes: cultural, 60–62; economic, 57; nation-state, 59–60, 61–62; USD processes and, 45
Schumpeterian workfare state, 12, 101
Seale, Bobby, 272–73, 278, 280n2. *See also* Black Panther Party (BPP)
Second National Hydraulic Plan (Spain), 121
Sen, Jai, 297n2
Severe Acute Respiratory Syndrome (SARS), 195, 199–200, 201–2, 203–4, 205–8
Sheppard, Eric, 8, 15, 16, 17, 65
Sierra Club, 256
Sikkink, Kathryn, 238
Silvern, Steven E., 153n4
Smith, Dorothy, 80
Smith, Jonathan M., 250, 262
Smith, Neil, 8, 9, 18, 19, 28–29, 57–58, 69, 75, 267, 277, 279

Smith, Richard, 14–15
social capital, 189, 190, 191–92
Social Forum of the Americas (SFA), 291
social movements: alliances, 234; Brazil, 293; construction of scale, 252–56; global, 271–72, 274; imaginaries, 249; indigenous, 294; international solidarity, 274; local mobilization, 240–41; and logic of political economy, 117; multiscalar politics, 249–50; networks, 47; non-elite social actors, 295; on Oak Ridges Moraine, 259; place-based differences, 298n11, 299n13; scalar strategies, 233–34; and scale, 19–20; shifts in relations, 296; solidarity, 241; spatial tactics, 236–39; strategies, 250; territorial structure, 40–41; of the WSF, 287, 289–90
social order, 72, 73, 75, 76, 78, 80–81, 96–97
social relations: place and, 8, 31, 41, 72, 75, 235, 283; scale and, 10, 31–32, 89, 122–23, 209; space and, 92–96, 98, 152, 282
social reproduction, 9–10; and capitalism, 266–67; multi-scaled, 267; neoliberal vs social democratic, 226–27; and politics of hunger, 106, 266, 272; and revolution, 268–69; scalar politics of, 267–69, 271–73
social space: boundaries, 53, 71–72, 178, 238; metaphorics, 32, 33; and nature, 10; polymorphic, 31–32; and social life, 72, 74; structure, 32–34; territorialization, 37
Social Union Framework Agreement (SUFA), 212, 213
sociospatial organization, 38–39, 45–46, 48, 72, 94, 98, 235

sociospatial positionality, 232, 242–44, 245
sociospatial processes, 32, 270–71
sociospatial theory, 32–34, 49
sociospatiality: of contentious politics, 244–45; dimensions, 28, 31–32, 47–48; metaphorics, 28, 31–32, 48; polymorphic, 29, 33, 49
Soja, Edward, 6, 7, 28, 30, 243, 282
space/spatiality: abstract, 77, 82n2; defined, 244n1; functions, 94; horizontal connections, 235; key categories, 93–102; and place, 7–8; of politics, 231–32; production of, 7; as site, 241; vs time, 5; umbrella concept, 93
Spain: censorship, 131–33, 134; educational propaganda system, 130–31; electricity companies, 128–29; elites, 133–34; financial aid/investment, 136–37; hydraulic development, 123–27, 128–29; hydraulic planning/management, 125; hydrosocial transformation, 125, 126(f), 127; networks of interest, 122 (See also networks of interest (Spain)); permanent ideal of autarchy, 133–34; post-Franco, 138; propaganda machinery, 124–25, 128, 130, 131–33; relations with US, 136–37, 139n2; scaling environments, 122–23; self-censorship, 130–31; sociohydraulic politics, 127–30
"Spanish Crusade," 129–31
spatial analysis, 90, 104n9
spatial determinism, 7, 73
spatial dialectic, 9, 29, 73–74, 92–93, 270
spatial fix, 34(f), 57, 67, 70, 278. See also scalar fix; spatiotemporal fix
spatial governance, objects of, 93–94; sites of, 94

spatial imaginary. See imaginaries, spatial
spatial politics, of colonization, 141
spatial relationships: and agency, 53, 63–64; globalized, 14–15; and space, 93, 123, 202, 283–84
spatial strategies, 30, 88, 96–97, 98, 104n6, 238, 242
spatial turn, 8, 282–83. See also scalar turns
spatiotemporal fix, 99–100, 179. See also scalar fix
spatiotemporality, 91, 93
Stanner, William E.H., 147
state. See nation-state
state power, 99, 192, 207–8, 283
state programs, goal, 143, 153n3
state spatiality, 99, 177–78, 178–79, 180, 192–94
statehood, 99, 102
Stöhr, Klaus, 200
strategies of localization, 233, 294
subsidies: to child care, 211, 220; to the talented, 160, 166, 169–71
supranational scale, 42, 196, 204, 233–34, 285
Supreme Court of Canada, 119n1
Swyngedouw, Erik, 8, 10, 12, 69, 210, 234, 270
systems competition. See Cold War
Sziarto, Kristin, 237, 244n4

Tarrow, Sidney, 277
Task Force on Children, 218
Taylor, Peter, 10, 44–45
technological capacity, 161
Telò, Mario, 104n10
terra nullius, 143, 145
territoriality: evolution, 37–41; and political contestation, 41; principle, 31; reterritorialization, 278; of WSF world event, 292

territory: defined, 95; extensiveness, 53–54; geographical extent, 56; and USD, 37–41
The Electors Action Movement (TEAM), 217, 227n6
Thrift, Nigel, 51
Tickell, Adam, 12, 59, 60, 210
Tilly, Charles, 277
time, as scale, 258–59
time-space, 51, 65n1, 82n1, 93. *See also* spatiotemporality
topological spatiality, 65n1, 92, 104n5
Toronto: City of Toronto, 255; Greater Toronto Area, 251–52, 260; relations with Asia, 203–4; SARS coronavirus crisis, 195, 199–200, 201–2, 203–4, 205–6; suburbanization, 247. *See also* child care provision (Toronto); greenbelt conflict (ON); Oak Ridges Moraine conflict
Toronto Children's Services, 215
Toronto Homebuilders Association, 262
Toronto and Region Conservation Authority, 255
totality, 68, 78, 79, 80–81
Trade New Zealand, 182, 183, 192, 194n2
transnational advocacy networks, 238–39
Tremblay, Richard E., 221

uneven spatial development (USD), 7, 267–69; concept, 27–28; deep structures, 30; patterns, 43; place-based, 34–37; scale-differentiated, 41–45; sources, 34(f); territory-based, 37–41; theory, 29–30, 31–32; urban growth, 175
United Airlines, 238
United States: dominance, 275, 285–86; and global economy, 164; legitimacy, 286; manifest destiny, 139n2;

military aggression, 285–86, 286–87; and repression, 286–87; welfare state, 270, 271; and WSF, 285–87
University of Auckland Fashion Project, 194n1
urban: as centrality/difference, 68; as dialectical unity, 67; as form and level, 70, 71; as level, 67, 74–82, 77, 81; as level and mediation, 71–74; as mediation, 72–74; as process, 69–70; as scale, 69, 70
urban/rural divide, 30, 35
Urban Development Institute, 262
urban economic development, 161–68
urban governance, 186–89, 197–98
urban movements, and class struggle, 76
urban question, 77–78, 82n1; and everyday life, 72, 79–80; and socialist revolution, 76
urban reform, 76–77, 222
urban regeneration, 178, 181, 186–89; privileged spaces, 188–89
urban social theory, 67, 77
urban society, 73–74
urbanization, 42, 69, 70, 72, 75, 77–78
Urry, John, 204

Vancouver Society of Children's Centres, 218
violence, 105, 113, 146, 208, 286–87

Waipareira Trust, 189
Wallace, Carey, 176
Wallerstein, Immanuel, 10
Walters, Vernon, 139n2
war on poverty, 211, 271
Washington, DC, 242
water economy, 121–22
Waterfront Regeneration Trust, 257
ways of life, 108–10, 112–13, 113–14
Wearable Arts Awards, 190

Index

Weber, Max, 113, 116
welfare state. *See* Keynesian welfare state
Wellington, 187
Westcoast Child Care Resource Centre, 218
Westphalian system, 3, 10, 11, 37–38, 196, 208
Williams, Fiona, 9
Williams, Landon, 266–67, 273
Witte, Jan Martin, 207
Wolfowitz, Paul, 285
Woodward, Keith, 16, 17, 18, 23n3, 51, 53
Wools of New Zealand, 182–83
World Economic Forum, 287
World Health Organization (WHO), 199–200, 204–6
world revolution, 76–77
World Social Forum (WSF), 235; Charter of Principles, 288, 290–91, 298n4, 298n7; as event, 287, 288, 290, 291, 292–93, 294, 298n8; indigenous presence, 294; International Council (IC), 288, 292, 298n5; national vs global strategies, 297n2; new spatiopolitical praxis, 281; and new worldwide left, 295; place-based dynamic, 293–94; polycentric, 288, 291–92; poor people's presence, 292–93; as process, 285, 289, 298n6; producing difference, 292; as space, 288, 290; spatial praxis, 281, 289–95, 297n1; trans-scalar character, 296–97; vs UN-sponsored gatherings, 290; vs World Economic Forum, 287
world systems theory, 10
World Wildlife Fund, 253, 256
worldwide: vs global, 75–76, 82n3

Yulong, Shi, 203

zero sum competition, 60
zero sum games, 174
zero sum process, 4
zones, 30, 35, 36, 37, 42, 43, 94
zones of impermissibility, 111–12, 114, 115–16

Printed and bound in Canada by Marquis Book Printing
Set in Giovanni and Scala Sans by Artegraphica Design Co. Ltd.
Copy editor: Dallas Harrison
Proofreader and indexer: Dianne Tiefensee